RETHINKING THE AMERICAN LABOR MOVEMENT

Rethinking the American Labor Movement tells the story of the various groups and incidents that make up what we think of as the "labor movement." While the efforts of the American labor force towards greater wealth parity have been rife with contention, the struggle has embraced a broad vision of a more equitable distribution of the nation's wealth and a desire for workers to have greater control over their own lives. In this succinct and authoritative volume, Elizabeth Faue reconsiders the varied strains of the labor movement, situating them within the context of rapidly transforming twentieth-century American society to show how these efforts have formed a political and social movement that has shaped the trajectory of American life. *Rethinking the American Labor Movement* is indispensable reading for scholars and students interested in American labor in the twentieth century and in the interplay between labor, wealth, and power.

Elizabeth Faue is Professor of History at Wayne State University.

AMERICAN SOCIAL AND POLITICAL MOVEMENTS OF THE 20TH CENTURY
Series Editor: Heather Ann Thompson, University of Michigan

RETHINKING THE AMERICAN LABOR MOVEMENT

Elizabeth Faue

Routledge
Taylor & Francis Group

NEW YORK AND LONDON

First published 2017
by Routledge
711 Third Avenue, New York, NY 10017

and by Routledge
2 Park Square, Milton Park, Abingdon, Oxon OX14 4RN

Routledge is an imprint of the Taylor & Francis Group, an informa business

© 2017 Taylor & Francis

The right of Elizabeth Faue to be identified as author of this work has been asserted by her in accordance with sections 77 and 78 of the Copyright, Designs and Patents Act 1988.

Library of Congress Cataloging in Publication Data
Names: Faue, Elizabeth, author.
Title: Rethinking the American labor movement / by Elizabeth Faue.
Description: New York : Routledge, 2017. | Series: American social and political movements of the twentieth century | Includes bibliographical references and index.
Identifiers: LCCN 2016048689 (print) | LCCN 2017007768 (ebook) | ISBN 9780415895842 (alk. paper) | ISBN 9780203081754 (ebook)
Subjects: LCSH: Labor movement--United States--History--20th century. | Labor--United States--History--20th century.
Classification: LCC HD8066 .F38 2017 (print) | LCC HD8066 (ebook) | DDC 331.880973--dc23
LC record available at https://lccn.loc.gov/2016048689

ISBN: 978-0-415-89583-5 (hbk)
ISBN: 978-0-415-89584-2 (pbk)
ISBN: 978-0-203-08175-4 (ebk)

Typeset in Bembo
by Taylor & Francis Books

For Carol

CONTENTS

EDITOR'S SERIES INTRODUCTION

Welcome to the *American Social and Political Movements of the 20th Century* series at Routledge. This collection of works by top historians from around the nation and world introduces students to the myriad movements that came together in the United States during the 20th century to expand democracy, to reshape the political economy, and to increase social justice.

Each book in this series explores a particular movement's origins, its central goals, its leading as well as grassroots figures, its actions as well as ideas, and its most important accomplishments as well as serious missteps.

With this series of concise yet synthetic overviews and reassessments, students not only will gain a richer understanding of the many human rights and civil liberties that they take for granted today, but they will also newly appreciate how recent, how deeply contested, and thus how inherently fragile, are these same elements of American citizenship.

Heather Ann Thompson
University of Michigan

ACKNOWLEDGEMENTS

Without engaging in intellectual autobiography, I cannot describe the origins and inspirations of this book, so I will leave that for another time. Instead, let me thank those directly and indirectly responsible. Heather Thompson, a friend and the editor of this series, recruited the book with the simple argument that it was time women set the narrative of labor history. We might harken back to predecessors such as Theresa Wolfson, Helen Sumner, and Caroline Ware; but in the great wave of scholarship that emerged in the 1970s as the new labor history, women have been identified chiefly as women's historians and their research on women workers largely ignored in the master narrative of labor and working-class history. This book, inspired by Heather's charge, employs gender analysis and speaks to women workers; but it is, first and foremost, a reconsideration of the American labor movement and U.S. labor history. The editors and staff at Routledge (Kimberly Guinta, Genevieve Aoki, Margo Irvin, and Eve Mayer) encouraged, rarely but importantly cajoled, and otherwise aided bringing this manuscript to press.

A core of die-hard friends can claim a piece of this book as well. I have to include my colleagues Tracy Neumann, Janine Lanza, and Karen Marrero, to which quartet I belong, and Kidada Williams, whose model of engaged scholarship I recommend. Joe Rector, who has been a friend and my doctoral student, read the manuscript and offered insightful comments. It became a better book from our conversations. I thank my graduate students over the past twenty-five years, especially Joe Turrini, Rob Gordon, Elizabeth Ryan, Louis Jones, Richard Fry, Andrew Hnatow, Amanda Walter, and the late Jake Hall. I would be remiss if I did not mention historian Sylvia Taschka, whose enthusiasm for writing is boundless, and Andrew Port, my colleague and her husband, who contributed insights, and their two daughters, Hannah and Rebekka.

There are others who need to be mentioned here. Most importantly, I want to thank the only U.S. labor historian who belongs in the mentoring category—Peter Rachleff, who became a peer and a brother when he was hired at Macalester College. His Pittsburgh School pals Shel Stromquist and Jim Barrett also befriended me. Horizon Books in Traverse City, a location that figured in the writing of this book, is mentioned here because such places are formative of the mind and restorative of the spirit. I'd also add Cambria Suites of Traverse City, which was the location for self-funded writing retreats, and several local coffeehouses, whose crews witnessed the completion of the manuscript. I also thank Bob Olender for his insights into legal history shared over meals at the Roadhouse.

The labor historians who belong in my acknowledgements are those I engaged along the way—Ruth Milkman, Nancy Gabin, Steve Meyer, Margo Anderson, Jan Reiff, Marcel Van der Linden, Diane Kirkby, Sylvia Hahn, Ardis Cameron, Alf Luedtke, Richard Greenwald, Toby Higbie, Caroline Merithew, Julie Greene, Cindy Hahamovitch, Craig Heron, Greg Patmore, and Terry Irving. It's an eclectic and incomplete list. No doubt I forgot to mention more than a few names, but each name is attached to a specific debt.

I owe my deepest debts in a different realm. I grew up in a blue-collar union family, learned from unionized teachers, and came of age in a world where unions provided American workers and citizens many benefits. Unions—good, effective, democratic unions—are owed their due. For myself, I received a good public school education from teachers who cared (a shout out to Francine Morgan and Elizabeth Borders Putjenter) in schools kept in good order by civil servants like my father, a stationary engineer and custodian. I read books at the public library, staffed by public employees; walked along roads and sidewalks paved by public employees and protected by unionized police and firefighters and by soldiers and sailors, some of whom were my family. I had my paperwork handled by unionized civil servants and went to a public university staffed by faculty and clerical workers employed by the public. I am a public employee, working at a public university that provides many first-generation college students with a good education. I understand the benefits of supporting the public sector. I have worked my forty, fifty, and even sixty hour weeks, knowing that I am a beneficiary of and a contributor to that world.

I owe my father and my maternal grandfather the implicit understanding of what good can come of public action, including the good that derives from democratic decisions of voters and taxpayers who care about the public good. The cost of such concerted effort is the taxes we pay and the respect due to those who contribute to our nation from their talents and their commitment. I remember here my mother and my maternal grandmother, because they taught me the pleasures of history, even if they were dubious about the benefits of politics.

Finally, I have other debts, whose keenness I feel because I know both what loneliness is and what connectedness brings. Long-time friends Natalie and

Robert, Paula and Steve, Patrice, Jill, Jan, and Anne, my sisters Annamarie and Deborah, my brother Greg, my late brother Jeffrey and his wife Alice, and my nieces and nephews have filled my life with love and laughter. My nieces Kate and Nora and my nephews Stephen and Rory in particular have tussled with me intellectually. My partner and now spouse Carol Acitelli and my stepchildren Christopher, Andrea, Sarah, Bryant, and LeeAnn changed my life utterly when they became part of it sixteen years ago. While they were not entirely appreciative of what it means to be a college professor, they made it possible for me to work and play in a happier place than I had been for some time. Carol taught me to take time to sing again, to breathe, to live with intention and appreciation. She has been an admirable nudge when needed. She sat through countless afternoons and evenings in coffee shops and bookstores while I wrote; luckily, she's addicted to reading good books and capable of striking up a conversation with anyone. There are many other reasons to thank her and my community of family and friends; but if there were no other than this—to experience life with love—that is plenty.

INTRODUCTION

"What Labor has fought to get, Labor must fight to keep." Those words, invoked by Minnesota Governor Floyd B. Olson in the depths of the Great Depression, are a good introduction into the history of the American labor movement. Throughout the past 150 years, labor movements at the local and national level have been organized to improve the conditions of employment, wages, and benefits. As today's workers know, organizing labor unions has not been easy. Even successful strikes and campaigns often result in only temporary victories. Yet, the struggle to achieve what many have called "Industrial Democracy" has embraced the vision of a more equitable distribution of the nation's wealth and prosperity, a sharing of cultural goods as well as material ones, and a bid for workers to have greater control over their own lives and those of their communities. While the labor movement has gained and lost, it retains influence and power in political and economic life. For these reasons, the legitimacy and power of organized labor continues to generate conflict in the workplace and in government. Even in the twenty-first century, despite the political clout of its conservative opponents, labor has played an important role in our national history and in the history of American democracy.

The labor movement, however, has not been a single, unified social movement. Rather, labor unionism has expressed itself in historical alliances among diverse groups of workers, their allies, and labor organizations. From its origins in early colonial guilds and the independent trades unions before the Civil War, to the working-class movement known as the Knights of Labor (KOL) and the radical syndicalism of the Industrial Workers of the World (IWW), the federated trades of the American Federation of Labor (AFL) and the railroad brotherhoods, the industrial unions of the Congress of Industrial Organizations (CIO) and the teamsters, and the public sector unionism of the American Federation of Teachers

(AFT), American Federation of State, County and Municipal Employees (AFSCME), and the Service Employees International Union (SEIU), the labor movement has taken a range of organizational forms and strategies. Just as significantly, labor historically rooted itself in communities as well as national campaigns and relied on the solidarities of class, gender, ethnicity, race, region, and occupation in its struggles.

Like other social movements, the labor movement has been divided over its goals and how to obtain them. Among workers and their allies, differences in how to address the problems of poverty, poor wages, hazardous working conditions, and workplace rights have led to sharp political and institutional conflicts. Internal struggles over policy goals and over legal and political strategies have undermined the unity of the labor movement and revealed the diversity of political, as well as social, opinion. Similarly, labor unions have struggled with changes in technology, the organization of work, and in what constitutes "the working class." Moreover, labor unions and individual workers have had to address changes in laws governing the workplace and in political organization and the growing power of the American state.

Labor's legacy from the turn of the twentieth century has been its belief in the value of labor and the dignity of working people, the strong bonds of solidarity among those who earn their living through wage labor, and their strategies for organizing politically. The shared knowledge of how workers and communities organized in the past and the "culture of unity and unionism" that inspired both labor leaders and rank-and-file workers were the inheritance of labor movements past and present.

This book is designed as a short and accessible overview of the labor movement during the twentieth century. It will focus on watershed moments in the history of the always diverse and often divided American working class. It explores major questions such as the labor movement's origins, its political agenda, its connections with other social movements, its impact on politics and society, and the labor movement's current status in the twenty-first century. The account integrates national labor leaders and major turning points in labor history, along with representative local activists and community-level struggles, into the story of labor's growth.

Rethinking the American Labor Movement further asks conceptual questions about the rise, decline, and rebuilding of the labor movement in crucial periods of the twentieth century. Echoing the perspective of recent labor scholarship, it will explore not just defeats and victories but also the missed opportunities for the labor movement to expand its membership and influence. It also makes central to labor's story questions about the impact of race and gender exclusion on the long-term fate of the labor movement and its declining, if still palpable, political and economic power in the early twenty-first century. It also will ask what the impact of globalization has been on the labor movement in the United States and how that labor movement connects with other global labor struggles.

To begin with, how do we define the American labor movement? And whom do we define as its principal constituents and members, its allies, and its organizational forms? According to John Commons, among the first and most significant historians of labor, the labor movement was the umbrella name for the loose coalition of organizations devoted to what, in the nineteenth century, was called "the Labor Question." That is, the American labor movement was concerned with the origins of class inequality, the source of and remedy for low wages, and the means to improve poor working conditions and the plight of working men and women. It addressed the consequences of workers' powerlessness, poverty, and lack of mobility in the United States. It also asked questions about labor value, and, like John R. Commons and his students, wanted to understand the moral foundations of capitalism and the meaning of democracy.[1]

Publicly allied with the labor movement, Commons worked for labor law reform and influenced the formation of the American welfare state. As historians, he and his students sought to track the history of working-class organization by exploring how workers, especially those in the skilled trades, organized unions and engaged in the public sphere. For Commons and his students, economic power and industrial democracy had an essential role to play in a democratic republic. Unions, like other elected representatives, were to give voice to the needs and aspirations of their members. Workplaces, like other public arenas, required orderly governance—contracts, rules, and procedures that allowed both for the authority of employers but also respected fairness in wages, conditions, and treatment of their employees. Citizen workers, like citizen employers, should be both orderly and respectful but also self-respecting and, to a limited extent, self-governing.[2]

By the twentieth century, the Labor Question expanded to encompass not just the short-term answers for low wages and dangerous working conditions but also larger questions about the organization of society and the distribution of political power. The increasing visibility of socialist parties in Europe, the rising tide of labor militancy and fainter stirrings of socialist political organizing at home, pushed labor reformers and activists to reconsider the future of American labor, among them, labor economist Selig Perlman. Perlman, Commons' most important student of labor history, focused on a question that had begun to haunt labor's partisans: Why was the American labor movement different from its European counterparts, and why had American workers, unlike their European peers, not organized politically into socialist party organizations? Why did they chiefly rely on economic means to settle labor problems? These questions took on increasing importance, as the vibrant labor militancy of the turn-of-the-century diminished in the quiet 1920s.[3]

Perlman's answer to what many considered labor's quiescence focused on the peculiarities—or the exceptional character—of the country. The United States had no feudal heritage of its own. It had vast tracts of sparsely settled land, which made land cheap and labor expensive; and it had several waves of immigration, which added new ethnic dimensions and competition to labor organization. Workers, at least white workingmen of European descent, achieved the vote far earlier than workers around the world. While British, French and German workers failed, repeatedly, to win the right to vote, their organizations were, by default, focused on both economic and political struggle. Perlman's arguments, which were predicated on the absence of a medieval past in the United States, strikingly did not address the impact of slavery, nor the power of slaveholders, on free labor in the United States. He also did not examine the long history of slave resistance that predated the Civil War. While Perlman's mentor, John Commons, attributed little political acumen or cultural resources to racial and ethnic minorities, Perlman omitted discussion of these crucial factors in his construction of a labor movement imbued not with racial- or class- but with "job consciousness."[4]

For decades, labor historians have grappled with these questions, providing answers for and rejoinders to the ideas put forward by Commons and Perlman. The rise of industrial labor unions in the 1930s and the growth of the New Deal allowed historians and labor economists to imagine a substantially different future. Trade and industrial unions then occupied a significant place on the economic and political stage, but less as a reform movement than as an institution that yielded power. While sociologist W.E.B. DuBois demonstrated cogently in *Black Reconstruction in America*, that the labor question must address what he called "the Wages of Whiteness," his book was largely ignored—not only by scholarly historians, but by labor activists and labor economists, whose view of labor's past suffered from a racial myopia.[5] Just as Perlman had not accounted for the impact and influence of slavery in his labor theory, the labor movement, and its chroniclers, did not incorporate DuBois's analysis of how racism had severely limited the horizons of the labor movement.[6] The uneven and often conflicted relationship between unions and African American and other minority workers was built on the silence around these issues.

The decades of the 1940s and 1950s saw a growth in industrial relations programs and a shift in emphasis away from the study of labor history except as a form of labor economics. It would take shifts within the academy, and in society, to restore labor history as a field. It was with the rise of the new social movements of the 1960s and 1970s that there came a revitalization of social history and a new labor history with it. Inspired by British historians E.P. Thompson and Eric Hobsbawm, sociologist Charles Tilly's work on quantifying collective action, and the cultural materials of anthropologist Clifford Geertz, the new labor history recaptured and expanded the interdisciplinary approach and comparative method of earlier labor economists and historians.

Like the Commons School, and their colleagues abroad, labor historians in the United States were engaged and committed scholars, whose work in the civil rights and student movements, in contemporary labor activism and in the emerging women's movement informed and fueled their studies. They searched for the origins of workingmen's politics and historical alternatives to what was, by the

1960s, an almost calcified labor bureaucracy, whose lack of concern for occupational safety, racial equality, environmental hazards, and parental leave appeared to reflect a fundamental disconnection between labor as an institution and the heroic labor movement of the past. Hundreds of studies of local labor movements were published in these years, as new labor historians found a past beyond the imagining not only of conservative labor leaders like AFL–CIO President George Meany and even progressive UAW President Leonard Woodcock but also beyond the reach of John Commons and Selig Perlman. These studies had, at their core, a fundamentally different vision of what the working classes—and unions—had been and could be.

What labor historians, sociologists, and economists have often missed is that the labor movement is, after all, a loose coalition. It has the character both of a social movement and of a coalition of organizations and institutions. Rooted in local workplaces and communities, the labor movement still has a national presence. And its institutional structure needs to be studied through organizational analysis and linked to its social movement roots. This means a concern for what social movement theorists call "resource mobilization"—that is, understanding how specific organizing campaigns, strikes, and unions have coalesced through strategic use of resources. A social movement perspective calls for us to consider how labor organizers and reformers have framed the labor question, and also how labor unions, once they became stable organizations, often became inflexible before change, bringing to the forefront of labor history a concern with what Roberto Michels (following Max Weber) called "the iron law of oligarchy," or how bureaucratization stymies democratic impulses.[7]

There are three other points to make here. First, the diversity of the working class means attention to the intraclass conflicts over gender, race, ethnic, religious, and sexual inequalities and differences. Second, masculinity and whiteness have set the parameters and limits of the institutional labor movement and its economic and political strategies. Third, labor history in the United States has been a transnational and global history. Created in a nation with a legacy of slavery, and high rates of immigration, the labor movement has sometimes defined itself against those workers who lack individual freedom; who do not have citizenship rights, and who are often embedded in national and international cultures distinct and isolated from their American counterparts. And yet, workers in the United States have shared common conditions and often participated in joint struggles.

As we survey the history of labor in the late nineteenth- and twentieth-century United States, it is important to remember that, while we should be informed by and learn from the past, it is equally important not to be governed by it. In many ways, the story that this book tells is about the hazards of being too wedded to traditions, customs, and practices that are historically rooted but increasingly distant from the realities of the contemporary workplace. Labor history can provide alternative models for labor organizing, inspiration for the struggle, and even resources in building and sustaining a social movement. What it cannot do is write the future.

Origins of the Labor Movement in the Nineteenth Century

The labor movement in the United States has no precise beginning. During the Middle Ages, trade guilds in Europe were created to protect the skills, customs, livelihoods, and rights of guild workers in such trades as brewing, shoemaking, weaving, and metal work.[8] While some contemporary unions in the United States can trace their origins to guilds, most have a far shorter history. They were a product of the developing relationship between employers and workers that emerged with the first stages of industrialization. Simply put, when work moved out of the household and into the public workplace, it shifted away from family labor and apprenticeship to public (private sector) employment. Work was organized in systematic routines, with greater use of tools and machines, and oriented largely toward the market. By the eighteenth century, the growth of large urban areas provided the conditions for craft production and market exchange to flourish. Wage work, even if in the context of year-long contracts and apprenticeship indentures, was the dominant form for landless laborers and craftsmen alike.[9]

As wage work emerged as the dominant form of employment, workers sought leverage in the workplace by demanding higher wages and better working conditions. They protested what they perceived as unfair treatment in informal and formal ways. As with other social movements, the labor movement has not been and is not now the product of massive widespread, pervasive, and daily discontent. Workplace protests, strikes, and working-class political organizations were not spontaneous responses to bad times. Rather, the labor movement developed over time as the contrasts between the prosperity of particular workplaces, specific jobs, and individual employers and the lack of working-class power and impoverishment led many to question workplace arrangements. These questions, however, were unsettled by the time of the Civil War, because wage work remained the experience of a small urban population and its rural counterparts.

For most of the nineteenth century, the United States, like most nations in the West, was primarily an agricultural nation. Small and large scale commercial farms were engaged in producing staple crops for the market (such as cotton, wheat, corn), as well as dairy products and vegetables and fruits; and farmers and workers also bought newly marketed consumer goods, such as ready-made clothing, shoes, and straw hats. Near urban and market centers, farm families subsidized their livelihoods through craft production and outwork in industries such as shoes and clothing for the mass market. In the developing areas of the North, South, and West, workers toiled in extractive industries such as coal, metal mining, and timber. In cities and along the developing frontier, workers were engaged in hauling freight, loading and unloading cargo at ports, digging canals or constructing roads or bridges, making high-skilled consumer goods for the market (tailoring, boot- and shoe-making, furniture manufacture, printing and book-making, among others), or in forms of service labor from waste collection and delivery to laundry work, cleaning, and the sex trade. Only a small minority of wage workingmen and workingwomen were employed in large manufacturing plants, where mass produced textiles, shoes and boots, or firearms were produced. Most industrial workers found employment in small to medium-sized workshops and mills that were engaged in producing cheap furniture, chemicals, and lumber largely through hand production.[10]

Protests against employers, whether in informal and sporadic strikes or in trade associations, were local or regional phenomena, occurring in small pockets of industrial development, such as shoe manufacturing in New England, or the textile mills of Lowell, Massachusetts, or among craftsmen in cities such as Boston, New York, and Baltimore. Before the Civil War, urban workers had begun to organize trade unions, organizations modeled in part on medieval trade guilds but with a growing resemblance to the fraternal organizations of the time. These early unions faced opposition from employers on the grounds that their withholding of labor was an illegal conspiracy; but this was not the only problem. Many trades that had been built through small workshops that employed apprentices and journeymen under the leadership of a master craftsmen were themselves transformed, first, by master craftsmen becoming entrepreneurs themselves, divorced from the shop floor and from the obligation to pass on the craft. Journeymen and apprentices, on the other hand, saw in the strong labor market (high demand for labor, short supply, and an abundance of cheap land in the West) an incentive to abandon their indentures and set up their own shop.[11]

The weakness of the early workingmen's movement was a product both of the small numbers of workers engaged in private enterprise and also the instincts of many workers to leave a job and even a city or state, if they were discontented with their wages or angry at their employer. This practice of "voting with their feet" meant that workers, like many other people in a mobile nation, moved rather than organized. Skilled trades workers, a much smaller group, became the basis of the emerging trade union movement. They were more inclined toward stable organizations and established communities, and they had a stake in the relationship between and among businesses and craft workers. In fact, many tradesmen moved between small business ownership and work in the skilled trades.[12]

The Civil War stands as a landmark in American labor history, because the war in the North and, more fundamentally, in the South altered the organization of work and the social and political relations of employment. Just as the Civil War provided the catalyst for the end of slavery as a system of labor, so too it resulted in the growth of free labor and the relative power of employed workers. It established the distinction between free labor and coerced labor (prison labor, immigrant contract labor, and debt peonage); and it opened up employment to a larger and more diverse working-age population. By emancipating 4 million African Americans from slavery, the Civil War and federal Reconstruction thus had long-term effects on employment and labor law in ways that were not foreseen. Most specifically, the Slaughterhouse cases led to greater corporate power in employment and to a strengthening of material property rights just at the time when property ownership of human beings (both in slavery and also in women and children within the family) was repudiated.[13]

The scale of capital investment, the dimension of industrial production, and the breadth of markets in goods and labor changed in the years following the conflict. Millions of dollars in federal and state spending in the war effort and through internal improvements during and after the Civil War laid the basis for the surge in mass production industry and international markets that followed.[14] The creation of railroads nationally, most specifically the transcontinental railroad, the construction of bridges, roads, and buildings, and the services provided to manual labor increased the demand for paid labor. And the need to build machines, factories, and shops to provide the physical scaffolding for the expansion of the capitalist economy and the growth of federal and state government also had increased labor demand to the point where it was no longer possible to depend on the native-born population alone. By 1864, the Congress felt compelled to act in encouraging immigration and the importation of foreign labor through the Contract Labor Act, which allowed firms to recruit European labor by covering transportation costs for term labor contracts.[15]

After the 1880s, immigrants from eastern and southern Europe became the new face of urban manufacturing work and an increasing presence in coal and hard-rock mining, timber cutting, agriculture, and railroad construction. The influx of immigrants from the developing areas of Europe and, increasingly, from Mexico and Asia as well as migrants from the South created a fragmented labor force. Ethnic and racial solidarities were, more often than not, stronger than the commonalities that bound together workers. This was particularly true in manufacturing, where employers actively recruited groups of workers from as many different countries and language groups as possible and fomented ethnic conflict through differential pay and hiring.[16]

In coal mining, these differences for the most part had little impact, in part because mining was dependent on collective survival, given the hazards of mining, and isolated within communities, many of long duration; but the traditions of mine worker solidarity also reflect how mine work was organized and the cultural traditions of mining. Distinctive among mine workers was their deep, collective, and successful resistance to the adaptation of new technology, like the steam drill. This distinctiveness gave mine workers' unions great longevity and strength at a time when the labor movement as a whole was fairly weak.[17] While mine workers' unions scored only sporadic victories, industrial workers, by contrast, remained divided and unorganized.

The Labor Crisis of the 1870s

This pattern of growth was interrupted when the United States suffered a major economic crisis in the 1870s. Banks and investment houses had become increasingly dependent on the monetization of silver. When railroad bonds began to fail, investors sought more secure markets. The ripple effects among private employers left hundreds of thousands of unemployed workers and the poor without recourse. City governments temporarily paid workers for street cleaning and road work, but the scale of the crisis was so large that local resources were inadequate. Indeed, the growing number of unemployed migratory workers, characterized widely as "the tramp problem," were the target of legislation that warned them out of towns and cities or pushed, instead, for imprisonment and gang labor as a solution to the economic woes of perhaps one-third of the population.[18]

Railroad workers, especially those in the skilled trades of locomotive engineers and firemen, bore much of the crisis head-on. For the years between 1873 and 1877, railroad workers were laid off or had their wages cut sequentially every time there was a company shortfall. Work loads were increased, and hiring and employment became more irregular. Railroad workers, who formed their own brotherhoods as leverage against employer retribution, teetered on the edge of strikes. Because there was no national railroad, but only a series of local and regional lines and routes, it was difficult to know where to pressure employers or how to address the mounting—if seemingly random and sporadic—grievances of the railroad men. Still, skilled railroad workers, who had strategic control over the running of trains, constituted less than 20 percent of the railroad work force. The vast majority of railroad workers, who built and maintained the roads and the machines, competed with other unemployed workers for these jobs. They had little power, and little incentive, to negotiate with employers, especially those who were seen both to cause and to prolong the economic crisis of the 1870s.[19]

Connected to the volatile labor situation on the railroads were the unstable and uncertain local communities who had become overly dependent on the prosperity of the railroad industry. Businesses that relied on rail transport of goods, and/or people, and firms that produced materials for the railroad or provided services to railroad workers faced the same gaping chasm of necessity that kept railroad workers working on the line. It was this relationship—between railroad workers and their communities—that increasingly led railroad workers to believe that they could use local power to force railroad companies to bargain.[20]

The economic depression of 1873 made railroad employment more precarious and increased the vulnerability of casual labor and working-class communities. When in 1877 railroad men on the Baltimore and Ohio were faced with new wage cuts, they finally rebelled. The wage cuts were yet another volley from employers who seemed to have emerged from the crisis even more powerful, despite political scandal and economic collapse. For urban working-class communities, however, the labor conflict on the railroads signified a coming of age after the cataclysms of war and depression. Protests against railroad wage cuts were but a small part of the massive rolling strike that followed.

Rapidly, though, strike and community protests followed in rail hubs such as Pittsburgh, Chicago, St. Louis, and Minneapolis–St. Paul. Employers called for police actions to end what increasingly looked like serial rioting. Elected officials called out the National Guard and militia units. The strike ended with the recall of federal troops from Southern states, the last army units engaged in the political Reconstruction, to suppress labor action in several cities. Some Civil War veterans, from both North and South, organized themselves into ad hoc militia units to deal with the massive public protests during the 1877 railroad crisis, as they did in St. Louis. The national crisis had shifted from slavery and emancipation to the control of labor and the city streets.

Contemporary observers viewed the railroad strike of 1877 as an American Paris Commune, paralleling the collective violence and revolutionary fervor in France of just a few years earlier. For some, the extent and level of collective protests called for new restrictions on movement and the creation of barriers to labor action. Police were reorganized for rapid response to urban disorder, as cities installed the call box system and turned away from neighborhood policing. Vagrancy laws were strictly enforced, as was the warning out of the homeless from villages and towns. Fears of labor conspiracy led to the building of military armories in central cities, and those who recalled the Molly Maguires sought to develop private and public detective forces to infiltrate organized labor.[21]

By the late nineteenth century, the stage was set for different forms of labor organization, necessitated by the changes in society. Secrecy at first governed their actions, as workers also harbored fears of unlawful imprisonment and arrest. They also feared the power of employers, in the wake of a major economic crisis, to blacklist and ban the leaders among them. Finally, the economy was changing. New technologies, first spurred by the necessities of wartime production, were introduced into several industries. New immigrants entered the country and began to compete for jobs. And new fears about the power of money and corruption in politics challenged those who believed in labor rights to find different means to organize and shape their lives.

The Outline of the Book

The chapters that follow take this story to the present and speculate, albeit briefly, at the future of labor organization. The first two chapters examine the foundations and character of trade unionism in the United States through craft unions and the American Federation of Labor and its opposite and opposing force, industrial unionism, through the history of the Industrial Workers of the World and the Western Federation of Miners. The third and fourth chapters examine the recuperation, rise, and success of industrial unionism in the middle decades of the twentieth century and consider how labor's strength in the 1950s contained the seeds of its weak response to the challenges of technological unemployment, the growth of the service and information economy, and the diverse character of the labor force after World War II. The fifth and sixth chapters examine the opportunities offered by the social movements of the 1960s and 1970s, the growth of public employee unionism, and the conservative attack on unions that began in the 1950s. In the sixth chapter, the discussion takes on how this legacy left the labor movement less capable of responding to new challenges and labor's efforts to survive in a hostile labor relations climate. The conclusion surveys contemporary developments in worker organization and addresses the future of the labor movement in the current political culture.

As I write, I am reminded of an article on the disappearing middle class that is trending through social media.[22] For the first time since the 1940s, the percentage of the population defined as middle class has dropped below 50 percent. At the same time, an article on the death of the white working class has hit similar nerves—and channels—as the media rediscovers that lower-income white men in particular have lost their demographic advantages over minorities in the United States—mortality and morbidity rates are rising, and life expectancy for white working-class men and women is declining due to alcohol, drugs, and suicide. Chronic degenerative diseases play a role as well, as diabetes, heart disease, and cancer disproportionately affect those chronically exposed to carcinogens in their work and community environments and poor diet and health care that signal widespread lack of employment benefits, irregular work histories, and stagnant wages.

These factors underlie the increasing gap between classes and the growth in American inequality on many grounds. Specifically, the deteriorating health and life prospects of the white working class, especially men, is a consequence not only of deindustrialization but corporate policies on and political opposition to the labor movement. They are not, however, the only collateral damage in what has become a running battle between political parties and the anti-democratic effect of Citizens United. Minority and women workers, so long left out of the equation of most labor leaders, are not even counted as losers in the labor movement's decline. They are affected, however, both in what work is available to them and as the labor movement's disappearing act affects all workers. Just as unions have positive effects on wages and salaries, their absence negatively affects the compensation and working conditions of all workers.[23]

Stagnant wages, irregular employment, disproportionate power of employers, deteriorating and hazardous working conditions, and the verbal and physical abuse by management—these are the reasons why labor unions organized in the past and why their history can guide us into the future. This book is not an instruction manual—a troublemaker's guide—but rather a history of those battles meant to inspire but also inform what ordinary workers and citizens can do in the realm of labor and what the limitations and opportunities for action might be.

Notes

1 John R. Commons, *Industrial Government* (New York: Macmillan, 1921); Roseanne Currarino, *The Labor Question in America: Economic Democracy in the Gilded Age* (Urbana: University of Illinois Press, 2010); see also Elizabeth Faue, "The United States," in Joan Allen, Alan Campbell, Malcolm Chase, and John McIlroy, eds., *Histories of Labour* (London: Merlin Press, 2010), 164–195.

2 For a recent overview, see Malcolm Rutherford, "Wisconsin Institutionalism: John R. Commons and His Students," *Labor History* 47 (2006), 161–188.

3 Selig Perlman, *A Theory of the Labor Movement* (New York: Macmillan, 1928); see also John R. Commons, *Races and Immigrants in America* (New York: Macmillan, 1907).

4 For recent efforts to grapple with the question, see Kim Voss and Rick Fantasia, *Hard Work: Remaking the American Labor Movement* (Berkeley: University of California Press, 2004); Seymour Martin Lipset and Gary Wolfe, *It Didn't Happen Here: Why Socialism Failed in the United States* (New York: W.W. Norton, 2000).

5 Francille Rusan Wilson, *The Segregated Scholars: Black Social Scientists and the Creation of Black Labor Studies, 1890–1950* (Charlottesville: University of Virginia Press, 2006) is a good place to begin. See also Aldon G. Morris, *A Scholar Denied: W.E.B. DuBois and the Birth of Modern Sociology* (Berkeley: University of California Press, 2015), which addresses DuBois's marginalization in sociology more broadly.

6 Following Barbara Fields, I would argue here that the issue is racism, not race. See Barbara J. Fields and Karen Fields, *Racecraft: The Soul of Inequality in American Life* (New York: Verso, 2012). On the racism-race distinction, see Barbara J. Fields, "Of Rogues and Geldings," *American Historical Review* 108:5 (2003), 1397–1405.

7 For a slightly different, albeit complementary, argument about bureaucratization, see Robert Brenner, "The Political Economy of the Rank-and-File Rebellion," in Aaron Brenner, Robert Brenner, and Cal Winslow, eds., *Rebel Rank and File: Labor Militancy and the Revolt from Below during the Long 1970s* (New York: Verso, 2010), 37–76, esp. 37–46.

8 There is no single text in labor history that discusses the roots of modern trade unionism's European origins. The reasons for this absence relate to the strong connection between labor history and institutional economics and the complex forms of labor control that made it difficult to assign class position to laborers and class politics to what seems to be informal collective and individual resistance.

9 For a recent review essay, see Jeffrey Sklansky, "Labor, Money, and the Financial Turn in the History of Capitalism," *Labor: Studies in Working-Class History of the Americas* 11:1 (2014), 103–119.

10 See Bruce Laurie, *Artisans into Workers: Labor in Nineteenth Century America* (New York: Hill and Wang, 1989); Theodore Hershberg, ed., *Philadelphia: Work, Space, Family, and Group Experience in the 19th Century: Essays Toward an Interdisciplinary History of the City* (New York: Oxford University Press, 1981); Seth Rockman, *Scraping By: Wage Labor, Slavery, and Survival in Early Baltimore* (Baltimore: Johns Hopkins University Press, 2008), on the gritty work of the urban working class.

11 William J. Rorabaugh, *The Craft Apprentice: From Franklin to the Machine Age in America* (New York: Oxford University Press, 1986); also Alan Dawley, *Class and Community: The Industrial Revolution in Lynn, Massachusetts* (Cambridge, MA: Harvard University Press, 1976), 42–72; Sean Wilentz, *Chants Democratic: New York City and the Rise of the American Working Class* (New York: Oxford University Press, 1984), 107–144, among others.

12 Stephen Thernstrom, *Poverty and Progress: Social Mobility in the Nineteenth Century City* (Cambridge, MA: Harvard University Press, 1064); Charles Stephenson, "'There's Plenty Waitin' at the Gates': Mobility, Opportunity, and the American Worker," in Charles Stephenson and Robert Asher, eds., *Life and Labor: Dimensions of American Working Class History* (Albany: SUNY Press, 1986), 72–91; Jonathan Prude, *The*

Coming of the Industrial Order: Town and Factory Life in Rural Massachusetts, 1810–1860 (Cambridge: Cambridge University Press, 1983).

13 W.E.B. DuBois, *Black Reconstruction in America* (1935) pointed the way to an integrated and interracial history of labor, but his capacious definition of labor revolt fell outside the interests of the Commons, or Wisconsin, School of labor history and has never quite found its place in labor history narratives. For perspectives on the connections between and among slave, wage, and family labor, see Amy Dru Stanley, *From Bondage to Contract: Wage Labor, Marriage and the Market in the Age of Slave Emancipation* (Cambridge: Cambridge University Press, 1998); Robert Steinfeld, *The Invention of Free Labor: The Employment Relations in English and American Law and Culture, 1350–1870.* (Chapel Hill: University of North Carolina Press, 1991); Alex Gourevitch, *From Slavery to the Cooperative Commonwealth: Labor and Republican Liberty in the Nineteenth Century* (Cambridge: Cambridge University Press, 2014).

14 See David Montgomery, *Beyond Equality: Labor and the Radical Republicans, 1862–1872* (New York: Vintage, 1972), and idem, *The Fall of the House of Labor: The Workplace, the State, and American Labor Activism, 1865–1925* (Cambridge: Cambridge University Press, 1987), on labor. For economic development generally, see Richard White, *Railroaded: The Transcontinentals and the Making of Modern America* (New York: W.W. Norton, 2012); William Cronon, *Nature's Metropolis: Chicago and the Great West* (New York: W.W. Norton, 1992); Sven Beckert, *The Monied Metropolis: New York City and the Consolidation of the American Bourgeoisie, 1850–1896* (Cambridge, Cambridge University Press, 2003), among many others.

15 Gunther Peck, *Reinventing Free Labor: Padrones and Immigrant Workers in the North American West, 1880–1930* (New York: Cambridge University Press, 2000) argues for the centrality of contract labor, especially in the West. Certainly, by the 1880s, these labor contracts became a major issue for the Knights of Labor and trade unions. See A. T. Lane, *Solidarity or Survival: American Labor and European Immigrants, 1830–1924* (New York: Praeger, 1987); Gwendolyn Mink, *Old Labor and New Immigrants in American Political Development: Union, Party, and State, 1875–1920* (Ithaca: Cornell University Press, 1990).

16 There are many sources for this paragraph, especially the work of economists such as Michael J. Piore, Richard Edwards, David Gordon, and Michael Reich.

17 Thomas Andrews, *Killing for Coal: America's Deadliest Labor War* (Cambridge, MA: Harvard University Press, 2008); see also Richard Fry, "Fighting for Survival: Coal Miners and the Struggle over Health and Safety in the United States, 1968–1988," doctoral dissertation, Wayne State University, 2010, specifically his synthesis of the literature on the eastern coal fields.

18 Heather Cox Richardson, *West from Appomattox: The Reconstruction of America after the Civil War* (New Haven: Yale University Press, 2007), 148–186; Michael B. Katz, *In the Shadow of the Poorhouse: A Social History of Welfare in America* (New York: Basic Books, 1986), 60–87; John C. Schneider, *Detroit and the Problem of Order, 1830–1880* (Lincoln: University of Nebraska Press, 1980); Eric H. Monkonnen, *Walking to Work: Tramps in America, 1790–1935* (Lincoln: University of Nebraska Press, 1984), among others.

19 Walter Licht, *Working for the Railroads: The Organization of Work in the Nineteenth Century* (Princeton: Princeton University Press, 1983); Shelton Stromquist, *A Generation of Boomers: The Pattern of Railroad Labor Conflict in Nineteenth Century America* (Urbana: University of Illinois Press, 1987); Jeffrey Marcos Garcilazo, *Traqueros: Mexican Railroad Workers in the United States, 1870–1930* (Denton, TX: University of North Texas Press, 2012); Ryan Dearinger, *The Filth of Progress: Immigrants, Americans, and the Building of Canals and Railroads in the West* (Berkeley: University of California Press, 2016); Peck, *Reinventing Free Labor.*

20 See Robert V. Bruce, *1877: Year of Violence* (Indianapolis: Bobbs-Merrill, 1959); David O. Stowell, ed., *The Great Railroad Strikes of 1877* (Urbana: University of Illinois Press, 2008).

21 Nell Irvin Painter, *Standing at Armageddon: The United States, 1877–1919* (New York: W.W. Norton, 1988); Troy Rondinone, *The Great Industrial War: Framing Class Conflict in the Media, 1865–1950* (New Brunswick, NJ: Rutgers University Press, 2009); Joshua Brown, *Beyond the Lines: Pictoral Reporting Everyday Life, and the Crisis of Gilded Age America* (Berkeley: University of California Press, 2002); Kevin Kenny, *Making Sense of the Molly Maguires* (New York: Oxford University Press, 1988); Sidney L. Harring, *Policing a Class Society: The Experience of American Cities, 1865–1915* (New Brunswick, NJ: Rutgers University Press, 1983); Sam Mitrani, *The Rise of the Chicago Police Department: Class and Conflict, 1850–1894* (Urbana: University of Illinois Press, 2013).

22 Gina Kolata, "Death Rates Rising for Middle-Aged White Americans," *New York Times*, November 2, 2015; Olga Khazan, "Middle-Class White Americans Are Dying of Despair," *Atlantic*, www.theatlantic.com/health/archive/2015/11/boomers-deaths-p nas/413971/; see also http://theweek.com/articles/459117/mysterious-decline-fema le-life-expectancy, on working-class women's declining life expectancy.

23 Jake Rosenfeld, *What Unions No Longer Do* (Cambridge, MA: Harvard University Press, 2014), shows that, while analyzing the impact on working women's wages is complicated, minority workers (male and female) have taken deep losses as a result of deunionization. See Rosenfeld, 100–130.

1

ORIGINS OF MODERN TRADE UNIONISM

In his autobiography, *Seventy Years of Life and Labor*, AFL head Samuel Gompers spoke of his trade and the labor movement as complementary aspects of his masculine identity. He was, at once, a son, a husband, a father, a skilled cigar maker, and a man. He was also a brother to those in his trade and to all men in the skilled trades, a category defined by kinship and racial and ethnic identity. Like fraternal twins, skilled craftsmen bore a family resemblance—whether they were coopers, butcher workmen, iron molders, or carpenters. They honored what they considered exclusively masculine—and white western European—traits of courage, self-reliance, and resilience. Their unions encouraged a strong work ethic, brotherly solidarity, craft autonomy, good citizenship and personal freedom. They saw the pursuit of happiness as a right embodied by family, home ownership, and the company of one's fellows. The ideal craftsman, Gompers wrote, exhibited virility, "self-government, self-reliance, and self-control," and "true patriotism." "The object, and the result" of trade unions, he argued, is "the making, not of paupers, but men, strong men, in body, mind, and spirit."[1]

In identifying trade unionism with "the making of men," Gompers echoed the language of his time. It equated individual standing with masculinity and whiteness. "Good, reliable white men" conducted trains, milled flour, hand-twisted cigars, cut or pressed fabric, wielded the cutting knife, made furniture joints, walked the high beams of skyscrapers, and fixed looms, to mention a few of the crafts they practiced. Each workman who entered a trade, usually through apprenticeship and family connections, learned the work through formal instruction and informal mentoring and polished his skills through experience and experiment. Often trades, and trade unions, had rituals to convey to apprentices and journeymen knowledge, collective identity and a sense of belonging. Like the fraternal associations on which they were modeled, craft unions combined a sense of high seriousness and shared secrecy with hazing rituals that tested and often humiliated those who sought entry into the craft. Trade union brotherhood was solidarity bound together with horseplay and peer pressure. The journey from apprenticeship to master craftsman was crosscut with tests showing how well individuals held together against an employer, a foreman, or on the picket line.

Skilled workers' collective identity was constructed as specifically ethnic and racial in character. While many men and some women possessed carpentry skills, only white men laid claim to the card of being a skilled union carpenter or shipwright and belonged to trade unions. African American and Mexican men might work on construction sites, laying bricks and crafting wood, or in shipyards constructing ships; but they were not members of the brotherhood. In similar fashion, there were, by the late nineteenth century, workers in cigar workshops and factories that produced cigars—hand-twisted or machine-molded; but only those who carried the union card were journeymen or master "cigar makers." In the South, black men who had been enslaved often possessed work skills that equaled or surpassed those of white craftsmen. Yet they did not belong and were not welcomed into the craft union brotherhood of their trades. Respectability in a racially segregated society meant, for white tradesmen, whites-only unions and the zealous protection of their rights as skilled white workers. Racial identity, with its political rights and cultural power, was forged onto trade unionism in the late nineteenth century by bonds that remained unbroken in the late twentieth.

The Trade Union Origins of the Modern American Labor Movement

Labor economist John Commons wrote an essay on American shoemakers. Like Commons, we can usefully learn about changes in work, and in workplace organization, from shoemaking, an ancient craft but also a mass production industry. In fact, one of the first trade unions to emerge after the Civil War was a fraternal organization of shoemakers, the Order of the Knights of St. Crispin.[2] Crispin was the patron saint of shoemakers, who embraced him as the symbol for their trade. The language of the trade union—a fraternal order of knights— echoed the medieval legacy of cobblers' guilds. Guided by the rules of behavior and the principles of manly bearing, brotherly support, and honor, the Knights of St. Crispin was in sync with other trade unions and labor orders of the day. Like other trade unions, it was built through bonds among workingmen who shared a common past and craft identity. Its union practices subjected its members to tests of courage and faith prior to joining the order and imposed obligations of reciprocity and mutual aid as a condition of membership. Peer judgment and communal enforcement of the rules spoke to the success or failure of members in their conduct both inside and outside the workplace.

Nineteenth-century trade unions embodied the masculine culture of skilled workers that labor historian David Montgomery captured in his classic book,

Workers' Control in America. Manly bearing, brotherly solidarity, and masculine independence—a refusal to bow to the authority of other men—were integral to the class and racial identity of skilled workingmen of the time.[3] Such men had their feet firmly planted in their craft—the skills that distinguished skilled workers from manual gang labor, slaves, and tramps who moved from one town—and job—to the next. Men who worked only for food and drink were cut off from the anchors of respectable manhood—work worthy of men, family and household, and the company of like fellows. Unemployment, whether due to economic crisis or just a run of bad luck, unmanned workingmen—and took from them the quality and character of citizens. As Samuel Gompers, AFL president, wrote,

> You meet a man on the street a man you knew years before as one in the crowd in your trade ... What has happened to this man? He may try to think he is the same, as a human being and a workman that he was when he fell out of his job ... [but] ... He has lost in self-respect, for he feels every hour that men may speak of him as not having made good. He has lost flesh and even strength ... He has suffered every day in his pride [and] if his chance hangs off too long, his fate is to "lay down." He is "gone." ... The real man having passed away, the poor body remains only to succumb, in its weakness, to one of the hundred forms of illness ...[4]

Only employment at one's trade created confidence and stability.

For skilled men in the late nineteenth century, there was little certainty in the length or place of one's employment. As Bruce Laurie and Alex Keyssar noted, skilled workers suffered longer periods of unemployment than semi-skilled or unskilled labor, even though they earned significantly higher wages.[5] The coming of machine production to industry displaced the majority of skilled jobs, even as industries continued to employ some skilled workers. The Knights of St. Crispin shared this common experience. The introduction of new machine technology in the production of shoes led to an industry-wide strike and related union losses in the mid-1870s. While the strike did not permanently crush shoe workers' unions nor reshape the gendered division of work and unionism, shoemakers shifted their tactics. By the 1880s, shoe workers had established new unions in Lynn, Haverhill, and other industrial towns. They joined or organized locals of the Knights of Labor, a national organization. Their labor newspaper, *The Awl*, was renamed *The Knight of Labor*. It incorporated much of the shared rhetoric of equal rights and labor republicanism.[6]

When the Knights of Labor failed to meet their expectations, a new Boot and Shoe Workers Union (BSWU) was formed. It was under that union umbrella that shoemakers entered the twentieth century. The BSWU captured the spirit of trade unionism that governed the labor movement. It stressed the skilled identity of shoe workers and, more importantly, organized men and women into different locals along occupational and skill lines. The BSWU was home base for many labor leaders, including John Tobin, its president and a foe of conservative AFL president Gompers, and Mary Anderson, later head of the Woman's Bureau of the Department of Labor.[7] The transformation of the Knights of St. Crispin into a more traditional trade union and its acceptance of greater machine production of shoes led to a new form of unionism—one modeled on stable British trades unions and their reliance on high dues, exclusionary membership, and targeted collective action to protect workers' rights and living.

As new technology altered work organization and the size and composition of the industrial work force, repeated strikes rocked the shoe industry.[8] Manufacturing companies were driven through competition to seek competitive advantages, and lowering the cost of labor was chief on the list. Replacing human labor entirely with machines was not possible, but machine production required far fewer workers. Breaking down labor into small, defined tasks, using machines to enhance the strength and speed of human workers, and then expanding employee workloads either by assigning workers greater numbers of machines (the "stretch-out") or increasing machine speed (the "speed-up") were the chief means to reduce costs. Scientific management, which intensified the pace and narrowed the scope of work assignments, was not fully implemented until the twentieth century, by which time new firms began to infringe on shoe production. Still, the basic concept—to reorganize work, standardize speed and performance, and exact greater labor from each worker—reflected common practices and attitudes among manufacturers.[9]

Workingmen in iron and steel production and working women in the collar trade witnessed similar changes in machine production in the late nineteenth century. In the cities of Troy and Cohoes, New York, men and women workers encountered the relentless innovation of industry as it reshaped work and transformed the labor force. In Troy, the "Collar City," the making and ironing of shirt collars from fabric was a major trade. Detachable collars, which allowed the wearer to switch out only the most visible piece of a garment, were widely worn among male clerks, skilled tradesmen, and small businessmen. Because shift collars were the hardest to clean and first to wear out, detachable collars placed white-collar respectability within the reach of every man, at a time when ready-made shirts were increasingly available but also relatively expensive.[10]

Women workers made, laundered, and ironed collars for the shirt industry in Troy. Like most women in wage work, the collar workers were unmarried young women, most of whom were immigrants and many of them Irish. Led by Kate Mulaney, women collar workers, in concert with the iron-molders of the city, formed a union to guarantee decent wages. The aftershocks of the Civil War, however, disrupted the industry. Firms quickly adopted the disposable collar as a means of limiting the costs of production. For the Collar Workers of Troy, it marked the end of an era of a visible and strong labor movement.[11]

Iron puddlers and molders experienced similar forces of technological innovation. In Troy and other cities, the introduction of new processes to make iron and shift the metal industry into steel production led to industrial conflict, the loss of jobs and standing, and the closure of plants. This innovation occurred in small cities like Troy, New York, and in Pittsburgh, Homestead, and surrounding areas. It was there that Andrew Carnegie began to consolidate steel production after the Civil War. At the Homestead Mill, he introduced Bessemer and open hearth furnaces to produce steel more efficiently than traditional blast furnaces, at greater speeds and in staggering quantities. Requiring a new organization of work, which increased labor and hours of individual workers, even as it diminished their control over work, the Bessemer process was not only a machine technology but a human one as well.[12]

New technologies for making metal existed simultaneously with older team-based forms of producing iron and steel. For the workers of the Amalgamated Association of Iron, Steel and Tin Workers, making iron had common customs and social practices that were inherited from earlier metal-forging and metal-working guilds. The master iron puddler headed a gang of workers who were subject to his authority. His workers included laborers and helpers, who lifted and moved materials; journeymen, who worked at improving their craft; and the puddler in charge of producing quality iron. The master craftsman doled out assignments and rewards. Working for iron manufacturers, these skilled craftsmen negotiated the conditions of work and the price of labor—for themselves and their men.[13]

From the perspective of industrialists such as Carnegie and Henry Clay Frick, who became Carnegie's partner in an expanding steel empire, the Iron Workers of the Amalgamated—indeed, of any trades union that effectively controlled how work was organized and paid—were obstacles to the innovation required of mass production industry. The conflict between skilled labor—whether the hatters of Danbury, the stove-makers of St. Louis and Detroit, the Iron Puddlers of Troy, the steelmakers of Homestead, or the Cigar Makers of Tampa—and employers over how goods should be produced and who had legitimate authority over workers became the chief industrial contest of the late nineteenth century.[14]

The Politics of Skill in an Age of Mass Production

Basing their labor activism on skill identity, craft unionists came to see new machine technologies as primary threats to their employment, social status, standard of living, and the unions that sustained their craft. Machine production was, however, only one side of the coin. In a much-cited anti-immigration tract, *Meat v. Rice*, the American Federation of Labor asserted that employers who put into place new machines and recruited unskilled workers to run them threatened the American way of life.[15] Immigration was thus also at fault for the plight of the skilled worker. Trade unionists believed that immigrant labor—Slavic, Italian, and Chinese in origin—lacked the exacting standards and customs of "American workers." Foreign workers, it was argued, accepted any working conditions in exchange for poverty wages. More importantly, their low wages denied skilled workers access to respectable family wages. Envisioned as "shoals of roast beef and apple pie," to echo German economist Werner Sombart, the American standard of living for skilled workers meant specific sustenance—a home of one's own, clean shirts, meat on Sunday, and schooling for children, a standard of living skilled workers believed was beyond the reach—and imagination—of the rude peasants at America's door.[16]

The skilled workers who dominated the labor movement at its outset—iron puddlers, printers, tailors, cigar makers, and barrel-makers (called coopers)—encountered the new age of mass production through the door of their own particular craft. While some skilled tradesmen (in shoe- and boot-making, to use one example) lost their privileged place in production to semi-skilled factory operatives, others, such as coopers, saw their industry become increasingly mechanized and slowly displaced. While unions of coopers lost much of their power in the 1880s, barrels as shipping containers for dry and wet goods continued to dominate the market until after World War I. Displacement, in terms of boxes and other containers, happened over decades. Still other trades, like cigar-making and furniture manufacture, adapted to a deeply stratified division of labor that distinguished a high quality product by the work process and created niche markets for skilled manufacture. The five-cent cigar and cheaper cigarettes that were machine-produced for the mass market contrasted in price and production with the expensive cigars that were the work of master craftsmen. The distinct differences and divisions between manual workers (in road and rail construction) and semi-skilled machine tenders (making cigarettes, mass produced clothing) on the one hand and workers in the skilled trades (printing, carpentry, iron manufacture) gave rise to different forms of union organization.[17]

By the 1880s, labor had coalesced into a broad-based, though highly localized, national movement. There were local trade unions, an emerging trades union movement, independent railroad brotherhoods of skilled workers, and a new organization—formed in the 1870s—the Knights of Labor. Belief in the labor theory of value and in the common interests of "the producing classes" against land speculators, bankers, and politicians was shared among these divergent groups. Organized workingmen in different regions supported Greenback politicians who believed in monetary solutions, workingmen's candidates who championed laws against prison and contract labor, advocates of the eight-hour day and promoters of cooperative stores and businesses. Still, while white workingmen voted for independent workingmen's tickets and plied for patronage and favor from different political parties, they accepted the principles of private property and a limited state. They, as did most white native-born men of their age, voted large majorities for one of two major political parties—whether the Republican party with its Civil War claims or the Democratic party, which depended on the urban working class vote.[18]

It was in workplace activism—demands for better wages, hours, and working conditions—that the distinctions among labor organizations revealed themselves.

While craft unions and the railroad brotherhoods relied on their skill monopoly to control the labor market, there were labor leaders who experimented with different models. In the years after the Civil War, the National Labor Union and the Eight Hour movement took an approach to labor organizing that emphasized worker self-organization, broadly defining who belonged in the labor movement and how to mobilize the communities and families in which workers lived. Organizing began, much as it did among skilled workers, with one-on-one relationships with other like-skilled workers and labor organizers. Much of the focus of the National Labor Union and of the Eight Hour movement, in contrast to trade unions, was outside the workplace. Campaigns for city- or state-wide eight hour laws, workingmen's tickets for city councils and state legislatures, Greenback party activism and forums to discuss the labor question were the first stages of building a social movement of working-class men *and* women. As the economy recovered in the late 1870s, new labor organizations emerged that used these local organizing efforts as a platform from which to launch a national labor movement.[19]

With a membership of over 700,000 at its peak in 1886, the Knights of Labor was the preeminent labor organization of its age. It came to represent a larger proportion of wage workers than any other labor union in American history. Formed in the years after the Civil War, the Knights were a transitional organization between the labor republicans' world of craft work and the emerging mass production economy. Tailors in Philadelphia, beset by the growth of the ready-made clothing industry, organized the first local assembly of the Knights of Labor in 1869. By 1873 the Knights established a sustained local assembly that functioned to organize workers in the city. The Knights proved resilient, outlasting the economic crisis of the 1870s, in part due to their secrecy. Focused on more than labor reform and political organization, the Knights fostered a vibrant labor culture that tapped familiar symbols, rituals, and demands for what was a largely native-born and northern European immigrant membership.[20]

The founding members of the Knights were trade unionists, skilled craft workers who embraced the labor theory of value and a community-based model of unionism. As the KOL expanded, its leaders welcomed a broad spectrum of workers and supporters; only liquor salesmen, land speculators, gamblers, bankers, and lawyers were excluded. There were reasons for all the exclusions—Terence Powderly, the second and longest serving Grand Master Workman of the Knights, was a teetotaler. Speculation on land or games of chance, and the risky business of banking, threatened to undermine workingmen's independence. More directly, bankers, lawyers, and speculators were not "productive" of value. Henry George's *Poverty and Progress*, a favorite among labor reformers, charged much of the corruption and moral decay of the United States to rank speculation. While all these ideas may seem a far cry from economic and political thinking that marked a social movement for change, the hallmark of the labor movement of the nineteenth century was that it, in fact, saw the labor theory of value as a moral as well as a political philosophy.[21]

The Knights of Labor as a hybrid labor union, to which workers without regard to skill and industry belonged, struck many trade unionists as an unnatural mingling of workers' interests, as American Federation of Labor president Samuel Gompers noted of the Knights. Like the fraternal organizations whose rituals it evoked, the Knights recruited on a one-on-one basis and educated their members through meetings and forums. They used elaborate rituals and imagery to communicate the ideas of "the Noble and Holy Order of the Knights of Labor" with a gravity similar to the Knights Templar. Yet, after the 1877 railroad strike, when local militias and police kept a close eye on workingmen's organizations, and employers were willing to fire workers who joined unions, the Knights' secrecy and ritual served a purpose. The fraternal culture of the Knights allowed the organization to maintain and even expand its membership at a time when there was little economic freedom or political support for unions.[22]

In 1881, the Knights of Labor put aside secrecy to become a public organization. Shortly after, the KOL inducted their first women members. By 1883, the Knights General Assembly was integrated by race and dared, in a segregating South, to hold integrated meetings, even while the majority of its black members were in segregated locals.[23] These changes, and the victories of Knights of Labor locals in such strikes as the Southwest Railway Strike of 1885, led to rapid growth in the 1880s.[24] Even as skilled trades unions were about to create their own national organization, the Knights captured much of the local stage—organizing among German craft workers in Cincinnati, stove makers in Detroit, carpet weavers in Yonkers, the granite cutters in Vermont, the sewing machine operatives in Minneapolis, and anarchist workingmen in Chicago.[25]

The Knights' broad definition of "the producing classes" meant that not only skilled workers, laborers, and their families were welcome but so, too, were the owners of small businesses.[26] Their labor republicanism—the belief that labor was the source of all wealth, an inclusive vision of "the producing classes," and the acceptance of small market capitalism—limited the tactics and strategies available to the Knights. Critical of the greed of corporations and the corruption of political leaders, the KOL turned to economic cooperation as an alternative. They supported worker-owned factories, stores, and home loans, much like the Populists. By the same token, the national Knights were risk-averse and sought to avoid strikes, engaging in them only where necessary. The Knights preferred other forms of collective action, including boycotts and political campaigns. Joining workingmen's parties, the Knights paid considerable time and attention to political pursuits. It was these activities, and conflicts over who owned local assets and who represented local workers, that dominated the last few years of the Knights of Labor as an active labor movement. It was this political turn that brought accusations that the Knights were hopeless utopians—"dreaming of what might be," instead of pursuing more practical aims.[27]

Struggles over basic resources such as local union treasuries and newspaper and journal editorship turned into personal battles, where each side charged the other with arrogance and greed. The reformist bent of Knights' leaders left them open to charges of allowing political ambition to trump the political interests of labor. For other observers, it was simply that the Knights had abandoned labor solidarity in favor of dual unionism, jurisdictional disputes, and local political spoils. The Cigar Makers' International Union (CMIU) was among the first affected by the battles between the Knights and skilled trades union locals. Faced with market trends toward molded and machine-produced cigars, the CMIU sought to use what power they had in the hand-crafted cigar market to sustain wages and workplace gains. In the midst of a CMIU strike in New York, the KOL inter-vened by sponsoring the Cigar Makers' Progressive Union's (CMPU) attempt to undermine CMIU contract negotiations in 1882. The CMPU, competing for the same members, claimed the right to represent the striking workers and altered strike demands in exchange for exclusive rights to represent the workers. For the leaders of the CMIU, Samuel Gompers and Adolph Strasser, the Knights and their efforts to take over existing union contracts had crossed the line. Other com-munities had different stories as trades unions and KOL local assemblies contested jurisdictional boundaries, political slates, and ownership of labor assets.[28]

By the mid-1880s, the only common ground left in the labor movement was the nation-wide campaign for the Eight Hour Day. Using the slogan, "Eight Hours for Work, Eight Hours for Rest, Eight Hours for What We Will," trade unionists and Knights advocates sought, through these efforts, to improve the working conditions and lives of workers as well as to create new work opportunities for the unemployed. Through Eight Hour rallies and legislative lobbying, and in strikes and protests against employers, labor leaders came into direct conflict with employers, who neither accepted unions nor believed that governments should intervene in the market. Many local governments, and police forces, saw the new Eight Hour activism and growth of the Knights of Labor as a threat to public order.

During an Eight Hour campaign in Chicago in 1886, this conflict between organized labor and employers reached an impasse. It also turned violent. By the mid-1880s, Chicago had become the center of a vibrant immigrant and working-class culture with a wide array of working-class organizations. A circle of German labor radicals, most of them anarchists, was at the center of the Eight Hour movement in the city. They believed strongly in worker self-organization and in confronting the state authorities and local employers in the right for better working conditions and a living wage, and engaged fully in the Eight Hour movement that had taken root. Demands for the Eight Hour day were at the heart of a strike against one of Chicago's most powerful employers, the McCormick Harvesting Machine Company, which adamantly refused to bargain with the union.[29]

While workers at the Harvester Plant confronted the immoveable force of Joseph McCormick, fellow workingmen gathered to strike against the plant. In early May, these demonstrations had drawn fire. City police and private guards had injured and killed some of the strikers, a fact that provoked responses from the wider working-class community.[30] Among those protesting was a group of anarchists, including Albert Parsons, a typesetter and former Confederate soldier, who edited the English-language newspaper, *The Alarm*; Michael Schwab and August Spies, who edited *Arbeiter-Zeitung*; and its typesetter, Adolph Fischer; Methodist minister Samuel Fielden; carpenter Louis Lingg; George Engel, who edited *Der Anarchist*, and labor organizer Oscar Neebe. On May 4, they organized a protest in Haymarket Square. Soon after the lead speakers, including Parsons and Spies, left the platform, someone in the crowd threw a bomb into a group of police standing in the square. Seven police were killed and sixty in the crowd injured in the blast. In the aftermath, the eight anarchists were arrested. Seven of the eight were sentenced to death in a trial that focused on the political beliefs—not the actions—of the anarchists. Two of the condemned had their sentences commuted; but after Louis Lingg committed suicide in prison, the remaining four were executed. Schwab, Fielden, and Neebe served several years in prison before Governor Altgeld pardoned them in 1893.[31]

For the labor movement, the Haymarket trial had two dramatic effects—a nation-wide campaign to round up anarchists and a precipitous decline in the Knights of Labor. The Knights figured in their own demise. The Grand Master Workman of the Knights, Terence Powderly, disavowed the Haymarket eight, even as local trade unions and Knights assemblies around the country protested the arrests. Many local assemblies shifted to political work, and competition with trade unions further undermined the national organization. As Richard Oestreicher argued in his *Solidarity and Fragmentation*, the Knights' rapid growth in the mid-1880s weakened the bonds that held it together. New Knights members had joined the organization in the wake of its victories over southwestern railroads but without fully understanding or accepting the Knights' movement culture. They had not joined or created cooperatives; they did not engage in political action. Trade unions moreover had become deeply suspicious of what they viewed as "dual unionism." While it would be over a decade before the Knights disbanded, these organizational weaknesses—and the strength of the new trade union federation—led to the Knights' decline.[32]

The Origins of the American Federation of Labor

Beyond the Knights of Labor, skilled workers began to explore other avenues of labor organization. Many who tried working with the Knights returned to the trade union of their craft. In 1881, thirteen international trades unions met in Cincinnati, Ohio, to discuss forming a new labor federation. The common theme was one of how the Knights had not addressed the grievances of skilled workers. In their quest for political power, trade union leaders argued, the Knights had abandoned the common ground of workplace grievances, conflicts, and wage disputes for the political office. Debates over which party to support and what religion to follow had been peripheral to labor solidarity but not so, trade unionists argued, if labor followed the workers to the more contested terrain of faith and political belief.[33]

By contrast, the Federation of Organized Trades and Labor Unions (FOTLU), an organization of trade unions, was established as a strictly secular and non-partisan organization. At a time characterized by widespread anti-Catholic, anti-Semitic, and nativist sentiments, it was important for workers of all trades to avoid strong partisan divisions and cultural differences. Sticking to what Samuel Gompers called "class feeling" made possible united action among workers. With this core understanding, the FOTLU reorganized as the American Federation of Labor in 1883. Its name change proclaimed Americanism as central to its identity. It reinforced the AFL's general aversion to anything—ethnic and racial identity, political and religious divisions, or even self-conscious consideration of gender—that might undermine a unified front among those who worked. Significantly, work for the AFL meant working for wages—not housework, contract labor, salaried employment, or the "work" of labor reform.[34]

The new American Federation of Labor grounded its organization in what was then a British model of trade unionism. In contrast to the Knights, the AFL was a federation, not an assembly or a congress. Its local affiliates and member international unions possessed self-determination in standards for membership eligibility, apprenticeship and hiring system, dues schedule, governing rules, organizational forms, and benefits. This craft autonomy severely limited the powers of national AFL leaders. Craft unions in practice held the AFL hostage to conflicting agendas and jurisdictional lines between and within unions. Only by understanding the power of the craft unions can one reconcile the conflicts within the AFL's national policy over such basic issues as how and whom to organize.

Publicly, the American Federation of Labor did support racial and gender equality, woman suffrage, and broad-based working-class solidarity. It also tolerated contradictory local, regional, and international union practices that were racially exclusive, discriminated on the basis of sex, and endorsed local anti-Prohibition— and anti-Woman Suffrage—political candidates. It wasn't that the AFL's heart was at war with its head. It was that the AFL's body was at war with each of its constituent parts. Yet it is also important to recognize the extent to which the "ideal worker" of the AFL, a skilled member of an AFL-affiliated trades union and a brother, embodied these contradictions. Craft unions were not egalitarian because, for the most part, their members did not see all workers or all work as equal. They defied, in daily practice, the AFL's public commitment to racial and gender equality.

By the 1880s, skilled tradesmen represented the best-paid and most stable group. Despite the introduction of machine production, most goods continued to be manufactured in small batches, in small to medium-sized workshops, and with master craftsmen as the lead—if not the only—producers. Skilled workers represented about 18 percent of the industrial labor force, and skilled work remained a crucial lynch pin in mass production processes. In iron manufacture, in tailoring and sewing, in the production of wagons, stoves, cigars, books and newspapers, beer, bread, and butchered meat, it was tradesmen who controlled craft knowledge, the transmission and training of skills, and the pace and organization of work. In the building of houses and commercial buildings, of bridges and roads, skilled tradesmen with skills in carpentry and metal work drew the heaviest paychecks. They handpicked their co-workers, helpers, and apprentices, often from friends and families. On railroads and in transport generally, there was equal power in the hands of the engineers, brakemen, firemen, conductors, captains, and navigators who controlled the journey. Coal miners held a monopoly on mining knowledge, and they passed it down to helpers and co-workers without the sanction or opposition of mine owners. Employers who had to deal with skilled workers as a whole had civil public relations with them but perhaps privately cursed a system that made businesses dependent on workers whose monopoly on skill guaranteed their power.[35]

Among the railroad brotherhoods and especially in the construction trades like carpentry, pipe-fitting, brewery, and metal-working, the path to full citizenship in the union was a much longer process. Along with work skills came trade rituals and customs. Initiation ceremonies had apprentice railroad brakemen and firemen standing blindfolded on a moving platform to show trust and fearlessness. Daily workplace practices, such as the reading of newspapers in cigar workshops or treating with beer, were an essential part of belonging. Some rituals were designed to humble future master craftsmen and give them a sense of how they were distinct from other workers employed at less skilled and less valued labor.[36]

Trade unions often began as mutual aid societies to provide unemployment insurance and death benefits. They became labor unions over time, as they engaged in collective bargaining and sought to control production. Trade unions took their cue from the fraternal organizations of the time, such as the Freemasons, Odd Fellows, Foresters, and Elks, not to mention the Knights of Labor. It is not surprising that most of the founders of the American Federation of Labor, including Samuel Gompers, Peter McGuire and Adolph Strasser, were members not only of their respective trade unions but also belonged to other fraternal organizations.[37] Like fraternal orders, trade unions embraced a code of manliness and honor. To be a member of a trade union, skilled workers were to be free men, independent of or not solely dependent upon wage employment, respectable family members (as current or future heads of households and families), and either current or future citizens. Citizenship, reimagined from Citizen-Soldier to Citizen-Worker, became the trope that distinguished the rabble, who engaged in labor protests but had little investment in community, and the skilled workers who claimed equal rights and citizenship for themselves.[38]

The fraternal culture of trade unions in the nineteenth century left traces on the landscape of unionism that were present in the Knights of Labor and in the AFL and are visible today. The language of labor, its form of address ("union brothers" and later "union sisters"), the initiation rituals that remain part of labor recruitment—especially in the skilled trades, the call for solidarity as a fraternal virtue and its emphasis on "masculine" values of courage, physical aggression, and comradely sacrifice: These attributes can be found in contemporary union language and guide the behavior of union members on the picket line and in the union hall. Sanctioned violence is neither frequent nor random in labor history, but the willingness to "strike a blow" for labor, and the celebration and com-memoration of labor struggles, embraces the past vision of brotherly solidarity (racially and ethnically defined as well as masculine by design) over all else.

The Reign of Gompers

The trade unions, despite resisting new technology, played an essential role in the modernization of industry. Even as some craft workers lost their foothold in manufacturing as machines replaced their work, others benefited from the evolving industrial economy. Trade unions also benefited from modern labor relations. Work relations and contracts were focused on and in the workplace, a place where skilled workers had both leverage and recognition. Public opinion was unreliable, communities divided, and police and courts focused more on law and order than on small workplace disputes. Employers often chose to bargain with the most valuable and hard-to-replace workers (tradesmen), rather than contend with semi-skilled operators and unskilled manual workers. For the most part, most firms did not bargain with ordinary workers, often immigrants who spoke different languages, possessed little leverage and had no monopoly on skills in their jobs. Factory hands and manual laborers were thought to be less predictable and less respectful of property rights and contractual law. Trade unions, while opposed by many employers, had a culture that honored the sanctity of property rights, shared a language and often membership in fraternal organizations with their middle-class and elite brothers.

Samuel Gompers, the president of the American Federation of Labor, was the public face of respectable labor. While he believed that trade unions were "born of the necessity of workers to protect and defend themselves from encroachment, injustice and wrong,"[39] he had a keen appreciation for property and a persistent desire for respectability. This was, no doubt, rooted in the loss of family fortune and his own standing as an outsider. He fought with the other immigrant boys in the London of his childhood, felt the sting of exile after being voted out as AFL president, and acquired and hoarded power as AFL president. He rarely spoke in public of his Judaism, even while he revered its moral authority. A naturalized citizen, Gompers persistently asserted his Americanism and his citizenship to ward off criticism. When he, in later years, joined wealthy allies in the National Civic Federation, the boy from the London streets must have felt vindicated. Still, even in the NCF, Gompers belonged to a small, elite group of trade unionists that joined its ranks.[40]

Family, religious, ethnic, and occupational experience colored the over forty years Gompers served as AFL president. His identity as a skilled tradesman, and his privileging fraternal bonds, put a damper on the democratic vision he brought to the federation. While Gompers insisted that AFL unions exclude non-workers from membership (diverging from Knights of Labor practice), he originally sought to abolish racial exclusion from trade union ranks. Gompers publicly supported woman's right to vote, advocated for equal pay, and withheld support from unions that restricted their membership on the basis of race. Self-taught in economics and politics, Gompers had an eye for the upwardly mobile within the labor movement and sought to mentor and bring along others with similarly open minds and strong instincts for working-class solidarity. In his autobiography, he is open about how the United States proved a poor ground for working-class identity and politics. At the same time, he well understood how important class feeling was in building solidarity and in defining worker identity. It is the early Gompers, and the broadly democratic union culture he represented, that is hardest to reconcile with the business unionism that ruled the AFL in the twentieth century.[41]

When one returns to the cultural context from which the AFL emerged, understanding how the AFL narrowed its goals is far easier. Men's authority, and the power of native white men in particular, governed much of what occurred in workplaces and communities. Paternal—even patriarchal—authority governed the lives of Gompers and other early trade union leaders. Within their families, it continued to govern the home. Skilled trade unionists were not, in this respect, unlike most "respectable" white men. They sought to govern their families, homes, and work relations with the power of their own authority, supported by like-minded men. Workers who came from different cultures were ungovernable, savages with little respect for order and anarchists prone to destroying rather than negotiating. The men who organized among these foreign workmen "would rush our people into a mad whirlpool of impractical doctrines only to be engulfed in a sea of turmoil, hatred, and possible bloodshed." They made "appeal[s] to the reckless, the unprincipled, the uneducated, the unstable." As "pernicious" "promoters of wild vagaries," they were "fanatics" who "perverted" the use of labor's most effective tool—the strike.[42]

Among skilled workers, white men's political and economic power and authority was believed to be rooted in the capacity for independence—from employers, from traditional authorities, and from the government. Craft ideology was coupled with "voluntarism," that sought to limit government action. While not averse to political action, trade unionists had a limited vision of what was possible and desirable. Deeply suspicious of government, due in part to police suppression of strikes, AFL trade unions perceived that a national law legislating minimum wages also might set maximum wages. Unemployment insurance, they speculated, might mean forced employment. Government wage and hour legislation, they believed, should only apply to public employment, where workers had considerably less autonomy, or to dependent classes, such as women, children, and workers in hazardous trades.[43] Beyond that, government assistance—for the unemployed, the elderly, the vulnerable—was seen to "soften […] the moral fiber of the people" and entail "the loss of red-blooded, rugged independence." Such dependency was for women, children, and the weaker races—those who did not possess requisite skill and who required the power of the state to ensure their standard of living and protection from dangerous labor. Women and children were the worthy objects of men's protection. They were seen not as equals in the workplace nor as brothers but rather as the source of lower wages and broken solidarity.[44]

In each case, the insurgent labor movements of the decades after the Civil War were primarily dedicated to the organization and mobilization of white men in the skilled trades. Because immigration threatened to both increase the labor pool and, thus, lower wages, many trade unionists and most unions adopted a cautious stance toward immigrant workers. Some, especially in areas where there was competition between immigrant and native-born labor, came to oppose all immigration. Differences in cultures and in identities, family status and education further gave rise to union hostility. All labor unions sought to restrict or ban contract and prison labor. Racially, trade unions, especially in the railroad craft trades and throughout the South, often excluded non-white members. Where African American or other racial minorities were admitted, they often belonged to segregated locals.[45]

Craft unionists had their own rituals of admission that emphasized these very traits. Did workers possess the requisite strength and knowledge to be trade union men? Were they capable of understanding and defending common interests? Did they share values of proper learning, that is, reading the newspaper, attending public lectures, and possessing craft knowledge and skill? Did they display proper conduct in the workplace and take their craft seriously, attending to authority but not being subservient? Did they engage in proper behavior in private life, demonstrating personal dignity, family respectability, and self-restraint? Did they also join in when it came to drinking, gambling and even sexual conquests? Could they keep secrets? Did they have proper standing in public life as citizens and voters? Did they attend public events and mass parades and participate in voluntary associations? For most craft unionists, unskilled and semi-skilled workers—whether the new immigrants, African American migrants, or women of any group—did not meet these standards.

The Risks and Limits of Railroad Labor

One group of respectable white men were skilled railroad workers, who constituted an independent conservative force in the labor movement and also the cutting edge of labor–state relations in the twentieth century. Since the advent of rail transportation, there had been a rigid hierarchy on the rails. Railroad construction was, apart from engineers and supervisors, semi-skilled manual labor, often performed by immigrant or contract labor and others who had few options for work. Laying and repairing tracks, however, was only one aspect. Those who repaired railroad engines and rail cars, in what was called "railroad shop crafts," had demonstrable skills but irregular employment. At the top of the labor hierarchy were the engineers, brakemen, firemen, and conductors who ran the trains. These skilled workers came to constitute the most skilled, and unionized, force of railroad workers—the railroad brotherhoods. These trade unions were entirely white and male in membership, and their labor activism was restricted to strikes of allied craft unions. They did not, by any stretch of the imagination, engage in broad-based protests, and they specifically barred non-white men from joining their organizations.[46]

Even as mass production industry introduced machines that intensified the pace of work and the injury rate, so too did the skilled workers on the railroads use their organizations to fight what they considered degraded and dangerous labor. The empowered railroad brotherhoods of firemen, engineers, signalmen/brakemen, and conductors were faced with technological changes that supposedly improved train performance and speed but also made railroad workers—skilled and unskilled—at risk of occupational injury and death. Railroad workers had, in fact, the highest occupational injury and mortality rates in the United States, even surpassing miners and steel workers. It is not surprising, then, that railroad workers were among the first groups to establish mutual benefit societies to provide death benefits and hazard insurance. At a time when employers had the upper hand legally in claims for liability and compensation, railroad unions led efforts to sue employers and establish workers' compensation. Working for what were most commonly interstate businesses, railroad workers played an important role in setting legal precedence for national labor legislation and federal mediation.[47] For the most part, however, the brotherhoods remained outside the mainstream of the labor movement; the legislation that applied to the railroad industry laid down the basic outlines of labor laws that evolved over the course of the twentieth century.

The Fiery Furnace: Labor Strife and Prudential Unionism

The splintering of class solidarity and the defeat of a more inclusive and community-based unionism came to a head in two epic strikes in the 1890s—the Homestead steel strike in 1892 and the Pullman strike in 1894. In the former, the Amalgamated Iron and Steel Workers went down to defeat when Carnegie Steel locked out workers and refused to sign contracts with the union. The conflict began as a narrow union protest and quickly accelerated into a community conflict, as the unemployed of Homestead and Pittsburgh joined forces with skilled workers. Pullman, in contrast, was begun when workers who were unaffiliated with any union organized to confront their employer in the wake of wage cuts and rent hikes. They were joined, after initial failure, by the forces of the American Railroad

Union, a broad-based industrial union of rail workers, who stood against and apart from the more conservative railroad brotherhoods. Both strikes took on the character of community-based actions and overran the boundaries of trade union action. For that reason, the strikes offered opportunities for employers to call in local police, state militia, and, in the case of Pullman, federal troops to defend the rights of workers and to arrest and imprison those who colored outside the lines of limited labor action. What were the costs and limits of broadly inclusive community-based struggles among workers, and did trade unionism, with its restrictions, offer some margin of protection against state action?

Originally on good terms with the Amalgamated Iron and Steel Workers, Carnegie Steel in the 1880s slowly reorganized production in line with new technology—the Bessemer and Open Hearth furnaces that promised to produce more steel, more quickly, and with fewer skilled workers. Carnegie also quickly sought to acquire iron ore mines, railroads and shipping lines, and coke plants to reduce the cost of factors of production. Ruthless with competitors, Carnegie established a partnership in 1881 with Henry Clay Frick, whose coke plants supplied the growing needs of Carnegie plants in Homestead, Braddock, and Pittsburgh. The new merger created the opportunity for Carnegie to end his long affiliation with the skilled workers of the Amalgamated.[48] Frick complained to his partner that the Amalgamated had kept the mills from "turn[ing] out the product they should ..."[49] For more than a decade, Carnegie Steel retained its contract with the Amalgamated. But while Carnegie took an extended trip to Scotland in 1892, Frick moved to close down the union. He first refused to negotiate terms and then moved to lock out union workers from steel plants he had encircled with fences, guards, and weapons.

The skilled workers of the Amalgamated were unprepared for the battle with Frick. While he mounted gatling guns on the steel mill walls, now nicknamed Fort Frick, the Amalgamated protested about the rights of citizens to their work. They surrounded the factory in Homestead and formed barriers to Frick's efforts to recruit and employ strikebreakers in the steel mills. Such efforts, supported by the community in Homestead, Braddock, and other mill towns, had little overall impact. When the strikers at Homestead forced barges of guards and strikebreakers to stop short of the stockade plant, they made them walk the gauntlet. On both sides, violence took its toll. Over the course of the Homestead battle, twelve died and more than twenty were seriously injured. With the intervention of the state militia, the Homestead strike was effectively over. The leaders of the strike were put on trial for conspiracy. Steel workers did not have effective unions again until the 1930s.[50]

The defeat of the Amalgamated at Homestead Steel Works signaled that mass protests had limited utility, especially in capital-intensive, well-funded and well-armed industries. The state courts that convicted the strike leaders gave little weight to claims that workers had property rights in their jobs. What is more, labor violence during the strike, including the gunshots fired from Pinkertons on the barges and beatings of strikebreakers, were charged not to the employer who hired guns and fortified his factory but to the workers who constructed barricades and obstructed movement through the factory gates. Alarmed by what they perceived as lawless and reckless strikers, elected officials, judges, and "public opinion" stood on the side of Carnegie Steel. It was a lesson to be repeated for decades.[51]

Pullman Strike

The economic crisis that began in 1893 would further change the labor movement and offer up yet another example of how widespread labor and community protests were increasingly ineffective. Once again, crises in the financial sector depressed employment, wages, and profits. Different sectors and agents within the sectors responded to the rapid decline of prices. In transportation, the costs were often born by railroad companies, which were volatile investments. On the outskirts of Chicago, one rail company, the Pullman Sleeping Car Company, faced declining demand as the economy continued to struggle. Its owner, George Pullman, had built his company on a model of paternalism, constructing a new town, Pullman, in which housing, stores, school, and church were owned by the company. Still, Pullman also wanted stable profits. He created privileged berths for managers and skilled workers, while he held down wages for the semi-skilled. The economic downturn, which saw employment levels rise and bankruptcies soar, provided him with the opportunity to cut his losses by cutting wages and not reducing workers' rents.[52]

Protests escalated as Pullman workers called on Eugene Debs and the American Railway Union (ARU), to support the strike. Debs had been a railway fireman and member of the Knights of Labor and of the Brotherhood of Locomotive Firemen. In his twenties, he had witnessed the defeat of railroad strikes, in large part fueled by the division among railroad crafts. The ARU, which Debs organized, sought to work on an industrial union model, recruiting from a range of railroad workers to create a stronger base for labor action. In building the ARU, Debs drew on the traditions of craft unionism in its celebration of skill, solidarity, and white manhood. In the course of the Pullman strike, Debs learned how inflexible craft unions had become in upholding the division of labor and how politically entrenched the railroads were. The time Debs would spend in prison reordered his priorities and altered his view of the world. He emerged from the Pullman conflict as a committed socialist, not antagonistic to trade unionism but rather seeing in socialism a broader and more inclusive agenda.[53]

While the Pullman workers were not originally part of the ARU's vision, Debs still took on their cause as his own, declaring a boycott on all trains with Pullman sleeping cars. He had originally advised against striking. The ARU, was, after all, only in its infancy as an industrial union of those employed in the operating crafts—engineers, firemen, brakemen, conductors. The union responded remarkably to the challenge. The 4,000 strikers at Pullman were joined by more than 100,000 workers nationally, as the Pullman strike mobilized railroad workers and their communities. It wasn't just about Pullman. The 1893 depression, an economic crisis on the scale of the 1873 depression, brought unemployment levels above 20 percent and caused massive dislocation of workers. Railroad workers knew better than most that the countryside was filled with poor farmers and the unemployed, an army of the discontented who blamed Pullman, the railroads and the banks for their plight.

In his refusal to negotiate with the workers and the ARU, Pullman was backed by the General Managers Association, an organization of twenty-four railroad lines, that wanted to avoid setting a precedent for railroad labor. They called on state and federal authorities to suppress the strike and, indeed, urged the federal government's intervention on the railroads. Under the Cleveland administration, Attorney General Richard Olney saw in the railroad conflict the seeds of further trouble. Each train that left the station in Chicago and elsewhere pulled a mail car, making boycotting Pullman operations and the regular railroad schedule a federal offense for those who now were obstructing the U.S. mail. Federal troops were mobilized to insure mail delivery by train. Justices in local and federal courts issued labor injunctions, prohibiting further picketing and boycotting of the rail line. Soon, Eugene Debs, ARU union leaders, and others were under indictment. Debs was later convicted (*In re Debs*), and the Pullman strike was lost. Once again, the sheer scope of the Pullman strike, involving possibly hundreds of thousands of railroad workers, community protesters, and the unemployed, pro-voked a severe legal and political response. The lesson, for conservative labor, was to retreat from the community-based actions of Homestead and Pullman to the narrower ground of craft unionism and focused, skill-based labor actions.

"Government by Injunction"

By the 1890s, employers, facing new political opposition and mass discontent, sought other means to control labor. Neither conspiracy laws nor overt political intervention had beaten back labor activism. It was the private guards at Homestead (later bolstered by state militia) and the federal troops in the Pullman strike that stifled workers' collective action. The labor injunction now became a primary means to disarm labor activists. This was particularly true in cases of strikes of skilled workers, where the chief strategy had been to withdraw labor and restrict or bar the employment of replacement workers with similar skills. In a Michigan case, *Beck*, teamsters had refused to work, contingent on negotiations with the employer. They withdrew their own labor and picketed the business to persuade other workers, by means that ranged from calm argument to physical coercion, to refuse to take their place in the shop. They otherwise sought to leverage their skills to stave off wage cuts and bolster their income.[54]

In *Beck*, as in what would amount to thousands of cases over the next thirty years, employers turned to the equity courts to ask for an injunction on labor union action, charging that the printers' union was responsible for damages to the employers' business—not only ongoing business but the firm's property in their reputation among other businesses, employers, workers, and the community at large. In equity court, defendants had no right to cross-examine and often did not know that they were being charged. Only if the judge (for there is no jury) issued an injunction was there public action, as the injunction was enforced. Labor unions—and their members—who violated the injunction were in contempt of court and liable for such damages as the judge awarded. The "judge-made law" of the labor injunction became the most effective way of closing down trade unions. It exempted the defendants from any regular means to challenge the charges and cost striking unions, their leaders, and members court costs, damages, and even jail time.[55]

The AFL had, since the late 1890s, assumed that the strike was a legitimate tool in labor conflict. It relied upon trade unionists' own ability to assert economic pressure on employers. Labor injunctions forced unions to confront the inherent inequality under the law. The judges who presided over the criminal and equity courts were, overwhelmingly, men of the middle and upper classes, deeply imbued with a commitment to property rights. Most disdained working men of any occupation, ethnicity or hue. Labor injunctions, which began as a trickle in the railroad strikes of the 1890s, became a familiar tactic of employers. There was little recourse, given the equity courts and the conservative bias of most judges in favor of the rights of property.

It was not simply the mass strikes that showed the limitations of the labor movement. Workingmen's parties and labor advocates proposed laws to restrict child labor, women's working hours, the exposure of workers to grinding machinery and dangerous trades, and the materials used by state and local government. The political friends of the workingman, whether in city and county government or in state legislatures, demanded work for the unemployed shoveling snow and cleaning streets, especially when there was no other form of outdoor relief. They also fought for state labor bureaus, statistics on employment, strikes, and family budgets; they demanded funding for public schools and sometimes defended parochial ones. They also asked, more pragmatically, that the competition of prison labor, contract labor, and immigrant labor be restrained from competing for jobs and work with good reliable white men. And in industries where home work prevailed—as in the sewing of garments or the producing of cheap cigars—labor unions and labor advocates pursued state legislation to prohibit the production of manufactured goods in private residences and in tenements, which were defined, significantly, as unclean, impure, and dangerous sites for production.

Because workingmen constituted, at least in major cities, a respectable margin in elections, workingmen's advocates sometimes succeeded. And yet, through the last few decades of the nineteenth century, workingmen also lost ground. If child labor was regulated, not the least through mandatory schooling, at the state level, there were greater and lesser mechanisms for enforcement. Dangerous workplace conditions or the length of hours women worked—regulation depended on reliable, honest state labor inspectors with sufficient hours to inspect industry. None of these were a given. What was more, as labor devised schemes for state regulation, it repeatedly came up against the limitations of the American judiciary. Was it constitutional to demand goods be produced in a particular environment? *In re Jacobs*, a decision that invalidated a tenement inspection law, showed that state governments could only regulate within fairly narrow bounds. Tenements may not have been clean and airy, but contemporary observers did not deem them dangerous. Labor unions found that labor laws promised little to labor that labor was not willing to demand on its own.[56]

The Labor Question in a New Age

Thirty years after the Civil War, the labor movement had become an important factor in local and state politics, creating new forms of labor organization that would shape the workplace and community in the new century. In the aftermath of the Homestead and Pullman strikes, few would have predicted that the labor movement would become a political force and enter the government arena. Responding to the crisis of the 1890s with a new pragmatic unionism, defined through stable union membership, formal labor contracts and limited political action, labor leaders allied themselves with forces that sought to rationalize the market, the workplace, and politics. The "horny-handed sons of toil" who led the American Federation of Labor, the United Mine Workers, and the railroad brotherhoods joined the corporate elite of the National Civic Federation in advocating immigration reform and workers' compensation and proposed federal regulation of seaboard and railroad work. They used their new political power to push for laws for shorter workdays and restrictions on child labor and fought to end widespread labor injunctions.

The political face of the labor movement, however, was limited by an ideology of voluntarism and the rejection of federal government power to intervene in routine labor relations. It was further restricted by the conservative and "pragmatic" vision of trade unionists. Protective labor laws regarding women workers, child labor, and hazardous trades were the only concessions to labor's commitment to the rights of independent workingmen and their self-reliance. Labor leaders such as Samuel Gompers, John Mitchell, and Andrew Furuseth fostered an image of craft autonomy and manly independence as well as deep aversion to the coercive power of the state. Homestead and Pullman deepened this aversion. They were traumatic losses for a labor movement that advocated the rights of Citizen-Worker and sought to protect property in skill. Facing armed company guards, private detectives, local police, state militias, federal troops, and court injunctions, the power of labor followed the law of diminishing returns.

Where the labor movement stood at the turn of the twentieth century was in fact divided—between the skilled worker and the machine operative, between native-born and naturalized citizen workers and immigrant labor, between men and women, white and black, long-term employees and migrant workers. While these lines were not hard and fast, the stratified labor movement provided skilled workers with limited bargaining power even while it neglected to provide industrial workers, harvest hands, and domestic servants with similar protection. As labor organizations and strikes began to fail along these divides, there was a call for a new unionism, one that would take on the challenges of organizing mass production industry and the now consolidated power and culture of labor's "aristocracy." All three elements—labor, capital, and the state—played roles in the tumultuous decades ahead, as new industrial workers and the trade union movement butted heads not simply with organized employers but also with each other.

Notes

1 Samuel Gompers, "Editorial: The 'Neighborhood Work' of Fellow Unionists," *American Federationist* 19:6 (June 1912), 472; idem, *Seventy Years of Life and Labor: An Autobiography*, ed. Nick Salvatore (New York: ILR Press, 1984, c. 1925).

2 John Commons, "American Shoemakers," was one of the earliest essays out of the Wisconsin school of labor history. In it, Commons emphasized trade union control over employment more than the cultural legacy of the Crispin past. Later scholars, such as Paul Faler, Alan Dawley, and Mary Blewett, focused on cultural symbols and work organization in the shoe industry. In *Class and Community*, Alan Dawley emphasizes that slogan of the Lynn shoemakers, "Equal Rights and No Favor," called for an equal rights society, a slogan that had meaning for both women and men, despite differences in work and circumstance. See John R. Commons, "American Shoemakers, 1648–1895," in *Labor and Administration*, reprint ed. (New York: Augustus Kelley, 1964), 219–266; Alan Dawley, *Class and Community: The Industrial Revolution in Lynn* (Cambridge, MA: Harvard University Press, 1976); Paul G. Faler, *Mechanics and Manufacturers in the Early Industrial Revolution: Lynn, Massachusetts, 1780–1860* (Albany: SUNY Press, 1981); Mary H. Blewett, *Men, Women, and Work: A Study of Class, Gender and Protest in the Nineteenth-Century New England Shoe Industry* (Urbana: University of Illinois Press, 1988).

3 Dawley, *Class and Community*; Blewett, *Men, Women, and Work*; David Montgomery, "Workers' Control of Machine Production in the 19th Century," in *Workers Control in America* (Cambridge: Cambridge University Press, 1979), 9–31; also see Paul Michel Taillon, *Good, Reliable White Men: Railroad Brotherhoods, 1877–1917* (Urbana: University of Illinois Press, 2009).

4 Editorial, *American Federationist* 18:4 (April 1911), excerpted in Samuel Gompers, *Labor and the Employer*, comp. and ed. Hayes Robbins (New York, 1920), 141–142.

5 Bruce Laurie, *Artisans into Workers: Labor in Nineteenth Century America* (New York: Hill and Wang, 1997), 129; Alexander Keyssar, *Out of Work: The First Century of Unemployment in Massachusetts* (Cambridge: Cambridge University Press, 1986), 54–55, 145–146ff.

6 Dawley, *Class and Community*; John T. Cumbler, *Working-Class Community in Industrial America: Work, Leisure and Struggle in Two Industrial Cities, 1880–1920* (Westport, CT: Greenwood Press, 1979), 57–61.

7 Dawley, *Class and Community*; Blewett, *Men, Women and Work*; Mary Anderson, *Woman at Work: The Autobiography of Mary Anderson*, as told to Mary N. Winslow (Minneapolis: University of Minnesota Press, 1951), 27–29.

8   Blewett, *Men, Women and Work*, 267–319; Keyssar, *Out of Work*.
9   David Montgomery, "Workers' Control of Machine Production in the 19th Century," *Labor History* 17 (Fall 1976), 485–509; Daniel Nelson, "Scientific Management, Systematic Management, and Labor, 1880–1915," *Business History Review* 48:4 (Winter 1974), 479–500; Jill Lapore, "Not So Fast: A Critic at Large," *New Yorker*, October 12, 2009: 114ff. For shoe production under the new welfare capitalism, see Gerald Zahavi, *Workers, Managers, and Welfare Capitalism: The Shoemakers and Tanners of Endicott Johnson, 1890–1950* (Urbana: University of Illinois Press, 1988).
10 Carole Turbin, "'And We Are Nothing But Women': Irish Working Women in Troy," in *Women of America: A History*, Carol R. Berkin and Mary Beth Norton, eds. (Boston, MA: Houghton Mifflin, 1979), 202–222; idem, *Working Women of Collar City: Gender, Class and Community in Troy, 1864–1886* (Urbana: University of Illinois Press, 1992); Daniel Walkowitz, *Worker City, Company Town: Iron and Cotton Workers' Protest in Troy and Cohoes, N.Y., 1855–1884* (Urbana: University of Illinois Press, 1978).
11 Turbin, "'And We Are Nothing But Women.'"
12 Paul Krause, *The Battle for Homestead, 1880–1892: Politics, Culture and Steel* (Pittsburgh: University of Pittsburgh Press, 1992), 47–80; Thomas J. Misa, *A Nation of Steel* (Baltimore: Johns Hopkins University Press, 1995), 5–38; David Montgomery, *The Fall of the House of Labor* (New York: Cambridge University Press, 1987), 9–44.
13 Montgomery, *Workers' Control in America*, 9–31; David Brody, *Steelworkers in the Non-Union Era* (Cambridge, MA: Harvard University Press, 1960), 60–68.
14 Montgomery, *Workers' Control* in America, 9–31; David Bensman, *The Practice of Solidarity: American Hat Finishers in the 19th Century* (Urbana: University of Illinois Press, 1985); Cooper, *Once a Cigar Maker: Men, Women, and Work Culture in American Cigar Factories, 1900–1919* (Urbana: University of Illinois Press, 1987); Nancy Hewett, "'The Voice of Virile Labor': Labor Militancy, Community Solidarity, and Gender Identity among Tampa's Latin Workers, 1880–1921," in Ava Baron, ed., *Work Engendered: Toward a New History of American Labor* (Ithaca: Cornell University Press, 1992), 142–67; Mary Blewett, "Manhood and the Market: The Politics of Gender and Class among the Textile Workers of Fall River, Massachusetts, 1870–1880," in Baron, ed., *Work Engendered*, 92–113.
15 Lawrence B. Glickman, *A Living Wage: American Workers and Consumer Society* (Ithaca: Cornell University Press, 1997), 61–92; Gwendolyn Mink, *Old Labor and New Immigrants in American Political Development: Union, Party and State, 1875–1920* (Ithaca: Cornell University Press, 1990), 45–112.
16 Mink, *Old Workers, New Immigrants*; Allen T. Lane, *Solidarity or Survival? American Labor and European Immigrants, 1830–1924* (Westport, CT: Greenwood Press, 1987); Catherine Collomp, "Unions, Civics, and National Identity: Organized Labor's Reaction to Immigration, 1881–1887," *Labor History* 29 (1988), 450–474; Elizabeth Faue, *Writing the Wrongs: Eva Valesh and the Rise of Labor Journalism* (Ithaca: Cornell University Press, 2002), 148–159.
17 Montgomery, *The Fall of the House of Labor*, 9–170; Walter Licht, *Industrializing America in the Nineteenth Century* (Baltimore: Johns Hopkins University Press, 1995), 102–132; Kim Voss, *The Making of American Exceptionalism: The Knights of Labor and Class Formation in the Nineteenth Century* (Ithaca: Cornell University Press, 1994), 105–135.
18 Richard Oestreicher, "Urban Working-Class Political Behavior and Theories of American Electoral Politics, 1870–1940," *Journal of American History* (1988), 1257–1286; Leon Fink, *Workingmen's Democracy: The Knights of Labor and American Democracy* (Urbana: University of Illinois Press, 1983), 3–17. On the Greenback party, which had strong support among working men, see Matthew Hild, *Greenbackers, Knights of Labor and Populists: Farmer-Labor Insurgency in the Late 19th Century South* (Athens: University of Georgia Press, 2007); Gretchen Ritter, *Goldbugs and Greenbacks: The Antimonopoly Tradition and the Politics of Finance in America* (New York: Cambridge University Press, 1997), 31–47.

19 David Montgomery, *Beyond Equality: Labor and the Radical Republicans, 1862–1872* (New York: Knopf, 1967); Lloyd Ulman, *The Rise of the National Trade Union: The Development and Significance of its Structure, Governing Institutions, and Economic Policies* (Cambridge, MA: Harvard University Press, 1966); David Roediger and Philip Foner, *Our Own Time: A History of American Labor and the Working Day* (New York: Verso, 1989), 97–99.

20 Robert Weir, *Beyond Labor's Veil: The Culture of the Knights of Labor* (University Park: Pennsylvania State University Press, 1996), is the best study of the Knights' organizational culture. See also Norman J. Ware, *The Labor Movement in the United States, 1860–1895: A Study in Democracy* (New York: Appleton, 1929).

21 Craig Phelan, *Grand Master Workman: Terence Powderly and the Knights of Labor* (Westport: Greenwood Press, 2000); Gerald N. Grob, *Workers and Utopia: A Study of Ideological Conflict in the American Labor Movement, 1865–1900* (Evanston, IL: Northwestern University Press, 1961), 87–88.

22 Weir, *Beyond Labor's Veil*, 19–102.

23 Susan Levine, *Labor's True Woman: Carpet Weavers, Industrialization, and Labor Reform in the Gilded Age* (Philadelphia, PA: Temple University Press, 1984); Joseph Gerteis, *Class and the Color Line: Interracial Class Coalition in the Knights of Labor and the Populist Movement* (Durham, NC: Duke University Press, 2007).

24 Theresa Ann Case, "Losing the Middle Ground: Strikebreakers and Labor Protest on the Southwestern Railroads," in Donna T. Haverty-Stacke and Daniel J. Walkowitz, eds., *Rethinking U.S. Labor History: Essays on the Working Class Experience, 1756–2009* (New York: Continuum, 2010), 54–81; idem, *The Great Southwestern Railroad Strike and Free Labor* (College Station: Texas A&M University Press, 2010).

25 Steve Ross, *Workers on the Edge: Work, Leisure, and Politics in Industrializing Cincinnati, 1788–1890* (1985); Richard Oestreicher, *Solidarity and Fragmentation: Working People and Class Consciousness in Detroit, 1874–1894* (Urbana: University of Illinois Press, 1986); Levine, *Labor's True Woman*; Fink, *Workingmen's Democracy*; Faue, *Writing the Wrongs*, 20–69; Richard Schneirov, *Labor and Urban Politics: Class Conflict and the Origins of Modern Liberalism in Chicago, 1864–1897* (Urbana: University of Illinois Press, 1998).

26 Voss, *The Making of American Exceptionalism*, 34–35, 43–44, 86–87, 215–221.

27 David Montgomery, "Labor and the Republic in Industrial America, 1860–1920," *Mouvement Social* 111 (1980), 57–80, outlined the ideological chasm between the Knights' labor republicanism and the class-based politics of the twentieth century. Gregory S. Kealey and Bryan D. Palmer, *Dreaming of What Might Be: The Knights of Labor in Ontario, 1880–1900* (Cambridge: Cambridge University Press, 1982) and more recent studies have been more respectful of the Knights' ideology. Robert E. Weir, *Knights Unhorsed: Internal Conflict in a Gilded Age Social Movement* (Detroit, MI: Wayne State University Press, 2000), brings us full circle. On cooperative work, see Steve Leikin, "The Cooperative Coopers of Minneapolis," *Minnesota History* 57:3 (December 2001), 386–405; idem, *The Practical Utopians: American Workers and the Cooperative Movement in the Gilded Age* (Detroit, MI: Wayne State University Press, 2005).

28 Weir, *Beyond the Veil*, 250–255. Competition between AFL-affiliated trades unions and the Knights of Labor became much more evident after 1886. In some cities and regions, the open break between trades unions and the Knights came later. See Grob, *Workers and Utopia*, 105–118; Voss, *The Making of American Exceptionalism*, 185–228; Faue, *Writing the Wrongs*, 95–116.

29 James Green, *Death in the Haymarket: A Story of Chicago, the First Labor Movement, and the Bombing that Divided Gilded Age America* (New York: Anchor, 2007), 102–125, 145–159.

30 Green, *Death in the Haymarket*, 160–173; Bruce C. Nelson, *Beyond the Martyrs: A Social History of Chicago's Anarchists* (New Brunswick: Rutgers University Press, 1988);

Schneirov, *Labor and Urban Politics*. A recent reinterpretation is Timothy Messer-Kruse, *The Haymarket Conspiracy: Transatlantic Anarchist Networks* (Urbana: University of Illinois Press, 2012).

31 Green, *Death in the Haymarket*, 274–299; Oestreicher, *Solidarity and Fragmentation*, 172–221.

32 Oestreicher, *Solidarity and Fragmentation*, 222–248.

33 Foner, *A History of the Labor Movement in the United States*, vol. 2 (New York: International Publishers, 1955), 78–83; Stuart B. Kaufman, *Samuel Gompers and the Origins of the American Federation of Labor, 1848–1896* (New York: Praeger, 1973), 160–167.

34 Standard accounts are Philip Taft, *The AFL in the Time of Gompers* (New York: Harper and Brothers, 1957); Philip Foner, *A History of the Labor Movement in the United States*, vols. 2 and 3 (New York: International Publishers, 1955).

35 Montgomery, *The Fall of the House of Labor*, 9–57; Andrew Dawson, "The Paradox of Dynamic Technological Change and the Labor Aristocracy in the United States, 1880–1914," *Labor History* 20 (Summer 1979), 325–351; idem, "The Parameters of Craft Consciousness: The Social Outlook of the Skilled Worker, 1890–1920," in *American Labor and Immigration History, 1877–1920: Recent European Research*, ed. Dirk Hoerder (Urbana: University of Illinois Press, 1983), 135–155. For specific individual trades, see Michael Kazin, *Barons of Labor: The San Francisco Building Trades and Union Power in the Progressive Era* (Urbana: University of Illinois Press, 1988); Cooper, *Once a Cigar Maker*; Bensman, *The Practice of Solidarity*; Taillon, *Good, Reliable White Men*.

36 Cooper, *Once a Cigar Maker*; Taillon, *Good, Reliable White Men*.

37 Mary Ann Clawson, *Constructing Brotherhood: Class, Gender, and Fraternalism* (Princeton: Princeton University Press, 1989); but see also Samuel Gompers, *Seventy Years of Life and Labor*, 12–13.

38 Faue, *Writing the Wrongs*, 143–163.

39 Florence Calvert Thorne, *Samuel Gompers, American Statesman* (Westport: Greenwood Press, 1969), 17–18.

40 Gompers, *Seventy Years of Life and Labor*, 383; see also Thorne, *Samuel Gompers*.

41 Dorothy Sue Cobble, "Pure and Simple Radicalism: Putting the Progressive Era AFL in Its Time," *Labor: Studies in Working Class History of the Americas* 10:4 (2013), 61–87; see, by contrast, Paul Buhle, *Taking Care of Business: Samuel Gompers, George Meany, Lane Kirkland, and the Tragedy of American Labor* (New York: Monthly Review Press, 1999), 17–34.

42 Gompers, *Seventy Years of Life and Labor*, 124–26; Samuel Gompers, *Labor and the Employer* (1920), 33–35, 70, 124–126, 194.

43 There is some argument about how apolitical and non-partisan AFL voluntarism was. Michael Rogin and other scholars have argued that there was a substantial bar to political action, following on Marc Karson's early work. Julie Greene, and most scholars since, argue that the AFL had a complicated stance that varied over time. By 1906, the AFL's economic and political fortunes were threatened by starkly pro-business courts, a fact that energized labor politics for more than a decade. See Michael Rogin, "Voluntarism: The Political Functions of an Antipolitical Doctrine," *Industrial and Labor Relations Review* 15:4 (July 1962), 521–525; Marc Karson, *American Labor Unions and Politics* (Carbondale: Southern Illinois University Press, 1958); Julie Greene, *Pure and Simple Politics*, 1–16, 49–70, 142–214.

44 Gompers, *Labor and the Employer*, 149–150, 151–153; Edward O'Donnell, "Women as Bread Winners: The Error of the Age," *American Federationist* 4:8 (1897), 186–87. See also Susan Levine, "Labor's True Woman: Domesticity and Equal Rights in the Knights of Labor," *Journal of American History* 70:2 (September 1983), 323–339; Alice Kessler-Harris, "Where are the Organized Women Workers?" *Feminist Studies* 3:2 (1975), 92–110; Ann Schofield, "Rebel Girls and Union Maids: The Woman Question in the Journals of the AFL and IWW, 1905–1920," *Feminist Studies* 9:2 (Summer 1983), 335–358; Faue, *Writing the Wrongs*, 148–159.

45 Robert H. Zieger, *For Jobs and Freedom: Race and Labor in America since 1865* (Lexington: University Press of Kentucky, 2007), 60–69, 75–91. For the historiography, see Joe William Trotter, Jr., "African American Workers: New Directions in U.S. Labor Historiography," *Labor History* 35:4 (1994), 495–523; David Roediger, *Towards the Abolition of Whiteness: Essays in Race, Politics and Working-Class History* (London: Verso, 1994), 21–38, 69–82.

46 Taillon, *Good, Reliable White Men*, 39–67; Eric Arnesen, "'Like Banquo's Ghost, It Will Not Down': The Race Question and the American Railroad Brotherhoods, 1880–1920," *American Historical Review* 99:5 (December 1994), 1601–1633; idem, *Brotherhoods of Color*.

47 John Fabian Witt, *The Accidental Republic: Crippled Workmen, Destitute Widows, and the Remaking of American Law* (Cambridge, MA: Harvard University Press, 2006); Taillon, *Good, Reliable White Men*; Jon R. Huibregtse, *American Railroad Unions and the Genesis of the New Deal, 1919–1935* (Gainesville: University of Florida Press, 2010).

48 Brody, *Steelworkers*, 50–60; Krause, *The Battle for Homestead*, 12–43, 284–314.

49 Quoted in Brody, *Steelworkers*, 53; George Harvey, *Henry Clay Frick: The Man*, reprint ed. (New York: Beard Books, 2002), 177.

50 Krause, *The Battle for Homestead*, 284–314.

51 Bruce Laurie, *Artisans into Workers*, argued that these two labor conflicts were the basis for the emerging strategy of "prudential unionism" that characterized the AFL. Laurie, 176–210.

52 Stanley Buder, *Pullman: An Experiment in Industrial Order and Community Planning, 1880–1930*, Reprint ed. (New York: Oxford University Press, 1970); Richard Schneirov, Shelton Stromquist, and Nick Salvatore, eds., *The Pullman Strike and the Crisis of the 1890s: Essays on Labor and Politics* (Urbana: University of Illinois Press, 1999); Troy Rondinone, *The Great Industrial War: Framing Class Conflict in the Media, 1865–1950* (New Brunswick: Rutgers University Press, 2009), 58–89.

53 Nick Salvatore, *Eugene V. Debs, Citizen and Socialist* (Urbana: University of Illinois Press, 1983), 114–146.

54 Elizabeth Faue, "'Methods of Mysticism' and the Industrial Order: Michigan Labor Law, 1870–1940," in *The History of Michigan Law*, eds. Paul Finkelman and Martin Hershock (Athens: Ohio University Press, 2006), 214–237.

55 The classic work on the labor injunction is Felix Frankfurter and Nathan Greene, *The Labor Injunction* (Gloucester, MA: Peter Smith, 1963, c. 1930). For a synthetic view of labor law in the period, see Leon Fink, "Labor, Liberty and the Law: Trade Unionism and the Problem of the American Constitutional Order," *Journal of American History* 74:3 (November 1987), 904–925.

56 Melvin I. Urofsky, "State Courts and Protective Legislation during the Progressive Era: A Reevaluation," *Journal of American History* 72:1 (June 1985), 63–91.

2

INSURGENT LABOR, 1905–1922

In 1905, what Bill Haywood called "the Continental Congress of the Working Class" gathered in Chicago. Labor leaders from across the nation attended—Eugene Debs, Mother Jones, and every socialist and radical trade unionist with a reputation, an idea, or an answer to the Labor Question was there. So was anyone who had the means to get to the meeting, the self-esteem to enter the debate, and enough popular backing to make themselves credible. The problem, writ large, was "Capitalism." The symptoms were widespread poverty, malnutrition, poor health and education, mass discontent, and a sense of powerlessness before the gears of the economic and political machine. Prescriptions to the diseases of the economic system varied—cooperative enterprises, communal living, popular education, social housekeeping, socialist political campaigns, mass strikes and worker resistance, everything from machine breaking and "soldiering" to mass picketing and grassroots rebellion.

One of the major issues was what many believed were social parasites—the 1 percent that owned the majority of the nation's wealth and lived off the body politic. Socialist Eugene Debs called them "Beasts of Prey," the businessmen who were the corporate elite of the National Civic Federation. Other villains more familiar to the radicals were leaders of the competing American Federation of Labor and the railroad brotherhoods. They were the "Aristocracy of Labor," who peacefully co-existed with the Capitalist Class. They undermined manual laborers, unskilled workers, and machine operatives, migratory farm workers, miners, and timber workers who constituted the bulk of the new working classes. Skilled trade union leaders, the IWW argued, not only betrayed ordinary workers in the search for power and stability but steered their attention away from the broader struggle for equality and justice toward phantom ills.

Caught up in what some termed, "Business Unionism," most trade union leaders resisted the call to organize the unorganized. This was especially true when the unorganized workers came to the United States from foreign lands, spoke a different language, practiced a different religion, wore skirts, or had work that did not fit the definition of "skilled." With some anger, radical labor activists in Chicago pointed out that existing trade unions not only excluded workers on the basis of ethnicity, race, and gender, but also required that workers within a single workplace join unions based principally on occupation or skill. Those who worked in the same industry had to be assigned to separate international unions based on slight differences in work assignments. Under these rules, sewing machine operators did not belong to the same union as those who cut fabric or ironed the final product. In a similar way, those charged with skilled machine repair could not join the same union as those who ran the machines or packed the goods; those who butchered the meat in a packing plant were members of a different local union than those who processed the meat as sausage and/or packed it for market. Skill differences, however, also ran along racial, ethnic, and gender lines.

Sociologist W.E.B. DuBois aptly described the differences among workers and the cost of their racial and ethnic conflicts as "the wages of Whiteness." Many white workers looked down on racial and ethnic minorities as unequal and inferior. Such racism among skilled workers, expressed as hostility to immigrants, African Americans, Asian workers, and Mexican migrants, plagued the labor movement. For native-born workers—and even those from more established immigrant groups—neither the new immigrants nor African Americans were deserving of the same pay or opportunity as "Americans." Rather, according to Samuel Gompers, these new workers became "a convenient whip placed in the hands of employers to cow the white man." Racial privilege undermined their ability to bond with and work alongside minority and immigrant workers. Even as job segregation allowed white men to monopolize skilled work, it also depressed earnings for all workers. These were the wages of whiteness but also the price of exclusionary and conservative unionism that barred gateways to well-paid jobs in ways that it could not bar entry into the United States.[1]

Mass Production Industry and the Modern American Labor Movement

From 1905 to the beginning of World War I, what we recognize as the modern American labor movement took shape. Responding to changes in the social division of labor and renewed industrial conflict, workers created new forms of organization and invented new tactics for collective action in the workplace. If they wanted to improve their wages and conditions, they could not have done otherwise. The average workplace was no longer the size of a family or a small gang of workers. Small focused strikes, even among skilled workers, lost their impact in large factory settings. Managers increasingly relied upon scientific management to organize production and slash wages. Moreover, the expansion of American industry relied on ever-changing technologies of machine and power.

By the turn of the twentieth century, the manufacture and mining of essential goods such as steel, lumber and wood products, coal and mineral ores like copper and lead, cotton and woollen textiles, clothing, and foodstuffs such as beef, pork, canned fish, and wheat flour were transformed by methods that reorganized production and deskilled work. Workplaces employed hundreds, and even thousands, of workers. As new managers redesigned work processes, they asserted stricter forms of control and speeded up production. In turn, the increasing pace of work and the introduction of new technology—including unstable rail couplings, blast furnaces prone to explosive fires, and new drilling machines that produced more coal and silicon dust and greater amounts of explosive gases and heightened the dangers of mine work—threatened workers in ways that unions began to address and protest.[2]

Who worked in industry was changing, but it was a change to which trade unions did not adapt. In each sector, new workers—immigrants from southern and eastern Europe, native-born and second-generation immigrant women, and white and black migrants from the rural South and Midwest—joined the labor force and expanded the reach of labor and working-class politics. The continuing dominance of craft union organizations restricted forms of collective action. Semi-skilled machine operators in meatpacking and light manufacturing had nowhere to turn for labor leadership. What unions did exist (the Butcher Workmen, the Amalgamated Iron and Steel Workers, or the United Garment Workers, to use a few examples) were indifferent to unskilled packers, machine operatives, and helpers. They ignored, to the point of derision, the clerks, typists, and secretaries who were employed in ever greater number as factories opened up personnel and billing offices. Trade unions were, for the most part, not for them, either.[3]

Among the skilled workers, labor's ranks grew rapidly between 1897 and 1903. Membership in the American Federation of Labor increased from 500,000 to nearly 2 million, and the railroad brotherhoods grew at a similar pace. Many of these gains were not in skilled manufacturing but in transport, the construction trades (stone masonry, bricklayers, carpenters), and among miners. The fastest growing union in 1890 was the United Mine Workers, which then had 20,000 members in bituminous coalfields. After a drop in the mid-1890s, the UMW became one of the nation's largest unions, with nearly 100,000 members. Nearly one in three coal miners belonged to the union. While union membership rose and fell with strikes, transport workers provided another rich field for labor organization. Freight haulers in the teamsters, streetcar workers, and railroad workers, especially in the railroad crafts, joined labor unions in growing numbers. In cities, where new buildings boomed alongside the growing influx of immigrants and migrants, construction workers, especially in structural iron work, joined unions at a fast pace and became among the most militant of workers in the period.[4]

The visible resurgence of the labor movement provoked two responses. First, upper middle class and elite men and women formed organizations that advocated some reforms expressed in protective labor laws and political work. Among employers, the Pullman strike sparked the formation of the Civic Federation of

Chicago and later of the National Civic Federation (NCF). Joined by such figures as politician Marcus Hanna and industrialist Andrew Carnegie, the NCF early on targeted employer liability laws as it sought to create workers' compensation as a means of controlling the spiralling costs of worker injuries and deaths. Its elite members understood the importance of an alliance with "respectable" labor. NCF head Ralph Easley courted AFL president Samuel Gompers and the UMW's John Mitchell for their ranks. Easley saw in the alliance a route to draw skilled workers' support and to make common cause with organized labor against protests in the workplace.[5]

For whatever benefit business leaders derived from their alliance with labor leaders, other employers began to organize themselves to confront and control the workplace. Through organizations such as the National Association of Manufacturers (NAM), the American Anti-Boycott Association, local Chambers of Commerce and city employers associations such as the Minneapolis Civic and Commerce Association and the Employers Association of Detroit launched campaigns to limit, if not completely eliminate, trade unionism and establish the open shop. Tactics ranged from blacklisting union activists and denying credit to union employers, to political campaigns and labor injunctions. Conservative in their approach, most employer organizations had little respect for "responsible" trade unionism. As NAM president John Kirby would proclaim in 1914, the labor movement was "an UnAmerican, illegal, and infamous conspiracy."[6] Opposition to labor was rooted in the belief that the private market should not be troubled by third party intervention. Business leaders insisted that individual workers needed to bargain individually and that the market should set wages.

As trade unions recruited new members and industrial workers began to organize, employers turned to state militia, local police, and private detective agencies as means to resist workers' demands. They re-organized workplaces to minimize the leverage of skilled workers, imported new technologies, and reassigned work to decrease the likelihood of a shutdown at any strategic point in the production process. Inspired by the work of scientific management guru Frederick Taylor and organizational engineers like Frank and Lillian Gilbreth, manufacturing firms conducted time-and-motion studies, subdivided tasks and increased repetition as a means to efficient production. They also stressed production quotas and shifted wages to piece-rate. Workers were filmed to capture their every movement, timed by stopwatches, and disciplined by an increasingly intense work pace set not by the average workers' output, but by the pace of the fastest workers. As a result, heightened conflict between labor and capital brought to a halt the energetic labor organizing of the 1890s. Unions gained only another half million members between 1903 and 1915.[7]

Trade Unions and Industrial Unionism

Divisions between skilled craft workers and semi-skilled operatives and between the native-born Anglo-, Irish- and German-American tradesmen and new immigrant workers from southern and eastern Europe were evident in strikes that rocked industry after the turn of the century. In Chicago, meatpacking plants had been hit in 1904, as butcher workmen and line workers took on the giant meat-processing companies. Skilled workers balked at efforts to join the greenhorn factory hands. Strategically, the big three packers (Wilson, Armour, and Hormel) brought in African American workers from the South to replace the operatives. The strike broke apart as workers were locked out of the factories, and racial tensions in Chicago neighborhoods grew. In what was a precursor of the 1919 riot, white and black workers assaulted one another and inflicted what damage they could to neighboring homes. After the strike, the union collapsed. Its leaders were barred from employment in the industry. Individual workers and leaders, such as John Kilkulski, who organized among the Polish immigrants, or Charles Ford, who organized black workers, were lost to the labor movement.[8]

Foreshadowing years of failed campaigns to organize mass production industries such as steel and electrical manufacturing, the 1904 strike summed up all that was wrong with craft unionism. Ethnic and racial conflict ruptured every fragile attempt to organize the industrial sector, and racial violence sporadically erupted in strikes that followed. During the 1905 teamster strike in Chicago, only eight months after the packinghouse strike, Montgomery Ward and other companies recruited black strikebreakers to drive delivery trucks. Although the strike involved only 10,000 of Chicago's 35,000 unionized teamsters, racial tensions rose and violence escalated between white and black workers and in working-class neighborhoods.[9]

Historian John Commons wrote that, "Even the ordinary Teamster looks upon his occupation as a craft, and the object of his union is to have it recognized as such." Craft, as Chapter 1 discussed, was central to trade union identity and also kept unions from recruiting members beyond their narrow base. Even when labor organizers sought to integrate new workers, the heritage of racial conflict, combined with cultural differences between native-born skilled workers and new immigrant and African American operatives, threatened to undermine the unions. Interracial unions, whether in the coalfields of Alabama or among longshoremen and dockworkers of New Orleans, had to maintain a delicate balance between labor solidarity and community divisions in a racially segregated and male-dominated society.[10]

Trade unions, by design, set skilled workers apart from the unskilled, but craft distinctions also allowed employers to pit higher-priced skilled workers against more easily replaced line operatives. As the IWW radicals argued, only a union that took seriously the need to organize all the unorganized and address working-class conditions on the basis that "an injury to one is an injury to all" could succeed against powerful corporations. Like the Knights of Labor whose slogan they echoed, the IWW was a hybrid and irregular form of organization, whose diverse membership was representative of the industrial working class as a whole. At the dawn of a new century, the IWW labor radicals believed that they could change the economic calculus and bring greater prosperity by opening the door to all workers across occupation and industry.[11]

What no one knew in 1905 was that it would be the 1930s before an industrial labor movement came of age and organized the core industries of steel, rubber, automobile, electrical, meatpacking and food processing, textile and garment manufacture, and the transport firms that served them. First, manufacturing firms were notoriously hostile to labor organizing and resilient in the face of any workplace protest. The work force in basic industry, and in extractive industries of mining and lumber, was predominantly immigrant and ethnic American, disproportionately male and white, but with significant groups of minority workers. Its hallmark, by employer design, was its diversity. Literally dozens of immigrant groups from southern and eastern Europe were employed in a single workplace, as they were in Pittsburgh steel mills, Chicago meatpacking plants, Lawrence woollen mills, and Ludlow coal mines. Hundreds of languages, made more complex by regional dialects and accented with American slang, turned manufacturing plants, mines, and steel mills into Towers of Babel. Faced with intense competition over jobs, small promotions, and wages, workers re-created homeland rivalries and slowed the development of workplace alliances.

In the renewed conflict between organized employers and organized labor, there were other obstacles to organizing among industrial workers. First, employers already made some accommodation for skilled workers, who remained in great demand. No streamlined production process was independent of the skills of machinists, pipe-fitters, tool-and-die makers, and machine fixers. Such workers were difficult to retain and hard to appease, but companies did seek to appease them. Welfare capitalism brought skilled workers perks—premium pay, employee stock purchasing, better company housing, company picnics, the solidarity of team sports and company newsletters. While skilled workers may have been skeptical of company motives, they knew that their jobs were more secure and better rewarded than those of the semi-skilled machine operatives, who had far less access to company benefits. This, too, created a challenge for those interested in industrial unionism.[12]

Second, because skilled trades unions were based on craft autonomy and on strict divisions based on occupation and skill, there were frequent, disruptive, and sometimes violent disputes about which workers belonged to what union and which unions had the right to organize specific industries. Even as manufacturers adopted new mass production techniques, their managers created deeper divides among the skilled workers in industry and the semi-skilled operatives who constituted the majority of the labor force in all industries. Skilled workers in wood, metal, and textiles saw their conditions and wages improve as the result of their monopoly of skill and expertise. Operatives who worked the production line— the blast furnace, the sewing machine, and the shovel—neither benefited nor did they belong to the skilled fraternity. The conditions of factory work for unskilled workers and their strength—or weakness—in collective bargaining could not be addressed through the same tactics and strategies of craft unions.

At their 1901 convention in Scranton, the AFL committed itself to exploring new forms of industrial unionism. At stake were several questions crucial to labor's vitality: First, should the AFL not only advocate for skilled workers in the trades, but take on the political role of representing all workers? Even while the AFL pursued policies to restrict immigration, the Federation rooted its demands, and its political legitimacy, in the claim that it represented all workers—especially, and ironically, the unorganized. In Scranton, the AFL proposed the creation of federal unions, a form of institutional holding company, for newly organized workers before they were formally admitted to a craft union. To those who saw any division as weakening workers, federal locals only made the problem worse by creating a similarly divided maze of unions within the labor movement. For the most part, these new federal locals had little autonomy. They were meant to be temporary solutions. Few of them became permanent, and most fell victim to an indifferent AFL leadership.[13]

As a matter of public record, the American Federation of Labor was an advocate for American workers and a supporter of workers' rights. Because it was a loose federation of international unions, which granted local as well as craft autonomy, the AFL had few means and little incentive to battle its constituent unions over race and gender discrimination. Neither the interracial unionism of waterfront workers and miners nor the racial exclusion of Southern locals were contested at the national level, nor did the AFL ask specific trades unions to open their doors to women workers. Instead, the AFL customarily spoke for gender equality in terms of equal pay, the right of and necessity for women workers to join unions, and endorsed national woman suffrage. It supported the rights of African Americans to join unions and opposed, on paper, the exclusion of workers from union membership based on race. It was these public declarations that made credible its claims on the loyalty and allegiance of workers across the nation.[14]

The public stance was not reflected in the AFL's long history of conflict with competing forms of organization, nor did it explain its lackluster record in organizing women, immigrant workers, and racial minorities. The problem the AFL faced was two-fold. First, craft unions based much of their institutional identity and politics on a defense of white male workers' rights. Craft brotherhoods in railroad, construction, metalworking, cigar and clothing production were defined as masculine in membership, solidarity, and practice. More than this, the definitions of skill that established the core of craft autonomy and defined who workers were and where they belonged were defined by gender and race.[15]

Second, national origin, citizenship status, political affiliation, and home ownership were essential building blocks of craft worker identity and came to define their political and labor activism. Line operatives, farm workers, sales clerks, and secretaries need not apply. When the Western Federation of Miners ridiculed the AFL as "the American Separation of Labor," they drew attention to the divisions that threatened to undermine labor economically and politically. The AFL embraced these values in public rhetoric and in policies that drew deep lines between citizen workers who were self-sufficient, independent workingmen and "dependent" others. Immigrant and child workers, women of all groups, and contract agricultural or gang labor, trade unionists believed, had neither the means nor the capacity to act as public agents. Craft unionism as an ideology echoed new theories of management that understood the utility of dividing workers along lines of skill and ability and reinforced those lines with ethnic rivalry, racial competition, and gender conflict in the workplace.

A New Model?

In 1902, a strike that illustrated the potential of organized labor to address these divisions occurred, unpredictably, in the eastern Pennsylvania anthracite coalfields. Miners fit uncomfortably within the AFL as a craft union. Skilled miners in coal and hard metal possessed skills that had to be learned on the job but remained intangible to those who had never worked underground. Knowing the ground where one worked, what a seam of coal looked like, or how to minimize the considerable risks in underground mining, such as water, unstable timbers, and the threat of gas explosions, were central to work in the mines. In most countries, this knowledge gave miners considerable power and status. In the United States, miners in coal retained this authority through most of the nineteenth century. Coal mines were slow to adopt technology, and coal miners resisted the introduction of steam drills. Miners maintained their hold on the jobs and fared better for not having to deal with the dust and explosive risks of the mine machinery. By 1900, though, mining and its work force began to change. From miners at the coal face to the breaker boys who picked slate from coal, new immigrants from southern and eastern Europe became a significant presence not only in Pennsylvania but in Colorado. In West Virginia, African Americans found a foothold in the industry.[16]

Coal operators were aware of how skilled miners lost leverage as the labor force grew and diversified. In Pennsylvania anthracite, an industry dominated by railroad ownership of the mines, operators calculated driving down wages with new immigrant workers. They lacked a family history of mining and a tradition of mine unionism. Coal operators cut wages, increased work demands, and let the conditions of the mines deteriorate. By 1902, immigrant mine workers had had enough. On the first day of the strike in May 1902, over 60 percent of the 143,000 workers in anthracite went out; by the end of the first week, more than 125,000 were on strike. By the end of the third week, only 15 of 39 collieries were operating. The nation was dependent on anthracite coal, a clean-burning hard coal, to heat homes and produce cheap iron and steel. When the anthracite miners walked out, they counted on this dependence to force mine operators to the bargaining table. The mine operators refused to budge, and the strike dragged on for five months.[17]

The National Civic Federation first turned to the AFL's Samuel Gompers and United Mine Workers' president John Mitchell to temper labor relations in coal.

Mitchell had been unable to stop the miners from walking out, and Gompers failed to persuade them to return. Pressure to provide heating fuel and keep prices in check for the alternative bituminous coal, a far smokier but quick-burning fuel primarily used in industry, brought corporate leaders into the mining conflict. They solicited the assistance of President Theodore Roosevelt to end the strike. It was a difficult task. Mine operators did not want to increase wages or improve conditions. They also did not want to bargain with miners or recognize the union. George Baer, president of the Pennsylvania and Reading, sought to break the strike without any concessions. The miners not only distrusted Baer; they hated him. Weeks later, President Roosevelt created the Anthracite Coal Commission to investigate. He then ordered the miners back to work. When the commission finished its task, miners received a 10 percent increase in wages and a nine-hour workday. The Commission, however, did not require the mine operators to recognize or bargain with the union. The Slavic miners had won a short-term victory. Any lasting solution would require formal government intervention in labor relations.[18]

Still, Roosevelt's negotiations were an important first step toward federal mediation of labor disputes. Labor–business–government cooperation resolved a conflict that had escalating costs and damages. Moreover, the anthracite strike had involved new immigrant groups who, prior to the strike, had little experience in collective bargaining in their new country. Yet the strike also exposed a deep fissure among workers. The American Federation of Labor saw itself as "the voice of labor" and its president as its leader, but the striking miners had followed the lead of neither the UMW's Mitchell nor President Gompers. The miners had, instead, acted in solidarity with each other. Neither side of labor's developing schism was invested in resolving the conflict.

By the turn of the century, newly politicized employer associations, anti-union hostility, and the splintering of industrial workers along ethnic and racial lines kept the AFL from growing in size and influence. Many of its constituent unions stopped growing or lost members, although their voting power within the labor federation was an obstacle to organizing along industrial lines. While the shift to new machine technologies fueled the growth of unions such as the International Association of Machinists (IAM), older, more narrowly defined craft unions took significant losses. The printing trades struggled against the introduction of women typesetters; the Cigar Makers' Union consigned its immigrant members to segregated locals. Those engaged in machine production of cigarettes were relegated to second-class status in the union.[19] Something had to change.

Workers in the West

Significant changes first appeared in the West, where the escalating conflict between employers and workers was especially sharp. While different conditions prevailed in each industry, mining, timber, and farming were all capital-intensive enterprises, requiring large capital outlays to make a farm or mine profitable. By the end of the nineteenth century, these costs had undermined family farming, shut down smaller mines and lumber operations, and encouraged company mergers. In southwestern Colorado, Rockefeller's Colorado Fuel and Iron (CF&I) consolidated coal mining in the region, and Anaconda Copper dominated Montana. Weyerhaeuser had more than 900,000 acres of timberland at its founding in 1900; twenty years later, at the death of its founder, the company owned over 2 million acres of forest. Other corporations in the West acquired monopoly control over natural resources, including land and mineral rights. They used their power to alter the organization and control of work.[20]

In Colorado, employer control proved deadly. Against workers' protests, and in contrast to eastern coal, Colorado F&I forcibly introduced the use of the mechanical one-man drill in the Western mines. It cut the number of workers per mine and thus increased the occupational hazards of mining. Acquiring an ever-larger proportion of the state's mineral lands and national market share, Colorado Fuel and Iron had a vested interest in cutting costs. It also backed a state government that controlled not only mineral rights but also militia that played a major role in controlling local disturbances. John D. Rockefeller brought to the table the political and economic resources to ensure mine workers slowly lost control over production. His indifference to the plight of immigrant workers played a role in stoking discontent among the miners he employed.[21]

Across the West, mine workers in Coeur d'Alene, the Black Hills, and Colorado turned first to existing trade unions and later to independent organizations. The treacherous conditions in mining, timber, and railroad construction presented challenges to union organizing. Mining and lumbering took place in sparsely populated, often isolated terrain. Hard rock mining companies introduced mine drills and work gangs that deskilled much of the work and made it possible to hire new workers to replace the discontented. Recruiting armies of contract laborers, many of them immigrants under the padrone system, companies suppressed wages and worker protests. Under the contract system, immigrants were effectively indentured. They owed the padrones the cost of a ticket and food and shelter while they worked off the debt. Living in ramshackle housing, often squalid bunkhouses, they had little time to organize and little incentive. Most were "birds of passage" committed to returning to their homeland after earning enough to return to their native country and buy property or pay for education. Still others never returned to their homeland, having found some kind of stability in the United States. A smaller number remained as industrial casualties—from mining disasters, construction collapses, or accidents in a steel mill or on a railroad line. With little leverage as unskilled labor, the immigrant labor force turned to individual remedies for their condition.[22]

At the same time, many workers, frustrated with the dangerous conditions and low pay, began to organize in the West. In May of 1893, after a stalemate in the Coeur d'Alene strike, mine workers created a new organization, the Western

Federation of Miners. They sought to address deteriorating and dangerous working conditions, script pay, child labor, and lack of dignity in the workplace. With little alternative to the harsh labor of the mines, mining camps were far from the power and purview of labor unions. The mining at Coeur d'Alene, like most hard rock mining, had particular challenges, including explosions from underground gases, cave-ins from inadequate timbering, and chronic lung diseases from toxic dust. Pressure to adopt mechanical drills forced workers into smaller crews and increased dangers for those working underground. The mining company, aware of growing discontent, had drawn on state government to police workers. Once the strike began, it turned violent as the company imported replacement workers and allowed armed guards to directly intervene.[23]

The bloody confrontation with police and militia inspired an energetic response from mine workers in the West. Miners gathered in Butte, Montana, in the copper mining region, to form the Western Federation of Miners (WFM). The WFM did not draw distinctions among the skilled and unskilled, or among those who worked in different mining operations. Specific metals and minerals were less important than creating solidarity among workers who had little but their own labor as leverage against employers. Inspired by distinctly American traditions of populism, "the Cooperative Commonwealth," and European syndicalism, the WFM was hybrid unionism. It gave an honored place to the labor theory of value and to a communitarian vision that drew on older labor traditions. It also possessed masculine stridency about the dignity of labor and the living wage that working men deserved and that they might demand from their employers. The WFM, in its origins, did not shy away from embracing armed resistance to industrial tyranny as one means to the end of greater equality. It employed a language not unlike that of employers who similarly envisioned themselves as generals leading an industrial army. The rank and file of the WFM held a different vision.[24]

The masculine images and traditions of Western mining and lumber were a page torn from the American labor playbook. They reflected Western Anglo American and European ideals about what constituted freedom in a Republic. For Ed Boyce, who led the WFM in the 1890s, the right to bear arms was part of that heritage. In an 1897 convention in Salt Lake City, Boyce declared that "Every union should have a rifle club" and that every member be provided "with the latest improved rifle ... so that in two years we can hear the inspiring music of the martial tread of 25,000 armed men in the ranks of labor."[25] As he later wrote, Boyce knew that advocating strikes led labor leaders to be "branded as criminals who aim to ruining [sic] the business interests of the country." But, he noted, labor couldn't "pursue the methods adopted by capitalists" either, for they would be "sent to prison for robbery or executed for murder." Even labor's basic demands for living wages were seen as "threats of violence against the rights of private property." He concluded, "Take what action you will in the interests of labor, the trained beagles in the employ of capital from behind their loathsome fortress of disguised patriotism will howl their tirade of condemnation." In defense of Boyce, a union brother declared, "The real revolutionists are those who have overridden all law in their effort to coerce workingmen. They have sown the wind, now let them seek their cyclone cellars."[26]

Not surprisingly, given this hostility, violence permeated labor conflicts in the West. Often at the instigation of mine owners who employed them, private guards and Pinkerton detectives protected private property with any means necessary. As strikes escalated, guns, brickbats, knives and clubs surfaced. Local police and sheriffs, National Guard troops and state militia might be called in, as miners refused to go back to work and also refused entry to the mines to their replacements. Dynamite, used in mining, lumber, and railroad construction, played a rare but real role in the drama of Western labor. Such violence provoked a response from the state but also strengthened the hands of the "law and order" forces that viewed the labor movement as lawless thugs.[27]

Apart from its public advocacy of armed protests, the WFM shared with the United Mine Workers and the American Federation of Labor an emphasis on male solidarity and masculine labor as core values, requiring an almost military discipline. But while mine work, especially in isolated mining camps, tended to exclude women, Western workers depended upon women's labor to sustain their work and their strikes. For every solitary male worker on the Western mining frontier, there were family members that both supported and were supported by him. Laundresses, female cooks, boarding-house owners, servants, and waitresses who provided meals and domestic labor; prostitutes who provided sexual services for single—and married—men; teachers who taught children and farm women who raised chickens, provided eggs and vegetables at market, or baked bread and pastries, sustained men's work in an environment that was often perceived as devoid of female labor. Still, for the IWW, worker solidarity was primarily mas-culine and born of workplace conditions. Men controlled the means not only to work but to protest the conditions of work and the underlying structure of inequality. Only in places like Cripple Creek, where miners lived in a town filled with working women and in a state that had woman suffrage, did women become a visible part of the labor movement.[28]

By 1905, the Western Federation of Miners became a powerful force for industrial unionism in the West. Through a series of strikes beginning in the 1890s through the Calumet and Hecla Copper Strike in Michigan in 1913, the WFM challenged employers to insure workers' safety, pay them a decent wage, bar child labor, and grant basic rights in the workplace. Fueled by a sense of injustice, the WFM, at great cost to many of its members, confronted armed guards, private detectives, and state militia in a long series of strikes. They were beaten, arrested, jailed and even murdered in their effort to return some measure of power to workers. Elizabeth Gurley Flynn's *Rebel Girl* is filled with stories of WFM members who served long prison sentences, often accused of crimes they did not commit, in the name of workers' justice.[29]

For its trouble, the Western Federation of Miners made powerful enemies and not simply among businessmen. The AFL, and its brother union, the United Mine Workers, saw the WFM as a renegade organization that threatened the legitimate trade union movement. In 1907, when WFM president "Big" Bill Haywood and two other WFM leaders, Charles Moyer and George Pettibone, were on trial for the murder of Frank Steunenberg, former governor of Oregon, the WFM's reputation for thuggery seemed justified. Mine owners hired James McParland, a Pinkerton detective, to find evidence that WFM leaders had hired an assassin to kill Steunenberg in retaliation for the deaths of miners in Coeur d'Alene. As defense lawyer Clarence Darrow later suggested, the state's star witness, McParland's informant Harry Orchard, who confessed his crime, was the real perpetrator. Haywood, Moyer, and Pettibone were acquitted, although never completely absolved of the murder. They had, it was believed, implicitly condoned worker violence, destruction of property, and the use of deadly force in strikes. Charged in an earlier strike in Cripple Creek with the bombing of a train station, WFM officers were found guilty, at least in public opinion, of instigating violence and mayhem throughout the West. For business leaders, the WFM remained a dangerous element in society. Ungoverned by civility and openly contemptuous of authority, the WFM required state control.[30]

After the Cripple Creek strike in 1903, the WFM struggled to maintain its membership. The Idaho trial brought publicity and the lingering shadow of lawlessness. In ways later echoed in charges against the IWW, the WFM's public anger, expressed in Boyce's call to arms, undermined efforts to win agreements on the Iron Range (1907), in the Homestead strike (1909), and in the Michigan copper mining strike (1913).[31] In this latter struggle, miners of the Hecla Mining Company in Calumet faced considerable opposition. A tragedy at the Italian Hall in Calumet, where dozens of children died in a fire behind locked doors, fueled miner resentment but also allowed employers to seek state intervention. Charles Moyer, who had long since abandoned radical WFM unionism, sought to negotiate an end to the strike. Instead, Moyer was arrested and deported from the state by rail. The strike collapsed in 1913. Miners returned to work.[32]

The AFL's Turn to Politics

Given employers' renewed hostility and the growth of semi-industrial unions like the WFM, the AFL turned between 1900 and 1910 to political means to augment its workplace presence. Labor leaders focused on what they considered to be the greatest threats to union power in the economy—competition from immigrant, women, and child workers; the coordinated attack of organized capital against unions, and the surge of industrial accidents as the casualties of mass production began to mount. It was the flood of labor injunctions that blocked even peaceful picketing and publicity about strikes and boycotts. Over 2,000 labor injunctions were issued in the years between 1890 and 1920, damaging, if not destroying, unions' ability to pressure employers to the bargaining table.

In the demand for labor legislation, organized labor was on its own against the formidable resources of the National Association of Manufacturers and the American Anti-Boycott Association. Speaker of the House Joseph Cannon and his congressional allies voted down other laws prohibiting child labor, limiting injunctions, and protecting federal employees and seamen.[33] In the courts as well the labor movement was stymied. Using the backdoor of equity courts, employers denied unions whatever recourse they had to challenging employer power. Indeed, equity court judges issued injunctions without a hearing. Labor unions and their leaders were held liable for employer losses, and they were held in contempt of court for violating the injunctions. In the landmark cases *Buck's Stove* (1906) and *Lawlor v. Loewe* (1908), the AFL and the Hatters' union challenged contempt citations and the labor injunctions on which they were based. The Supreme Court upheld the lower court findings.[34] *Buck's Stove* proved to be a turning point for the AFL. Given the judicial climate, the AFL shifted its priorities to court reform as the most significant issue facing existing trade unions.[35]

The two Supreme Court decisions prompted the AFL to engage in election campaigns to unseat anti-union congressmen. Beginning in 1906, they campaigned for Democratic party candidates and coordinated local and federal political efforts. The AFL further worked to elect legislators more friendly to its concerns. In 1908, the Federation backed Democratic party candidate William Jennings Bryan with a "full dinner pail" campaign that aimed to bring labor's agenda to the forefront of congressional concerns. Hiring over 100 organizers in 1908, the AFL distributed more than 5 million pieces of literature highlighting its legislative agenda and pushed for broad changes in public policy, most forcefully in immigration policy and judicial reform. Republican nominee William Howard Taft, a former judge who had a record of issuing labor injunctions, won the presidency. Labor's failure to loosen employers' grip on Congress, despite local and state successes, forced the AFL to return to an earlier strategy of congressional lobbying as its principal political weapon.[36]

On the issue of immigration restriction, the AFL found ready allies among elite groups. Already working with the National Civic Federation on workers' compensation and other labor issues, the AFL joined with the Immigration Reform League, established in 1894, to bring about legislation at the state and federal level. The new immigration that brought millions of new workers into the American economy provoked this broad-based response. Trade unions, since their beginnings, had leaders—and, indeed, members—who were predominantly of native-born Anglo-American stock or of Irish, Scottish, Welsh, or German origin. The railroad brotherhoods had a similar profile. Norwegians, Swedes, Dutch, Czechs, and Austrian Germans occupied the margins of these unions, but the new immigrants from eastern and southern Europe did not. Asian immigrants— whether from China, Japan, or the Philippines—found no place alongside working-class brethren but rather were viewed as alien competitors. In the words of an AFL pamphlet, it was a war of 'Meat versus Rice', where good laboring men had to compete against—and fight—subservient coolies. As industrial work became increasingly deskilled and removed from workers' control, new immigrant workers presented a threat to organized labor's ability to shape the market and bargain effectively with employers.[37]

For employers, there were few economic reasons to restrict immigration. Indeed, most corporations recruited broadly from the new immigrant groups. There were, however, more visceral reasons to back new restrictions. Business owners were not only capitalists but also public figures, men who had either experienced upward mobility or who were born to wealth and position. They were members not only of a class and gender but also of a racially and ethnically defined group in society. Many of them belonged to elite clubs and harbored interests in genealogy and heraldry and laid claim to being descended from original Anglo-Saxon, Scotch-Irish, or Dutch settlers, a category that was endowed with cultural power and privilege.[38]

Fear of radicalism among the new immigrants had prompted quick responses. Leaders of business and labor alike feared the presence of anarchists, socialists, and syndicalists among the mass of industrial workers, a fear that emerged time and again in national politics and in the court system. After the McKinley assassination, Congress passed the Immigration Act of 1903, or Anarchist Exclusion Act, to bar radicals like Leon Czolgosz from American shores. More laws followed. In 1907, the Expatriation Act barred Asian immigration and provided the legal means to deport immigrants, even those naturalized, for their political beliefs. In 1917, the Immigration Act required those seeking residence in the United States to pass a literacy test. In 1920 and 1924, the Quota Act and the National Origins Act slowed immigration through the use of quotas, in the latter keyed to the 1890 census. The quotas drastically reduced or eliminated immigrants from southern and eastern Europe, Asia, the Middle East and Africa. In each case, the AFL saw restricting the number of workers competing for jobs as beneficial. And yet, for most of the twentieth century, restricting formal immigration did not prevent the recruitment of contract laborers, guest workers, and other undocumented workers by American employers. While it was not clear that organized labor benefited from these restrictions, the passage of such laws sent a message about labor's indifference to the plight of immigrants.[39]

Anti-immigration policy had, as its close associate, a protectionist stance toward trade and a pro-tariff agenda. Both labor unions and trade associations had an interest in creating tariff barriers to the importation of cheap goods. The "foreign-made" and the "foreign-born" had more than a subconscious link between them. Restricting access to the United States fit well within a vision that saw American labor as uniquely endowed with characteristics of manliness and American-made goods as superior. For the labor movement, advocacy of immigration restriction and hostility to immigrant workers already in country did risk alienating growing sectors of the work force. Moreover, it was not at all clear that tariffs on imported goods benefited the mass of American workers. With little margin for economic or personal disaster, working-class families had little discretionary money for clothing or cigars made abroad; high tariffs maintained high prices on goods that they did buy, including bread and meat. Agricultural goods, including wheat, corn, cotton, and processed meat, constituted the bulk of U.S. exports, although manufactured goods made up a larger share of exports by 1900. High prices for agricultural commodities did not primarily benefit the American farmer, either, but rather the food corporations such as National Brands (Nabisco) or the four big meatpackers—Armour, Hormel, Wilson, and Swift. Yet, the American Federation of Labor continued to support high domestic tariffs.[40]

For the most part, the AFL engaged in national politics in ways that captured their lack of power in the private sector. While skilled trade unions and individual workers could negotiate with companies dependent on their labor, the AFL's declining base within industry meant that the labor federation had to focus on the fights that were removed from the local context. The passage of contract and child labor laws, which were unenforceable and later seen as unconstitutional; the regulation of federal employee hours and wages; the Seamen's Act, and the progressive campaign to limit labor injunctions, culminating in the Clayton Act in 1914—these issues were central to labor's national agenda.[41] On the state level, AFL-affiliated central labor unions lobbied for and often won workmen's compensation laws, the first step in rationalizing occupational injury and death.[42] In progressive cities like Milwaukee, Minneapolis, and New York, labor—and socialist—candidates for city council, the state legislature, and the mayor's office won gains.[43] For the most part, however, divisions weakened the labor movement in 1912. Those who believed that the political system offered a path to change saw their opponents as naïve and even dangerous. Those who thought that only workplace and community struggle could create change advocated collective action beyond the ballot box and without a picket line. They viewed those who hewed to political convention and craft unions as dangerously out of touch with workers.

American Syndicalism

The weakness of the American Federation of Labor was not lost either on socialists or on the majority of rank-and-file workers. The Western Federation of Miners was organized to challenge not only employers but also conservative trade unions. Confronting the savage conditions of the industrial workplace, the WFM and its allied union, the Industrial Workers of the World, sought to level the playing field of industrial relations. For radical trade unionists, the heart of the issue was workers' lack of power in the workplace. The lack of living wages and the poverty of working-class lives stemmed from workers' inability to control working conditions and to earn fair wages. Maternal and child mortality, petty crime and social violence, emaciated bodies and impoverished spirits, family dissolution and urban disease—all were the products of an economic system that paid little attention to workers' bodies, let alone their minds. Beneath the social disorder visible in cities and in the countryside were structures of authority that kept demands for social justice at bay. The rights of property—and of those who owned property—to mandate working conditions, dictate what workers would earn, and steal from workers the pittance they were offered, undermined democracy and called for radically different solutions.[44]

To begin with, the WFM and the IWW relied not on direct challenges to national authorities but decentralized protests in slowing down the pace of work, work stoppage, and the practice of machine-breaking, or "sabotage" from the use of wooden shoes (or sabots) to stop the gears. These informal means of challenging authority—called "soldiering" among scientific managers and "sabotage" among radical unionists—were not original. Both unfree labor and free-born workers engaged in a silent tug-of-war over the conditions of work. What was new were the ideas behind their resistance. Working-class radicals were drawn toward what became known as "syndicalism," a wide-ranging critique of power and authority in society and the workplace that had, as its solution, the organization of workers into "syndicates"—unions to control the means of production and through them the economy and the government. Popularly, this form of organizing society was portrayed in a diagram called "Father Haggerty's wheel," where society was divided into industrial cohorts that governed together and provided for all.[45]

The "Continental Congress of the Working Class" in 1905 produced a manifesto that declared renewed war on capital. They bemoaned "the displacement of human skill by machines" and noted workers' servitude and loss of skill and employment. The only answer was for workers to organize collectively and bring their power to withhold labor to bear on employers. The IWW was committed to organizing industrial unions to replace moribund AFL unions that had "shatter[ed] the ranks of the workers into fragments." Indeed, "the power of resistance [was] broken by craft division." Its inevitable end was that, "Union men scab upon union men; hatred of worker for work is engendered, and the workers are delivered helpless and disintegrated into the hands of the capitalists." They sought nothing less than to empower workers to challenge these conditions. Workers had to find new means to confront capital, even as employers presented "a united front in their war against labor."[46]

The Chicago meeting, while inspirational, had little immediate impact. The failure of several important strikes in 1905, along with the failed revolution in Russia, had a dampening effect on Chicago's pledges. An economic recession in 1907, with massive layoffs in core industries like steel, further lowered expectations of workers, even as an important steel strike came to an end. Sporadic protests and organizing campaigns kept the IWW idea alive, especially in the West. Without organizing among the immigrants in Eastern industry, however, there was little hope that the industrial union ideal could take hold. It was in McKees Rock, Pennsylvania, that it had its first test.

McKees Rock was home to the Pressed Steel Car Company, a firm that made railroad cars for both passengers and freight. Its largely semi-skilled labor force was comprised of eastern European immigrants, many of whom were workers on a migratory round. They sought work and money in the United States but intended to return to their home villages. The Pressed Steel Car Company had little interest in its workers' homes, welfare, or migratory patterns. In a competitive market, its owners sought to draw more profit from its operations. It continually increased the workload of employees and pace of its production line. In 1909, the introduction of new equipment cranes, and speed-ups and stretch-outs, steeply increased the rates of worker injury and death to one a day. Workers who saw their peers' broken bodies removed from the factory on a regular basis nicknamed the company "the Slaughterhouse" and "Last Chance." In defense, the company replied, "Working with technology is an inherently risky business. We can reduce risks by learning and through technological progress, but perfection is an elusive and unrealistic goal." Corruption in the wage system, and charges of sexual abuse of women and children by company agents, surely stoked workers' anger. Short pay envelopes finally pushed workers over the edge.[47]

On July 10, 1909, 5,000 workers of the Pressed Steel Car Company struck; they were joined by the 3,000 workers of Standard Pressed Steel Car. Joined by IWW leaders William Trautmann, Joe Ettor, and Bill Haywood, the workers stymied efforts to bring in substitute workers. A month and a half later, at least twelve men were killed and several wounded in a confrontation at the company, after the manager had brought in the Pennsylvania State Constabulary. With these deaths, the strike drew public attention. Eventually, on September 8, the company settled with the workers, granting a pay raise, the posting of rates, and new company housing policies.[48]

At McKees Rock, the workers who organized the strike and their IWW allies broke from the staid, conservative, and even corrupt practices of the trade union establishment. Rather than being focused on skill distinctions, their union was organized along industrial lines—capable of bringing together the bobbin boy and the weaver and the machinist in a textile factory; of uniting the gang labor of the steel mill with the roller of steel and the tool and die man; of organizing the pattern cutter, the presser, and the sewing machine operator in a garment factory, and the lumberjack and sawmill hand in the timber industry. Instead of dividing workers by minute classifications, industrial unions sought to be a voice for all workers. The IWW adopted, again, the old Knights slogan of "An Injury to One Is an Injury to All," and proclaimed a broad solidarity across the working class and not merely victory for the skilled and powerful few.

The militant trade unionism of the IWW borrowed heavily from popular anti-government traditions and saw much political activism, especially elections and party politics, as useless to workers, many of whom could not or did not vote. Corruption, they believed, was a defining characteristic of a system in which millionaires bought and sold senators and governors and called on their lackeys to unleash their police dogs whenever the workers went on strike. It was a view of the state, and of politics, that comfortably fit within the voluntarist traditions of the craft union AFL. But there was this difference. Radical trade unionists, at least syndicalists, did not see citizenship or voting participation as essential either to workers' manhood or to the labor movement. But while most workers in the IWW viewed politics as corrupt and elections as diversions, they saw the importance of the protection that labor allies in government and society could give. Further, the radicalism of the IWW owed much to socialist visions of a better future and a people's democracy, complete with the conflicted racial legacy of those visions.[49]

The New Unionism Spreads

These years were characterized by what historian David Montgomery called, "the Syndicalist moment," two decades of radical union activism from the industrial labor force. What became known as the Uprising of the 20,000 among shirtwaist makers, strikes in Lawrence textile factories, the lumber camps and iron and copper mines of Minnesota and Michigan, the coal mines of Ludlow, on the waterfront in Philadelphia, and among hop pickers in Wheatland revealed a new activism among immigrant and migrant workers. Industrial unionism was the banner that united Belgian weavers and Hungarian spinners, Irish labor leaders like Elizabeth Gurley Flynn and the Finns of the Iron Range. Activists such as William Foster, Carlo Tresca and Rose Schneiderman joined forces with and challenged traditional trade union leaders. They introduced new strategies and forms of labor organization better suited to mass production industry.[50]

For workers in the garment trade, the process of organizing was torturously slow. Ready-made clothing was a relatively new industry in turn-of-the-century New York. Women had previously sewn much of their own clothing, but clothing styles and cultural changes—the existence of a female labor force—made ready-made shirtwaists, a popular article of clothing but one that had little profit margin; volume, not quality, was the key. Garment manufacture also was a labor- but not capital-intensive business, with little barrier to entry and heated competition for the retail market. Small shops far outnumbered larger garment concerns. Indeed, while the production of cotton and woollen textiles occurred in factories that employed thousands of mill hands, garment workshops often employed as few as 20 or 25 workers. There continued to be a good deal of outwork— home garment manufacture through subcontracting. Larger garment workshops, like Triangle Shirtwaist Company, which employed a few hundred workers, were rare. Conditions of garment manufacture were not unlike that of most competitive light industry. Low-wage production work was conducted in factories that were poorly ventilated, often dusty, fire-traps, located in the same tenement districts on the lower East Side where the workers lived.

By the turn of the twentieth century, New York had become the largest center of garment manufacture in the nation. In December 1909, over 20,000 workers went on strike in a combination of small and large garment workshops and factories. Few of the workers cutting, sewing, and pressing shirtwaists, cloaks, and men's shirts were native-born American citizens. The vast majority of women working in shirtwaist manufacture were eastern European Jewish immigrants, with some Italian women immigrant sewing machine operators and some German Jewish immigrant men working as pressers, cutters, and cloakmakers. Only among skilled men was there any evidence of union affiliation. What was present was a vibrant Jewish immigrant culture that sheltered socialist workingmen's circles, socialist newspapers like the *Jewish Daily Forward* and the *New York Call*, and forums that taught workers socialist ideals and trade unionism. Jewish immigrant women, among them Rose Schneiderman, Clara Lemlich, Pauline Newman, and Fannia Cohn, participated in the early days of the union. They turned, intermittently, to trade union men and to a new force in society—organized women from the middle and upper classes. This new elite group found common cause in working women's plight. The National Women's Trade Union League came in to support the garment strike by supporting, joining the picket line, and arousing public opinion. Despite a growing public support, the strike dragged on for months. The women refused to go back to work without union recognition. Even as smaller shops returned, there was the steadfast refusal of larger companies to come to terms with the striking workers. In the end, the strike ended with victories in a few shops. The larger factories, including Triangle, which was the original scene of the strike, hired new workers and refused to sign a contract. Generally considered an early and important victory for working women, the uprising of the 20,000 still left a majority of the garment industry unorganized.[51]

The Triangle Shirtwaist Company, the most intractable employer, spent the next year fending off union organizing. Locking doors against employee theft—and against labor organizers, the owners sought to prevent a repeat of the 1909 strike. Conditions in the factory had not changed. There were but few exits, a small fire escape, and only one stairwell. Located in a poorly ventilated tenement on the lower East Side, the factory had significant hazards—dust from clothing, scraps of fabric, poor construction. On March 25, 1911, the Triangle Shirtwaist factory, the scene of the first walkout in the Uprising, caught on fire. Of its workers, the majority—123 women and 23 men—died in the fire or jumping to escape; more than 70 others were injured. This tragedy is seen as the origin of the International Ladies Garment Workers' Union. In fact, it was the activists from the 1909 strike who took meaning from this tragedy. Within three years, firms in New York City signed the Protocols of Peace that unionized garment work and made the ILGWU a bulwark of the new unionism—inspired by radical ideals but also pragmatic in its use of mass protest, public opinion, and a broad, inclusive organizing strategy.[52]

Immigrants and the Lawrence Strike

In 1912, the new unionism drew national attention again with the strike of American Woolen Company workers in Lawrence, Massachusetts. More than 25,000 workers, 40 percent of them women, and nearly 20 percent children, struck American Woolen in protest over wage cuts. Before the strike, the state of Massachusetts implemented a fifty-four hour law that reduced the number of working hours from nearly sixty in most factories. In Lawrence, the woolen companies that had fought the law politically now turned to wage cuts to compensate for the loss of working hours. Pay envelopes in early January showed the cost: Most workers lost the equivalent of five loaves of bread per week. In Lawrence, a city of immigrant workers, the wage cuts only further deepened the poverty of an immigrant labor force already suffering from high rates of malnutrition, childhood mortality, and chronic respiratory disease. The poorly ventilated, damp, and fiber-filled factory air created an atmosphere in which malnourished and sleep-deprived workers became ill and died at alarming rates. Dr. Elizabeth Shipleigh noted in her report on Lawrence that

> 36 out of every 100 men and women who work in the mill die before, or by the time, they are 25 years of age. That means that out of the long line which enters the mill you may strike out every third person as dying before reaching maturity. Every fourth person in line is dying from tuberculosis. And further, every second person, that is one alternating with a healthy person, will die of some form of respiratory disease.

There had been, in the face of these conditions, efforts to organize the skilled workers. With the short pay, the vast majority of workers walked out of the factory in protest.[53]

What followed was a three-month long strike of more than 25,000 workers. In the midst of a New England winter, strikers in Lawrence marched, protested, organized and maintained a mass moving picket line. Prior to the strike, workers had been divided and isolated from one another. Representing nearly sixty different ethnic groups, they now found a common voice in the strike committee of one hundred. Despite few resources and semi-starvation, workers did not return to the factories. The arrest of some of their number, in what turned out to be trumped up dynamiting charges, and the death of a woman protester, did not impede the strike. When they were accused of starving their children, strikers organized to send them to foster families while the strike persisted. In a much celebrated move, IWW supporter Margaret Sanger, a trained nurse, accompanied the first group of children to Grand Central Station, where sympathetic labor families waited to house the children for the duration of the strike. In a subsequent attempt, state militia and local police tried to stop the children from leaving Lawrence. They beat women and children at the train station, causing public outcry. Eventually, political pressure and its failure to bring back workers brought the company to the bargaining table.[54]

What made Lawrence important was that it succeeded where other mass strikes in the period failed. There were peculiar circumstances in Lawrence, including the pre-existence of skilled workers committed to industrial unionism—the weavers who had formed the first IWW local in Lawrence. The quick response of the national IWW and its allies, including Margaret Sanger, anarchist Emma Goldman, Mary Heaton Vorse, an experienced writer turned labor reporter; Elizabeth Gurley Flynn, Irish American socialist and IWW leader, who, with Big Bill Haywood, used her speaking voice and personal charisma to draw public attention to the cause; and Joe Ettor and Arturo Giovanetti, skilled organizers who, despite their unjust imprisonment and public martyrdom, held the line—helped steer the strike. Even when a company agent tried to tar workers as dynamiters and assassins, the strike leadership managed to control tempers and limit violence. The dependence of American Woolen and the woolen industry on the protective tariff made them more vulnerable—and responsive to public claims. For the most part, the living drama of the Lawrence strike, reported in newspapers nation-wide and remembered decades later in the memoirs of those who witnessed it, put the Labor Question in the forefront of the times. Would the captains of industry continue to tyrannize over the army of labor, or would the latter achieve an industrial democracy that might allow workers not only a living wage but more freedom in the workplace and in government?

The Ludlow Massacre and the Power of Public Opinion

In Colorado, the United Mine Workers, which had organized coal miners in West Virginia and Pennsylvania, had a new stage of action. In Colorado's southwestern coal fields, miners faced the introduction of new mechanical drills in order to lower labor costs. Miners were expected to work alone, which added to the dangers of mining; the drills also increased coal and mineral dust in the already stagnant air. Gas in the mines, increased dust, and the heat of drills meant greater risk of explosions and long-term threats to miners' lungs and general health. All of these factors stirred discontent among miners. Their activism by 1912 had brought the miners and employers into frequent and repeated conflicts. Labor activism spread throughout Colorado, as it had among lead, gold, and silver miners at the turn of the century. The difference was the employer.

By 1912, John D. Rockefeller, who had significant holdings in oil and petroleum, also owned the major stake in Colorado Fuel and Iron (CF&I). It was Rockefeller who demanded that managers get labor costs under control. The slow ratcheting up of conflict led to a series of strikes. Finally, there was a fourteen-month strike in the southern Colorado coal fields, most owned by CF&I. Many of the 1,200 workers at CF&I's Ludlow mine were immigrants from southeastern Europe and veterans of the wars that rocked that region. Under the leadership of Greek immigrant Louis Tikas, the miners went out on strike over the continued wage cuts and the ever-more dangerous conditions of the Colorado mines. As with many other mining companies, CF&I owned the houses miners lived in and the land on which they lived. As the strike progressed, miners were evicted from their homes and went to live in tent settlements near the mines they struck. Hundreds of workers were clustered in about 200 tents at Ludlow, including women and children. Under the threat of violence from the Colorado militia, UMW miners at Ludlow had dug trenches underneath the tents. One night, a train of 150 militia turned their guns, including mounted gatling guns, on the tent colony, as miners turned shotguns on their attackers. Fire consumed many of the tents, even as other strikers were struck by rifle fire. The violence left two women and eleven children dead, along with five strikers. Louis Tikas, the strike leader, was among them, and four militiamen.[55]

As news of the deaths at Ludlow spread, the managers of Colorado Fuel and Iron quickly responded with their own version of the strike. Radical trade unionists had turned their weapons not only on company guards but on the Colorado militia. Still, the warfare in the Western coal fields continued. As historian Thomas Andrews relates the tale, Ludlow occurred about midpoint in a long campaign. In other towns, for months on end, miners confronted the company and its armed support.

By 1912, the escalation of violence in labor conflicts prompted President Taft and his congressional allies to create a Commission on Industrial Relations to investigate working conditions throughout the United States. Working from 1913 to 1915, the CIR published its report in eleven volumes, using testimony from business, labor, and government leaders that had been gathered in 154 days of hearings. There were reports on lumbering in the Northwest, migrant workers in California, Paterson silk mills, the mines of Ludlow and in the Copper Country of Michigan. Commission president Frank Walsh, called by his detractors "Mother Jones in trousers," targeted employer violence in suppressing strikes, a violence that seemed to call for government intervention. Yet, dominated by corporate representatives and their political allies, the CIR argued less for industrial democracy than for advisory boards, less for a complete welfare state than the gradual implementation of new labor laws. The court of public opinion, for the most part, was far tougher on Rockefeller than the commission.[56]

Wheatland and the Reach of Industrial Unionism

The public had little interest in migrant harvest workers, most of whom were transient single men. But the IWW, which had its origins among miners and timber workers, reached out to the harvest hands and agricultural workers whom no union claimed. What trade unions existed in an agricultural nation avoided farmers and the issue of farm labor, which was often unregulated, sometimes coerced, and intertwined with family and even convict labor. The late nineteenth century had seen a flowering of farm organizations, some political, others economic, that attempted to address the ills of farmers. These organizations, however, saw a fundamental opposition between farm and labor interests. Indeed, agricultural workers fit into neither group, since trade unions exempted farm labor from the demand for an eight-hour day; and farmers saw agricultural workers as migrant, temporary, and distinct. Harvest hands were almost disembodied in the imagination and politics of both farmers and workers.[57]

From its origins, the IWW addressed farm labor in the same terms and with the same language of all migrant workers. The "bindle stiffs," migrant workers, were a part of the IWW's base constituency, workers upon whom much of the nation depended and who were, by virtue of their poverty and unsettled status, disenfranchised and beyond the margin of respectability. Among agricultural workers, there were enormous differences—Chinese, Japanese and Filipino hands often worked in family groups; native-born workers, of Anglo-American and immigrant ancestry, resembled more closely Wobbly folklore. All of them worked in a system that kept them hidden from public discussion and lacking protection from employer abuse.[58]

In northern California, harvest hands were hired for a range of tasks—from harvesting wheat to picking grapes and vegetable crops. No worker earned much in any one harvest. Indeed, most harvest hands were busy for months with a constantly rotating cycle of crops and broad geographic range. They also were underpaid and badly treated, despite the centrality of agricultural produce in domestic and foreign markets. In 1913, the epicenter of agricultural production for the market was in the Western Plains, California, and the Pacific Northwest. The wheat farms and ranches of South Dakota, Nebraska, and Kansas and the hop fields and vineyards of California and Oregon employed thousands of migrant workers.[59] On the Durst ranch, in Wheatland, California, hands were brought in every year to harvest hops for breweries nation-wide. In 1913, Durst advertised he needed workers for the harvest, only to find himself inundated with harvest hands. As more workers showed up, wages dropped. The living conditions of the workers, always poor, deteriorated. That year, however, IWW members organized the hop pickers into a union, one which demanded that Durst pay better wages and improve the shacks they lived in. The crowd of workers did not intimidate the owner, who brought in the sheriff and deputies to control the crowd. In what came to be called "the Wheatland riot," four men were killed and many more injured, including one of the sheriff's men. Within days, leaders of the strike, including Richard "Blackie" Ford and Herman Suhr, were arrested and charged with murder. A California judge sentenced them to life imprisonment. Activists demanding their release worked for decades before Ford and Suhr were finally released but not exonerated of their "crimes."[60]

With the exception of Lawrence, the IWW left a legacy filled with losses of a particular kind. IWW strikers resisted the imposition of wage cuts, the introduction of longer hours or new machinery, and deteriorating working conditions. The strikes often lasted for weeks or months at a time. But having little respect for contracts or government mediation, IWW locals often lost everything they had won on the picket line. Moreover, strikes led or aided by the IWW often drew out the long arm of the law. In the cases of its most successful strikes, there still were losses—strikers killed by police, labor leaders jailed for incitement to riot, and even murder. Both engaged workers and innocent bystanders became part of the industrial "butcher's bill," the casualties of industrial warfare when there were no rules of engagement nor practices of mediation.

By contrast, other organizing strikes, such as the Shirtwaist Strike in 1909–1910, the Chicago-based garment strikes that formed the basis of the Amalgamated Clothing Workers, and the garment strikes that led to the International Ladies' Garment Workers' Union and the Protocols of Peace, left behind an institutional structure that lasted through the long years of World War I and even, despite internal schism and conflict, through the doldrum 1920s. The longshoremen's union in Philadelphia, IWW Local 8, and its leader Ben Fletcher, succeeded in sustaining an interracial union in the midst of a racially divided society; only World War I changed that. Industrial democracy made tentative inroads in competitive industries such as mining and textile manufacture early on, but over all, the IWW and other industrial unions remained unable to maintain strike gains when employers brought the state to the table.[61]

Industrial Democracy and the Coming War

As the world spiralled into military conflict in 1914, the wave of immigrants to the United States slowed. Even as manufacturers geared up to meet European defense needs for arms, clothing, and food, labor was increasingly in short supply. Industry's need for workers led firms to tap new sources, especially in the South. African American migrants soon sought places in Northern factories; Southern whites also made the trek to Northern cities and jobs. This Great Migration had an important impact on urban industry and on the labor movement. Leaving the Jim Crow South for opportunities up North was a rational first step for African Americans looking for equality and a better life. Still, racist attitudes extended beyond the South, and economic competition, which drove racial conflict among the working class and poor, haunted the relations of whites and blacks in Northern industry. White workers remembered that African Americans had worked as strikebreakers in steel mills and packing plants. Tensions between African Americans and European immigrant workers stirred whenever competition for jobs intensified. More than that, the desire of many immigrants to acquire racial privilege, the "wages of whiteness," served as a road block to worker solidarity across racial and ethnic lines.[62]

The wartime boom kept much of these tensions muted. As the need for materials and foodstuffs in wartime Europe escalated, Northern manufacturers hired greater numbers of workers, even those who often had been excluded on racial grounds from industrial jobs. Like new immigrant workers before them, migrant black workers were hired to fill jobs at the bottom of the ladder. In the steel plant, they worked in the hottest and dirtiest sections of the mill. In automobile manufacture, where Henry Ford was in the vanguard in employing black workers, they worked in the forge, which was dangerous both in heat and in the fumes. In meatpacking plants, black workers were often put on the killing floor, not as butcher workmen but as those who cleaned up the offal and lifted heavy carcasses and in the tannery, where toxic chemicals processed the raw hides. Most black workers of this generation did not advance past the bottom rung. Still, racial and ethnic diversity in the labor force increased with each passing year. Conflicts among workers, caught up in the risks and tension of industrial work, challenged labor unions to unify them in workplace struggles.[63]

Wartime presented other challenges. While the United States remained neutral in 1914, many public officials, including former president Theodore Roosevelt and AFL president Samuel Gompers, called for "preparedness" as a prelude to American entry into the war. Major cities had Preparedness Day parades and rallies in support of the Allied war effort. It was to such an event in San Francisco in July 1916 that socialist and labor leader Tom Mooney and his assistant Warren Billings went, despite their belief that "preparedness" would end in the United States joining the Allied forces in Europe. That day, while more than 50,000 marched through the streets of San Francisco, a bomb went off on the parade route, killing ten and wounding forty. Tom Mooney was arrested, as were his wife, Rena Mooney, Billings, and Israel Weinberg. On the basis of scant evidence, Mooney and Billings were convicted and given death sentences; Rena Mooney and Weinberg were exonerated. Mooney and Billings had their sentences commuted to life imprisonment. Decades of activism to free the pair ended with their release in 1939 and eventual pardon.[64]

Impending war, and the lasting conflict between radical trade unionism and organized employers, had determined Mooney and Billings' fate. By 1917, the Wilson administration and its congressional allies all but conceded to the inevitable. Elected on a "He kept us out of the war" platform, Woodrow Wilson declared war on Germany and its allies in April of 1917. Congress moved swiftly to implement measures to ensure domestic cooperation. What followed, in rapid succession, were federal laws barring anti-war protest, speech, and publications, all actions defined as sedition under the Sedition, Espionage, and Trading with the Enemy Acts. The U.S. Army conducted domestic surveillance; civilian "citizens" organizations kept tabs on local unions, and the Justice Department arrested thousands of resident aliens, political activists, and labor radicals in a broad sweep. Civil liberties, in yet another crisis time, were suppressed with vigor. Local, state and federal officials, often in collaboration with or at the behest of employer-led groups, determined who represented a plausible threat to the war effort. Those targeted included hundreds of IWW members, anti-war socialists such as Kate O'Hare and Eugene Debs, and even naturalized citizens who failed to support the war by buying bonds or serving in the armed forces. World War I and the growing power of the federal surveillance state changed the context in which labor organizations and workers themselves acted.[65]

Widespread opposition to American participation in the war in Europe began as early as the fall of 1914, across a wide spectrum of the people. Many workers assumed it was a European conflict, probably of short duration. Ordinary workers may have read the news from the front at work, but it was not a foregone conclusion that the war would last or that the United States would find it necessary to intervene. Anti-war socialists viewed the war as a massive effort to disrupt revolutionary movements and undermine worker solidarity. "A rich man's war and a poor man's fight" summed up the growing conflict in Europe. In the IWW, there was no hard line on the war. Most IWWs, though, believed strongly that it was wrong for workers to fight workers. Other labor leaders followed the lead of Samuel Gompers, to whom the war presented opportunities to further his agenda. Openly courting advocates of U.S. participation in the war, many union leaders emphasized their willingness to join forces against the country's foes. From AFL trade unions came the pledge not to strike if the United States entered the war, a promise that elicited both opportunity to shape defense policy and contempt. Many workers saw the AFL's pledge as a foolish betrayal of their rights and a pre-emptive move that would undermine labor's bargaining power.[66]

What had been true since Wilson's election was that AFL president Gompers had newfound access to the administration. In Congress, the Clayton Act and other labor legislation passed with strong progressive support. The AFL in turn denounced the IWW and socialists in general. This stance kept Gompers and his supporters in line with the Wilson administration, a support acknowledged by the appointment of labor leader William B. Wilson as labor secretary. The creation of the Commission on Industrial Relations, shortly after the tragedy in Ludlow and the collapse of the Calumet and Hecla mine strike, signaled labor's new power. The CIR investigations, in which labor lawyer Frank Walsh played a major role, did little more than confirm the weakness of organized labor in the industrial field; they also laid the groundwork for new initiatives in industrial relations during the war.[67]

During World War I, the AFL and its leader Gompers had greater access to wartime administrations such as the National War Labor Board, owing to the AFL's "No strike" pledge. While labor remained a minor voice, this access guaranteed that some effort was made to "bring labor in" to government planning for mobilization and defense production. The creation of a Federal Mediation Service, and the direct intervention of government in the labor relations of the meatpacking, steel, and ammunitions industries, meant that workers received some wage improvement and some access to federal oversight boards. In Chicago's meatpacking plants, this access made a difference during the war. A wartime commission rewarded packinghouse workers with a raise that addressed escalating wartime prices. On the railroads, similar government intervention staved off strike action and granted railroad workers improved wages and conditions.[68]

Wartime conditions—European (or, more specifically, Allied) demand for ammunition and weaponry, war materiel, textiles and clothing, and agricultural commodities and processed meats and canned goods—created new opportunities for American manufacturers and farmers at the same time that they began to drive domestic inflation. For workers, higher demand meant greater employment but also greater inflation, even before the United States entered the war. It is not surprising, then, that the war years saw increased industrial action and the highest level of strikes in the United States until World War II and its aftermath caused similar reaction.

Even as the federal government opened the doors to government mediation of labor relations, the newly emerging national security shifted the ground for labor organization. State bureaus and private detective agencies kept track of union organizing in factories and in the community. Wartime legislation specifically barred, with great penalties, speech that was critical of the government or that opposed the draft and the financing of the war through public bonds. Within months of entering the war in 1917, the Wilson administration had arrested and imprisoned hundreds of radical trade unionists, anti-war protesters, and free speech advocates.[69] During the Bisbee deportation dozens of miners were left in locked boxcars in the Arizona desert. IWW supporters, strikers, and anti-war protesters in Spokane and Centralia, Washington, and Missoula and Butte, Montana, were beaten and killed by police and militia. Frank Little, an IWW organizer, was lynched. Forty-eight IWW offices in the country were raided, as Wobblies were arrested and their pamphlets and newspaper confiscated. While Elizabeth Gurley Flynn and Carlo Tresca, who faced trial in New Jersey, fought the charges, others—including socialists Eugene Debs and Kate O'Hare, Big Bill Haywood and over 100 IWW organizers—were convicted and given long sentences.[70] The scenario was repeated many times over the next decade, as criminal syndicalism and criminal anarchism laws, the "Red Raids" that rounded up alien radicals during and after the war, and persecutions of labor union members suppressed labor action and civil liberties.[71]

Industrial Democracy: Victory and Defeat

In the aftermath of the war, as government contracts were canceled and the army demobilized, labor organizers sought to make wartime gains permanent. The work that William Z. Foster and John Fitzpatrick had been doing in the meat-packing and steel industries was a case in point. During the war, workers had been sold on the idea of industrial democracy—of workers having a say not only in wages but on the shop floor and how production should be organized. The break-back pace of steel mills and packing plants was reflected in high rates of worker injuries and deaths. Punitive managers pressed workers for still greater effort, even as wartime inflation stubbornly persisted and fears of unemployment grew.

Foster and Chicago labor leader John Fitzpatrick sought to capture this pent-up energy to unionize the packing and steel plants, a goal that had eluded labor organizers for over a generation. The problem was that craft union restrictions on who could join the Amalgamated Meat Cutters and Butcher Workmen or the Amalgamated Iron and Steel Workers prevented the majority of the labor force from joining. Even once a union was created for other workers, the lack of coordination between the skilled unions and unions for line and assembly workers caused friction.

At first these fears seemed ill-founded. The experiment with industrial democracy in wartime plants had benefited workers in the meatpacking plants. Ethnic divisions had been worked out—even, tentatively, among some African American workers, but the harsh economic realities—combined with the "red summer" of 1919—undermined the fragile Stockyard Labor Council that had been built during the war. The Chicago riot that summer stripped away the fragile solidarity among black and white workers. A strike of the Amalgamated Meat Cutters Union in 1921–1922, isolated from the Back of the Yards community, was defeated. Packinghouse workers did not unionize until the 1930s.

In the steel industry, there were even higher barriers to organizing. There were, in contrast to the Chicago packinghouse drive, differences in the racial and ethnic make-up of the communities around the Pittsburgh, Chicago, Cleveland, and Youngstown steel plants. What the steel communities shared in common was the fact of division, a history of racial and ethnic antagonisms that undermined common interests of steel workers and their families. What was more, in Pittsburgh, Homestead, and Braddock ethnic differences only doubled down on the pre-existing conflicts between native-born skilled workers and the semi-skilled steel workers who tended the furnace and rolled molten steel. The steel strike of 1919 failed in part due to these divisions, in part because steel employers made effective use of the news media to spread false information, and also because the AFL stood adamantly opposed to a blurring of skill lines. Successful organization of industry required not just a calming of ethnic and racial division but a resolution of the fundamental conflict between trade union leaders and the industrial unionism that offered hope to industrial workers.

By 1922, with the defeat of national strikes in meatpacking, steel, textiles, mining, and rail, the labor movement lost its momentum and, rapidly, many of its members. The collapse of fragile industrial unions in core industries, and the ramped up opposition of employers, meant that the battle for workplace control had been ceded, at least temporarily, to those who owned factories and ran the shopfloor. Internal divisions in labor unions and among unions contributed to the demoralization of workers. Further, the sense that trade union leadership had compromised labor's political position, fed reaction against foreign-born workers, and undermined industrial organizing campaigns led to popular disinterest in the labor movement. Big labor, even small labor, was seen as subversive, corrupt, and ineffective. Workers were better off on their own, voting with their feet, using informal resistance in the form of slowdowns and poor work, rather than joining a traditional union. In fact, it was the mavericks, the heirs and comrades of syndicalist working-class hero William Z. Foster, who led some of the largest, best-known, and most fiercely contested labor battles of the interwar period.

"The Lean Years" of the 1920s thus began with the labor movement in disarray and the conservative forces behind the Open Shop nation and the American Plan having regained momentum. Even as workers had engaged in widespread strikes during the war, and found new support in the federal government, they encountered armed resistance in the form of military surveillance, the Federal Bureau of Investigation, state and local police, and a court system dominated by conservative judges who most often viewed labor organizers and especially immigrant workers as outside the law. The IWW, which had been a radical voice for workers, was largely silenced, its Continental Congress of the Working Class forgotten, and its members disbursed—some into prisons, some into private life, and others into political activity. Many with experience among the Wobblies would become a source of experience and ideas for the labor movement of the 1930s, even while they remained dormant for many years. The memory of the labor movement before the Great War, and its collapse in the postwar years, remained in the possession of individual workers, who would keep alive labor traditions in the long decade between the war and the Great Depression.[72]

Notes

1 W.E.B. DuBois, *Black Reconstruction in America* (New York: Harcourt Brace and Company, 1935). While DuBois was focused on the South and its racial conflict, his perspective on native-born white working men, and their belief in white racial superiority, has since been more widely applied. See David Roediger, *The Wages of Whiteness: Race and the Making of the American Working Class* (London: Verso, 1991); Neil Foley, *The White Scourge: Mexicans, Blacks, and Poor Whites in Texas Cotton Culture* (Berkeley: University of California Press, 1997); Eric Arnesen, *Brotherhoods of Color: Black Railroad Workers and the Struggle for Equality* (Cambridge, MA: Harvard University Press, 2001), among others. Notably, DuBois wrote his book in the 1930s, when many industrial unions in the North promoted a "gospel of unity and unionism" that sought to overcome racial divisions in the workplace. In the South, racial segregation continued to pay dividends to employers and cost workers in textiles and other industries.

2 David Montgomery's *The Fall of the House of Labor: The Workplace, State and American Labor Activism, 1865–1925* (New York: Cambridge University Press, 1987) focuses on the central shifts in production, labor force, and labor organization. See also Daniel Nelson, *Managers and Workers: Origins of the Twentieth Century Factory System in the United States, 1880–1920*, second ed. (Madison: University of Wisconsin Press, 1995); Bruno Ramirez, *When Workers Fight: The Politics of Industrial Relations in the Progressive Era, 1898–1916* (Westport: Greenwood Press, 1978); David Roediger and Elizabeth Esch, *The Production of Difference: Race and the Management of Labor in U.S. History* (New York: Oxford University Press, 2014).

3 David Brody, *The Butcher Workmen: A Study of Unionization* (Cambridge, MA: Harvard University Press, 1964); idem, *Steelworkers in America: The Non-Union Era* (Cambridge, MA: Harvard University Press, 1960); Philip Foner, *History of the Labor Movement in the United States*, vols. 2–3 (New York: International Publishers, 1955, 1964); Roslyn

Feldberg, "'Union Fever': Organizing among Clerical Workers, 1900–1930," in James Green, ed, *Workers Struggles, Past and Present: A Radical America Reader* (Philadelphia: Temple University Press, 1983), 151–167.

4 Leo Troy, *Trade Union Membership, 1897–1965* (Washington DC: National Bureau of Economic Research, 1965), 1–10; Perry K. Blatz, *Democratic Miners: Work and Labor Relations in the Anthracite Coal Industry* (Albany: SUNY Press, 1994); Scott Molloy, *Trolley Wars: Streetcar Workers on the Line* (Dover: University of New Hampshire Press, 2007); Sidney Fine, *"Without the Blare of Trumpets": Walter Drew, the National Erectors Association, and the Open Shop Movement, 1903–1957* (Ann Arbor: University of Michigan Press, 1995); Michael Kazin, *Barons of Labor: The San Francisco Building Trades and Union Power in the Progressive Era* (Urbana: University of Illinois Press, 1987); Kenneth Fones-Wolf, *Glass Towns: Industry, Labor, and Political Economy in Appalachia, 1890–1930* (Urbana: University of Illinois Press, 2006).

5 See James Weinstein, *The Corporate Ideal in the Liberal State, 1900–1918* (Boston MA: Beacon Press, 1968), 7ff; Marguerite Green, *The National Civic Federation and the American Labor Movement, 1900–1925* (Washington DC, Catholic University of American Press, 1956); Christopher J. Cyphers, *The National Civic Federation and the Making of a New Liberalism, 1900–1915* (New York: Praeger, 2002).

6 Philip Nicholson, *Labor's Story in the United States* (Philadelphia: Temple University Press, 2004), 189. See also Weinstein, *The Corporate Ideal in Liberal America*, which distinguishes between the small businessmen engaged in the National Association of Manufacturers, and the corporate leaders who belonged to the National Civic Federation. See also Thomas Ralph Clark, *Defending Rights: Law, Labor Politics, and the State in California, 1890–1925* (Detroit: Wayne State University Press, 2002); William Millikan, *A Union Against Unions: The Minneapolis Citizens' Alliance and Its Fights Against Organized Labor, 1903–1947* (St. Paul: Minnesota Historical Society Press, 2003); Daniel Ernst, *Lawyers Against Labor: From Individual Rights to Corporate Liberalism* (Urbana: University of Illinois Press, 1995); Thomas A. Klug, "The Roots of the Open Shop: Employers, Trade Unions, and Craft Labor Markets in Detroit, 1859–1907" (Ph.D. diss., Wayne State University, 1993).

7 Fine, *"Without the Blare of Trumpets"*; Ernst, *Lawyers against Labor*; David Montgomery, *Workers' Control in America* (Cambridge: Cambridge University Press, 1979); Mike Davis, "The Stop Watch and the Wooden Shoe: Scientific Management and the Industrial Workers of the World," *Radical America* 9:1 (January-February 1975), 69–86; Daniel Nelson, *Frederick W. Taylor and the Rise of Scientific Management* (Madison: University of Wisconsin Press, 1980); idem, *Managers and Workers*. On labor statistics, see Leo Troy, *Trade Union Membership, 1897–1962* (New York: National Bureau of Economic Research, 1965).

8 Brody, *The Butcher Workmen*; James Barrett, *Work and Community in the Jungle: Chicago's Packinghouse Workers, 1894–1922* (Urbana: University of Illinois Press, 1987).

9 James R. Grossman, "The White Man's Union: The Great Migration and the Resonance of Race and Class in Chicago, 1916–1922," in Joe William Trotter, Jr., ed., *The Great Migration in Historical Perspective: New Dimensions of Race, Class, and Gender* (Bloomington: Indiana University Press, 1991), 83–105; John Commons, "The Teamsters of Chicago," in idem, ed., *Trade Unionism and Labor Problems* (New York: McGinn and Co, 1905), 36–86; David Witwer, *Corruption and Reform in the Teamsters' Union* (Urbana: University of Illinois Press, 2003), 20–37; Warren C. Whatley, "African American Strikebreaking from the Civil War to the New Deal," *Social Science History* 17:4 (1993), 525–558.

10 Daniel Letwin, *The Challenge of Interracial Unionism: Alabama Coal Miners, 1878–1921* (Chapel Hill: University of North Carolina Press, 1998); Eric Arnesen, *Waterfront Workers of New Orleans: Race, Class and Politics, 1863–1923* (New York: Oxford University Press, 1991).

11 Scholarship on the Industrial Workers of the World has been shaped by Melvyn Dubofsky's path-breaking study, *We Shall Be All: A History of the IWW* (New York: Quadrangle Books, 1969). Dubofsky's purpose was to refute the long-held assumption that foreign-born radicals created the IWW and root the IWW in traditions of western labor radicalism. He was left with the problem of explaining immigrant workers in struggles that were equally important at Lawrence, McKees Rock, and Paterson.

12 Stuart D. Brandes, *American Welfare Corporatism, 1880–1940* (Chicago: Chicago University Press, 1976); Andrea Tone, *The Business of Benevolence: Industrial Paternalism in Progressive America* (Ithaca: Cornell University Press, 1997).

13 Dorothy Sue Cobble has argued for the flexibility that AFL unions provided and for the better match between trade unions and the growth sectors of the current labor force. See Dorothy Sue Cobble, "Lost Ways of Unionism: Historical Perspectives on Reinventing the Labor Movement," in Lowell Turner, ed., *Rebuilding the Movement: Labor's Quest for Relevance in the 21st Century* (Ithaca: Cornell University Press, 2001), 82–98. Arguments against this position stress the diversity and precarity of workers in the postindustrial economy and in the need for greater flexibility in organizing.

14 William H. Harris, *The Harder We Run: Black Workers since the Civil War* (New York: Oxford University Press, 1982); Robert Zieger, *For Jobs and Justice: Race and Labor in American since 1865* (Lexington: University Press of Kentucky, 2007); James Kenneally, *Women and American Trade Unions* (St. Albans, VT: Eden Press, 1978); Philip Foner, *Women and the American Labor Movement*, vol. 1 (New York: International Publishers, 1979).

15 There are now two decades of scholarship to support this contention, most recently in Paul Michel Taillon's *Good, Reliable White Men: Railroad Brotherhoods, 1877–1917* (Urbana: University of Illinois Press, 2009) and Steve Meyer's *Manhood on the Line* (Urbana: University of Illinois Press, 2016). See the opening volleys in Ava Baron, ed., *Work Engendered* (Ithaca: Cornell University Press, 1991); Foley, *The White Scourge*, among others.

16 Thomas G. Andrews, *Killing for Coal: America's Deadliest Labor War* (Cambridge, MA: Harvard University Press, 2008); David Corbin, *Life, Work and Rebellion in the Southern West Virginia Coal Fields, 1880–1922* (Urbana: University of Illinois Press, 1981); Joe W. Trotter, Jr., *Coal, Class and Color: Blacks in the Southern West Virginia, 1915–1932* (Urbana: University of Illinois Press, 1990).

17 Victor Greene, *The Slavic Community on Strike: Immigrant Labor in Pennsylvania Anthracite* (South Bend: Notre Dame University Press, 1968); Blatz, *Democratic Miners*; Gwendolyn Mink, *Old Labor and New Immigrants in American Political Development: Union, Party, and State, 1875–1920* (Ithaca: Cornell University Press, 1986), 172–177.

18 Greene, *The Slavic Community on Strike*; Blatz, *Democratic Miners*; Peter Roberts, *Anthracite Coal Communities* (New York: Arno Press, 1970, c. 1904).

19 Philip Foner, *The History of the Labor Movement in the United States*, vol. 3, has as its theme the moribund status of the AFL after 1900. See also the somewhat more nuanced argument of Montgomery, *The Fall of the House of Labor*.

20 Elizabeth Jameson, *All That Glitters: Class, Conflict, and Community in Cripple Creek* (Urbana: University of Illinois Press, 1997); Andrews, *Killing for Coal: America's Deadliest Labor War*; David M. Emmons, *The Butte Irish: Class and Ethnicity in an American Mining Town, 1875–1925* (Urbana: University of Illinois Press, 1989); Mary Murphy, *Mining Cultures: Men, Women, and Leisure in Butte, 1914–1941* (Urbana: University of Illinois Press, 1997); Eric Rutkow, *American Canopy: Trees, Forests, and the Making of a Nation* (New York: Scribner, 2012).

21 Andrews, *Killing for Coal*, 240–286; Jameson, *All That Glitters*, 21–49, 87–113.

22 Gunther Peck, *Reinventing Free Labor: Padrones and Immigrant Workers in the North American West, 1880–1930* (Cambridge: Cambridge University Press, 2000); Melvyn Dubofsky, "The Origins of Western Working Class Radicalism, 1890–1905," *Labor*

History 7:2 (Spring 1966), 131–154; William D. Haywood, *The Autobiography of Big Bill Haywood* (New York: International Publishers, 1977, c. 1929), 70–173.

23 Mark Wyman, *Hard Rock Epic: Western Miners and the Industrial Revolution, 1860–1910* (Berkeley: University of California Press, 1979); J. Anthony Lucas, *Big Trouble: A Murder in a Small Western Town Sets off a Struggle for the Soul of America* (New York: Simon and Schuster, 1998).

24 Dubofsky, "Origins of Western Working Class Radicalism"; see also Haywood, *The Autobiography of Big Bill Haywood*, 70–89.

25 *Rocky Mountain News*, May 11, 1897, cited in Vernon H. Jensen, *Heritage of Conflict: Labor Relations in the Nonferrous Metals Industry up to 1930* (Ithaca: Cornell University Press, 1950), 67; *Salt Lake City Tribune*, May 13, 1897, cited in *The Samuel Gompers Papers*, vol. 4, *A National Movement Takes Shape, 1895–1898*, eds. Stuart B. Kaufman, Peter J. Albert, and Grace Palladino (Urbana: University of Illinois Press, 1992), fn. 14, 258.

26 Quoted in George Suggs, Jr., *Colorado's War on Militant Unionism: James H. Peabody and the Western Federation of Miners* (Detroit: Wayne State University Press, 1972), 24.

27 Richard Slotkin, *The Fatal Environment: The Myth of the Frontier in the Age of Industrialization, 1800–1890* (New York: Macmillan, 1985), 477–498; Troy Rondinone, *The Great Industrial War: Framing Class Conflict in the Media, 1865–1950* (New Brunswick: Rutgers University Press, 2009), 38–89.

28 Jameson, *All That Glitters*, makes this point, as do other Western community studies. On the masculine character of WFM and IWW imagery, see Ann Schofield, "Rebel Girls and Union Maids: The Woman Question in the Journals of the AFL and IWW, 1905–1920," *Feminist Studies* 9:2 (Summer 1983), 335–358; Vincent DiGirolamo, "The Women of Wheatland: Female Consciousness and the 1913 Wheatland Hop Strike," *Labor History* 34:2–3 (Spring–Summer 1993), 236–255; Francis Shor, "'Virile Syndicalism' in Comparative Perspective: A Gender Analysis of the IWW in the United States and Australia," *International Labor and Working Class History* 56 (1999), 65–77.

29 Elizabeth Gurley Flynn, *The Rebel Girl: An Autobiography, My First Life, 1906–1926* reprint ed. (New York: International Publishers, 1973), 160–163, 177–180, 194–195, 225–229, 252–254, 297–312; see also Lukas, *Big Trouble*.

30 Lucas, *Big Trouble*, 240–345; Haywood, *The Autobiography of Big Bill Haywood*.

31 Neil Betten, "Strike on the Mesabi," *Minnesota History* 40 (Fall 1967), 340–347; Robert M. Eleff, "The 1916 Minnesota Miners Strike against U.S. Steel," *Minnesota History* 55 (Summer 1983), 63–74; Peck, *Reinventing Free Labor*, 204–216; William A. Sullivan, "The 1913 Revolt of the Michigan Copper Miners," *Michigan History* 43:3 (September 1959), 294–314; William Beck, "Law and Order during the 1913 Copper Strike," *Michigan History* 54 (1970), 275–292.

32 Sullivan; Beck.

33 William Forbath, *Law and the Shaping of the American Labor Movement* (Cambridge, MA: Harvard University Press, 1991), 90ff; Julie Greene, *Pure and Simple Politics: The American Federation of Labor and Political Activism, 1881–1917* (New York: Cambridge University Press, 1998), 73–88.

34 Melvyn Dubofsky, *The State and Labor in Modern America* (Chapel Hill: University of North Carolina Press, 1994); Ernst, *Lawyers Against Labor*, 124–146.

35 Weinstein, *The Corporate Ideal in the Liberal State, 1900–1918*, 16; Greene, *Pure and Simple Politics*, 107–180.

36 Marc Karson, *American Labor Unions and Politics, 1900–1918* (Carbondale: Southern Illinois University Press, 1958); Julie Greene, "Dinner Pail Politics: Employers, Workers, and Partisan Culture in the Progressive Era," in Eric Arnesen, Julie Greene and Bruce Laurie, eds., *Labor Histories: Class, Politics, and Working Class Experience* (Urbana: University of Illinois Press, 1998), 71–96; Faue, *Writing the Wrongs*, 144–152.

37 Mink, *Old Labor, New Immigrants*, 71–112; see also Mae F. Ngai, "Chinese Gold Miners and the 'Chinese Question' in Nineteenth Century California and Victoria,"

Journal of American History 101:4 (2015), 1082–1105; idem, *Impossible Subjects: Illegal Aliens and the Making of Modern America* (Princeton: Princeton University Press, 2004), 96–165.

38 John King Van Rensselaer, *The Social Ladder* (New York: Henry Holt, 1924), but also see Elizabeth Marbury, *My Crystal Ball* (New York: Boni and Liveright, 1923); Sven Beckert, *The Monied Metropolis: New York City and the Consolidation of the American Bourgeoisie, 1850–1896* (New York: Cambridge University Press, 2001), 237–272, 293–322. John Higham's *Strangers in the Land: Patterns of American Nativism, 1860–1925*, reprint ed. (New Brunswick: Rutgers University Press, 2003), remains the best on nativism and immigration restriction.

39 Mink, *Old Labor and New Immigrants in American Political Development*, 45–70; Allen T. Lane, *Solidarity or Survival: American Labor and European Immigrants, 1830–1924* (Westport, CT: Greenwood Publishers, 1986), chapter 9; Catherine Collomp, "Unions, Civics, and National Identity: Labor's Reaction to Immigration, 1881–1897," *Labor History* 29 (1988), 450–474.

40 Mary H. Blewett, *Constant Turmoil: The Politics of Industrial Life in Nineteenth Century New England* (Amherst: University of Massachusetts Press, 2000), 338–387, discusses the politics of the tariff in the context of industrial conflict; "Tariffs and Labor," in Robert E. Weir, ed., *Workers in America: A Historical Encyclopaedia* (New York: ABC-CLIO, 2013), 753–755; Dana Frank, *Buy American: The Untold Story of Economic Nationalism* (Boston MA: Beacon Press, 1999), 33–55.

41 Greene, *Pure and Simple Politics*, 85, 247–248.

42 Price Fishback and Shawn Everett Kantor, *A Prelude to the Welfare State: The Origins of Workers' Compensation* (Chicago: University of Chicago Press, 2000); John Fabian Witt, *The Accidental Republic: Crippled Working Men, Destitute Widows, and the Remaking of American Law* (Cambridge, MA: Harvard University Press, 2004).

43 Bruce M. Stave, *Socialism and the Cities* (Port Washington, NY: Kennikat Press, 1975); Shelton Stromquist, *Reinventing "the People": The Progressive Movement, the Class Problem, and the Origins of Modern Liberalism* (Urbana: University of Illinois Press, 2006).

44 Davis, "The Stop Watch and the Wooden Shoe," and Shor, "Virile Syndicalism," are suggestive here.

45 Paul F. Brissenden, *The IWW: A Study in American Syndicalism* (1919), first discussed the new ideas. See also Salvatore Salerno, *Red November, Black November: Culture and Community in the Industrial Workers of the World* (Albany: SUNY Press, 1989); Jennifer Guglielmo, *Living the Revolution: Italian Women's Resistance and Radicalism in New York City* (Chapel Hill: University of North Carolina Press, 2010), 139–175, for a rich and fascinating discussion of anarcho-syndicalism among European immigrants.

46 Joyce L. Kornbluh, ed., *Rebel Voices: An IWW Anthology*, reprint ed. (Chicago: Charles H. Kerr, 1998), has the manifesto and other relevant documents.

47 Dubofsky, *We Shall Be All*, 202–208.

48 Davis, "The Stop Watch and the Wooden Shoe"; Dubofsky, *We Shall Be All*, 202–208.

49 Despite its opening salvo, the IWW's "Continental Congress of the Working Class" did not have a coherent ideology. An organization that appreciated dues but did not require them, rejected contracts, and promoted inclusive membership, the IWW did not imagine, and did not impose, any specific political beliefs on its members. Its ideology has to be understood through its members' language, imagery, and practice.

50 David Montgomery, "The 'New Unionism' and the Transformation of Workers' Consciousness in the United States, 1909–1922," *Journal of Social History* 7:4 (May 1974), 509–529.

51 Meredith Tax, *The Rising of the Women: Feminist Solidarity and Class Conflict, 1880–1917* (New York: Monthly Review Press, 1980), 205–240; Nancy Schrom Dye, *As Equals and As Sisters: Feminism, Trade Unionism, and the New York Women's Trade Union League* (Columbia: University of Missouri Press, 1980), 91–104; and a more recent

account, Annelise Orleck, *Common Sense and a Little Fire: Women and Working-Class Politics in the United States, 1900–1965* (Chapel Hill: University of North Carolina Press, 1995), 31–86.

52 Richard Greenwald, *The Triangle Fire, the Protocols of Peace and Industrial Democracy in the Progressive Era New York* (Philadelphia: Temple University Press, 2005); Daniel Bender, *Sweated Work, Weak Bodies: Anti-Sweatshop Campaigns and the Language of Labor* (New Brunswick: Rutgers University Press, 2004), 105–154.

53 Flynn, *The Rebel Girl*, 127–151; Tax, *The Rising of the* Women, 241–275. Bruce Watson, *Bread and Roses: Mills, Migrants and the American Dream* (New York: Viking, 2005), is a recent account of the strike. See also the insightful analysis by Ardis Cameron in *Radicals of the Worst Sort: Laboring Women in Lawrence, Massachusetts, 1860–1912* (Urbana: University of Illinois Press, 1993), 117–169; and Guglielmo, *Living the Revolution*, 176–198.

54 Watson, *Bread and Roses*, 141–198.

55 Andrews, *Killing for Coal*, 233–286; Scott Martelle, *Blood Passion: The Ludlow Massacre and Class War in the American West* (New Brunswick: Rutgers University Press, 2008).

56 Joseph McCartin, *Labor's Great War: The Struggle for Industrial Democracy and the Origins of Modern American Labor Relations, 1912–1921* (Chapel Hill: University of North Carolina Press, 1998), 12–37, sees the CIR as a first step toward industrial democracy, though conservative members modified its recommendations. Still, Frank Walsh carried the experience with him into the War Labor Board, where he became a chief advocate for federal mediation of labor disputes.

57 Alex Gourevitch, *From Slavery to the Cooperative Commonwealth: Labor and Republican Liberty in the Nineteenth Century* (New York: Cambridge University Press, 2014), gives some counter-examples of farmer-labor organizing, in particular among sugar cane workers.

58 Carey McWilliams, *Factories in the Field: The Story of Migratory Farm Labor in California*, reprint ed. (Berkeley: University of California Press, 2000), 66–133; Frank Tobias Higbie, *Indispensible Outcasts: Hobo Workers and Community in the American Midwest, 1880–1930* (Urbana: University of Illinois Press, 2003), 25–65.

59 Higbie, *Indispensible Outcasts*, 134–172; McWilliams, *Factories in the Field*, 134–151; Mark Pittenger, *Class Unknown: Undercover Investigations of American Work and Poverty in the Progressive Era to the Present* (New York: NYU Press, 2012), 78–116.

60 Flynn, *Rebel Girl*; McWilliams, *Factories in the Field*, 152–167; DiGirolamo, "Women of Wheatland," 236–255.

61 On Philadelphia, see Peter Cole, *Wobblies on the Waterfront: Interracial Unionism in Progressive-Era Philadelphia* (Urbana: University of Illinois Press, 2007). Studies of the garment trade are instructive here. See Roger Waldinger, "Another Look at the ILGWU: Women, Industry Structure, and Collective Action," in Ruth Milkman, ed., *Women, Work and Protest: A Century of U.S. Women's Labor History* (Boston MA: Routledge and Kegan Paul, 1985), 86–109; Alice Kessler-Harris, "Problems of Coalition-Building: Women and Trade Unions in the 1920s," in Milkman, ed., *Women, Work and Protest*, 110–138; Steve Fraser, *Labor Will Rule: Sidney Hillman and the Rise of American Labor* (New York: Free Press, 1991), 146–237.

62 Roediger, *The Wages of Whiteness*; Thomas Guglielmo, *White on Arrival: Italians, Race, Color, and Power in Chicago, 1890–1945* (New York: Oxford University Press, 2003).

63 Trotter, ed., *The Great Migration in Historical Perspective*; Beth Tomkins Bates, *The Making of Black Detroit in the Age of Henry Ford* (Chapel Hill: University of North Carolina Press, 2012), 15–38.

64 Curt Gentry, *Frame-Up: The Incredible Case of Tom Mooney and Warren Billings* (New York: W.W. Norton, 1967).

65 Christopher Capozzola, *Uncle Sam Wants You: World War I and the Making of the Modern American Citizen* (New York: Oxford University Press, 2008), 117–205.

66 Dubofsky, *We Shall Be All*, 349–375; Montgomery, *The Fall of the House of Labor*, 330–385.

67 McCartin, *Labor's Great War*, 12–37.

68 McCartin, *Labor's Great War*, 94–146.

69 McCartin, *Labor's Great War*, underplays this aspect of labor's experience in World War I; but federal surveillance and the arrest of union and radical activists undermined the labor movement and contributed to labor's weak response in the 1920s. See Dubofsky, *We Shall Be All*, 376–444.

70 Flynn, *Rebel Girl*, 217–296; Montgomery, *The Fall of the House of Labor*, 393–395; Dubofsky, *We Shall Be All*, 385–392.

71 William Preston, *Aliens and Dissenters: Federal Suppression of Radicals, 1903–1933*, reprint (Urbana: University of Illinois Press, 1994), 88–152, 238–272.

72 Allen M. Wakstein, "The Origins of the Open Shop Movement, 1919–1920," *Journal of American History* 51 (December 1964), 460–475; Irving Bernstein, *The Lean Years: A History of the American Worker, 1920–1933* (Boston MA: Houghton Mifflin, 1960), 83–143.

3

REBUILDING THE MOVEMENT, 1922–1945

The Independent Union of All Workers, formed in Austin, Minnesota, was the brainchild of former Wobbly Frank Ellis, a labor organizer and packinghouse worker at the local Hormel plant. When Ellis wanted to turn Hormel's company town into a union city, he encountered the same problems that had dogged unionists in meatpacking and mass production industries since the late nineteenth century. He faced a politically powerful anti-union employer, a work force divided by skill, ethnicity, race and gender, a history of failed organizing and broken strikes, and a local government hostile to labor. Nonetheless, Ellis managed to organize not just the Hormel meatpacking plant but most of the workers of Austin, Minnesota, in the depth of the Great Depression. This organizing feat was secured by the growth and stability of union power and sustained gains in wages, working conditions, and benefits during World War II.[1]

The Independent Union of All Workers was only one of labor's successes in the early 1930s. Community-based organizing campaigns, unemployed councils, and working-class political activism at the local level made significant gains for the American labor movement, which had suffered tremendous losses in the years following World War I. The question that continues to stir debate among those interested in labor and in social movements is how workers during the Great Depression acted contrary to every expectation and rebuilt the labor movement. They gained political and economic power when unemployment was high, competition for jobs intense, and employers powerful. They made those gains despite ethnic, racial, occupational, and gender divisions. How did working men and women find their voice in the workplace and in politics, given the obstacles they faced?

The labor movement was in a state of disarray in 1922. Catastrophic union losses opened the door to a decade of what many commentators have called "quiescence," that is, a slowing down or cessation of active labor organization. Following the disastrous strike defeats of 1919–1922, rank-and-file workers harbored legitimate fears of unemployment, poverty, and, among immigrant activists, deportation. Racial and ethnic hostilities and political conflicts undercut what gains had been made. The Supreme Court decision in *Duplex Printing v. Deering* (1921) voided protections against labor injunctions. New union organization slowed to a crawl, as labor reformers focused on third-party political strategies and labor legislation.[2]

Some labor historians have faulted the prosperity of the 1920s and the greater availability of consumer goods for lulling workers into a false sense of security. After a short period of post-war unemployment, they argue, workers joined in the good fortunes of the time. Decent wages, readily available durable goods, mass-produced clothing, and consumer confidence meant that workers no longer looked to strikes or collective bargaining to improve their lot. A shared sense of progress and well-being put the ragged fear of poverty far behind and made the idea of class warfare—and even labor organizing—seem irrelevant to many wageworkers. Many who still belonged to unions saw them torn apart by internal conflict. Trade unionists retreated to high ground, maintaining union strength through union label campaigns and conservative bargaining.

The experience of second-generation immigrant workers in Passaic, Gastonia, and Harlan County and urban migrants in cities like Norfolk, Akron, and Minneapolis provide a striking contrast to this picture. First, not only were coal mining, textile manufacturing, and agriculture depressed industries, but the South and rural Midwest faced economic challenges that stemmed from overproduction and troubling debt. Hundreds of thousands of young workers migrated from rural farms and towns to cities to take jobs in auto, rubber, steel, and electrical manufacturing. Here workers—both old and new—faced challenging conditions. Unemployment stubbornly remained above 14 percent. In some regions, joblessness was at depression levels.[3]

As manufacturers upgraded equipment to meet new consumer demand, they continued to reduce labor costs by hiring fewer workers, intensifying production, and paying lower piece-rates and take-home wages. What came to be called technological unemployment was a factor in the deteriorating economic conditions of the late 1920s. The evolution of management science and industrial psychology added to employer power in the workplace. The adoption of more efficient machine production and widespread open shop campaigns meant fewer workers, smaller unions, and lower wages.[4] Fewer and lower-paid workers meant fewer consumers could afford to buy goods, even with new credit schemes. The market for durable consumer goods (such as cars and refrigerators) that led the way to prosperity in the early 1920s was in decline by the end of the decade. The drag of these factors on the national economy contributed to growing uncertainty.[5]

The labor movement was neither invisible nor inactive in these years. While it faced formidable opposition in what was called "the American Plan," unions organized and revitalized institutions that supported the labor movement. Among these were labor and consumer advocacy groups, the labor press, worker- and consumer cooperatives, independent unions, and working-class political organizations. While it is difficult to measure the impact of these groups, the labor movement that launched massive strikes in the 1930s would not have been possible without community organizations that kept labor's traditions alive and its human and institutional resources intact. Intermittent activism, sustained institution building, and even failed struggles provided resources for labor's explosive growth.[6]

This chapter will focus on the rebirth of labor organization in the 1920s and the emerging industrial union movement of the 1930s and 1940s. Exploring the political culture of the labor movement, shared understandings about common problems, and networks of communication, the chapter shows how the 1920s was a rebuilding decade during which central institutions of organized labor were recreated and their influence restored. As grassroots leaders rebuilt labor unions, the new activism gave rise to an energetic national labor movement in the Congress of Industrial Organizations (CIO) and the revitalized American Federation of Labor (AFL).

Despite inter-union rivalries and political divisions, the decades of the 1930s and 1940s established the labor movement as a powerful political and economic voice. Labor's "turbulent years" stabilized the power of a new union bureaucracy in alliance with organized capital and a federal government willing to regulate labor relations. During World War II, demand for labor and generous defense contracts further solidified the power of a newly centralized labor movement. Taking the no-strike pledge, CIO leaders were able to secure union jobs, despite the entry of millions of new workers into defense production. By routinizing how unions interacted with employers, national labor unions slowly exchanged community-based unionism for workplace contractualism. Minority and women workers who emerged during the war as leaders did so in a union context where ordinary workers had less of a voice. The labor movement emerged from World War II more powerful but significantly less democratic.

The Meaning of Victory and Defeat

As we saw in the previous chapter, the call for industrial democracy inspired broad-based labor organizing during World War I. By the end of the war, discontent about the speed of production, unsafe working conditions, and low wages brought workers in to conflict with employers. Across the country workers in steel, meatpacking, coal, railroads, textiles, urban transit, and telephone walked out in protest. Local police, the National Guard, federal troops, and private security guards used armed force to put down strikes, even where there was significant community support. Wartime propaganda about growing radicalism and the arrest of immigrant activists was held against the labor movement, as organizing campaigns in mass production industry went down to defeat.[7]

Labor's wartime alliance with the Wilson administration held little meaning after the war. The fragile relationship between the national AFL and the Democratic party unraveled as the troops came home and the economy spiraled into a postwar recession. The withdrawal of federal mediators from the meatpacking industry in 1919 signaled that labor no longer had a place at the president's table. Instead, the Democratic party sought support from conservatives opposed to Wilson's foreign policy and hostile to labor. Facing defeat in the 1920 election, some Democratic candidates flirted with the Ku Klux Klan, which had added anti-unionism, anti-Catholicism, and fear of immigrants to its agenda of racial segregation and violence. The Democratic party's return to business-friendly policies emphasized free markets and opposed government regulation. Little wonder that conservative trade unionists like John Lewis of the United Mine Workers chose to ally with the ascendant Republican party and its "return to normalcy." Other labor leaders temporarily turned toward the Non-Partisan League and the Farmer–Labor party. If the Wilson years had proven to be a disappointment for labor's political agenda, union leaders argued, there was the sustaining tradition of craft unionism and the strength of skilled workers in the labor market to uphold industrial democracy.[8]

In the wake of several defeats, the labor movement fell into disarray. The councils that led the effort to organize steel and meatpacking were gone; the coal industry was in depression. The United Mine Workers, one of the workhorses of labor, saw a rapid decline in membership and resources. The IWW, which had stimulated trade unions and workers to organize, was decimated. Most importantly, the labor movement had lost its most vital channels of communication. The wartime Trading with the Enemy Act and the Espionage and Sedition Acts, the Postmaster General's censorship of the U.S. Mail and publishing delays hit labor and foreign language newspapers hard. When wartime censorship of mailed publications ended, the damage had been done. The increased price of paper during the war, reduced circulation, and the loss of mailing privileges forced hundreds of labor weeklies and foreign language newspapers to close. Wartime restrictions and the new Red Scare made news reporting more difficult. Independent labor papers had difficulty paying their staff and relied on a shrinking number of volunteer reporters.[9]

What was more, mass circulation newspapers, often owned by conservative open shop advocates, dedicated little space to covering labor news. Strikes and labor conflicts, union meetings and Labor Day parades—all disappeared from front pages and even lists of local events. When news media did cover strikes, labor leaders were represented as radicals and thugs and striking workers as individual troublemakers and criminals. As the Interchurch World Movement found in its investigation of the 1919 steel strike, local newspapers falsified strike information and led the public to believe that remaining picketers were malcontents, immigrant and homegrown subversives who sought to destroy the economy and undermine the civil order. The smear campaign contributed to anti-union sentiment and the belief that the labor movement was inherently dangerous and defeated.[10]

The labor movement was internally divided on political grounds and on organizing strategies. The question was whether labor should continue to pursue an agenda of reform dependent on state action, or return to the militant trade unionism of the 1910s. Would labor activism enhance chances for court reform and social provision or simply provoke the national security state to declare all labor organization—and not simply criminal syndicalists and anarchists—illegal? Was it even possible to organize mass production industry, given the ethnic and racial hostilities among workers? The return to normalcy that heralded the election of Republican presidents and congresses in the 1920s left the labor movement demoralized and without a strong federal voice.[11]

Lingering labor unrest surfaced in the civil war that erupted in West Virginia mines. Mingo and Logan counties, the center of labor conflict for nearly two decades, witnessed clashes between the mining companies and their Baldwin-Felts guards and the fragile locals of the United Mine Workers. Frank Keeney, a native West Virginian, had been organizing in the coal fields since before the war. Along with the legendary organizer Mother Jones, Keeney created interracial alliances among Southern miners and the immigrant Italian workers who had been recruited to replace them. For African American and immigrant workers, the mines had represented rare opportunities for equal employment. White miners, despite their own racial and ethnic prejudices, learned to overcome them in recruiting new workers for the sake of the union.

"Bloody Mingo" became the scene of prolonged battles between mine guards and armed miners that escalated into street gunfights and assaults on tent colonies of evicted mine families. Machine guns and dynamite marred the landscape, as mine tipples and railroad cars were destroyed, and workers and guards murdered. In response to the "armed insurrection" against mine owners, the state governor sent in the National Guard. After the conflict ended, the coal industry entered a decade-long depression that gave surviving mine companies an even tighter grip on the lives of miners and their families.[12]

The railroad shopmen's strike that same year marked the end of widespread labor conflict that had stretched from the Seattle General Strike to New England textile mills. As *Minnesota Union Advocate* editor William Mahoney wrote, "the greatest industrial struggle that ever occurred in America" began that summer after a wage cut and changes in work rules fed workers' discontent.[13] During the war, the railroad unions had benefited from progressive Secretary of the Treasury William McAdoo, who directed the United States Railroad Administration during the First World War. In contrast to the heavy-handed rule of other government officials, McAdoo recognized the critical importance of railroads to the war effort. He also understood the power of railroad workers, who had won an eight-hour day with the Adamson Act. With the dissolution of the Railroad Administration at war's end, control of labor relations was left to the newly created United States Railroad Labor Board, which negotiated with private railroad companies, and the Interstate Commerce Commission.[14]

Railroad shop craft workers constituted about 20 percent of the railroad labor force. They were faced with different conditions than among the railroad operating crafts, such as engineers, firemen, trainmen, and conductors. Maintaining the rails and rail beds, the rolling stock, and right-of-way, railroad shop workers such as machinists, boilermakers, sheet metal and electrical workers were ineligible for membership in the railroad brotherhoods. While engineers and firemen kept the trains running, the maintenance of the lines relied on a different, and less valued, set of skills and workers outside the realm of conservative labor. As the war ended, railroad shop workers faced escalating unemployment and surplus labor. Employers filled maintenance jobs much more easily than railroad operating trades, and they did not hesitate to cut wages and lay off workers. Inflation and the abrupt return of railroad control to private hands disrupted the labor peace. A new wage cut directed at shop craft workers amounted to 12 percent of their pay, but the operating trades were unaffected. When railroad unions called for a vote, the railroad brotherhoods voted no. In the strike, the railroad shop crafts were on their own.[15]

More than 400,000 railroad workers went on strike. In cities and towns such as Buffalo, Cleveland, Wilmington, North Carolina, and Needles, California, there were outbreaks of individualized violence. Compared to the mass actions in Chicago meatpacking and Pittsburgh steel, the railroad strike was relatively peaceful.[16] Local National Guard units and U.S. Marshals were on hand when sporadic violence occurred. After the strike began, Attorney General Harry M. Daugherty urged President Harding to intervene. While Secretary of Labor James Davis and Secretary of Commerce Herbert Hoover argued for mediation, Daugherty sought and won a federal injunction against the strikers barring any form of strike activity, including picketing and public gathering, near railroad lines. The Justice Department hired 2,200 new marshals to enforce the injunction. Federal troops were assigned to protect replacement workers and keep the peace in affected towns and cities.[17]

Government intervention fatally undermined the ability of the railroad shop craft unions to sustain the strike. A proposed settlement promised to respect worker seniority, but the majority of railroad shop men remained unemployed at strike's end. More than three-quarters had been replaced; only about a third of the strikers went back to their jobs. Railroad superintendents such as Northern Pacific's H.M. Curry saw the strike as an opportunity to "rid the service of chronic agitators, fault finders, time servers, etc." Other railroads targeted "undesirables" for permanent dismissal.[18] While the strike paved the way for the Railway Labor Act of 1926, it also demonstrated the continued willingness of the federal government to use troops and the judiciary to suppress labor protests, a harbinger for labor troubles ahead.

The Narrow Limits of Labor's Power and Organized Employers

The decisive defeat of the railroad shop craft strike discouraged further labor protests. Compared to the peak year of 1917, when 4,450 strikes involved over a million workers and nearly 7 percent of the labor force, the number of strikes in 1922 dropped to just over a thousand.[19] By 1925, that number had risen to just over 1,300, but more importantly, strikers represented only 2 percent of the labor force, or about 428,000 workers.[20] The railroad shop craft strike also revealed the limits of labor's political power. The Coolidge administration, hastily created after the death of President Harding in 1923, had little support for or from the labor movement. As governor of Massachusetts during the Boston police strike, and during the trial of immigrant radicals Nicola Sacco and Bartolomeo Vanzetti, Coolidge was openly hostile to working-class organization. He was moved neither by concerns for civil liberties nor for individual rights beyond the economic realm. Like many men of his time, Coolidge believed in the capacity of markets to address all social ills. He saw private employment as beyond state regulation and government as principally a force for maintaining public order.[21]

Organized employers eyed government at all levels as the means to limit labor power. Even before World War I ended, state legislatures passed laws to prohibit criminal syndicalism, a broadly defined term that targeted the Industrial Workers of the World and the emerging Communist party. More than twenty states eventually passed similar legislation. Sponsored by employer associations and conservative groups, the laws had a broader mandate than just jailing Wobblies. Rather, "criminal syndicalism" laws cast doubt on the legitimacy of all trade unions. Public trials, such as those of communists William Z. Foster and Anita Whitney, further eroded public support for the labor movement. Faced with fines and imprisonment for the act of labor organizing, workers often chose not to organize. Those who had already served time in jail or were threatened with arrest were less likely to engage in public organizing campaigns.[22]

A Supreme Court case put labor's most important victory, which exempted labor from anti-trust legislation, in jeopardy. Employers increasingly sought labor injunctions to block boycotts and strikes. After the war, employers interested in outlawing the union, or closed shop, funded a court challenge of the Clayton Act. They found a vehicle in a relatively obscure strike in Michigan, which pitted union machinists against an anti-union firm. In 1920, the machinists went out on strike against the Duplex Printing Company, one of only four firms nation-wide that manufactured printing presses and the only non-union company. Located in Battle Creek, Duplex's owners insisted upon operating an open shop. They had the backing of business organizations and Battle Creek's powerful C.W. Post. After calling a secondary boycott, the machinists' union faced a labor injunction that barred picketing. Employers argued that the strike was causing irreparable harm to their reputation, market, and ability to operate. Strikes, the argument went, hampered the freedom of individual workers to contract their labor. The union argued that the injunction violated the Clayton Act. The court's decision in *Duplex Printing v. Deering* invalidated key provisions of the Clayton Act. In its aftermath, businesses and employer organizations pursued broad injunctions in strikes and boycotts. More labor injunctions—approximately 2,000—were issued in the 1920s than in any other decade. Union campaigns fell apart as court-ordered injunctions effectively ended organizing efforts.[23]

As part of the American Plan, labor injunctions undermined the limited power of unions in the workplace. Businesses were virtually assured of an open shop. Faced with barriers to strike action, trade unions turned to union label buying campaigns, legislative work, and political work not in direct conflict with organized employers. Beyond the workplace, organizations such as the Citizens' Alliance of Minneapolis and the Employers' Association of Detroit had targeted labor's allies. They denied credit to unionized employers and funded election campaigns to unseat union supporters from public office.[24] Company unions proliferated to compete directly with union benefits and reinforce divisions among workers. National Cash Register, U.S. Steel, and REO, to use but a few examples, offered skilled workers stock purchases, subsidized home loans, and opportunities to join company sports teams and hunting clubs. New bonds between companies and skilled workers created new barriers to industrial unions that would have to be overcome, if mass production industries were to be organized.[25]

Consumer Culture and Worker Cohesion

As contemporary observers noted, a major reason for strike failure in mass production industries were the ethnic and racial conflicts among workers that flared into violence during several strikes and race riots in 1919. The Great Migration of African Americans from the South led to greater diversity in the labor force and increased racial tension among workers in steel, rubber, and meatpacking. Cultural differences meant that there was little shared experience among the operatives on the same assembly line. Everyday life, from where one bought groceries and what one ate, to the neighborhood or type of home one lived in and the music and movies one enjoyed in leisure time, differed from group to group. But with the spread of Hollywood movies, mass-produced records and radios, chain stores, banks, and newly active ward politics in the 1920s, workers had a greater range of experiences and social bonds in common. What is more, the language they spoke, and images they used, increasingly reflected these cultural experiences.[26]

There was another common ground. The 1920s was an associational decade. Membership and participation in voluntary associations was at an all-time high, whether that was in church membership, community organization, or political activism that opened the door for a new political coalition.[27] Grassroots urban politics had, by 1928, contributed to these changes, as the children of immigrants turned to the Democratic party and its ward politics. Ethnic organizations were active but in ways that provided community access to the political goods of the New Deal. By 1934, African American voters also began to defect from the party of Lincoln to join the new coalition.[28]

In the 1920s, labor unionists turned to state politics and government as arenas for activism. Despite defeat for labor's Non-Partisan League in the Midwest, there was strong support for farmer–labor politics, as seen in the campaigns of 1920 and 1924. At the state level, labor unions worked to secure unemployment insurance and used union label campaigns to build community ties. Continuing campaigns for the reform of the court system, to pass protective labor laws for women, and to ban labor injunctions showed that working-class men and women remained committed to political action. Indirectly, the fight for the Soldier's Bonus, central to many working-class veterans, reflected renewed interest in the welfare state.[29]

Voluntary associations helped nurture the incipient labor organizing of the 1920s. In San Francisco, New York, Minneapolis, and Detroit, there was a revival of community organization that provided new bases for labor action. In cooperative housing, ethnic fraternities and auxiliaries, worker education programs, singing and theater groups, dairy and consumer cooperatives, and socialist summer camps could be found the roots of labor activism for the next decade. Neighborhood solidarities were not, as some have assumed, detached from the world of work, but rather complementary to it.

The Brotherhood of Sleeping Car Porters is a case in point. The railroad brotherhoods operated as white fraternities of the craft workers. They resisted the industrial unionism of the American Railway Union and opposed organizing railroad workers in construction and maintenance of way. More than that, the railroad brotherhoods refused to recognize or support the organization of service workers in railroads, most significantly the Pullman Porters. Such policies embraced a definition of skill and solidarity that was racially and gender exclusive. Pullman Porters were, by employer choice, African American men. They were also among the best-paid workers in their communities. They performed an essential role in luxury rail travel by providing personal service to sleeping car patrons. They maintained the car interiors, turned down and made beds, provided food service and security for railroad travelers. Like other service workers, porters had a job that was part emotional labor—listening to complaints, addressing personal needs, offering service with a smile, polite language, and gestures of subordination to a largely elite clientele—all requiring skill and experience that were implied in the employment contract. Despite this level of skill, and their status within the African American community, Pullman porters were shunned by the skilled railroad brotherhoods.[30]

In 1925, socialist Asa Phillip Randolph decided to organize Pullman Porters. Porters, Randolph learned, had no regular hours and often no layover time between railroad runs. What followed was sleep deprivation, rigid, on-call work schedules, and 24/7 service. There were few protections against passenger abuse. Using the motto, "Fight or Be Slaves," Randolph brought 500 porters to Harlem to organize the Brotherhood of Sleeping Car Porters (BSCP). With over 15,000 porters in 1928, the BSCP had its strongest presence in the railroad hubs of Chicago, St. Louis, and Oakland and represented more than half of all porters. Despite its vital presence in the community, neither the AFL nor National Mediation Board accepted BSCP claims to represent the Pullman porters in collective bargaining. It was not until 1935 that the union was recognized; in 1937, the BSCP negotiated a national labor agreement.[31]

Through the BSCP, Pullman porters sought to improve their working conditions. Like other skilled unionists, they relied on their wives and families to raise funds and support union activities. Even in the doldrums of the 1920s, the BSCP and other craft unions had vibrant and active women's auxiliaries.[32] The Brotherhood served another purpose. Its porters became conduits of information about and among African American communities. They learned about other communities on train routes in communicating with rail passengers, trainmen, and other porters. Belonging not only to the Sleeping Car Porters brotherhood but to other African American fraternal orders and organizations, BSCP porters provided resources to nascent civil rights work. They thus became an important voice for racial equality in the labor movement and in the workplace.

The Great Migration that had brought growing numbers of African Americans and Mexican migrants into primary industries continued through the 1920s. Workers who had been targeted by postwar ethnic and racial violence now constituted a crucial segment of industrial workers. In steel and rubber production and meatpacking, automobile and tobacco manufacture, and coal mining, African Americans—and women workers of all races—became a strategic plurality in the manufacturing labor force. If mass production industries were to be organized, the labor movement needed to find a way to integrate them.[33]

Women Workers

For women workers, the decade of the 1920s provided a contrast with the progressive-era activism that had sparked the creation of the National Women's Trade Union League (WTUL) and the formation of garment workers' unions. By the 1920s, however, the WTUL and its ally, the National Consumer League (NCL), had shifted their focus from workplace action to lobbying for federal and state labor laws for women wage-earners. Middle- and upper-class women saw themselves as voicing working women's demands. At another remove, organizations like the Young Women's Christian Association (YWCA) engaged young working women with worker education programs and workplace clubs. The School for Workers in Industry at the University of Wisconsin, Brookwood Labor College, and the Bryn Mawr School for Women Workers trained women to be labor leaders. Within garment workers' unions, women leaders pursued similar programs in labor education—among them Fannia Cohn, Pauline Newman, and Rose Schneiderman in the International Ladies' Garment Workers' Union (ILGWU), and Agnes Nestor of the Amalgamated Clothing Workers.[34]

The emergence of a new generation of women union activists was significant for the labor movement. By the 1930s, nearly a third of all adult women were in the labor force. Crucially the new workers included women whose labor force participation bridged marriage and motherhood. The percentage of women who worked grew steadily over the course of the century and had a disproportionate impact on key industries. If there were no women employed in steel mills, coal mines, or behind the wheel of a truck, electrical, textile, and automobile plants often employed up to 40 percent women. Women worked, moreover, not only in clerical positions or inspection but in the production of auto parts, electrical motors, the packaging of bacon, and the making of fabric. The growing numbers of women in hotel and restaurant service, industrial laundries, commercial cleaning, and in teaching, nursing, and social work meant that there was a steady demand for women who could work and for women who might join and even lead unions.[35] For the 1930s labor movement, these women leaders proved essential not only to women joining unions but to the support of sit-down strikes, organizing campaigns, relief protests, and get-out-the-vote efforts.[36]

Organizing in the Periphery: Labor Stirrings

There were signs, mid-decade, of new labor organization. Despite bitter defeats in steel and meatpacking, syndicalist William Foster, now a member of the Communist party, formed the Trade Union Education League and the Trade Union Unity League to serve as umbrella organizations for left unionists in textiles, coal, and the auto industry. Many city and state labor federations put renewed energies into their political organizing to combat the public assault on labor unions. They rebuilt alliances between community and labor organizations and reestablished communication networks.

The Federated Press, a labor news network that provided copy to labor, radical, cooperative and farm newspapers across the country, played a crucial role in these efforts. Established in November 1919, the Federated Press (FP) expanded the reach of the labor movement. With money from the Garland Fund, FP editors Carl Haessler and Harvey O'Connor and reporters such as Art Shields, Esther Lowell, Jessie O'Connor, Laurence Todd, Louis Lochner, and Mary Heaton Vorse covered the major strikes of these decades. The FP daily news service and *Federated Press Labor Letter* connected the activism of Detroit autoworkers, engaged in a struggle to ward off technological unemployment, with the miners of Harlan County, German workers on strike, and efforts to create an India independent of British rule. Copy from the FP found its way into alternative and labor newspapers and helped to foster, among its readers, a sense of a movement that encompassed local conflicts and international struggles.[37]

By 1926, workers in textiles and in mining began to chafe under depressed wages and greater management demands. In towns such as Passaic and Gastonia, textile workers sensed both the incipient recovery and the possibility that workers might again have some leverage against management. Years of patient organizing, with the support of veteran labor unionists, laid the groundwork for renewed labor militancy. Workers, now more secure in their jobs, were willing to press management. Serial wage cuts, mandatory overtime, bad working conditions, and increasing workloads set the stage for the massive walkouts that followed.

The legacy of syndicalism, and the leadership of communists such as William Z. Foster, Albert Weisbord, and others, played an important role. Although craft unions continued to dominate the labor movement, the Trade Union Education League (TUEL) renewed efforts to organize mass production industry, whether in the automotive industry, which saw sporadic strikes in the 1920s, or in the woolen industry in Passaic, New Jersey. Workers in the woolen mills in Passaic and surrounding towns were first- and second-generation ethnics, many of them women. Their employers sharply cut wages and regularly laid off workers. The halting economic recovery of the mid-1920s brought the hope that workers would no longer be asked to accept whatever management offered. On January 25, 1926, 6,000 workers struck the Botany Woolen Mill in Passaic. The strike quickly spread to mills in Garfield, Clifton, and Lodi. Within days, there were over 20,000 woolen workers on strike. They demanded employers reverse the 10 percent cut in wages, limit hours to forty-four per week, and improve working conditions. They also sought union recognition. When the Passaic City Council passed an ordinance to prohibit workers from picketing, strikers continued to picket and to be arrested.

The strike in Passaic attracted national publicity and the support of liberal and left organizations. The relief committee raised over $500,000 to aid strikers. By summer, however, lost wages were taking a toll among workers. To divert growing criticism, the Communist party asked the United Textile Workers, an AFL union, to take over leadership of the strike. The UTW demanded, as a condition, that organizer Albert Weisbord leave. Once Weisbord withdrew, the strike began to fall apart. Relief funds slowed, and the UTW began to negotiate with employers. In late 1926, some of the mills came to terms with the strikers. These mills avoided the wage cuts but failed to gain union recognition. The strike's failure left them, and the organized labor movement, without recourse to collective bargaining in the textile industry.[38]

The Passaic strike was only the first of a series of strikes to affect the textile industry. The migration of textiles to the Piedmont South had left Northern companies disadvantaged and Northern unions vulnerable. Passaic, however, set a pattern for how subsequent strikes would be fought. First, it was the first strike to have an organized public relations campaign, which veteran labor journalist Mary Heaton Vorse headed. The lack of clear communication had been a contributing cause of the failure of the 1919 steel strike. Courting the media, and getting information to the general public and to labor organizers and workers, was now understood to be a key ingredient for strike success. Vorse helped to systematize strike communication, with techniques she employed later in other strikes. Her labor reporting and her press releases to the broader media stamped strikes she covered on the national consciousness. They became the iconic labor struggles of a cheerless decade.[39]

By early 1929, workers in Southern textiles seemed ready to join their Northern peers. The Loray Mill strike in Gastonia burst into the national press as the first of a rolling wave of textile strikes. On April 1, 1929, 1,800 workers left their workplace in protest of recent wage cuts. Led by Fred Beal and Ellen Dawson of the National Textile Workers' Union, the strike grew to 3,500 workers. It was met with armed force, including the Committee of One Hundred, whose purpose was to break the strike. On April 3, the state governor sent 250 National Guardsmen to Gastonia to protect the mills. When a masked mob destroyed strike headquarters, the union moved to a tent city on the outskirts of town. Still, there was no let-up of the strike. Within weeks, the strikers in Gastonia were joined by thousands of other textile workers in the region.

At first, the Loray Mill strike resembled other organizing campaigns. Workers had contacted labor organizers for the United Textile Workers seeking labor support for a walkout. On the ground, the majority of workers wanted to strike the mill, especially given speeded up machines, heavier workloads, and wage cuts. Many workers carried powerful resentments against mill owners who viewed them as rednecks and condemned their evangelical religion, political loyalty, and their speech. Yet the same employers hired mill hands at such low pay that families had to sacrifice children's education in exchange for their wages. The brutal regime of the mill—exhausting ten-hour workdays, dangerous machinery, and respiratory illness (tuberculosis and brown lung, a debilitating disease associated with inhaling cotton fibers)—had no relation to the value of the textiles they produced or the physical and mental labor of its production.[40] When employers found a decline in consumer demand and a corresponding need to increase profits, they asked even more of their workers—that they supervise more machines at a faster pace and accept lower piece-rates.

After the strike had lasted two months, local authorities sought to force the workers' hand. The local sheriff and three other officers went to the union's tent city to demand the strikers surrender their guns. The confrontation ended with the sheriff dead and a few strikers and officers wounded. Following the confrontation, sixteen strike leaders, including organizer Fred Beal, were put on trial for the death of the sheriff. During the trial the violence did not abate. Gunmen, later identified as mill employees, ambushed a car of strikers in the hills outside of town. Ella Mae Wiggins was killed, and others wounded. While seven men were convicted of the sheriff's murder, and had to flee the country, no one was convicted of Wiggins' death. Eventually, the strike broke, as workers faced empty cupboards, evictions from company housing, and the fear of repeated violence. Throughout the region, the textile strikes failed, even as mill orders began to decline and unemployment rose.[41]

Gastonia was only one of a series of strikes to hit the Piedmont textile industry in 1929 but became the most enduring loss for the southern labor movement. The subject of novels and autobiographical writings, Gastonia had strong support from labor radicals across the country. Public opinion about the strike was deeply divided. Strikers faced both the opposition of local government authorities and community members who saw the involvement of outside organizers, and suspected communists, as violating Southern racial norms. While the mill labor force was no longer racially exclusive, the segregation among black and white communities played a central role in delegitimizing the strike leaders. Among those was Ella Mae Wiggins, a single mother who emerged in the early days of the strike as a leader. She became, through news reports, the voice of the strikers in her folk song, "Mill Mother's Lament." She also was a symbol of the marginalized population of textile workers, as a single mother and a woman whose sexual morality became the subject of gossip and speculation. Strike leaders Beal, Dawson, and others were similarly condemned for violating racial and sexual norms.[42]

Gastonia left many labor activists with the sense that the racial problem of the South, and the violent anti-unionism of the region, made failure inevitable. The South, they would argue, could not be organized. This sentiment was to be proven wrong in the Depression-era and wartime militancy of Southern sharecroppers, tobacco workers, steel workers, and shipyard workers. Still, the race line, and the association of racially integrated unions with communism, weakened, undermined, and even destroyed some of the work of the labor movement in the South. If the labor movement came to serve as a voice for racial equality, it proved problematic for unions in the segregated South.

Workers and the Economic Crisis, 1929

The onset of the Great Depression serves as a watershed in United States history and the history of the labor movement. Millions of workers were unemployed and underemployed, and they and their families suffered the effects of one of the greatest economic crises in modern history. For many workers, the Great Depression was felt not as a hammer blow or a falling axe but as the slow disappearance of life as they had known it. Most working people did not encounter the crisis as the stock market crash or the lightning strike of a closed factory or a pink slip. Rather, they saw the crisis deepen in smaller paychecks, fewer hours, and less food on the table. In major industrial cities like Pittsburgh and Detroit, steel and auto workers experienced the Depression first in wage and work hour cuts and then, and only then, unemployment. Skilled workers were less likely to be let go than semi-skilled factory operatives. Young and old workers were more likely to lose their jobs than experienced factory hands and office workers.[43]

Household budgets were trimmed in parallel fashion. Small indulgences disappeared. Installment bills were not paid, and consumer goods were repossessed. Then, and only then, did the unfortunate unemployed face homelessness. Even then, people adapted. Young workers at risk moved back to their family homes; older workers facing eviction asked their children for rent, and tapped-out families set up house in shantytowns or in tents and abandoned buildings. For the majority of workers, the economic crisis brought not homelessness and permanent unemployment but temporary deprivations and longer periods of uncertainty. These conditions made blue collar and white collar workers less likely to protest wage and hour cuts and more willing to accept new demands at work. Fearing unemployment, many people in the late 1920s and early 1930s became more vulnerable to employer abuse and less receptive to union appeals.

The Great Depression occurred in the context of workers who were already accustomed to short pay and rising uncertainty. By 1926, unemployment rates had already begun to increase. In so-called "sick" industries like mining and textiles, workers experienced repeated attempts to replace workers with machinery and supervisors who demanded that workers work more machines at a faster pace. The stretch-out and the speed-up were familiar tactics in businesses trying to keep afloat in the flooded market for cotton and wool textiles and coal.

The discontent of workers expressed itself in a growing wave of small protests during the deepening crisis from October 1929 to November 1932. As businesses cut hours and then began to lay off employees, working-class men and women turned from strategies of adaptation and self-help toward collective organization, protest, and political activism. Faced with growing poverty, they formed neighborhood groups to advocate for greater city and county relief. Witnessing neighbors being evicted from apartments and homes, ward locals fought evictions and forced landlords to restore possessions. Seeing the problem as homelessness and hunger, communist and labor organizations forced the hand of city and county officials to provide more bread, more beds in shelters, and more temporary work for the unemployed. They demanded old age pensions for the elderly poor. Most importantly, ward clubs and neighborhood groups pushed for political solutions to the growing crisis. They voted in ways that elected a Democratic Congress and a Democratic president. No one party encompassed the interests and issues of the working class; but the national Democratic party, running on a platform that targeted the business indifference of the Hoover administration, established a new tone in the federal government and sponsored the politics of experimentation that was the New Deal.[44]

By 1933, with the election of Franklin Delano Roosevelt, there was some conviction that circumstances had to change and, in fact, had changed. Urban workers, many of them second-generation ethnics, came out to vote for the Democratic party in rising numbers in 1928 and 1932. They expected that the new president would address the crisis that restricted their lives and undermined their capacity for progress. While FDR had run as a mainstream politician, his reputation as a Democratic reform governor of New York and his campaign led to rising expectations. Roosevelt's inaugural promise of persistent experimentation, the Fireside Chat message that "the only thing we have to fear is fear itself," created an implicit bond between FDR and the majority electorate that persisted throughout his presidency.[45]

Under FDR's leadership, the hundred days from his March inauguration to June saw Congress pass major landmark legislation targeting the economic causes of the Depression and the social consequences of high unemployment. The banking crisis, during which thousands of banks had failed and hundreds of thousands of depositors had lost their savings, was addressed head-on with banking and financial reforms. The Agricultural Depression, over a decade in duration, was met with the Agricultural Adjustment Act that sought to restore farm price parity and stave off further farm losses. For the manufacturing sector, weakened by low consumer demand and the fractured calculus of employment, Roosevelt's administration created the National Recovery Administration. The NRA sought to restore the economy through industrial codes with production quotas, wage and hour formulas, and employee representation. At first this was imagined as company unions but instead became an industrial union movement. Out of sync with expectations that labor gains can only be made when employment security is at its zenith, the NRA strike wave shocked businessmen and politicians alike. In such places as Chicago's Back of the Yards, along the waterfronts of New York and San Francisco, in tobacco and textile factories and garment shops, and among truck drivers and coal miners, there was recognition that unity and not division was the only way to counter the power of employers. What was to follow in the heady years between 1934 and 1939 were waves of labor militancy that sporadically but regularly disrupted cities, workplaces, and government councils. The turbulent years, while never reaching the levels of strikes witnessed during either world war, rocked the economy and changed labor relations for the following fifty years.[46]

It began with the passage of the National Industrial Recovery Act in 1933. Ostensibly designed to balance economic production and consumption, profits and wages, the NIRA included section 7(a), which was widely interpreted as sanctioning collective bargaining and union membership. NRA "babies" flooded the labor movement, as coal, textile, and garment unions quickly sprang back to life. Hundreds of thousands of workers believed that "the president wants you to join a union." Nascent labor organizations in the national textile industry, shipping and transportation, and light manufacturing came on line.[47]

The United Mine Workers, the International Ladies' Garment Workers Union, the Amalgamated Clothing Workers, and the Textile Workers Union witnessed explosive growth in membership. Joined by semi-industrial unions like the Typographical Union and the Mine, Mill, and Smelter Workers, they turned resources to other industries. But the wave of organization placed industrial workers and their "rogue" leaders in the midst of old battles about how workers should be organized. As workers formed new upstart locals in electrical and rubber industries, in the same plants where labor conflict had smoldered during the war, older trade unionists argued about who had jurisdiction. Trade union stalwarts Matthew Woll of the Photo Engravers, Bill Hutcheson of the Carpenters, John Frey of the Metal Trades, Dan Tobin of the teamsters, and Arthur Wharton of the Machinists worked to block the formation of new industrial unions and sought to channel new members into craft unions.[48] But like new wine in old vessels, they would not hold.

The Uprisings of 1934

Where unions catapulted to national attention was in a series of critical strikes in 1934. Beyond new unions under the NRA, there were general labor uprisings in three cities—San Francisco, Minneapolis, and Toledo—and an industry-wide textile strike. In San Francisco, the International Longshoremen's Union (ILWU) organized the waterfront under the formidable skills of Harry Bridges, an Australian, a former Wobbly and likely communist, as were many of the waterfront organizers. Bridges understood, as earlier radicals had, that transport industries had strategic leverage against their employers. They could force firms to bargain, in ways that directly contradicted the practices of the craft union AFL. Controlling hiring was one key; so too was being able to regulate the transport and distribution of goods. Longshoremen mobilized their membership and the community. The strike hit major ports along the entire West Coast. Erupting in sporadic actions from May to July of 1934, the longshoremen's strike came to encompass the entire city of San Francisco in a four-day general strike to protest the death of strikers. The general strike thus led the way for the unionization not only of the waterfront but of the city itself.[49]

In Minneapolis, militant trade unionists like Bill Brown and Trotskyists Carl Skoglund, the Dunne Brothers (Miles, Vincent and Bill), and Farrell Dobbs conducted a similar organizing campaign to that of the longshoremen's union. They understood the power of truckers and warehousemen in a transportation hub like Minneapolis. As a marketing center, the city provided rail and truck transport and distribution of goods to an entire region. The teamsters capitalized on this advantage in what was a slow but impressive organizing campaign that eventually unionized not only trucking but the entire city of Minneapolis and the vast majority of drivers in the Upper Midwest.[50] The teamster rebellion began with a coal drivers' strike in February of 1934, an action that provided the resources and pattern for a broader strike, which was called in May of that year. Like in San Francisco, collective action was sporadic, often taking place in response to or anticipation of the movements of trucking firms, the Citizens' Alliance of businessmen, and the local police and state National Guard. Politically, the teamsters benefited from the presence of Farmer–Labor governor, Floyd B. Olson, on the scene. While Olson did not support the strike directly, neither did he back the Citizens' Alliance in its efforts to suppress the strike. If the strike headquarters was raided, so too were the offices of the business organization. Federal intervention played an important role in providing political and economic incentives for businesses to settle strikes.

The national textile strike that occurred that year was both similar in its causes and different in outcome. Unlike the community-based collective action in Toledo, San Francisco and Minneapolis, the textile strike took place in several communities, many of them in the union-hostile South. Occurring at some of the same mills that struck in 1929, the 1934 strike also had a familiar cast of characters—and strikingly disparate resources from one community to another. In the Northeast, textile workers won contracts in cities like Woonsocket, Rhode Island. South of the Mason-Dixon line, militant trade unionists called down the wrath of anti-union local police and hostile state governments. The political weakness of the strike was not the only issue. Textile production, like garment manufacture, was an industry with a disproportionately female labor force. Without the same level of capital investment as core industries like steel, rubber, electrical, and auto, textile plants had a history of capital flight. They lacked the tactical advantages of transportation industries and the strategic leverage that plants like Auto-Lite in Toledo (which produced key components of durable goods) possessed. The defeat of the textile strike had long-lasting effects on the labor movement and on the capacity of the South to organize.[51]

The strikes in 1934 and subsequent labor victories were based on political and social forces that were, for the time, wholly new. The combination of experienced and militant labor organizers, nascent labor voices in the press, second generation ethnics who bridged community and workplace organization, a resurgent belief in industrial democracy, and the emerging New Deal coalition assured that labor conflict would be addressed differently. State and local governments that depended on working-class votes promoted programs that insulated individual workers from the labor market, such as unemployment insurance, workers' compensation, and old age pensions. Most importantly, mayors, governors, and other elected officials had in some ways to honor legal guarantees of the right to organize unions, to strike, and to bargain collectively. The NRA's section 7(a) and other legislation opened up new possibilities for labor unions.

Labor's New Deal: The Wagner Act and the Rise of the CIO

The turning point was in 1935. The mid-term elections the year before provided a larger Democratic majority in Congress that backed the central programs of the New Deal. That same Congress passed the Wagner National Labor Relations Act. The law affirmed the right of workers to join a union without penalty, to vote for union representation, and to participate in collective bargaining with employers. It established the National Labor Relations Board (NLRB) to administer and enforce these rights. While not without limitations, the Wagner Act gave support to a broad swath of union organizing campaigns. It became the mechanism by which unions were certified, contracts were ratified, and grievances pursued. Institutionally, it gave workers protections against the unfair labor practices of employers and routine abuses on the shop floor. While organizing strikes often required political allies to insure success, it was the Wagner Act that provided both the inspiration and structure for these victories. The New Deal's robust second act, in which the NLRB played a central part, forced elected officials to act as neutral mediators between employers and workers, rather than as primary defenders of private property.

Amidst the chaotic growth of grassroots unions across the country was the realization of union leaders like John Lewis of the UMW that the door was open for a national organizing campaign in critical industries. Under his militant leadership and the coalition of radical organizers he employed, the CIO targeted the critical industry of steel, which had tentacles in the coal industry and many others, including rubber, electrical, oil, and, most significantly, auto. It was not just the captive mines owned by U.S. Steel that motivated Lewis but rather the constant threat that U.S. Steel and allied companies had presented to the labor movement. Lewis envisioned forcing the AFL to commit to the industrial organization of primary industry. In the end, the effort would require a newly formed Congress of Industrial Organizations to employ the resources of organized sectors to bring a revolution in labor relations and fully implement the Wagner Act.[52]

It was not steel but rubber and auto that led the way. Mary Heaton Vorse, the premiere labor journalist of the age, captured some of the driving forces behind labor's rebirth in reporting on cataclysmic struggles. Along with ILGWU organizer Rose Pesotta, Vorse witnessed first-hand the Akron rubber strike of Goodyear Tire in February and March 1936. The strike began when Goodyear laid off 700 workers due to a decline in tire sales. Over 10,000 men and women eventually picketed the plant. As part of a series of sitdowns in rubber that year, the Goodyear strike pushed the industry toward union recognition, despite the sustained efforts of local police and the Law and Order League to break the union. The United Rubber Workers was able to negotiate a successful conclusion to the strike with an agreement that promised layoffs would respect worker seniority, a return to six-hour shifts, and new grievance procedures.[53]

As witness to the wave of sit-down strikes that followed, Mary Heaton Vorse captured the emergence of the labor movement nationally as struggles in the automobile industry came to the fore. Her vantage point among the women of Pengally Hall in Flint allowed her to see how the components of collective action—the use of sitdowns and flying squadrons, women's auxiliaries, and strategic picketing—made victory possible. In the fall of 1936, Flint, Michigan, home to General Motors, the largest corporation in the United States, was the epicenter of the struggle. GM effectively owned the city, as housing, schools, city government and the police force all depended on the company's revenues and support.[54] Union veterans later recounted that it was difficult to escape the company's vigilant surveillance of its members. Workers joined the union silently and kept their union buttons hidden. They attended meetings under cover of darkness. A series of short strikes that began in 1933 with the Briggs Manufacturing Company set the stage for the unionization of the Big Three.[55]

The auto industry had not been a priority for the UMW or the nascent CIO. Steel was considered the crucial priority target for the CIO, and the Steel Workers Organizing Committee (SWOC) launched a well-funded organizing drive. It was, however, Flint, Detroit, the auto industry, and the emerging United Auto Workers that sparked massive sit-down strikes in the winter of 1936–1937.

The strike began in Flint on December 31st. General Motors workers sat down for forty-four days before GM recognized the United Automobile Workers (UAW). Central factors in the victory were skilled autoworkers, an interracial coalition of African Americans and second-generation ethnic Americans, and a leadership cadre of militant trade unionists, including communists and socialists. The UAW Women's Auxiliary (the red berets of Flint) played a crucial strategic role as well. The Flint strike, and not the stalled steel campaign, created a template for organizing mass production companies in the industrial heartland. The decision of Michigan governor Frank Murphy to limit state intervention in the strike also contributed to the outcome.

The core strategy, beyond building grassroots support through one-on-one organizing, was to use what power workers had at hand. The sit-down strike was adopted to leverage workers' physical presence to gain union recognition and worker demands. Sitting down on the job, refusing either to use the machinery or to move from the plant, kept the employer from using the machinery and replacing the labor force. With some strategic picketing, and the closing of one final Chevrolet plant, the strike was won. In the short season of the sit-down, this tactic would win dozens of strikes and bring into the labor movement thousands of workers. After the Flint strike, UAW-CIO membership soared. In February 1937, it was 88,000; in March 1937 it grew to 166,000. By the end of 1937, the membership rolls had grown to more than 230,000 members.[56]

The sit-down strike became the labor movement's principal weapon in organizing mass production industry. As *Time* magazine proclaimed, "Sitting down has replaced baseball as the national pastime." In January 1937, 74,748 workers participated in 25 sit-downs. A month later, 31,236 workers conducted another 47 sit-downs. By March 1937, 167,210 workers sat down in 170 additional strikes, including waitresses at a Detroit Woolworth diner, tobacco workers in Raleigh-Durham, and hospital laundry workers in Brooklyn. Labor unions called nearly 5,000 strikes that year and won favorable terms in 80 percent of them.[57]

The rise of mass production industrial unionism in the mid-1930s capitalized on the talents and resources of new leaders such as John Brophy, Philip Murray, James Matles and James Carey, and Rose Pesotta, many of whom identified as socialists, communists, and syndicalists. As Len De Caux recalled, "There was light after darkness in the youth of the movement—youth that was direct and bold in action, not sluggish and sly in long compromise with the old and the rotten …"[58] But the experience of union veterans from the strike waves of the 1910s and the war years played a crucial role as well. As shown in the 1934 strikes, those who had witnessed those strikes recalled how governments—and employer organizations—responded to militant trade unionism. They recognized the importance of employing whatever leverage—political, economic, and spatial—that workers had. Sit-downs were a spatial strategy as well as an economic one. Urban workers constituted the base of the New Deal coalition, and that was now used to advantage. Strike victories depended as well on the resources that the

United Mine Workers and its CIO allies had in steering relief funds and political support to striking workers. The season of sit-downs lasted only about a year, but industrial unions dominated most of the decade, as the core steel industry, electrical manufacturing, cannery workers, and packinghouse plants all unionized.[59]

Conservative Backlash and the End of Labor's New Deal

While successful labor organizing campaigns continued throughout the decade and well into the 1940s, labor encountered obstacles to its goal to organize the unorganized. Union membership had reached nearly 9 million by 1940 but represented less than 30 percent of all wage workers. A major obstacle was the presence of a conservative trade union organization, the American Federation of Labor, which continued to compete over jurisdiction in several industries. The AFL and the CIO unions were both capable of arguing to employers that they could channel worker discontent at the same time they engaged in industrial conflict. Moreover, in some cities and industries, the contest between AFL and CIO union representation in NLRB elections led to workplace violence and mutual defeat. Sometimes workers chose no union.

Another major barrier to labor organization was continued racial conflict among workers. In the meatpacking industry, racial violence had undermined and then destroyed initial organizing in the packinghouses of Chicago. The Packinghouse Workers Organizing Committee (PWOC) actively worked to overcome racial competition and prejudice among workers. Aiming to organize a labor force that included nearly 40 percent women in some meatpacking plants and a disproportionate number of African American workers made the advocacy of racial equality and equal pay crucial to the success of the United Packinghouse Workers. Its integrated leadership embraced the CIO's "Gospel of Unity and Unionism" as a central part of its appeal.[60]

By contrast, the UAW had a more difficult time overcoming the racial divide in the automobile industry, both in the South and in trying to organize Ford Motor Company. At Ford Motor, they had to confront a racially segmented labor force, the chief architect of whom was Henry Ford. Dearborn, where company headquarters and the large River Rouge plant were located, was a white city. Inkster was the segregated suburb where black workers lived. Ford recruited African Americans for his foundry and employed more black workers than either GM or Chrysler. He supported black churches, whose conservative preachers viewed the labor movement with skepticism and hostility. Working-class communities and labor unions, many black leaders argued, excluded African Americans, demanded employers fire them, threatened black strikebreakers, and organized violence against black homeowners and workers.[61]

This history was played out in the organizing campaign for Ford. In 1937, after successfully organizing GM and Chrysler, Walter Reuther and Richard Frankensteen led a campaign to organize Ford. Focusing on the River Rouge plant, they led a leafleting campaign ("Unionism, Not Fordism") that met with bloody opposition in what was known as "the Battle of the Overpass." The company's security force turned its weapons on the labor leaders and their followers; sixteen were injured, including seven women from Reuther's home Local 174. While employer violence played a major role in short-circuiting the organizing drive, conflict between white and black workers at the Rouge undermined the campaign still further. Black workers were more suspicious of the UAW than most white workers, partly because Ford was more willing to hire black workers than GM or Chrysler and partly because some perceived the UAW as a "white" organization. Still, in the years between 1936 and 1941, African Americans became increasingly disillusioned with Ford's discriminatory labor practices, speed-up, and declining wages in the foundry. Black union leaders such as Robert "Buddy" Battle, Shelton Tappes, Horace Sheffield, and Joseph Billups argued that the labor movement was the means to expand opportunities for African Americans and a potential weapon in the struggle for civil rights. Overcoming the opposition of black workers, the UAW signed Ford to a union contract after a short strike in 1941. Rouge Local 600 remained the most integrated local in the UAW and pushed the union to address issues of discrimination and segregation.[62]

Beyond racial division, there was a committed, well-connected, and well-financed resistance to labor organization. The United Steel Workers of America-CIO, which organized in core U.S. Steel plants, ran into substantial opposition in Little Steel, the misnamed sector of the steel industry that encompassed Republic, Midland, and Bethlehem Steel and rivaled U.S. Steel in size and production. In 1938, the failed strike in Little Steel led to the deaths of ten marchers and the shooting or beating of more than one hundred others in the Memorial Day Massacre in Chicago. On that day, thousands of strikers and their families had gathered to march in protest against the steel companies.[63] Other organizing campaigns collapsed as resources ran out or local opposition undermined strike actions. As the LaFollette Committee later documented, business opposition to the labor movement found expression in violence against strikers, labor spying, and political and economic blackmail of union employers and union members.[64]

Workers outside mass production industry also joined labor unions and engaged in collective action during the 1930s. Among sharecroppers and tenant farmers, the early 1930s brought new forms of organization; among farm workers on the East Coast, there were efforts to organize. Clerical workers, newspaper reporters and pressmen, workers in hotels and restaurants, laundries, and in state and municipal government were successful in establishing unions and in winning strikes. Indeed, many workers came to enjoy union wages and benefits that had previously been denied them. For the most part, however, the great union victories of the decade remained in primary industries. During the war years, it was these unions that benefited from the labor movement's new prominence and also were constrained by wartime experience.[65]

By the end of the 1930s, the anti-union fortress that was mass production industry had capitulated to the forces of labor. The terms of its surrender, however, have long been in dispute. The membership of the labor movement had more than doubled, and the proportion of workers who belonged to unions rose above the level during World War I. What was the role of community-based organizing drives in jumpstarting a labor movement when the nationally coordinated efforts in mass production industry had failed? Did they leave a lasting legacy? Would the bureaucratization of labor unions, seemingly required by the vast numbers of workers and the vast powers of the corporations for which they worked, lead to a strong labor movement or rather undermine the grassroots rebellions that might have led to a more capacious, social democratic state?

While grassroots campaigns and community-based unionism made possible the emergence of a new and powerful industrial labor movement, a federally mediated system of labor relations, created by the Wagner Act, required that labor lose its social movement character and acquire the habits of institutions. Under the new system, unions needed routine communications, protocols for democratic action, tools of political power, and agreements that would be honored, even if they did not allow for the fullest freedom of expression and action.[66] To have a regular paycheck, health insurance, and a pension made a significant difference for workers who joined the CIO.

Recognizing that power requires responsibility and even a modicum of bureaucracy does not, however, require that one be blinded to the power of employer opposition, the divisiveness of workers along race and gender lines, or the capacity of entrenched union leaders to ignore the demands of popular democracy and democratic principles. The labor movement that had, with great and deliberate intent, overcome the barriers of race and gender in Chicago packinghouses and Detroit auto factories also overlooked the racial exclusion and gender discrimination of countless employers and unions. They did not take on these issues, with the excuse that their members were not ready for such policies. It was, however, convenient to believe that organizing men like themselves was sufficient to creating a new future for all American workers.

The Coming of World War II and Defense Industry

The economic crisis of the 1930s absorbed the energies and resources of a generation of labor activists and political leaders. The labor movement had a vibrant presence in unionized workplaces and an important role in the New Deal order. Still, neither the New Deal nor the resurgent labor movement resolved the structural problems that had led to the Great Depression. Unemployment remained stubbornly high until 1940. When unemployment began to decline, it owed much to increased government defense spending. While there was widespread support for remaining neutral, the Roosevelt administration and Congress had begun to prepare for war. Japanese expansion in the Pacific, Italian and German intervention in

Ethiopia and in Spain, and German incursions into the Rhineland, Austria, and Czechoslovakia alarmed many observers. Some American corporations already were intervening, specifically by investing in the Axis military build-up.[67] The majority of American citizens, including labor leaders John Lewis of the CIO and William Green of the AFL, preferred that the United States distance itself from the growing global conflict. The question that dogged the president and the country was how long it would be possible to remain insulated from the tumultuous violence abroad.

The United States in 1939 had an aging fleet, poorly prepared armed forces, and little or no stockpile of defense goods. With popular anxiety about war at an all-time high, Congress had passed three separate neutrality acts aimed at keeping President Roosevelt from supporting European allies and from intervening in the Spanish Civil War. Despite opposition at home, the Roosevelt administration had to act to mobilize forces and war materiel, recruit domestic support, and rally its allies with whatever resources were available. Indeed, Roosevelt seemed to act with caution abroad but also to gather political and economic resources for the world war ahead. His efforts for defense, first undertaken as cash-and-carry provisions for arms sales and the passage of the Lend–Lease Act that sent munitions and ships to Great Britain, had an immediate impact on the economy. Unemployment, still at 17 percent in 1939, declined in 1940 to 14.5 percent. In 1941, it fell to under 10 percent.[68]

Despite business resistance to converting industry to a wartime footing, new defense production was underway by 1940. Federal support for the construction and conversion of defense plants and government contracts for arms, munitions, vehicles and planes improved the economic climate. The effect on unemployment numbers was immediate, as the demand for labor soared. Not only did employers seek to extend the hours and increase the pay of their work force; they were willing to hire, train, promote and pay new workers to increase production for the war effort. Skilled workers in particular saw a significant increase in their salaries.[69]

As diplomatic relations with Germany and Japan deteriorated, Congress passed legislation to lay the groundwork for the defense effort. First among these was the Burke Wadsworth Selective Training and Service Act, which reinstated the military draft in 1940. Eventually, over 16 million men served in the armed forces, creating a drain on the work force that could not be met by the shrinking unemployed reserve. Rather, new workers were needed—rural migrants from the South and Midwest, black and white; new women workers of all races, who joined 11 million women already in the labor force; young workers trained by the National Youth Administration, and older workers brought back from unemployment and retirement. The federal government began a Bracero program in 1942 to help shore up the dwindling labor supply. Recruited from Mexico and Jamaica, and employed mostly in farm labor, the braceros lacked access to stable employment or basic labor protections. Employers held deportation as means of control. Overall, though, employers hoarded skilled labor and sought deferments for skilled workers in industry, resisted the hiring of minority and women workers, and reluctantly accepted training of young male workers.[70]

By 1941, there was a new call for equality in the workplace. A. Philip Randolph, head of the Brotherhood of Sleeping Car Porters, threatened to organize a march on Washington DC, as the government prepared its defense efforts. Calling on President Roosevelt to address mounting inequality, Randolph, NAACP head Walter White, and National Youth Administration advisor Mary McLeod Bethune persuaded the president to address the need for oversight in war industries. With Executive Order 8802, issued in June 1941, Roosevelt prohibited race discrimination in employment under federal contract. He also created the Committee on Fair Employment Practices (FEPC) with powers to investigate and resolve complaints against specific employers. While the Executive Order took more than a year to implement, the FEPC held out the promise that African Americans—and Latinos and women workers of all races—could find well-paid, unionized, and skilled jobs in defense. It was a pragmatic policy in a time of labor shortages. It was also, given continued racial hostility and political opposition, visionary in its goal of racial parity in the workplace.

By the end of the war, despite the FEPC's weak enforcement powers, it showed results. In Detroit, for example, UAW Local 600 at the River Rouge was central to the operation of the FEPC. In 1942, about 3 percent of the labor force in defense industries was African American; by 1945 this proportion had risen to 9 percent. By the end of the war, the number of African American workers in defense industries had increased to 1.2 million and black union membership doubled to 1.25 million. Further, the domestic labor shortage gave urgency to the recruitment of female workers. By 1945, some 19 million women were in the labor force, 6 million of them new workers. Women constituted about one-third of war industry workers and more than 20 percent of the 15 million union members in 1944. Because defense jobs were disproportionately unionized, the proportion of African American workers—and women workers—who belonged to unions and earned union wages also grew.[71]

Labor and Equality of Sacrifice in Wartime

Workers on the home front generally understood the priorities of defense production. They complained about the scarcity of gasoline, sugar, textiles, and new automobile tires; but for the most part, civilian workers understood necessary sacrifice. It was, instead, disparity between the sacrifices of business and labor, government employees and those in private industry, that was at issue. The labor movement seized the moment in 1941, when CIO head Philip Murray took a no-strike pledge in support of the war effort. This was not, in the end, a neutral act. In exchange for the government agreeing to maintain union jobs, the CIO promised to refrain from strikes and other workplace protests. Labor unionists supported the war effort by serving in the armed forces and in civilian war bond and scrap drives, with patriotic language and enthusiastic public rallies. Workers met and often exceeded wartime production goals in defense industries, as labor newspapers reported. Labor was rewarded for its war efforts by representation on government committees, and Sidney Hillman, president of the Amalgamated Clothing Workers and a vice president of the CIO, weighed in on vital defense matters. By contrast, the AFL played a less public role in the war effort. Its constituent unions were reluctant to promise the same restraint.[72]

Still, the needs of the nation for plant and factories, heavy equipment and transportation, and labor power to produce military weaponry, transport, and other war materiel gave workers and their unions new leverage in bargaining for wages and working conditions. John L. Lewis, president of the United Mine Workers after he resigned as CIO head, understood that these conditions were unique. He asserted that workers also made sacrifices—in military service and in factories and mines. In 1941, Lewis balked in response to pressure from the National Defense Mediation Board to settle a national mine strike. With 53,000 miners on strike, the board finally negotiated union contracts for so-called "captive mines," which had been non-union. Later that year, more than 400,000 miners went on strike for higher wages. In 1943, the UMW called a national strike over mining wages. When Secretary of the Interior Harold Ickes instructed troops to take over 3,300 mines, Lewis taunted, "What will they do–dig coal with their bayonets?" Labor conflict during the war, one writer argued, "was irresponsible and unpatriotic, no matter what the miners' grievances." The Army newspaper, *Stars and Stripes*, went farther: "Speaking for the American soldier—John L. Lewis, damn your coal-black soul." A pilot declared, "I'd just as soon shoot down one of the strikers as shoot down a Jap—They're doing just as much to lose the war for us."[73]

Neither the newspapers nor the labor board paid attention to the fact that in 1943, before the United States armed forces were fully engaged in Europe, the casualty numbers for coal miners and defense workers outnumbered combat injuries and deaths. Such injuries were incurred in private employment and remained hidden from view. By the end of the war, nearly 140,000 workers were killed in defense production. More than a half million were permanently disabled. These statistics fueled the determination of workers and their unions to demand more from employers and the government and to accept, as the price of their loyalty, mandatory overtime and deteriorating conditions. The problem of the labor movement during the war was that any collective bargaining, in the wake of calls for wartime sacrifice and patriotic participation, had to be moderate, reasoned, and fairly invisible. Thus, when labor spoke out against dangerous working conditions or wages that did not keep pace with inflation, it provoked charges of opportunism, greed, and even treason. While few employers were attacked for hard bargaining on government contracts, labor was in a different category. Workers were individuals who were more receptive to calls for sacrifice, especially when they had brothers, husbands, and sons in the fight.[74]

In response to Lewis's strike, Congress, acting on the wartime emergency, passed the 1943 Smith-Connally Act. The law gave the federal government the power to shut down illegal and wildcat strikes, take over and run private industry in support of the war effort, and imprison workers who resisted. Labor also learned that civil liberties were as imperiled as they were during the First World War. During the war, labor unions pursued—and lost—court cases that argued that picketing was a form of free speech. This was, however, the time when Japanese Americans were interned on the West Coast and political dissenters and conscientious objectors were jailed. The Smith Act trial of the leaders of the teamster rebellion was a sign that labor's liberties were not secure.[75]

United in War, Divided in the Workplace

Wartime labor shortages brought more than bargaining power to the workplace. New workers in defense industry, more often than not, were outsiders. Both white and black Southerners migrated to Northern cities to work in defense industry. Women left jobs in restaurant, retail, and domestic service to work in tank assembly, airplane production, munitions manufacture, and ship welding. Mexican Americans in Texas and in California took up defense jobs. When new workers did so, they entered a manufacturing labor force that before the war was predominantly white and male. They often stepped into jobs that had belonged to men who joined or were drafted into the armed services. That women workers, Southerners, Mexican migrants, and African Americans now took jobs once held by white men—and union brothers—was not lost on the working men they joined. There was a good deal of workplace intimidation, insults, and harassment. The white "dollies" and "lipsticks" who dared to wield a rivet gun and the black men and women who assembled tanks were not often welcomed. Given that long hours, higher prices, dangerous working conditions, and unresponsive labor leaders were par for the course, workers rebelled—sometimes in concert with new workers, often not. There were nearly 14,500 wildcat strikes during World War II, and some targeted the presence of women and minority men working in defense plants.[76]

In Mobile, Alabama, the Addsco shipyard began to employ increasing numbers of workers at the beginning of the war. The city's population grew from 79,000 in 1940 to 125,000 in 1943. Rural white migrants found work in the shipyards, as did a growing number of black workers. Conflict between white and black workers broke out when the company promoted some skilled black welders to the same job as white workers. Ten thousand white workers went on strike, as the fighting spread across the shipyard. Workers armed with bricks, clubs, and bats attacked the welders and injured eleven of them. One worker explained, "We realize the fact that they are human beings … but we don't want anymore to work or want our women to work alongside a negro." Fear of social equality between the races sparked violence, a scene that played out, with different outcomes, in defense plants across the nation and even on city transit, as the employment of black drivers provided the spark for a streetcar strike in Philadelphia in 1944.[77]

Racial conflict was, however, not only a workplace problem. World War II saw some of the greatest geographic mobility in U.S. history. Rural workers moved to cities, Southerners moved into Northern industries, and workers in the Midwest moved to the West Coast to find defense jobs. Aircraft plants and shipyards were constructed and set into motion, often without improving community services. In Ypsilanti, Michigan, the Ford Company built a plant in Willow Run to produce B-24 Liberation bombers. Covering more than seven acres, it employed 42,000 workers. Those workers had to live somewhere. They moved into communities that viewed them as intruders adding to the burden of city government, schools, and local transportation. Even when they lived elsewhere, they still encountered racial hostility and competition over scarce housing. Racial violence at the Sojourner Housing Development and at Belle Isle in Detroit, or the Mobile, Alabama, shipyard, flared not only on the job, but in the neighborhoods and streets where locals battled outsiders for space and resources.[78] Confronting these racial divisions became one of labor's most important challenges in the post-war years.

Conclusion

Historians of the labor movement argue that World War II had three effects. First, it solidified the acceptance of government intervention in labor relations, both by employers and by unions. Second, it gave labor new resources, including maintenance of membership agreements, payroll dues collection, expanded union membership, and greater access to government agencies. Third, because labor's demands were limited by government policy and union agreements for the duration of the war, there was pent-up demand for wage increases and improvements in working conditions. There was anger about runaway inflation and the rationing of consumer goods, and resentment against employers. Big business had gained generous contracts, upgraded facilities, and new equipment at government expense, and outsized profits as well. Workers did not understand why corporations, and employers, the Tories who opposed the New Deal and defense production, were the primary beneficiaries of wartime profits. They also did not always understand why labor leaders, especially the notorious John L. Lewis, did not cooperate with government in the midst of the "Good War." These factors would fuel working-class discontent and give rise to the highest level of strikes in industry in the twentieth century. They also fed middle-class resentment of and hostility to labor unions, a response that gave support to anti-union conservatives in the postwar era.

There were several ironies in the success of industrial unionism in the interwar decades. Despite barriers to organizing mass production industry, and the strength of employer opposition, the labor movement reasserted itself in the most unlikely context—the economic crisis of the 1930s. It did so in large part because it was able to rely upon the expertise of veterans of the labor movement and the institutions that they rebuilt in the 1920s. Labor and radical newspapers and organizations survived the hostile political environment of that decade to support resurgent unions in 1933 and 1934. Still, as many commentators have said, the labor movement became the victim of its own success. Millions of workers entered the labor movement, encouraged by the idea that the NRA and the president "want you to join a union." Their activism was sparked by years of unemployment and disillusionment with the failed promises of employers. The passion and commitment of militant trade unionists and young activists no doubt contributed. But an organizing campaign is most often a one-time occurrence. There's difficulty in maintaining the level of commitment, especially when labor union procedures like local elections and contract bargaining became more routine.

Second, even as the labor movement drew on the strength of ethnic, racial, and community organizations, it emphasized the "gospel of unity and unionism." For the broad constituency of American labor, unity meant that differences among workers, long a source of division, were submerged under the language of the labor movement. Differences among workers, however, were not and are not rooted only in cultural preferences but in structural inequalities and social practices. Even when white and black union brothers shared a union meeting or a hiring hall, they rarely shared neighborhoods. So it was that while the CIO celebrated its commitment to racial, ethnic, and even gender equality through its demands for equal pay, it did not address how the basic demand for seniority rights disadvantaged women and minority workers. Nor did labor leaders fully understand the consequences of employers continuing to classify jobs by race and gender, because they shared many of the same prejudices. Even the symbols of the labor movement in action—the iconography of male workers and the language of fraternal solidarity—excluded the majority of the working class. Solidarity was defined in relatively narrow terms and portrayed in the mainstream press—as well as in labor and left newspapers—as male and white.

As organized labor became rooted in institutions, and acquired economic and political power in bargaining and in elections, it abandoned its community roots. Women workers, ethnic and racial minorities, the unemployed, agricultural and domestic labor, and unorganized workers in the South and the rural West became marginal to the main thrust of the labor movement's agenda. The institutions of "Big Labor" were focused on maintaining their membership, protecting the rights of unionized workers, and in improving the pay, benefits and conditions of union workplaces.

It was not, however, that the labor movement was unaware of the mass of unorganized workers in the country. Rather, these groups of workers seemed to always be beyond the reach of labor, for reasons that seemed unalterable. How would workers in the South, whose racial divisions had destroyed so many promising union campaigns, ever be brought into the labor movement? How could women, whose primary allegiance was assumed to be to marriage and family, ever be equal participants in a labor movement that required lifetime work force participation? How would farm laborers and domestic workers, whose occupations and workplaces were both diffuse and beyond the domain of national labor law and even removed from the protections of social security, ever be equal players in the labor movement? How could they even be organized? Finally, whatever changes and challenges lay before labor in terms of changing employment conditions and a continually evolving work force, how could labor, that must pay attention to its political challenges, also find time and resources to organize the unorganized and integrate them into the labor movement's ranks?

Notes

1 Peter Rachleff, "Organizing Wall to Wall: The Independent Union of All Workers, 1933–1937," in Staughton Lynd, ed., *"We Are All Leaders": The Alternative Unionism of the Early 1930s* (Urbana: University of Illinois Press, 1996), 51–71; Larry Engelmann, "We Were the Poor People: The Hormel Strike of 1933," *Labor History* 15:4 (1974), 483–510.

2 Irving Bernstein, *The Lean Years: A History of the American Worker* (Boston MA: Houghton Mifflin, 1960), 190–244. For a view of the politics of the period, see Robert K. Murray, *The Harding Era: Warren G. Harding and His Administration* (Minneapolis: University of Minnesota Press, 1969); idem, *The Politics of Normalcy: Government Theory and Practice in the Harding–Coolidge Era* (New York: Norton, 1973).

3 John W. Hevener, *Which Side Are You On? The Harlan County Coal Miners, 1931–1939* (Urbana: University of Illinois Press, 1978), 1–32; Jacquelyn Dowd Hall, James L. Leloudis, Robert Rodgers Korstad, Mary Murphy, Lu Ann Jones, and Christopher B. Daly, *Like a Family: The Making of a Southern Cotton Mill World* (Chapel Hill: University of North Carolina Press, 1987), 183–236; Earl Lewis, *In Their Own Interests: Race, Class and Power in Twentieth Century Norfolk, Virginia* (Berkeley: University of California Press, 1991), 29–65, 110–125; Elizabeth Faue, *Community of Suffering and Struggle: Women, Men and the Labor Movement in Minneapolis, 1915–1945* (Chapel Hill: University of North Carolina Press, 1991), 39–46; Daniel Nelson, *Farm and Factory: Workers in the Midwest, 1880–1990* (Bloomington: Indiana University Press, 1995), chapter 5.

4 Bernstein, *The Lean Years*, 16–36; William Millikan, *A Union Against Unions: The Minneapolis Citizens' Alliance and Its Fight Against Organized Labor, 1903–1947* (St. Paul: Minnesota Historical Society Press, 2003), 159–180.

5 Frank Stricker, "Affluence for Whom? Another Look at Prosperity and the Working Classes in the 1920s," *Labor History* 24:1 (1983), 5–33; see also Winifred D. Wandersee, *Women's Work and Family Values, 1920–1940* (Cambridge, MA: Harvard University Press, 1981), 18–32.

6 See Mary Heaton Vorse, *Footnote to Folly: Reminiscences* (New York: Farrar and Rinehart, 1935), 199ff, on the elements of a strong labor movement. On the history, see Philip S. Foner, *The History of the Labor Movement in the United States*, vol. 7 *Postwar Struggles, 1918–1920* (1988), vol. 8 *The TUEL to the End of the Gompers' Era* (1991), vol. 9 *The TUEL, 1925–1929* (New York: International Publishers, 1994); David Montgomery, "Thinking about American Workers in the 1920s," *International Labor and Working Class History* 32 (1987), 4–30, Susan Porter Benson, "The 1920s through the Looking Glass of Gender," *International Labour and Working Class History* 32 (Fall 1987) 31–38.

7 Mel Dubofsky, *We Shall Be All: A History of the Industrial Workers of the World* (Chicago: Quadrangle Books, 1969), 420–468; David Brody, *Labor in Crisis: The Steel Strike of 1919* (Philadelphia: Lippincott, 1965); David Montgomery, *The Fall of the House of Labor* (Cambridge: Cambridge University Press, 1987), 370–410; Joseph A. McCartin, *Labor's Great War: The Struggle for Industrial Democracy and the Origins of Modern American Labor Relations, 1912–1921* (Chapel Hill: University of North Carolina Press, 1997), 193–220; James R. Barrett, *Work and Community in the Jungle: Chicago's Packinghouse Workers, 1894–1922* (Urbana: University of Illinois Press, 1987), 240–268; Stephen H. Norwood, *Labor's Flaming Youth: Telephone Operators and Worker Militancy, 1878–1923* (Urbana: University of Illinois Press, 1990), 156–215.

8 McCartin, *Labor's Great War*, 173–220; Montgomery, *The Fall of the House of Labor*, 411–464; John D. Hicks, *The Republican Ascendency, 1921–1933* (New York: Harper Torchbooks, 1963), 50–105.

9 Elizabeth Faue, "Labor Journalism," in Melvyn Dubofsky, ed., *The Oxford Encyclopedia of American Business, Labor and Economic History*, vol. 1 (New York: Oxford University Press, 2013), 429–431.

10 Brody, *Labor in Crisis*, 147–178; Interchurch World Movement of North America, *Public Opinion and the Steel Strike* (New York: Harcourt, Brace, 1921).

11 Bernstein, *The Lean Years*, 47–82; Robert H. Zieger, *Republicans and Labor, 1919–1929* (Lexington: University of Kentucky Press, 1969).

12 David Alan Corbin, *Life, Work and Rebellion in the Coal Fields: The Southern West Virginia Miners, 1880–1922* (Urbana: University of Illinois Press, 1989), 195–235; James Green, *The Devil is Here in These Hills: West Virginia's Coal Miners and their Battle for Freedom* (New York: Atlantic Monthly Press, 2015).

13 Colin J. Davis, *Power at Odds: The National Railroad Shopmen's Strike of 1922* (Urbana: University of Illinois Press, 1997); Jon Huigbretse, *American Railroad Labor and the Genesis of the New Deal, 1919–1935* (Tallahassee: University Press of Florida, 2010), 22–50.

14 Huigbretse, *American Railroad Labor*, 22–33; Davis, *Power at Odds*, 48–63.

15 Davis, *Power at Odds*, 9–25, 60–61.

16 Davis, *Power at Odds*, 64–82.

17 Davis, *Power at Odds*, 83–115.

18 Davis, *Power at Odds*, 133–166; www.workdayminnesota.org/articles/big-strike.

19 See Alexander M. Bing, *Wartime Strikes and Their Adjustment* (New York: Dutton, 1921); Montgomery, *Fall of the House of Labor*, 370ff.

20 David Montgomery, *Workers Control in America* (Cambridge: Cambridge University Press, 1979), 93–101; P.K. Edwards, *Strikes in the United States, 1881–1974* (New York: St. Martin's Press, 1981), 12–51.

21 Murray, *The Politics of Normalcy*, 130–146; Francis Russell, *A City in Terror: Calvin Coolidge and the 1919 Boston Police Strike* (Boston MA: Beacon Press, 1930, reprint 1975); Joseph Slater, *Public Workers: Government Employee Unions, the Law, and the State, 1900–1962* (Ithaca: ILR Press, 2004), 13–38.

22 Eldridge Foster Dowell, *A History of Criminal Syndicalism Legislation in the United States* (Baltimore: Johns Hopkins University Press, 1939); Edward Johanningsmeier, *Forging American Communism: The Life of William Z. Foster* (Princeton: Princeton University Press, 1994), 188–192; Jacob Kramer, *The New Freedom and the New Radicals: Woodrow Wilson, Progressive Views of Radicalism, and the Origins of Repressive Tolerance* (Philadelphia: Temple University Press, 2015), 144–147.

23 On Michigan and the Duplex Printing case, see Doris McLaughlin, *Michigan Labor*, 50–73; see also George I. Lovell, *Legislative Deferrals: Statutory Ambiguity, Judicial Power, and American Democracy* (Cambridge: Cambridge University Press, 2010), 99–160, on the lack of political will behind the Clayton Act.

24 George Tselos, "The Labor Movement in Minneapolis in the 1930s," Ph.D. dissertation, University of Minnesota, 1970, 34–35, discusses Wilbur Foshay, whose hiring of

union workers provoked the Citizens' Alliance; Millikan, *A Union Against Unions*, 227–243.

25 Lizabeth Cohen, *Making A New Deal: Industrial Workers in Chicago, 1919–1939* (Cambridge: Cambridge University Press, 1989), 99–158; Dowd Hall et al., *Like a Family*, 237–288; Lisa M. Fine, *The Story of REO Joe: Work, Kin and Community in Autotown U.S.A.* (Philadelphia: Temple University Press, 2004).

26 Cohen, *Making a New Deal*, 323–360.

27 Lynn Dumenil, *The Modern Temper: American Culture and Society in the 1920s* (New York: Hill and Wang, 1995); Nancy Cott, *The Grounding of Modern Feminism* (New Haven: Yale University Press, 1989).

28 Samuel Lubell, *The Future of American Politics* (New York: Doubleday Anchor, 1952), 29–43; Cohen, *Making a New Deal*, 253–261, 283–289.

29 Alexander Keyssar, *Out of Work: The First Century of Unemployment in Massachusetts* (Cambridge, Cambridge University Press, 1986), 222–298; Dana Frank, *Purchasing Power: Consumer Organizing, Gender and the Seattle Labor Movement, 1919–1929* (Cambridge: Cambridge University Press, 1994), 108–138, 212–246; Jennifer D. Keene, *Doughboys, the Great War, and the Remaking of* America (Baltimore: Johns Hopkins University Press, 2003), 161–178; Stephen R. Ortiz, *Beyond the Bonus March and GI Bill: How Veteran Politics Shaped the New Deal Era* (New York: NYU Press, 2009), chapter 1.

30 Jack Santino, *Miles of Smiles, Years of Struggle: Stories of Black Pullman Porters* (Urbana: University of Illinois Press, 1989); Beth Bates, *Pullman Porters and the Rise of Protest Politics in Black America, 1925–1945* (Chapel Hill: University of North Carolina Press, 2001).

31 Santino, *Miles of Smiles, Years of Struggle*; Andrew E. Kersten, *A. Philip Randolph: A Life in the Vanguard* (Boston MA: Rowman and Littlefield, 2006), 25–46.

32 Melinda Chateauvert, *Marching Together: Women of the Sleeping Car Porters* (Urbana: University of Illinois Press, 1998); Susan Levine, "Workers' Wives: Gender, Class, and Consumerism in the 1920s," *Gender and History* 3:1 (Spring 1991), 45–64.

33 See Robert H. Zieger, *For Jobs and Freedom: Race and Labor in America since 1865* (Lexington: University of Kentucky Press, 2014), 70–105; Zaragosa Vargas, *Proletarians of the North: A History of Mexicans in Industrial Detroit and the Midwest* (Berkeley: University of California Press, 1998). I see "strategic plurality" as an important factor in the rise of the CIO. It is derived, in part, from Rosabeth Moss Kanter, *Men and Women of the Corporation* (New York: Basic Books, 1977). It describes the critical point at which women and minority workers had to be incorporated if the industry were to be organized and when women and minority workers have access to leadership positions. See Elizabeth Faue, "Anti-Heroes of the Working Class: A Response to Bruce Nelson," *International Review of Social History* 41 (December 1996), 75–88.

34 Stella Nowicki, "Back of the Yards," in Alice and Staughton Lynd, eds., *Rank and File: Personal Histories by Working-Class Organizers*, 2nd ed. (Princeton: Princeton University Press, 1981), 77; Joyce Kornbluh and Mary Frederickson, eds., *Sisterhood and Solidarity: Workers Education for Women, 1914–1984* (Philadelphia: Temple University Press, 1984); Agnes Nestor, *Woman Labor Leader: The Autobiography of Agnes Nestor* (Rockford, IL: Bellevue Books, 1954).

35 Claudia Goldin, *Understanding the Gender Gap: An Economic History of American Women* (Oxford University Press, 1990), 10–57; Alice Kessler-Harris, *Out to Work: A History of Wage Working Women in the United States* (New York: Oxford University Press, 1982), 217–272.

36 Dorothy Sue Cobble, *The Other Women's Movement: Workplace Justice and Social Rights in Modern America* (Princeton: Princeton University Press, 2003), places this development in the 1940s; but it was the 1930s wave of labor organizing that first offered opportunities for a new generation of women leaders to emerge.

37 Harvey and Jessie Lloyd O'Connor, *Harvey and Jessie: A Couple of Radicals* (Philadelphia: Temple University Press, 1988); Art Shields, *On the Battle Lines, 1919–1939* (New York: International Publishers, 1986); Dee Garrison, *Mary Heaton Vorse: The Life of an American Insurgent* (Philadelphia: Temple University Press, 1989), 153–212; Tracy B. Strong and Helen Keyssar, *Right in Her Soul: The Life of Anna Louise Strong* (New York: Random House, 1983).

38 Weisbord, *A Radical Life*, 100–136; Paul Murphy, Kermit Hall, and David Klaasen, *The Passaic Textile Strike of 1926* (Belmont, CA: Wadsworth Publishing, 1974); David Lee McMullen, *Strike!: The Radical Insurrections of Ellen Dawson* (Gainesville: University Press of Florida, 2010), 75–95.

39 Mary Heaton Vorse, *The Passaic Textile Strike, 1926–1927* (Passaic, NJ: General Relief Committee of Textile Strikers, 1927).

40 Dowd Hall et al., *Like a Family*; see also Liston Pope, *Preachers and Millhands: A Study of Gastonia* (New Haven: Yale University Press, 1965).

41 See John A. Salmond, *Gastonia, 1929: The Story of the Loray Mill Strike* (Chapel Hill: University of North Carolina Press, 1995); Dowd Hall et al., *Like a Family*, 214ff.

42 First-hand and literary accounts of the strike include Fred Beal, *Proletarian Journey: New England, Gastonia, Moscow* (New York: Hillman, Curl, 1937); Tom Tippett, *When Southern Labor Stirs* (New York: Jonathan Cape and Harrison Smith, 1931); Vera Buch Weisbord, *A Radical Life* (Bloomington: Indiana University Press, 1977), 173ff; Mary Heaton Vorse, *Strike!*, reprint ed. (Urbana: University of Illinois Press, 1991); Fielding Burke, *Call Home the Heart*, reprint ed. (New York: Feminist Press, 2002). On boundary-crossing, see Jacquelyn Dowd Hall, "Disorderly Women: Gender and Labor Militancy in the Appalachian South," *Journal of American History* 73:2 (September 1986), 354–382.

43 Important accounts include Robert S. McElvaine, *The Great Depression: America, 1929–1941* (New York: Crown, 2009, c. 1984); T.H. Watkins, *The Great Depression: America in the 1930s* (Boston MA: Little, Brown, 1993); David Kennedy, *Freedom from Fear: The American People in Depression and War* (New York: Oxford University Press, 1999).

44 Elizabeth Faue, "'Blurred Subfields': Irving Bernstein and the History of the Worker as U.S. History," *Labor History* 37:1 (1996), 77–83.

45 William Leuchtenberg, *Franklin Delano Roosevelt and the New Deal* (New York: Harper Torchbooks, 1963), captures this sensibility. See also Douglas B. Craig, *Fireside Politics: Radio and Political Culture in the United States, 1920–1940* (Baltimore: Johns Hopkins University Press, 2000), 126–127, 154–157, on FDR's media appeal.

46 Bernstein, *The Turbulent Years*, 126–171, 217–317, 432–634; Melvyn Dubofsky, "The 'Not So' Turbulent Years: A New Look at the 1930s," in Charles Stephenson and Robert Asher, eds., *Life and Labor: Dimensions of Working-Class History* (Albany: SUNY Press, 1986), 205–223. See also Christopher L. Tomlins, "The AFL Unions in the 1930s: Their Performance in Historical Perspective," *Journal of American History* 65:3 (March 1979), 1021–1042.

47 The NIRA has not been well-served by historians. For an exception, see Sidney Fine, *The Automobile under the Blue Eagle* (Ann Arbor: University of Michigan Press, 1963).

48 David Milton, *The Politics of U.S. Labor* (New York: Monthly Review Press, 1982), 70–71.

49 Bernstein, *The Turbulent Years*, 217–317; Bruce Nelson, "'Pentecost' on the Pacific: Maritime Workers and Working Class Consciousness in the 1930s," *Political Power and Social Theory* 4 (1984), 141–182.

50 Charles Rumford Walker, *American City: A Rank and File History of Minneapolis*, reprint ed. (Minneapolis: University of Minnesota Press, 2005); Farrell Dobbs, *Teamster Rebellion* (New York: Monad Press, 1973).

51 Janet Irons, *Testing the New Deal: The General Textile Strike of 1934 in the American South* (Urbana: University of Illinois Press, 2000); Gary Gerstle, *Working Class Americanism:*

The Politics of Labor in a Textile City, 1914–1960 (Cambridge: Cambridge University Press, 1989), 127–150; Philip A. Korth and Margaret Beegle, *"I Remember Like Today": The Toledo Auto-Lite Strike of 1934* (Lansing: Michigan State University Press, 1988).

52 Bernstein, *The Turbulent Years*, 352–398; Milton, *The Politics of U.S. Labor*, 69–89; Robert H. Zieger, *The CIO* (Chapel Hill: University of North Carolina Press, 1995), 22–65.

53 Milton, *The Politics of U.S. Labor*, 79–82; Vorse, *Labor's New Millions*, 5–11; Pesotta, *Bread Upon the Waters*, 195–207; Daniel Nelson, *American Rubber Workers and Organized Labor, 1900–1941* (Princeton: Princeton University Press, 1988), 170–233.

54 Vorse, *Labor's New Millions*, 59–90.

55 For accounts of the strike, see Sidney Fine, *Sit-Down: The General Motors Strike of 1936–1937* (Ann Arbor: University of Michigan Press, 1969); Henry Kraus, *The Many and the Few: The Chronicle of the Dynamic Auto Workers*, 2nd ed. (Urbana: University of Illinois Press, 1985), among many others.

56 Fine, *Sit-Down*, 331; Bernstein, *The Turbulent Years*, 554. Three years later, in 1941, the UAW would have more than 450,000 members, due to the unionization of Ford and expanded defense production.

57 Fine, *Sit-Down: The General Motors Strike of 1936–1937*, 331; United States Department of Commerce, *August 1938 Survey of Current Business* (Washington DC: United States Department of Commerce, 1938), 29. See also Dana Frank, *Women Strikers Occupy Chain Stores, Win Big: The 1937 Woolworth's Sit-Down* (Chicago: Haymarket Books, 2012).

58 Len De Caux, *Labor Radical: From the Wobblies to the CIO* (Boston MA: Beacon Press, 1970), 230.

59 See, among others, Ronald Schatz, *The Electrical Workers: A History of Labor at General Electric and Westinghouse, 1923–1960* (Urbana: University of Illinois Press, 1983); Vicki Ruiz, *Cannery Workers, Cannery Lives: Mexican Women, Unionization and the California Food Processing Industry, 1930–1950* (Albuquerque: University of New Mexico Press, 1987); Rick Halpern, *Down on the Killing Floor: Black and White Workers in Chicago's Packinghouses, 1904–1954* (Urbana: University of Illinois Press, 1997); James D. Rose, *Duquesne and the Rise of Steel Unionism* (Urbana: University of Illinois Press, 2001).

60 Halpern, *Down on the Killing Floor*; Roger Horowitz, *Negro and White, Unite and Fight: A Social History of Industrial Unionism in Meatpacking, 1930–1990* (Urbana: University of Illinois Press, 1997).

61 August Meier and Elliott Rudwick, *Black Detroit and the Rise of the UAW* (New York: Oxford University Press, 1979).

62 Meier and Rudwick, *Black Detroit and the Rise of the UAW*, 82–107ff; Beth Tomkins Bates, *The Making of Black Detroit in the Age of Henry Ford* (Chapel Hill: University of North Carolina Press, 2012), 199–250.

63 Ahmed White, *The Last Great Strike: Little Steel, the CIO, and the Struggle for Labor Rights in New Deal America* (Berkeley: University of California Press, 2016); Carol Quirke, *Eyes on Labor: News Photography and America's Working Class* (New York: Oxford University Press, 2012), 149–185; see also Joseph M. Turrini, "The Newton Steel Strike: A Watershed in the CIO's Failure to Organize Little Steel," *Labor History* 38:2–3 (1997), 229–265.

64 Jerold S. Auerbach, *Labor and Liberty: The LaFollette Committee and the New Deal* (Indianapolis: Bobbs-Merrill, 1966).

65 Robin D.G. Kelley, *Hammer and Hoe: Alabama Communists during the Great Depression* (Chapel Hill: University of North Carolina Press, 1990), 34–56; Cindy Hahamovitch, *The Fruits of Their Labor: Atlantic Coast Farmworkers and the Making of Migrant Poverty, 1870–1945* (Chapel Hill: University of North Carolina Press, 1997), chapter 6; Sharon Hartman Strom, "Challenging 'Woman's Place': Feminism, the Left and Industrial Unionism in the 1930s," *Feminist Studies* 9 (Summer 1983), 359–386; idem, "'We're

No Kitty Foyles': Organizing Office Workers for the Congress of Industrial Organizations, 1937–1950," in Ruth Milkman, ed., *Women, Work and Protest: A Century of U.S. Women's Labor History* (Boston MA: Routledge, 1984), 206–234; Robert R. Korstad, *Civil Rights Unionism: Tobacco Workers and the Struggle for Democracy in the Mid-Twentieth Century South* (Chapel Hill: University of North Carolina Press, 2003), 142–166.

66 Clearly, this is an issue of contention in the field, the one side of which is best represented by Staughton Lynd, ed., *We All Are Leaders*, and Christopher L. Tomlins, *The State and the Unions: Labor Relations, Law, and the Organized Labor Movement in America, 1880–1960* (New York: Cambridge University Press, 1980), 103–147, and the other of which is characterized by the work of historian David Brody and his students.

67 See Edwin Black, *IBM and the Holocaust: The Strategic Alliance Between Nazi Germany and America's Most Powerful Corporation* (New York: Crown Publishers, 2001); Stefan Link, "Rethinking the Ford–Nazi Connection," *Bulletin of the German Historical Institute* 49 (2011), 135–150; Reinhold Billstein, Karola Fings, Anita Kugler, and Nicholas Levis, *Working for the Enemy: Ford, General Motors, and Forced Labor during the Second World War* (New York: Berghahn, 2000); Jacques R. Pauwels, "Profits 'Über Alles!': American Corporations and Hitler," *Labour/Le Travail* 51 (Spring 2003), 223–249.

68 Kennedy, *Freedom from Fear*, 166. For employment figures, see Stanley Lebergott, "Annual Estimates of Unemployment in the United States, 1900–1954," in National Bureau for Economic Research, eds., *The Measurement and Behavior of Unemployment* (Princeton: National Bureau of Economic Research, 1957), 215–216, available at: www.nber.org/chapters/c2644.pdf.

69 Paul A.C. Koistinen, "Mobilizing the World War II Economy: Labor and the Industrial-Military Alliance," *Pacific Historical Review* 42:4 (November 1973), 443–478; idem, *Arsenal of World War II: The Political Economy of American Warfare, 1940–1945* (Lawrence: University Press of Kansas, 2004), 370–418.

70 Nelson Lichtenstein, *Labor's War at Home: The CIO in World War II* (New York: Cambridge University Press, 1982), 44–66; Milkman, *Gender at Work*, 65–83, 99–127; Zieger, *For Jobs and Freedom*, 70–138; Zaragosa Vargas, *Labor Rights are Civil Rights: Mexican American Workers in Twentieth Century America* (Princeton: Princeton University Press, 2004), 276–280; Cindy Hahamovitch, *No Man's Land: Jamaican Guestworkers in America and the Global History of Deportable Labor* (Princeton: Princeton University Press, 2011), 22–66.

71 Andrew E. Kersten, *Race, Jobs, and the War: The FEPC in the Midwest* (Urbana: University of Illinois Press, 2000); Emilio Zamora, *Claiming Rights and Righting Wrongs in Texas: Mexican American Workers and Job Politics during World War II* (College Station: Texas A&M University Press, 2009).

72 Lichtenstein, *Labor's War at Home*, 44–66; Andrew E. Kersten, *Labor's Home Front: The American Federation of Labor during World War II* (New York: NYU Press, 2006), 1–40. See also Steve Fraser, *Labor Will Rule: Sidney Hillman and the Rise of American Labor* (New York: Free Press, 1991), 444–491; Kevin Boyle, "Auto Workers at War: Patriotism and Protest in the American Auto Industry, 1939–1945," in *Auto Work*, eds. Robert Asher and Ronald Edsforth (Albany: SUNY Press, 1995), 99–126.

73 Quoted in David Kennedy, *Freedom from Fear*, 643.

74 Gerald Markowitz and David Rosner, "More than Economism: The Politics of Worker Safety and Health, 1932–1947," *Millbank Quarterly* 64:3 (1986), 341–346; Allison Hepler, "'And We Want Steel Toes like the Men': Gender and Occupational Health during World War II," *Bulletin of the History of Medicine* 72:4 (Winter 1998), 689–713; Kersten, *Labor's Home Front*, 166–188.

75 Donna T. Haverty-Stacke, *Trotskyists on Trial: Free Speech and Political Persecution since the Age of FDR* (New York: NYU Press, 2016).

76 Martin Glaberman, *Wartime Strikes: The Struggle against the No-Strike Pledge in the UAW during World War II* (Detroit: Bewick Editions, 1980), 35–60; Meier and Rudwick,

Black Detroit and the Rise of the UAW, 125–134, 165–172; Milkman, *Gender at Work*, 65–83.

77 Bruce Nelson, "Organized Labor and the Struggle for Black Equality in Mobile during World War II," *Journal of American History* 80:3 (December 1993), 952–988; Glaberman, *Wartime Strikes*, 35–60; James Wolfinger, *Philadelphia Divided: Race and Class Politics in the City of Brotherly Love* (Chapel Hill: University of North Carolina Press, 2007), 142–175.

78 Lowell J. Carr and James E. Stermer, *Willow Run: A Study of Industrialization and Cultural Inadequacy* (New York: Harper, 1952).

4

STABILITY AND RETREAT, 1945–1960

Labor's "Men of Power," the Cold War, and the State

In his widely read book on the American labor movement, Thomas Geoghegan memorably imagined "Big Labor" in the 1990s as a mastodon—a gigantic, lumbering, thick-headed yet menacing, and extinct form of life that terrorizes in shape but does not exist. The labor movement today is at best a creature the size of a pterodactyl and a small one at that. It still "menaces" but doesn't cover the same territory. The threat that Labor presents to shareholder profits, economic prosperity, political power, or the American Way of Life was and continues to be a product of the conservative imagination. They argue today that Labor is no less real in its power, even if exaggerated in imagination.[1] As a labor lawyer for Phelps-Dodge Copper once argued, "The entire working force of the Nation will eventually become a subservient group dependent on labor bosses for its livelihood. Thus the way is paved to labor dictatorship."[2] In reality, labor unions had limited influence in shaping the postwar labor accord. Rather, labor leaders responded, like dinosaurs, rather slowly, despite the rapidly changing economic and political environment of the postwar years.

Depictions of labor organizers as menacing predate the rise of the CIO in the 1930s. Anti-union newspapers historically drew parallels between subversive foreign agents and union conspirators.[3] Strike coverage often focused on violent pickets that threatened the safety of life and the sanctity of property. The National Association of Manufacturers demonized labor as the enemy of economic freedom, a view that has persisted from the conspiracy cases of the 1830s and the injunction-prone equity courts of the early twentieth century to the contemporary Business Roundtable and the American Legislative Exchange Council. Conservative media often has focused on the scariest individuals, as it did with anarchist Albert Parsons, Wobbly Big Bill Haywood, "Red" Kate O'Hare, and communist Harry Bridges. Dividing labor against labor has worked remarkably well. Pitting labor "contra mundum"—against the world—has been an effective strategy to undermine unions.

In the decades after World War II, it was the scale of Big Labor—specifically CIO unions like the United Steel Workers and the United Automobile Workers— that concerned corporations and employer associations. Corporate spokesmen blamed the massive strikes in 1946 for short-circuiting the postwar reboot of the economy. It was, however, labor's "New Men of Power," in the words of C. Wright Mills, that most concerned conservatives. John Lewis of the United Mine Workers, Walter Reuther of the UAW, and the Teamsters' Jimmy Hoffa could halt coal production, freeze the assembly line, and stop shipping in its tracks and have a seat at the government's table. While sociologist Daniel Bell saw the rise of labor in more benign terms, labor's power—in postwar politics and in the workplace—sparked attacks from conservatives and corporations alike.[4]

This chapter focuses on the gains and losses of the postwar labor movement, its fight over labor law reform, and the changing landscape of labor relations in the last half of the twentieth century. Against the growing economic and political influence of the labor movement, symbolized by the massive postwar strikes of 1946, there was a coordinated business offensive against Big Labor. By the 1950s, labor unions represented 35 percent of the non-agricultural labor force. Union workers voted, and unions gained significant strength. Bolstered by the wartime no-strike pledge, the dues check-off, and maintenance of membership agreements, labor leaders occupied a place at the government table. They demanded a role in defining domestic policy. Innovations in health care and insurance, expanded private pensions and social security, struggles for racial and gender equality, and a continuing—if weaker—effort to organize the South made the labor movement a powerful political force. While workers were not the only beneficiaries of wartime gains, labor unions emerged from the war with greater numbers, more visibility, and considerably more bargaining power, even as defense production declined and the economy briefly sagged during the postwar conversion.

By the end of the 1950s, struggles over control of production were to be resolved in what many saw as a massive compromise for the labor movement. While work rules continued to be contested in contract negotiations, most industrial unions conceded management prerogatives on the shop floor. Postwar labor contracts, echoing what Daniel Bell called "the Treaty of Detroit," secured short-term union gains in membership and wages and benefits. They also cost working-class people—and their representatives—any power in shaping the workplace.[5] More significant were corporate strategies for reductions of the work force, plant relocation, and anti-union campaigns that combined economic blackmail with marginal—and temporary—relief of workers' grievances. Automation and greater intensity and speed on production lines contributed to rising productivity but also loss of production jobs and increased occupational risks.[6]

The largest industrial unions survived—and even thrived—during the 1950s, despite political losses; but there were greater stakes in the postwar decade than maintenance of membership or higher wages. While pattern-bargaining and productivity-linked wage increases bolstered the living standards of workers in auto, steel, rubber, electrical production, and construction, unions largely ignored the signs of change. Whether the labor movement would organize the South, continue to advocate for racial equality, and recruit new immigrants and women workers across ethnic and racial barriers, or whether labor would extend its wartime and postwar gains by organizing them—these questions remained unanswered. The challenges of an economy in which knowledge work, social service, and public employment played an increasingly significant role remained unmet. Postwar prosperity, stemming from a robust manufacturing sector, obscured the narrow provenance of labor.

Labor in the Postwar World

The postwar economy in the United States was, with brief interruptions, strong, prosperous, and expansive. The country emerged from the war with more resources and far fewer losses than other combatants. Even as the United States assisted in the rebuilding of western Europe and Japan through the Marshall Plan and other foreign aid programs, it benefited from pent-up consumer demand and the absence of competitors in global markets. Manufacturing and construction increased by leaps and bounds, and services that maintained the market—from clerical and maintenance work within industry to the expanding realm of government and financial services—grew at an even faster pace. While some feared the return of high unemployment, the economy of the United States recuperated rapidly. Allied economies were bolstered as well, as foreign aid and American-made products became the carriers of postwar prosperity to the West.[7]

The political context for this prosperity was contradictory at best. Abundant goods, a buoyant economy, and burgeoning good will were matched with widespread social fears about postwar shortages, looming economic problems, and the piracy of communism. Like the character in William Goldman's *Princess Bride*, Dread Pirate Stalin became a bogeyman who threatened to make all the uncomfortable realities of the war years permanent. The American Way of Life was insecure, under the communist threat abroad and at home. The possibility of war with the Soviet Union, the increased visibility of women in the workplace, and the subversion of juvenile delinquents, homosexuals, and reefer-smoking musicians eroded the workings of American Democracy. The fast spread of information through mass culture—radio, television, movies and newsreels—made the public more aware of these perceived threats. Necessarily, these dangers meant that labor unions, long-affiliated with marginal forces and tinged with radicalism, must be brought to heel. While popular support for this nightmarish vision of postwar America was not what anti-communist politicians claimed, laws requiring loyalty oaths and expelling radicals undermined labor influence in Congress and state and local governments.[8]

Despite increasing tensions with the Soviet Union after the war, there were few signs that the New Deal political coalition and its labor allies had weakened. Progressives had placed policy proposals for full employment, civil rights, and health insurance before Congress. Some women's advocates, with the backing of the Republican party, re-introduced the long-abandoned Equal Rights Amendment in response to women's wartime contributions. Popular support for expanded veterans' benefits under the GI Bill complemented the call for expanded worker rights. Labor leaders, especially from the UAW and other industrial unions, lobbied for measures to ensure that wartime gains would not be lost. Moreover, workers across the country made clear that wartime inflation, coupled with wage controls, required a peacetime fix.[9]

The strength that the labor movement represented became evident as the war wound down in August 1945. Workers in the United States conducted a series of strikes that involved 3 percent of the non-farm labor force, the largest strike wave in United States history. Government defense contracts had raised wages to new levels, and pent-up demand for new housing and consumer goods promised to stave off the anticipated postwar recession. Businesses began hiring. By 1946, inflation had skyrocketed to over 18 percent. Wages, still suppressed from wartime controls, could not keep pace with prices. Most important, during the war, there had been relatively little labor protest. In the light of the no-strike pledge, industrial unions had held the line. There had been wildcat strikes against increased production quotas, harsh management, and new—minority or women—workers; but these had been few in number. These grievances had percolated to the surface with the coming of peace.[10]

After the war ended, labor protests that had been sporadic and localized became national and routine as workers went out on strike in major industries and cities across the country. Anticipating rising costs of living, workers demanded that employers raise their wages. Nearly 5,000 strikes, involving over 5 million workers, demonstrated that workers understood their newfound power in the market. Their willingness to answer the wartime call for sacrifice had ended with the war.

The 1946 strike wave affected most industries, occupations, and regions. There were citywide general strikes in Rochester, New York; Stamford, Connecticut; and Lancaster, Pennsylvania. More important for the national economy were the 200,000 auto workers, 300,000 meatpackers, and 750,000 steel workers who went on strike in 1946, along with hundreds of thousands of miners and electrical workers, streetcar employees, and railroad workers.[11] CIO president Philip Murray had warned that "Only chaos and destruction of our industrial life will result if employers look to the war's end as an opportunity for a union-breaking, wage-cutting, open shop drive and if labor unions have to resort to widespread strikes to defend their very existence and the living standard of their members."[12] Murray was right. As the war ended, employers tried to reassert prewar wage rates and increased work loads. Labor leaders, citing workers' wartime service and constraint, demanded increases in wages and benefits.

The power of labor was demonstrated during the long tense months between the end of the war and the fall of 1946. Millions of work hours were lost as hundreds of thousands of workers took their grievances to the picket line in one of the largest strike waves in U.S. history. Strikes and unions, however, were and are dependent upon the public's good will. In making postwar gains in wages, pensions, and benefits, large industrial unions proved their clout but provided a stark contrast to workers in secondary industry, poorly paid service work, and manual labor. The gains of union labor overshadowed those of the respectable middle class, who viewed the labor movement with an increasingly critical eye. Postwar inflation, shortages of essential goods, and growing fears of communist subversion and personal corruption undermined the public trust. In these crucial years, Jack Metzgar noted, the giant-killer CIO lost its luster and its visibility. "The union" was no longer the labor movement or the CIO, but the union to which individual workers belonged. The steel workers, the autoworkers, and the electrical workers became separate organizations. The labor movement gradually lost its collective identity and the broad social agenda that fueled the CIO.[13]

Postwar Effects: The Other Working Class

The prosperity of the war years offered opportunities to organize new workers in the defense industry. It also revealed vulnerabilities in union labor. After the war, the CIO looked to the South, which had provided an economic haven for anti-union employers. Labor leaders hoped at long last to organize the textile industry, in which non-union firms competed with unionized factories in the Northeast. The CIO wanted to increase its membership in construction and steel and to expand its hold in tobacco manufacturing in the South. Elsewhere in the country, white collar workers had begun to organize. Clerical and retail workers, and those employed in service work, soon attracted the attention of labor's most forward-looking unions. Agricultural workers, specifically excluded from the National Labor Relations Board under the Wagner Act, provided another target of opportunity for an expansive labor vision, even as migrant workers from Jamaica and Mexico—brought in under the Bracero program or other like initiatives—swelled the numbers of those harvesting the nation's abundant crops.[14]

Labor's renewed energy attracted a younger generation of organizers, many of them participants in, or witnesses to, the rise of the Popular Front in the 1930s and 1940s. They possessed broad visions of American democracy in which labor played a pivotal role. Inspired and mentored by labor organizers like Lucy Randolph Mason, rank-and-file members of the CIO entered the postwar years with hope that the labor movement would expand its horizons and make a firm commitment to social and economic equality. The young activists had come of age in a world where the Communist party participated in electoral politics, John Lewis heroically led the CIO, and industrial unions were the good guys. Some, like Clinton Jencks, had their first taste of organizing in youth organizations and migrated into unions like Mine Mill. They joined anti-war groups, engaged in early civil rights (Congress of Racial Equality, CORE) activism, and organized unions. Subsequently, their lives were threatened by conservative attacks and loyalty pledges. Some activists were lost permanently to labor in light of their political loyalties. Jencks was among the first prosecuted under the Taft–Hartley Act. Others learned pragmatically to adapt to the new labor bureaucracy and its constituency.[15]

The same generation that encountered anti-communism faced changes in the labor force that demanded a new approach. First, wartime labor shortages brought rural migrants, African American men, and women of all races onto the factory shop floor but also into ranks of organized labor. The muscular image and masculine face of labor in the 1930s now gave way to wartime conditions that opened doors to Rosie the Riveter and a postwar generation of women labor leaders. They found positions in support and social functions such as labor education, worker welfare, and community relations. As the labor force changed, and the CIO and the faster growing AFL unions moved to adapt, women unionists had fewer barriers to entering the leadership ranks than they had at any time prior to the 1980s. Whether labor economists, social workers, or adult education teachers, they had skills that many working men, eager to rise in labor's ranks—and focused on collective bargaining and strike tactics—lacked.[16]

Women's skills—in community organizing, network-building, adult education, writing for popular audiences, assessing social needs, even calculating measures of productivity and wage formulas—were not particularly valued by workers or labor leaders. And yet, they were essential to sustaining the CIO and labor's political power. Even as CIO unions established recreation, education, women's, and community relations departments, there was a glass ceiling between local women and minority labor leaders and national executive boards. But it was more than that. The shop floor and the union hall were the poles of labor's world. As in the military, there was disproportionate weight placed on labor's might—the power of the picket line, the confrontational style associated with tough negotiations, and the public bond of brotherhood, compared to the less dynamic force of labor education and union social welfare. That the language of labor celebrated manly strength and masculine values and measured solidarity by muscle weight was not a matter leaders perceived or, if perceived, addressed. As Daniel Bell later noted, this language was off-putting to women workers and to any workers not accustomed or attracted to its stridency. For a brief moment in the postwar world, however, the labor movement made room for a different experience.[17]

In the postwar decades, a crucial cohort of women labor leaders—including Addie Wyatt of the Packinghouse Workers; Olga Madar, Caroline Davis, and Lillian Hatcher of the United Auto Workers; Myra Wolfgang of the Hotel and Restaurant Workers; and Ruth Young of the United Electrical Workers—came to the fore. They were influential in setting the policy agenda of the labor movement and in directing attention to the gaping holes of the social contract. The UAW's Millie Jeffrey made essential connections between labor's economic presence and the political power of working-class votes. The UAW's Caroline Davis and the UPWA's Addie Wyatt led the charge in addressing racial inequality. Connecting labor to community networks and political activism, women leaders occupied ground that male labor leaders both acknowledged to be of central importance and at the same time denied sufficient resources. Although the UAW had a women's department, a civil rights department, a veterans department, and a recreation department, it lacked consistent policies toward or commitments to constituencies it viewed as marginal and unessential.[18]

As World War II came to a close, labor signed on to reconversion plans that denied employment opportunities to those hired during the war and sent women and minority male workers packing. There were, with or without union consent, reasons for the rapid departure of new defense workers after the war: the retooling of factories and shift to civilian production that laid off wartime employees; the return of discharged military personnel who had veterans' preference and union seniority to reclaim positions on the shopfloor; and the postwar recession that, even though brief, saw employers return to prewar hiring customs unregulated by the Committee on Fair Employment Practices or the War Manpower Commission. With a large pool of potential employees, and no responsibility to answer to local or federal authorities, private employers returned to familiar patterns. That meant that by an overwhelming margin, most well-paid union jobs were held by white men, and industrial unions were led by the same group.[19]

While the American Left understood the importance of addressing racial inequality, racial and ethnic divisions had undermined the labor movement almost from its origins. The wartime struggles, from the Committee on Fair Employment Practices to hate strikes, revealed the continuing salience of race. Left-led unions from the communist faction of the United Auto Workers to the Packinghouse Workers and the UE gave some priority to addressing the problems. It was not an easy sell to workers who had come of age in an effectively segregated and discriminatory labor force. Still, union organizers had succeeded in the Back of the Yards in creating an interracial union of packinghouse workers. In Winston-Salem, they had sustained a union of black and white tobacco workers in Local 22. Even as the postwar years saw a retrenchment of initiatives for racial and gender equality, labor activists continued to believe that they could transform the Piedmont South, unionize textiles, and forge stronger bonds between Northern and Southern workers. While black workers were confined to the most dangerous and dirty jobs in manufacturing and encountered barriers to skilled employment, the CIO marched into the South confident that they could transform the region and recruit young Southern workers to the union cause. Parochial interests were not of their concern.[20]

Labor's New Power and the Postwar Paradox

Under the Truman presidency, the conditions for labor organizing deteriorated; and the role of left unionists received new scrutiny. There were several reasons for the changing political context. The National Labor Relations Board tightened its rules, especially around the organization of supervisors and foremen. The NLRB also altered its priorities and processes subtly in the direction of a more neutral process. The Smith-Connally War Labor Disputes Act (1943) and the Little-Steel wage formula, which instituted federal control over the bargaining process during the war, had restricted labor actions. Massive postwar strikes further eroded public support. As the number and impact of strikes in coal, steel and rail grew, many citizens—and political leaders—questioned the right of labor to manage its own affairs, strike at will, and refuse to cross picket lines. If strikes in shipping or an essential industry like steel disrupted the national economy, should workers be able to strike? When miners refused to mine coal, they left consumers without heat and industry without fuel. They involuntarily left other workers idle. When railroad or shipyard workers abandoned their duties, other workers lost their way to work. Factory machines stood still, due to the lack of raw materials. Agricultural produce and manufactured goods slowed their progress to store shelves. The unbroken picket line called into question whether unions or individual workers had the right to strike and to grieve in the context of an unchecked and unregulated union leadership.[21]

These questions were not settled even within the ranks of labor. While on strike, workers could understand the reasons the union struck. "The Company" (whether U.S. Steel or General Motors) was at fault. Most workers stood behind "the union" (the steel workers, auto workers, or the Brotherhood of Electrical Workers), but those on strike did not always understand or even see that workers in other sectors had needs and interests that directly conflicted with their own. The labor movement of the 1940s and 1950s thus was divided—not only between the American Federation of Labor and the CIO, but between organized labor and the majority of workers, who remained unorganized even at the peak of the labor movement.

Factions of the labor movement, organized along political and occupational lines, debated the extent to which the labor movement could or would sustain a program of "social unionism," as UAW leader Walter Reuther understood it. That is, could union leaders—at least in the CIO—pursue jobs *and* justice, economic expansion *and also* economic equality? Would it devote resources and political capital to address stubborn issues of working-class parochialism, sexism, and racial and ethnic prejudice? Addressing these issues was not simply a matter of asking for token public commitments in a culture of unity and unionism. Tolerance— and pragmatic workplace solidarity—could only go so far. Labor leadership needed to take the next step and bridge the division, as sociologist Ira Katznelson noted, between the identities of men and women who were "workers at work and ethnics at home." Accepting African American or Hispanic or women workers of all races as union members was one thing. Supporting measures to give them greater equity in the workplace, a track to promotion, and compensation for prior discrimination was quite another.[22]

In a perceptive contemporary study, sociologist Daniel Bell argued that the labor movement had reached its saturation point by the end of the Second World War.[23] Industrial unions had organized the heartland of American manufacturing, with the vast majority of workers (mostly white and male) in primary industry belonging to unions. The only potential areas for growth, significantly, were attached to those regions and occupations that had proved resistant to organizing or where the labor movement was reluctant to organize—that is, the South, minority workers in extractive, manufacturing and service work, and in the information sector, including higher education and the expanding public sector of the postwar years.[24]

Central to any organizing effort was the need to overcome cultural barriers between union culture and practice on the one hand and the workers who remained outside labor's domain: White collar workers, who believed unions served workers chiefly in physical—even when skilled—labor; women, who were employed in service and clerical jobs and in the caring professions, many of whom were alienated by the rough masculinity labor unions projected; undocumented and immigrant workers, who saw the labor movement as domestic and nativist in culture; African American and Hispanic workers, who saw the labor movement as a white man's club, and many of whom spurned labor organizations. The CIO's call for racial equality and the interracial unionism of the United Packinghouse Workers and the United Mine Workers did not—and could not—completely resolve decades of suspicion and fear.

Most importantly, many white workers, especially in the South, were antagonized by union efforts to challenge racial segregation and inequality in the workplace. They saw labor's alliance with radical causes, including civil rights, as dangerous. The ambivalence and hostility of working-class whites mattered, as Truman desegregated the military and legal challenges to the Jim Crow system wound their way through the courts. The residual anti-statism of Southern workers was rooted both in the states' rights tradition and in light of the New Deal's failure to protect Southern workers and their unions.[25] There was, in fact, a fundamental contradiction between the labor movement's need to organize the unorganized and the strategies that labor unions used to recruit them.

Operation Dixie: Expanding Labor's Domain?

It was to the South that Big Labor turned in the late 1940s. There were two reasons for this decision. First, after the death of Roosevelt, the Democratic party strove to maintain its national majority and hold on Congress. Southern Democratic power might be shored up, if the labor movement could organize the South. More importantly, employers were adapting to competitive markets by moving South. Upgrading equipment and facilities could be more easily accomplished in a new factory than in an old one and with fewer consequences. Differences in regional wages made Southern workers a bargain. Textile companies had been moving South since the beginning of the twentieth century. By the 1950s, employers saw, in the anti-union states of North and South Carolina, Tennessee, Alabama, Mississippi, and Georgia, a region with no entrenched union leadership and considerable hostility to external interference. Electrical manufacturing companies soon followed.[26]

The CIO and its affiliate Textile Workers Union of America (TWUA) knew that it had to organize the South in order to protect fragile gains in Northern factories. The textile industry was only the most obvious target. In every occupation in the South, workers were lower paid and disproportionately unorganized. Construction, steel manufacturing, and coal mining had fewer union members in the South than the population warranted. The first step in maintaining and extending union power nationally, CIO president Phil Murray declared, was to take on Southern industry, "the best place for the CIO to undertake organizing."[27]

Among the obstacles to a unionized South were continuing inter-union rivalries. Both the AFL and the CIO competed in the drive to organize the South, as the AFL charged a committee the same year as the CIO. The AFL sought to forestall any loss of members from its unions, so it invested in areas where it had secure dominance. The CIO focused on the Piedmont and the Deep South, where they had been defeated a decade before. In cities like Birmingham (steel) and Mobile (port labor), the CIO sought to branch out into the hinterland. It brought to the table resources on a scale it believed matched the problem. The CIO budgeted $1 million for the campaign in the twelve-state region and employed 200 organizers at the campaign's peak in 1946 and 1947.[28]

The South had not been without union representation. In addition to the robust United Mine Workers, which had half a million members in 1946, there were over 225,000 union members in the South, including 42,000 members of the TWUA. Most Southern unionists were concentrated in the urban areas, where they were scattered through a handful of unions, including the steel workers. The CIO appointed steelworker Van Bittner to head Operation Dixie. Even with his second-in-command coming from the TWUA, Van Bittner and his staff had little connection with the region or the workers they were organizing. Little understanding the powerful grip of segregation and the politics of whiteness on Southern workers, they did not understand how interracial unionism had to be faced in segregated communities nor that failure to address the racism would undermine the campaign. Fueled by the association of labor unions with civil rights, anti-union and anti-communist rhetoric hardened opposition to Operation Dixie. Competition with the AFL's Southern organizing drive, which escalated into union raiding, cost the labor movement even more.[29]

The hostility provoked by Operation Dixie surfaced throughout the South. In Birmingham, Alabama, steel workers rejected the Mine, Mill and Smelter Workers Union. In Winston-Salem, a smear campaign that red-baited union organizers led to defeat of Local 22 of the Food, Tobacco, Agricultural and Allied Workers' Union. Workplaces unionized during the war then encountered a backlash in the wake of the CIO's failures, and antipathy to unions and the Democratic party deepened. By 1948, Operation Dixie was a clear failure. It engendered opposition from nearly every sector—state governments, newly competitive unions in steel and automobile manufacture (the International Association of Machinists contested several union elections), and anti-union employers. The new anti-communist barrage linked CIO unions with the outlawed Communist Party of the U.S.A. In 1955, unions enrolled a slightly smaller percentage of non-agricultural workers of the South that year than they had in 1945—about 18 percent, compared to 35 percent nationally.[30] Throughout the campaign, Northern-based unions were caught in the contradictions between the need to organize the South and how the CIO purge had cost them effective organizers and unions, many of which had successfully pursued interracial union organizing.[31]

The Taft-Hartley Act: Employers and Labor at Impasse

Operation Dixie was played out against the backdrop of the emerging conflict with the Soviet Union and renewed anti-communism at home. Calls for investigations of the federal government, military, unions, and the new medium of television to smoke out the "enemy within" challenged the loyalties of union members. Charges of union corruption, radicalism, and incompetence sapped labor's strength and provided fodder for legal and political battles that lasted for decades. While Wisconsin's Senator McCarthy used his bullhorn to decry communist subversion, he was not the only one. Both Democrats and Republicans vied for the microphone when it came to confronting the Soviet threat. The House Un-American Activities Committee hearings (HUAC) strained the conflicted relationship between the labor movement and the Democratic party, with its increasingly tenuous hold on the political loyalties of working-class people.[32]

To define labor's opponents in these years as limited to small businessmen, paranoid rural anti-communists, Southern racists, and Western conservatives is to forget the most important source of opposition to the labor movement: big business. Corporate leaders such as General Electric's Lemuel Ricketts Boulware and Pierre Dupont found labor's power threatening not only at the bargaining table but in the workplace and the voting booth. Among the most vocal opponents of the postwar labor order, corporate executives were hostile to interference in management, transparency in record-keeping, and across the board wage hikes. Few demands upset the corporate world more than union leaders asking to take a look at the books or federal officials mediating labor disputes. Most business owners and managers were solid conservatives, whose party affiliation often was on the right of the Republican Party.[33]

The high level of strikes after the war brought new pressure on Congress and the presidency to bring the labor movement under control. The argument was that the Wagner Act had bent too far in the direction of labor unions and left unions and workers unregulated. The National Labor Relations Board had been designed to restrict the anti-union practices of businesses. Many employers believed that it was time to limit union activities as well. President Truman had expressed deep reservations about the extent of labor power in the workplace and politics. When he instituted loyalty oaths from federal employees, Truman further fueled anti-communist and anti-union sentiments and effectively sparked a domestic cold war. His response to the postwar strike wave deepened Truman's alienation from rank-and-file labor Democrats. With 400,000 coal miners and 250,000 railroad engineers and trainmen on strike in May 1946, Truman had issued executive orders for troops to take over the mines and railroads. Between 1946 and 1950, the federal government took over mining operations some half-dozen times. Truman damned UMW head John Lewis as a traitor and called railroad executives "effete" in their response to the walkouts. The number of work stoppages and walkouts in the strategic industries like coal and steel brought new pressure on Congress and the administration to impose limits on unions' ability to engage in strikes.[34]

Opening the door to anti-labor congressmen and senators bent on breaking the New Deal coalition, President Truman faced the possibility that he would lose the labor vote in the 1948 election by a combination of labor inaction and anti-union hostility. He quickly moved to block proposed legislation that imposed new regulations on labor unions and undercut the ability of labor leaders to force strike settlements. Opposed by even anti-communist union leaders like John L. Lewis, the newly proposed law, named the Taft-Hartley Act, had the support of the American Federation of Labor. For some time, the AFL had contended that the Wagner Act and the National Labor Relations Board had favored the CIO. With Taft-Hartley, AFL leaders argued, the renegade CIO might be brought to heel. They did not foresee the consequences of the law.[35]

For conservatives, the Taft-Hartley Act promised to reassert management rights in the workplace. Moreover, as a Republican congressman argued, the bill was "anti-abuse, not anti-labor." It saved American workers from "the dictators who have so effectively enslaved him." Indeed, language in support of the bill repeatedly charged that labor leaders had become "power-drunk bosses" and "dictators." The only way to keep the nation safe from the economic strangle-hold of labor, and its chief villain, UMW president John Lewis, was to institute controls on the ability of unions to call strikes at will and with the purpose of crippling commerce.[36]

In Washington DC, the labor movement waged an uphill battle against the bill. Not only did they face a hostile, Republican-controlled Congress, but an anti-communist mood colored the discussion of democratic initiatives for full employment and the creation of national health insurance. Some Democrats, like John F. Kennedy of Massachusetts, declared that the Taft-Hartley bill promoted "widespread class warfare, industrial chaos, and economic depression" in its wake and strengthened the influence of the Communist party. Truman similarly argued that a weakened labor movement cost the United States "a strong bulwark against the growth of totalitarian movements." Such arguments animated congressional debate but failed to persuade either legislators or the public to oppose the new law.[37]

Designed as a union parallel to National Labor Relations Act regulation of "unfair labor practices," the Taft-Hartley bill instituted new restrictions on labor unions. First, it narrowed the applicability of the Wagner Act and firmly excluded groups of workers, such as foremen, who did not fit within the narrow definition of "employee."[38] It outlawed the closed shop, which had been an effective tool for the recruitment of new workers and maintained union membership levels, and imposed a mandatory eighty-day cooling-off period for strikes. The cooling-off period was a crucial intervention that threatened to undermine worker solidarity in the face of mass grievances but also offered, to management, the opportunity to avoid or subvert strike actions. Section 304 of the Taft-Hartley Act prohibited unions from making direct contributions for political purposes, which had immediate consequences for the 1948 presidential campaign. It also undermined press favorable to labor, such as the independent news service, the Federated Press, which was committed to political reporting from a labor perspective. Taft-Hartley further called for affidavits from union leaders denying membership in or affiliation with the Communist party. It required that union officers swear that they "did not believe in, nor were a member or supporter of any organization that believed in or taught the overthrow of the U.S. government by force or by any illegal or unconstitutional methods." While Communist party members were a small minority of union leaders and members, the affidavits had a devastating impact on union democracy.[39]

President Truman vetoed the original bill, but there were strong currents in favor of more restrictive labor laws. While the Democratic party at the grassroots was partially staffed by the CIO Political Action Committee, the New Deal coalition that sustained it was weak. Not surprisingly, the Republican-led Congress overrode Truman's veto. There, too, politics governed the process. The response of the labor movement was both direct and immediate. Ordinary unionists and leaders alike called Taft-Hartley "the Slave Labor Act." Yet, the provisions were such that there was little recourse to accepting Taft-Hartley whole cloth. Unions that refused to cooperate with Taft-Hartley and its provisions lost bargaining rights and access to National Labor Relations Board hearings. Companies that had contracts with renegade unions lost their government contracts.[40]

Realigning Labor and Anti-Communism

Most importantly, the new law and the anti-communist purge that followed led to unions cannibalizing other unions. AFL unions, especially the International Association of Machinists (IAM), raided CIO unions in manufacturing. Anxious to preserve their access to the National Labor Relations Board and their base, the CIO complied with the law by issuing affidavits and expelling communist members. Between 1947 and 1952, 232,000 anti-communist affidavits were filed. The CIO followed with a purge of unions whose leadership and membership would not take loyalty oaths and created new unions to raid the older, supposed "red" unions like the Mine, Mill and Smelter Workers and the United Electrical Workers (UE). Between 1949 and 1950, the CIO expelled eleven unions representing more than a million members for the ostensible cause of "communist domination." Those unions purged included the Mine, Mill and Smelter Workers, the UE, Farm Equipment Workers, UOPWA, ILWU, United Public Workers, American Communications Association, National Union of Maritime Cooks and Stewards, and the Food, Tobacco, Agricultural and Allied Workers. The International Fur and Leather Workers withdrew from the CIO before being expelled.[41]

Winston-Salem's Food, Tobacco, Agricultural and Allied Workers Local 22, an important union that had emerged as a leader in the wartime South, faced a series of challenges. After a successful strike against Reynolds Tobacco in 1947, it steadily lost ground. An interracial union whose influence extended beyond its boundaries, Local 22 divided into factions over political campaigns. Its leaders faced expulsion from the CIO due to their refusal to sign anti-communist affidavits required by the Taft-Hartley Act. Finally, the workers at Reynolds lost their union in an NLRB election, where the company had stacked the cards. Workers new to the plant and hostile to the union were added to the bargaining unit, and "no union" won the election by sixty-six votes.[42] National labor leaders did little to stop such depredations. In fact, the UAW and other industrial unions faced their own internal conflicts over the role and place of communist organizers in their ranks. As long as the industrial core held, most labor leaders clung to their belief that labor could withstand any political opposition.[43]

Organizations such as FTA, Mine, Mill and Smelter Workers, and the United Electrical Workers, in which communist trade unionists played crucial roles, remained vibrant and successful as long as labor unions proved useful political allies for the Democratic party. The labor movement of the 1930s had benefited from the organizing talent and social vision of radical trade unionists—whether syndicalists, communists, or Trotskyists. Although most working men and women balked at third-party politics, the Democratic party under the New Deal took up the demands of the earlier generation of American radicals—including unemployment and old age insurance, federally mediated labor relations, and housing policies. As early as 1928, urban workers aligned themselves with this emerging Democratic majority. Social security and unemployment insurance disproportionately benefited white, male, and middle-class workers, but these programs also breached the wall of resistance to the limited welfare state. These policies, later augmented to include welfare provisions for single parents, health insurance for the elderly, and anti-poverty programs, were the product of the left imagination and its powers of advocacy and imagination. The Left, in fact, shaped the New Deal and the labor movement along with it.[44]

In this context, it is not surprising that the CIO Executive Board purged union officers who did not endorse its political agenda, including support for the Marshall Plan and opposition to the Progressive Party. Sixty percent of AFL and CIO unions banned communists as officers, and 40 percent barred communists as members. By the time of the AFL-CIO merger in 1955, over 200,000 union officers had taken a pledge that they were not, nor had they been, members of the Communist party. The exclusion of militants from the labor movement had long-lasting effects. Several unions failed; others, such as the United Electrical, Machine, and Radio Workers, and Mine-Mill faced cataclysmic splits. White collar unions such as the United Office and Professional Workers were dealt fatal blows by expulsion. The anti-communist provisions of the Taft-Hartley Act thus undermined progressive unionism and reinforced the power of union bureaucracy.[45]

The Right to Work in Corporate America

In the United States, conflicts between employers and labor unions ran along political lines as the assault on Big Labor became a principal target not only of anti-communist conservatives but also of those who wished to re-establish the conservative movement's position in the wake of the New Deal. Congressional investigations were only one aspect of conservative attacks on labor. The public employee strikes of the immediate postwar period and the national railroad, mining, and steel strikes of the 1950s set the stage for political confrontation. Investigations into featherbedding, challenges to union work rules, and reactionary reforms to labor law intensified internal political divisions in labor. New media campaigns against unions gave cultural support to employers' challenges to labor organizing and union representation.[46]

Right to work campaigns, labor law reform aimed at "labor monopoly," racketeering charges of the 1950s and 1960s set the stage for a broad-based assault on labor rights. Congressional investigations into "featherbedding," that is, union mandates for the number of workers employed in specific job contexts—such as the number of workers on a train run or the number of workers required to tend a steel furnace—sought to evoke images of workplace slackers in a Soviet-style economy. Employers' opposition to these practices added up to major investments to de-certify unions and undermine union organizing. Labor unions were attacked as special interests. Congress had a duty to intervene to investigate union financial abuses and intervene in internal union affairs. This political attack was a major factor in declining labor membership and power.[47]

Labor unions encountered renewed political challenges from business organizations, anti-communist organizations, and conservative circles. Forging a critique of unions that stemmed from the Wagner Act, opponents of labor, such as the rejuvenated National Association of Manufacturers, argued that the National Labor Relations Board had given labor too much power and that labor leaders were abusing that power. Unions, in this perspective, forced unwilling employees to pay dues that they did not choose for activities they did not support. Moreover, there was little government oversight of union leaders, pension funds or political contributions. Labor's critics embraced the language of individual rights, most specifically "the right to work," as an attack on what was construed to be union overreach in the workplace.[48]

Resurrecting open shop arguments about freedom of contract, the Right-to-Work movement made substantial gains at the state level and in federal labor law reform. Conservative opponents of labor, including up-and-coming Arizona senator Barry Goldwater, gathered allies by eroding public confidence in and support for labor.[49] Small business owners played a role in supporting the new anti-labor offensive. They had been sidelined during the Second World War, less able to compete for defense contracts and subject to tighter labor markets and empowered labor unions. The labor movement had made significant gains in wages and benefits. Strongholds of anti-union sentiment now claimed the "right to work" as a first liberty for both worker and the small businessman. Preceded by restrictive labor laws in pro-labor states such as Michigan and Minnesota, right-to-work laws became a Southern regional and then national phenomenon within years of labor's most decisive victories.[50]

Consolidation: Powerhouse Labor

After a decade of escalating political hostilities, labor's response was to consolidate its forces. The rebel CIO, which had broken from the stodgy AFL in 1935, now returned to the fold in a move that left many unionists mystified. In 1956, the AFL, represented by George Meany, its president and a member of the plumbers union, and the CIO, led by dynamic UAW president Walter Reuther, merged. A symbol of labor's increasingly defensive position, the merger brought the embattled and decimated ranks of the industrial unions of the CIO under the wings and leadership of the more traditional trade unions of the AFL. There were, some argued, good reasons for the merger. Labor needed to be as big and as well-endowed as its opponents in the political arena. The merger brought together the two national labor federations and their considerable resources and ended decades of conflict between and among its affiliated unions. The problem then was to what would the now-merged union turn its attention? Would the disproportionate weight of the skilled trade union voting bloc stifle any efforts at new organizing campaigns or new political work?[51]

As George Meany was fond of reminding his membership, they had no particular interest in or concern for the unorganized, except where they stood in direct competition with union labor. The AFL-CIO did not, as a consequence of the merger, launch new efforts among farm workers, domestic labor, or in the public sector. Rather, it devoted its resources to serving its current membership and limited its organizing campaigns to a relatively narrow channel of the work force. In national convention and in the public media, unionists presented a unified and stable front. Only in local campaigns and in state and local politics did labor seem to direct its efforts toward broader goals. One of those, as we shall see in the next chapter, was organizing public sector workers and challenging legal barriers to public employee unionism. Fairly consistent with its political past, the labor movement presented a united front in its conservative foreign policy, opposition to lowering trade barriers, and fulsome support of the defense budget. Wartime and then postwar jobs in the defense sector generally were union jobs—mostly employing white men—and they were to be protected.[52]

Structural changes in the work force began to erode the strength of labor representation. The most significant growth in the postwar labor force was in clerical, managerial and technical, and service employment—both in the private and public sectors. After the purging of white collar unions from the CIO, there were few advocates and no new resources dedicated to organizing the staggering numbers of women and men who became retail clerks, office secretaries and clerical workers, middle management and technical workers, or administrative staff. It may have been that battling the public relations war over existing unions took the lion's share of the AFL-CIO's time and energy; but these choices had long-term consequences for labor. Its weak and ambivalent organizing strategy and failure to meet the race and gender challenges of a changing work force left the country's largest labor federation hemorrhaging members and losing its tenuous foothold in the new sectors of the economy.

Blue Collar Workers in the Postwar Years

For most observers, blue collar workers were the heart and soul of the labor movement of the 1950s and 1960s. Many saw rising incomes, even in economic uncertainty, and their children benefited from greater economic security. Others experienced labor loyalty and strike participation as double-edged. Cheri Register's father, a packinghouse worker in Albert Lea, Minnesota, took a job in the local Wilson & Co. plant during World War II, when packing plants struggled to maintain their labor force. A relatively young worker, Gordy Register became a millwright, responsible for maintaining and repairing packing plant machinery. Descended from immigrant farmers and agricultural workers, Register believed that his work, and the physically exhausting and dangerous work of butchering, curing, and packaging meat, was important because it supported his family, church, and community life. It also provided Register with status. He was a trustworthy, experienced, and skilled worker, loyal friend, dependable employee, and family man. These qualities did not protect him, however, when the company defeated workers in an 109-day strike in 1959. Caught on camera during the strike, Register was charged with property damage and laid off until he was found innocent of the charges. His delayed return to work signaled a loss of status and a loss of material resources. It played havoc with his predictable future, seen as a life without deprivation, in which the roles of son, brother, husband, and father were well-defined and his place in the community secure. The strike drove deep rifts in the community of Albert Lea, as it exposed the vulnerabilities of even the most secure union worker and the vagaries of management and the market.[53]

For blue collar workers who returned to the industrial labor force during or after World War II, strong unions provided the security recounted in Register's tale. While consumer demand was high, and the company stable, union jobs offered a better standard of living and access not only to the public social security system but to private pensions. Employment security, overtime pay, vacation days, protection against managerial abuse and random workplace discipline gave the postwar working class stability and predictability. Only in such a world could working-class men and women and their families plan on home ownership and retirement; union jobs and wages thus provided a bulwark against the precariousness of individual and family lives. This security was possible only as long as there was relative peace between unions and employers, an implicit pact that kept union demands in check and limited management's actions.

Strengthened by this postwar pact, unionized industrial workers became, for the most part, more prosperous in these decades and their children socially mobile. This prosperity was clearly relative, seen in the differences between unemployment during the Depression and postwar stability. Before the rise of the CIO, industrial workers had little power on the shop floor or in the community. By the 1950s, the labor movement changed the equation through union rules that protected seniority and granted benefits and gave workers an education in politics and a political vision that overrode voter apathy. Organized labor mobilized workers at the ward level to participate in elections and to support funding for public education, highway and bridge construction, and the local "commons" of public libraries and museums. Despite what seemed like minor losses for the labor movement, the expansion of the public sector—including public sector employment—occurred even as the political influence of labor leaders grew.[54]

Prior to this, workers' social horizons had been limited by a skewed wealth distribution and by public education that failed to provide more than marginal social mobility. Tracked not only by ability but by family background, working-class kids were directed toward a school curriculum that focused on basic work force and vocational skills or toward general courses that more often than not spurred early exit and incomplete schooling. In fact, learning on the job was considered the best education. Even upwardly mobile working-class children learned occupational skills through employment, not formal training. With the expansion of the public sector, this too began to change. Sons and daughters of blue collar workers often finished high school. Many went to university; some became managers and professionals.[55]

The economic crisis and the war altered the educational landscape for working-class men and women by providing disincentives for early school leaving and veterans' benefits that funded, at least for white men, vocational training and even college education. Military service offered some veterans skills that translated into careers in engineering, management, and other white collar jobs after the war. While this may have diverted organic working-class leaders away from service to the labor movement, it also gave working-class families incentives to seek union jobs and wages. The possibility of funding college education for their children motivated many workers to work overtime, and the labor movement better educated workers to serve as stewards and union officials.

Working-class women also played a major role in the improving social conditions and upward mobility of their families. Women's labor force participation across the class spectrum increased, and married women and women with children rejoined the labor force in the 1950s and 1960s. While this trend was evident from the 1930s, its growth in the postwar period reflected new opportunities for women. The growing dependence of manufacturing concerns and financial institutions on technical and managerial workers in engineering, human relations and personnel, marketing, advertising, banking, and insurance called for an equal or greater number of support staff. Women of this generation, often better educated than their mothers and with business skills learned in new high school curricula, easily found employment in these new sectors. Family incomes rose as a consequence; so too did the need for women to work in retail as cashiers, sales women, stock clerks, and bookkeepers. The expansion of health care and government services had a similar impact, vastly increasing demand for secretaries, typists, and clerks. The postwar baby boom also called for teachers, nurses, and social workers; and the growing number of dual wage-earner households meant that there were jobs in restaurant food service, cleaning, and child care.[56]

Union Men and "Mad Men"

Observers of the blue collar world often commented on the complacency and belligerency among newly entitled blue collar workers. Second- and third-generation white European immigrants had traversed the harrowing ground from poverty and dislocation to a stable and settled location in the lower middle class. Union auto workers, some exclaimed, earned more than semi-professional workers and even salesmen, managers, and the owners of small business. Grating, in particular, was the idea that an auto worker could own a boat, take their vacation in a cottage at the lake, and send their children to college. Even as plant foremen were excluded from the National Labor Relations Board procedures, they took umbrage at the aggressive tactics among union workers and shop stewards. For plant supervisors, foremen, and professional workers such as engineers and designers, the new power of workers in demanding and strictly obeying work rules and filing grievances took company time and slowed production. Masculinity on the shop floor seemed to call for confrontation in a middle-class world that demanded cohesion and cooperation. An escalating intensity of labor and employer conflict was the inevitable result. Managers consistently distanced themselves, using the differences between the physical and mental content of work to justify wage cuts and right-to-work campaigns.[57]

In *Striking Steel*, Jack Metzgar, the son of a United Steel Workers organizer and griever, recounts the experience of two generations with the labor movement at its prime. In telling the story of his father, Johnny, Metzgar intertwined the public war of labor—fought on the picket line, in the voting booth, and in public opinion—with the private war of the strike. Strikes were fought against workers' own inertia, their precarious hold on middle-class status, and the calculus of money earned, saved, spent, and reserved for catastrophic layoffs and walkouts. The 116-day steel strike in 1959 was one such struggle. The long strike was sustained against the expectations of short-term planners, but it had consequences similar to the Albert Lea strike in the same year.

As in Albert Lea, labor relations in the steel industry had deteriorated by the end of the 1950s. Contract negotiations began with firm resolve by management and labor. At the end of their contract, the United Steel Workers (USW) sought wage increases due to increased productivity and anticipated some improvement over the previous contract. Steel manufacturers, seeking to cut labor costs, opposed union wage demands and insisted that rules that protected union jobs be modified. The Steel Workers argued such work rule changes would endanger worker health and safety. Despite months of negotiation from mid-July to mid-October, the two parties arrived at an impasse. The USW went out on strike across the country. Using his powers under the Taft-Hartley Act, President Eisenhower asked the Justice Department to seek a labor injunction. The Steel Workers fought the injunction until November, when the Supreme Court sustained the injunction. The strike was declared over in January 1960.[58]

Steel companies were prepared to resume production after the injunction ended. Both sides agreed to end the strike with a contract that satisfied neither. That agreement, many have argued, was the cause of long-term changes in the steel industry and the labor movement. Over the short term, the contract deferred workers' pay raise, but there were no work rule changes, the union's primary demand. In *Striking Steel*, Jack Metzgar suggested that the work rule concession, Section 2(B) of the contract, led to the long-term decline of steel and steel unionism. In this, he agrees with other industry commentators such as John Hoerr, who believed that the intransigence of the steel industry helped sow the seeds of industrial decline. More to the point, labor unions in the steel industry, as well as automobile and rubber, could make substantial gains in wages and benefits for their members, protect workers' rights in grievance procedures, and create short-term employment security. They could not, however, intervene in corporate responses to changing conditions. When industries chose to move production facilities, or alter the production in ways that cut jobs or instituted a tiered wage system, unions often stood to gain in the short term. In the long term, they had little recourse but protest, even as companies cut their labor force, shifted production, and left communities.[59]

Teamsters and Longshoremen: Union Transformations in the 1950s

By contrast, one of the fastest growing unions in the postwar economy was the International Brotherhood of Teamsters (IBT), whose influence and power increased over the course of the twentieth century. The postwar world saw local and regional shipping integrated into an expanded transportation system that combined overseas shipping with railroad cars and interstate highways. With the introduction of container shipping, manufacturing and shipping firms shifted much of their freight from rail cars and ships to over-the-road trucking. An overall decline in oil prices encouraged this growing dependence on diesel fuel in an increasingly petroleum-based economy. It also led to the slow decline in port labor and in the power of these two respective unions.[60]

The origins of the Teamster union were in horse-drawn cart hauling. In 1905, a crucial trucking strike in Chicago established the union. Long-term Teamster president Dan Tobin presided over a decades-long membership growth beginning in 1907. After successful organizing drives in Minneapolis, Detroit, the Upper Midwest and Pacific Northwest, the Teamsters gained tens of thousands of members. And in 1952, with over a million members, the Teamsters vied with the United Auto Workers as one of the largest unions in the country. Under Tobin's successor, Dave Beck, the Teamsters gained another 500,000 members.[61]

The Teamsters served as a major force in the regeneration of craft unionism, as they adapted to new jobs and workers. Expanding union membership in food processing, packaging, and retail only bolstered the Teamsters' strong craft union identity and their use of benefits unionism—the Teamster pension fund in particular—to recruit and retain members. Teamsters also played a vital political role. To use only one example, the Teamsters played a major role in opposition to the passage of the Taft-Hartley Act. They also launched the DRIVE (Democratic Republican Independent Voter Education) campaign in the 1950s. This move, which asserted party independence, echoed Samuel Gompers' earlier insistence that labor "elect friends and defeat enemies." And, like Gompers, Teamster politics focused on the workplace. There was little room for the social unionism of the liberal UAW. With close to 200,000 African Americans in its ranks, the Teamsters had one of the largest and most integrated unions. The union also retained discriminatory policies. Nearly 80,000 women belonged to the union in the 1960s, but the growing number of women members did not alter the fact that the Teamsters were, for all intents and purposes, "a man's union."[62]

Their robust use of the secondary boycott, a tactic specifically banned later under Taft-Hartley, had been an effective tool for organizing workers. In the 1930s and 1940s, the IBT aided the organization of the auto industry into the UAW; and in Minneapolis, the Teamsters' local supported organizing campaigns and strikes throughout the city. By the 1950s and 1960s, the Teamsters moved to organize employers, rather than focusing on individual recruitment, a tactic later questioned in congressional investigations. The Teamsters modeled new organizing strategies throughout the postwar period, and it was among the first unions to adopt national contracts. For the most part, however, the Teamsters came to represent the conservative bent of business unionism. They were not constrained by jurisdictional lines in organizing workers or in the tactics they used to win organizing drives and strikes. By the late 1950s, Robert Kennedy, a rising congressional counsel, attacked "the labor bosses" behind the Teamsters and launched a full scale attack on former Teamster president David Beck and its then president, Jimmy Hoffa. They were, Kennedy asserted, labor racketeers and, in effect, *The Enemy Within*. In 1957, following on Beck's indictment, the AFL–CIO expelled the Teamsters.[63]

Jimmy Hoffa's tenure as Teamster president coincided with a time many viewed as "the glory years" of the union. Hoffa began his career with the IBT when he began organizing into Local 299 (strawberry workers) and Local 337 in Detroit. He later claimed to have modeled his organizing tactics on those of Minneapolis Teamsters leader, Farrell Dobbs. Hoffa expanded the territory of the Teamsters through strategic boycott but also an expansive organizing policy, bringing in the car haulers in the auto industry. More than that, Hoffa used his leverage in one region to gain territory in another. In 1964, the Teamsters negotiated a national freight contract for 400,000 workers. Following on earlier membership gains, Teamsters expanded membership to over 2 million members by the 1960s.[64]

The growth of the Teamsters is connected to the revolution that took place in the 1950s and created the new globalized economy of today—that is, the changes in shipping and transportation known as "containerization." Prior to these changes, longshoremen and stevedores and their unions were a central part of organized labor. Goods shipped to and from the United States passed through ports, where they were loaded onto or unloaded from wooden pallets and moved from ship to truck to railroad cars. Goods then finished the distance to warehouses and stores via local truck transportation. Teamsters—truck drivers and warehouse workers—were important to freight shipment but mostly along these secondary routes. This changed with two important developments—the creation of the interstate highway system begun in 1956 and the adoption of containerization as the most cost-efficient means for transportation to, from, and within the United States.[65]

Companies that first innovated this process viewed port labor—longshoremen and warehousemen—as an obstacle to transportation of goods. The International Longshoremen and Warehousemen's Union (ILWU), they argued, placed shippers under a constant threat of strikes, vulnerable to port and harbor corruption, and unable to adjust their payrolls to reflect the labor required to handle and ship goods. In order to lower shipping costs, manufacturers and distributors looked to cut the amount of ship and rail transport. Piggy-backing semi-containers on rail cars, entailing the loading of cars on one end and the unloading of semis on the other, proved an effective means to lowering labor costs across the board.[66]

The creation of the container system reduced costs associated with overseas shipping and the port labor force. In 1956, a signal year, the aging tanker ship, *Ideal-X*, took on fifty-eight aluminum truck bodies as cargo in Newark, New Jersey. Five days later, the ship sailed into Houston harbor, where fifty-eight trucks took on the metal boxes to haul them to their destination. In 1961, ocean freight costs constituted 12 percent of value of US exports and 10 percent of value of US imports, as each shipment was handled by as many as a dozen vendors. The process was considered as more of an obstacle to international trade than tariffs. With the introduction of containerization, there was a significant drop in labor costs that, over the short term, benefited the trucking industry and the Teamsters. Later, through innovation in trucking with the introduction of automated terminals and diesel trucks, even these costs would drop.[67]

Loading and unloading freight in ports had been a major source of jobs for working-class men. In the decades before unionization, longshoremen and stevedores were faced with uncertain employment in a dangerous and physically brutal industry. Indeed, before the ILWU organized in 1934, longshoremen and warehousemen were subjected to a "shape up" hiring system for jobs that were poorly paid and riddled with corruption. The 1934 San Francisco General Strike gave the West Coast union its footing in the industry, as did port strikes in New York, but unions did not eliminate the dangers of port labor. As Marc Levinson writes, "Because the [longshoremen] had to bend over to [unload cargo from pallets], you'd see these fellows going home at the end of the day kind of like orangutans ... I mean they were just kind of all bent, and they'd eventually straighten up for the next day." Work on the docks took place in sweltering weather and heavy rain; heavy equipment, dangerous loads, and slippery docks led to high rates of worker injury and death. In 1950 alone, there were 2,208 serious accidents in the port of New York.[68]

Automation began to change these statistics but only alongside cuts in the number of jobs. During World War II, shipping depots adapted forklifts, cranes, and conveyors to reduce muscle strain and give dockworkers some protection against nearly daily injuries. Still, port-related employment was about 400,000 workers in the port of New York alone. When the ILWU and the International Longshoremen's Organization fought against further mechanization by unions, such resistance opened the door to containerization. To reduce costs, the Sea-Land Service was created in 1955–1958 and later turned to railroads to complete the system. The process led to the decline of older ports and expansion, as in New York, to the non-union port facilities in New Jersey. It further expanded the trucking labor force and saved railways from extinction. And it gave, to the Teamsters, an even stronger foothold in the economy.[69]

While both the Longshoremen's Union and the Teamsters were accused of corruption, it was only the ILWU that had been tarred with a radical brush. But while federal authorities seemed intent on either imprisoning or deporting ILWU head, and accused communist, Harry Bridges, there was somewhat less concern in the early 1950s about the Teamsters' growing influence. That changed with the indictment and imprisonment of David Beck, former IBT president. His successor, Jimmy Hoffa, also faced criminal indictments for corruption and became the target of a congressional investigation with the McClellan Committee Hearings. The outcome, in the end, was not only the imprisonment of Hoffa but the passage of another labor reform law that proved detrimental to labor. Under Hoffa's leadership, the IBT grew to over 2 million members in 1970 and continued to grow after his imprisonment. Hoffa remained a major figure in the Teamsters after his release from prison until he disappeared in 1975.[70]

Conservative Powers and Labor Law Reform

The postwar era saw industrial unions stabilized, even as the American economy began to shift toward greater emphasis on service and information sectors. Changes in the demand for labor, growth in non-production jobs in manufacturing, and the vast expansion in service and in government employment led to declines in private sector unionization but also new opportunities for the labor movement. The question was whether labor leaders would capitalize on these changes or spend their resources on retaining influence and power in primary industry. They chose the latter course. These structural changes were but the backdrop to the political and cultural changes with which labor was faced.

By 1957, many voices called for the reform of labor law. A small group of these voices spoke to the damage the Taft-Hartley Act had brought to labor relations. Still, the Hearings of the Senate Select Committee on Improper Conduct in Labor and Management Field brought forth a different call. Congress rapidly became a platform for further restrictions on the labor movement even as labor unions lost the public relations war. Over 75 percent of those polled approved of labor unions before the McClellan committee hearings. Public support declined first to 64 percent then to 56 percent after the committee published its findings. The committee drew attention to the corruption and undue political influence of labor, echoing the criticism of corporate leaders and organized employers. As anti-communism began to wane, anti-unionism took its place.[71]

Robert Griffin, Republican from Michigan, and Philip Landrum, Democrat from Georgia, sponsored the Labor Management Reporting and Disclosure Act of 1959. It was the first labor law since 1938 Fair Labor Standards Act to present reform as possibility. By the end of congressional debates, Landrum-Griffin doubled down on Taft-Hartley Act restrictions of labor union financial and political power. Originally designed as a reform of labor law to liberalize labor relations, it achieved the opposite, firmly cementing into place the limits of labor union organizing. Congress clearly understood that public opinion had changed and no longer supported labor law liberalization. These changes isolated labor from the liberalization of civil rights and civil liberties. Landrum-Griffin restricted union financial practices and instituted government oversight of union internal affairs.

The law also enlarged the definition of secondary boycotts, and it weakened union solidarity by instituting a "bill of rights" for individual workers, in effect a "right to work" for individuals. It further weakened labor unions in the private sector and opened the door for other opportunities.[72]

The response of labor unions to the conservative political climate was not unified. The international AFL-CIO continued to pursue a conservative policy, ignoring shifts in the labor force and the opportunities presented by civil rights activism in the South and the growth of the public sector. At the state level, however, these changes did not go unnoticed. The investment of the labor movement in the Democratic party, especially at the state level, offered resources to meet the challenges of right-to-work laws and Landrum-Griffin. More specifically, labor unions began to pay attention to how state races and state legislatures set the context for public sector employment and opened the door to public sector unionism. There was much work to be done.

Conclusion

In one of the great ironies of the postwar world, the American labor movement, weakened by internal division, hampered with restrictive labor laws, and facing an aggressive employer campaign aimed at dismantling labor's influence, remained a powerful political force. By the 1960s, labor votes had restored the Democratic party's control over Congress and the presidency, even as labor unions lost influence in the workplace. It would be labor's political power that sustained it in union-friendly states such as Michigan, Illinois, and New York. Union Democrats voted for, and supported, new labor laws that expanded union protections to the public sector. And the working-class base of the Democratic party enabled it to legitimize public employee unionism, to sponsor the expansion of the American welfare state in the Great Society, and to address longstanding social and economic inequality. None of these achievements altered the slow erosion of private sector unionism and the declining representation of union labor in the economy. Ironically, labor's continuing political power put it repeatedly in the sights of conservative politicians and lobbying groups.

For those who worked in unionized factories, offices, ports, warehouses, and transport, the labor movement guaranteed higher pay, greater benefits, and, for some, employment security. There were long-term and intergenerational benefits to the labor movement's continued strength as well—including greater educational opportunity for working-class sons and daughters and even the possibility of unionized employment in the second and third generation. That meant something in postwar America—home ownership, access to private or public transportation at low cost, better nutrition, and, for most, healthier and longer lives. For men and women who lacked that good fortune, American society offered few compensations and little support.

It was with the growth of public sector unions in the 1960s and 1970s that labor experienced a resurgence comparable to, if not surpassing, the turbulent years of the 1930s. The troubled Teamsters and Steel Workers, the powerful Auto Workers, and declining Mine Workers all experienced upheavals in their ranks, with widespread wildcat strikes and internal dissenters alike seeking to dislodge an entrenched labor bureaucracy. At first, the contradictions between the prosperity of the 1960s and the brutal pace of the shop floor fed worker discontent. Faster production lines and more dangerous machinery threatened the lives and livelihoods of workers. But the steep declines of the 1970s, in the context of new trade policies and a global energy crisis, smothered the flames. How labor confronted the social movements of the 1960s and 1970s, and how they suppressed their own internal movements for change, is the subject of the next chapter.

Notes

1 Thomas Geoghegan, *Which Side Are You On? Trying to Be for Labor When It's Flat on Its Back* (New York: Farrar, Straus and Giroux, 1991), 3–4.
2 Charles Kuzell, testimony, *Hearings before the United States Congress, House Committee on Education and Labor, Matters Relating to the Labor-Management Relations Act of 1947*, 83rd Congress, 1st sess., 1953, quoted in Kim Phillips-Fein, "Business Conservatism on the Shop Floor: Anti-Union Campaigns in the 1950s," *Labor: Studies in Working Class History of the Americas* 7:2 (Summer 2010), 15.
3 For insight into the negative media coverage of unions, see Troy Rondinone, *The Great Industrial War: Framing Class Conflict in the Media* (New Brunswick: Rutgers University Press, 2010); Lawrence Richards, *Union-Free America: Workers and Anti-Union Culture* (Urbana: University of Illinois Press, 2008); Elizabeth Fones-Wolf, *Selling Free Enterprise: The Business Assault on Labor and Liberalism, 1945–1960* (Urbana: University of Illinois Press, 1994); David Witwer, *Shadow of the Racketeer: Scandal in Organized Labor* (Urbana: University of Illinois Press, 2009).
4 C. Wright Mills, *The New Men of Power: America's Labor Leaders* (New York: Harcourt Brace, 1948); Daniel Bell, *The End of Ideology* (Cambridge, MA: Harvard University Press, 1988, c. 1960); Howell John Harris, *The Right to Manage: Industrial Relations Policies of American Business in the 1940s* (Madison: University of Wisconsin Press, 1982); Kim Phillips-Fein, *Invisible Hands: The Making of the Conservative Movement from the New Deal to Reagan* (New York: W.W. Norton, 2009); Nelson Lichtenstein and Elizabeth Tandy Shermer, eds., *The Right and Labor in America: Politics, Ideology, and Imagination* (Philadelphia: University of Pennsylvania Press, 2012); Elizabeth Tandy Shermer, *Sunbelt Capitalism: Phoenix and the Transformation of American Politics* (Philadelphia: University Pennsylvania Press, 2013).
5 Daniel Bell, "The Treaty of Detroit," *Fortune* (July 1950), 53–55; Nelson Lichtenstein, "From Corporatism to Collective Bargaining: Organized Labor and the Eclipse of Social Democracy in the Post-War Era," in Steve Fraser and Gary Gerstle, eds., *The Rise and Fall of the New Deal Order, 1930–1980* (Princeton: Princeton University Press, 1989), 152–182.
6 Tami J. Friedman, "Exploiting the North–South Differential: Corporate Power, Southern Politics, and the Decline of Organized Labor after World War II," *Journal of American History* 95:2 (September 2008), 323–348; idem, "'Acute Depression … in the Age … of Plenty': Capital Migration, Economic Dislocation, and the Missing 'Social Contract' of the 1950s," *Labor: Working-Class History of the Americas* 8:4 (2011), 89–119; Thomas J. Sugrue, "'Forget About Your Inalienable Right to Work':

Deindustrialization and Its Discontents at Ford, 1950–1953," *International Labor and Working Class History* 48 (1995), 112–130.

7 Robert J. Gordon, *The Rise and Fall of American Growth: The U.S. Standard of Living Since the Civil War* (Princeton: Princeton University Press, 2016), credits overall increases in standard and quality of living to mid-century governmental and technological innovation during the New Deal and World War II; see also Joel Seidman, *American Labor from Defense to Reconversion* (Chicago: University of Chicago Press, 1953).

8 Gordon, *The Rise and Fall of American Growth*, 409–421; Elaine May, *Homeward Bound: American Families in the Cold War Era* (New York: Basic Books, 1988), 10–29, 163–185; Thomas Doherty, *Cold War, Cool Medium: Television, McCarthyism, and American Culture* (New York: Columbia University Press, 2003), 1–18, 105–133, 215–230; Richards, *Union-Free America*, 38–88.

9 Nelson Lichtenstein, *Labor's War at Home: The CIO in World War II*, 2nd ed. (Philadelphia: Temple University Press, 2003), 203–232.

10 Lichtenstein, *Labor's War at Home*, 133–135, 157–177, 189–200.

11 George Lipsitz, *Rainbow at Midnight: Labor and Culture in the 1940s* (Urbana: University of Illinois Press, 1994), 99–154; Joshua B. Freeman, *Working Class New York: Life and Labor Since World War II* (New York: New Press, 2000), 3–6; Robert Self, *American Babylon: Race and the Struggle for Postwar Oakland* (Princeton: Princeton University Press, 2003), 24–25; Colleen Doody, *Detroit's Cold War: The Origins of Postwar Conservatism* (Urbana: University of Illinois Press, 2012), 19–45.

12 CIO 1943 convention; quoted in Lichtenstein, *Labor's War at Home*, 216–217.

13 Jack Metzgar, *Striking Steel*, 30–31.

14 Barbara Griffith, *The Crisis of American Labor: Operation Dixie and the Defeat of the CIO* (Philadelphia: Temple University Press, 1988); Sharon Hartman, "'We're No Kitty Foyles': Organizing Women Office Workers for the CIO, 1937–1950," in Ruth Milkman, ed., *Women, Work, and Protest: A Century of U.S. Labor History* (Boston MA: Routledge, 1984), 206–234; Mark McColloch, *White Collar Workers in Transition: The Boom Years, 1940–1970* (New York: Praeger, 1983); Daniel J. Opler, *For All White Collar Workers: The Possibilities of Radicalism in New York City's Department Store Unions, 1934–1953* (Columbus: Ohio State University Press, 2007); Zaragosa Vargas, *Labor Rights Are Civil Rights: Mexican American Workers in Twentieth Century America* (Princeton: Princeton University Press, 2005), 276–280; Cindy Hahamovitch, *No Man's Land: Jamaican Guest Workers in America and the Global History of Deportable Workers* (Princeton: Princeton University Press, 2011).

15 Historians have viewed this world from the perspective of the Red Diaper babies who were active in social movements of the 1960s. The second generation of industrial unionists who came of age during the war at the height of CIO influence were their parents. For mentors, see, among others, John A. Salmond, *Miss Lucy of the CIO: The Life and Times of Lucy Randolph Mason* (Athens: University of Georgia Press, 1988); James J. Lorence, *Palomino: Clinton Jencks and Mexican-American Unionism in the American Southwest* (Urbana: University of Illinois Press, 2013).

16 See Amy Bromsen, "'They All Sort of Disappeared': The Early Cohort of UAW Women Leaders," *Michigan Historical Review* 37:1 (Spring 2011), 5–40; also Dorothy Sue Cobble, *The Other Women's Movement: Workplace Justice and Social Rights in Modern America* (Princeton: Princeton University Press, 2003); Daniel Horowitz, *Betty Friedan and the Making of the Feminine Mystique: The American Left, the Cold War, and Modern Feminism* (Amherst: University of Massachusetts Press, 1998), 102–152.

17 For its origins in the 1930s, see Elizabeth Faue, "'The Dynamo of Change': Gender and Solidarity in the American Labour Movement of the 1930s," *Gender and History* 1:2 (Summer 1989), 138–158.

18 Cobble, *The Other Women's Movement*; Nancy F. Gabin, *Feminism in the Labor Movement: Women and the United Auto Workers, 1935–1970* (Ithaca: Cornell University

Press, 1990); Ruth Milkman, *Gender at Work: The Dynamics of Job Segregation by Sex during World War II* (Urbana: University of Illinois Press, 1986); Dennis Deslippe, *Rights, Not Roses: Unions and the Rise of Working-Class Feminism* (Urbana: University of Illinois Press, 2000); Lisa Kannenberg, "The Impact of the Cold War on Women's Trade Union Activism: The UE Experience," *Labor History* 34 (Spring-Summer 1993), 309–323. For a more recent work, see Marcia Walker-McWilliams, *Reverend Addie Wyatt: Faith and the Fight for Labor, Gender, and Racial Equality* (Urbana: University of Illinois Press, 2016).

19 Ruth Milkman, "Rosie the Riveter Resorted: Management's Postwar Purge of Women Automobile Workers," in Nelson Lichtenstein and Steve Meyer, eds., *On the Line: Essays in the History of Auto Work* (Urbana: University of Illinois Press, 1989), 129–152; idem, *Gender at Work.* 99–127; Daniel Kryder, *Divided Arsenal: Race and the American State during World War II* (Cambridge: Cambridge University Press, 2000), conclusion; Zieger, *For Jobs and Freedom*, 123–138.

20 See Robert Korstad, *Civil Rights Unionism: Tobacco Workers and the Struggle for Democracy in the Twentieth Century South* (Chapel Hill: University of North Carolina Press, 2003), 276–300; Horace Huntley, "The Red Scare and Black Workers in Alabama: The International Union of Mine, Mill and Smelter Workers, 1945–1953," in *Labor Divided: Race and Ethnicity in United States Labor Struggles, 1835–1960*, ed. Robert Asher and Charles Stephenson (Albany: SUNY Press, 1990), 129–150; Laurie Mercier, *Anaconda: Labor, Community, and Culture in Montana's Smelter City* (Urbana: University of Illinois Press, 2001); Ronald Filipelli and Mark McCulloch, *Cold War on the Working Class: The Rise and Decline of the United Electrical Workers* (Albany: SUNY Press, 1995); Steven J. Rosswurm, *The CIO's Left-Led Unions* (New Brunswick: Rutgers University Press, 1992). On the Democratic Party link, see Mike Davis, *Prisoners of the American Dream: Politics and Economy in the History of the U.S. Working Class* (London: Verso, 1986), 52–101.

21 Recent memoirs reveal this side of strikes. Jack Metzgar, *Striking Steel: Solidarity Remembered* (Philadelphia: Temple University Press 2000); Cheri Register, *Packinghouse Daughter: A Memoir* (Minneapolis: Minnesota Historical Society Press, 2000); and Robert Bruno, *Steel Workers Alley: How Class Works in Youngstown* (Ithaca, NY: ILR Press, 1999) read as elegies to the working-class past, revealing the contradictions and divisions within labor struggles and expressing grief for lost working-class worlds. These memoirs of upwardly mobile working-class sons and daughters are bittersweet and ambivalent about how the working class came to be and how it was undone.

22 Robert H. Zieger, *The CIO, 1935–1955* (Chapel Hill: University of North Carolina Press, 1997); Ira Katznelson, *City Trenches: Urban Politics and the Patterning of Class in the United States* (Chicago: University of Chicago Press, 1982).

23 Daniel Bell, "Prospects for Union Growth," *Contemporary Labor Issues*, edited by Walter Fogel and Archie Kleingartner (New York: Wadsworth, 1964), 225–228; Irving Bernstein, "The Growth of American Unions," *Labor History* 2:2 (Spring 1961), 131–157; Sidney Lens, *The Crisis of American Labor*, (New York: A.S. Barnes, 1961).

24 For critiques of Bell's arguments about industrial workers, in *The End of Ideology* and more fully in Bell's *The Coming of Post-Industrial Society: A Venture in Social Forecasting* (New York: Basic Books, 1973), see Tracy Neumann, *Remaking the Rust Belt: The Post-Industrial Transformation of North America* (Philadelphia: University of Pennsylvania Press, 2016), 8–9, 12, 28, 78–79, 212–213. Neumann shows that Bell, in his arguments about post-industrialism, got many things wrong about inequality. His ideas influenced policymakers in the Carter and Reagan years who favored the Sun Belt over the Rust Belt, and prioritized services for professionals over blue-collar workers.

25 See Jacquelyn Dowd Hall, Robert Korstad, and James Leloudis, "Cotton Mill People: Work, Community, and Protest in the Textile South, 1880–1940," *American Historical Review* 91 (1986), 245–286; Michelle Brattain, *The Politics of Whiteness: Race, Workers, and Culture in the Modern South* (Princeton: Princeton University Press, 2001); Bryant

Simon, *The Fabric of Defeat: The Politics of South Carolina Millhands* (Chapel Hill: University of North Carolina Press, 1998).

26 After World War I, a steady stream of companies moved to the South in an industrial migration that continued through the 1970s. See Tamara K. Hareven and Randolph Langenbach, *Amoskeag: Life and Work in an American Factory-City* (New York: Pantheon, 1980); Jefferson Cowie, *Capital Moves: RCA's 70-Year Quest for Cheap Labor* (New York: New Press, 2001); William Adler, *Mollie's Job: A Story of Life and Work on the Global Assembly Line* (New York: Scribner's, 2000). See Joseph B. Atkins, *Covering for the Bosses: Labor and the Southern Press* (Oxford: University Press of Mississippi, 2011), on capital mobility and postwar industrial development in the South.

27 Zieger *The CIO*, 231.

28 Griffith, *Crisis of American Labor*, 22–45.

29 Korstad, *Civil Rights Unionism*, 276–300; Zieger, *The CIO*, 233–241.

30 James T. Patterson, *Grand Expectations: The United States, 1945–1974* (New York: Oxford University Press, 1996), 53; Korstad, *Civil Rights Unionism*, 290–300.

31 Judith Stepan-Norris and Maurice Zeitlin, *Left Out: Reds and America's Industrial Unions* (Cambridge: Cambridge University Press, 2003).

32 David M. Oshinsky, *Senator Joseph McCarthy and the American Labor Movement* (Columbia: University of Missouri Press, 1976); Ellen Schrecker, *Many Are the Crimes: McCarthyism in America* (Boston MA: Little, Brown, 1998).

33 Shermer, *Sunbelt Capitalism*, 283–290; Phillips-Fein, *Invisible Hands*, 97–105; Fones-Wolf, *Selling Free Enterprise*, 257–284; Harris, *The Right to Manage*, 129–158.

34 Barton J. Bernstein, "The Truman Administration and the Steel Strike of 1946," *Journal of American History* 52 (March 1966), 791–803; Kim Phillips-Fein, "'If Business and the Country Will Be Run Right': The Business Challenge to the Liberal Consensus, 1945–1965," *International Labor and Working-Class History* 72:1 (Fall 2007), 192–215.

35 Rondinone, *The Great Industrial War*, 151–165.

36 Melvyn Dubofsky, *The State and Labor in Modern America* (Chapel Hill: University of North Carolina Press, 1994), 199–207, quote 202.

37 Dubofsky, *The State and Labor in Modern America*, 203–205.

38 Jean-Christian Vinel, *The Employee: A Political History* (Philadelphia: University of Pennsylvania Press, 2013), discusses the implications of this exclusion and how reclassification of employees to subcontractors undermined labor law.

39 Mari Jo Buhle, Paul Buhle, and Dan Georgakas, eds., *Encyclopedia of the American Left*, rev. ed. (New York: Oxford University Press, 1998), 813; Rondinone, *The Great Industrial War*, 151–165. See also R. Alton Lee, *Truman and Taft-Hartley: A Question of Mandate* (Westport: Greenwood Press, 1966); Arthur F. McClure, *The Truman Administration and the Problems of Postwar Labor, 1945–1948* (Rutherford, NC: Fairleigh Dickinson University Press, 1969); Tracy Roof, *American Labor, Congress, and the Welfare State, 1935–2010* (Baltimore: Johns Hopkins University Press, 2011), 38–44.

40 Lichtenstein, *Labor's War at Home*, 233–245.

41 Steve Rosswurm, "An Overview and Preliminary Assessment of the CIO's Expelled Unions," in idem, ed., *The CIO's Left-Led Unions* (New Brunswick: Rutgers University Press, 1992) 1–18; Ellen Schrecker, *The Age of McCarthyism: A Brief History with Documents* (New York: Bedford St. Martin's, 2002), 58–62; David M. Oshinsky, *A Conspiracy So Immense: The World of Joe McCarthy*, 2nd ed. (New York: Oxford University Press, 2005), 53–71.

42 Robert Korstad, *Civil Rights Unionism*, 413.

43 See Stepan-Norris and Zeitlin, *Left Out*, 95–158; Nelson Lichtenstein, *The Most Dangerous Man in Detroit: Walter Reuther and the Fate of American Labor* (New York: Basic Books, 1995), 248–269.

44 Michael Denning, *The Cultural Front: The Laboring of American Culture* (New York: Verso, 1996), champions this argument, as do Nelson Lichtenstein, *The State of the*

Unions; Margaret Miller, "Negotiating Cold War Politics: The Washington Pension Union and the Labor Left in the 1940s and 1950s," in Robert W. Cherny, William Issel, and Kieran Walsh, eds., *American Labor and the Cold War: Grassroots Politics and Postwar Political Culture* (New Brunswick: Rutgers University Press, 2004), 190–204; Richard Oestreicher, "Urban Working-Class Political Behavior and Theories of American Electoral Politics, 1870–1940," *Journal of American History* 74:4 (1988), 1257–1286.

45 Schrecker, *Many Are the Crimes: McCarthyism in America*, 379–382.

46 Elizabeth Tandy Shermer, "Origins of the Conservative Ascendancy: Barry Goldwater's Early Senate Career and the De-legitimization of Organized Labor," *Journal of American History* 95:3 (December 2008), 678–709; Richards, *Union-free America: Workers and Antiunion Culture*, 62–88.

47 Henry Hazlitt, "Uncurbed Union Power," *Newsweek* February 23, 1959, 84; "A Day's Work and Dollars Is Industry's Worst Irritant," *Newsweek* September 21, 1959, 102–104; "Where Employers Are Pressing the Fight Against Featherbedding," *U.S. News and World Report* July 20, 1959, 94–95; "What to Look for in a New Labor Law," *U.S. News* August 3, 1959, 82ff; E.J. Manley, "Labor Monopolies—Successors to Trusts?" *U.S. News* August 10, 1959; "A Cry from the Grass Roots for Labor Reform Law," *U.S. News* August 10, 1959, 89. On the featherbedding crisis, see Robert D. Leiter, *Featherbedding and Job Security* (1964); Porter Matteson, *Whose Feather Bed?* (Rochester, NY: Mohawk Press, 1963). On union corruption, see Donald R. Richberg, *Labor Union Monopoly* (Chicago: Regnery, 1957); John L. McClellan, *Crime Without Punishment* (New York: Duell, Sloan, and Pearce, 1962); *The Menace of Restrictive Work Practices* (Washington DC: Labor Relations and Legal Department, 1963).

48 Joseph M. McCartin, "Probing the Limits of Rights Discourse in the Obama Era: A Crossroads for Labor and Liberalism," *International Labor and Working Class History* 80:1 (September 2011), 148–160, discusses the limits of rights talk for labor.

49 Kim Phillips-Fein, "Business Conservatism on the Shop Floor: Anti-Union Campaigns in the 1950s," *Labor: Working-Class History of the Americas*, 7:2 (2010), 9–26.

50 Gilbert Gall, *The Politics of the Right to Work: The Labor Federations as Special Interests, 1943–1979* (Westport, CT: Greenwood, 1988); Elizabeth Tandy Shermer, "Counter-Organizing the Sunbelt: Right-to-Work Campaigns and Anti-Union Conservatism, 1943–1958," *Pacific Historical Review* 78:1 (2009), 81–118; idem, "Origins of Conservative Ascendancy: Barry Goldwater's Early Senate Career and the De-Legitimization of Organized Labor," *Journal of American History* 95:3 (2008), 678–709.

51 "Text of the AFL-CIO Merger Agreement," *Monthly Labor Review* 78:4 (April 1955), 428–430; Arthur J. Goldberg, *AFL-CIO: Labor United* (New York: McGraw-Hill, 1956); Zieger, *The CIO*, 357–371.

52 Kim McQuaid, *Uneasy Partners: Big Business in American Politics, 1945–1990* (Baltimore: Johns Hopkins University Press, 1994), 73–101; Naomi Baden, "Developing an Agenda: Expanding the Role of Women in Unions," *Labor Studies Journal* 10:3 (1986), 229–249; Peter B. Levy, *The New Left and Labor in the 1960s* (Urbana: University of Illinois Press, 1994), 48–53.

53 Register, *Packinghouse Daughter*.

54 Richard Oestreicher, "The Rules of the Game: Class Politics in Twentieth-Century America," in Kevin Boyle, ed., *Organized Labor and American Politics, 1894–1994: The Labor-Liberal Alliance* (Albany: SUNY Press, 1998), 19–50; Oestreicher, "Urban Working-Class Political Behavior," 1257–1286.

55 The extent of social mobility in these decades has been often asserted but measured only infrequently and with difficulty. Many of the baby boom generation, children of Depression-era parents, had greater educational opportunity than their parents but also higher barriers to employment in terms of certification and degree requirements. This mobility varied by cohort, region, race, ethnicity, and gender. Richard A. Easterlin,

Birth and Fortune: The Impact of Numbers on Personal Welfare (Chicago: University of Chicago Press, 1980), is a starting place. What we do know is that the expansion of low-cost and relatively accessible higher education in the 1960s and 1970s increased the college-educated population and without the debt-load of recent student cohorts.

56 Kessler-Harris, *Out to Work*, 300–319. For recent case studies, see Venus Green, "Race and Technology: African American Women in the Bell System, 1945–1980," *Technology and Culture* 36:2 (April 1995), 101–144; Vicki Howard, "At the Curve Exchange: Postwar Beauty Culture and Working Women at Maidenform," *Enterprise and Society* 1:3 (September 2000), 591–618; Victoria T. Grando, "A Hard Day's Work: Institutional Nursing in the Post-World War II Era," *Nursing History Review* 8 (2000), 9–184; Premilla Nadasen, *Household Workers Unite: The Untold Story of African American Women Who Built a Movement* (Boston MA: Beacon Press, 2015).

57 Vinel, *The Employee: A Political History*; Barbara Ehrenreich, *Fear of Falling: The Inner Life of the Middle Class* (New York: Harper Collins, 1990).

58 Metzgar, *Striking Steel*.

59 John P. Hoerr, *And the Wolf Finally Came: The Decline and Fall of the American Steel Industry* (Pittsburgh: University of Pittsburgh Press, 1988).

60 Marc Levinson, *The Box: How the Shipping Containers Made the World Smaller and the World Economy Bigger* (Princeton: Princeton University Press, 2008).

61 Lester Velie, *Labor U.S.A.* (New York: Harpers, 1959), 289; David Witwer, *Corruption and Reform in the Teamsters' Union* (Urbana: University of Illinois Press, 2008), 131–146.

62 Leah F. Vosko and David Scott Witwer, "'Not a Man's Union': Women Teamsters in the 1940s and 1950s," *Journal of Women's History* 13:3 (Autumn 2001), 169–192.

63 Witwer, *Corruption and Reform in the Teamsters*, 183–211; Robert F. Kennedy, *The Enemy Within: The McClellan Committee's Crusade against Jimmy Hoffa and Corrupt Labor Unions* (New York: Da Capo Press, 1994, c. 1960).

64 Robert E. Weir, *Workers in America: A Historical Encyclopedia, Vol. 2* (Santa Barbara, CA: ABC-CLIO, 2013), 761–764.

65 Shane Hamilton, *Trucking Country: The Road to America's Wal-Mart Economy* (Princeton: Princeton University Press, 2008), 99–134; Levinson, *The Box*, 135–169.

66 Ibid.; Colin Davis, *Waterfront Revolts: New York and London Dockworkers, 1946–61* (Urbana: University of Illinois Press, 2003), 141–178.

67 Levinson, *The Box*, 11, 68; Edna Bonacich and Jake B. Wilson, *Getting the Goods: Ports, Labor, and the Logistics Revolution* (Ithaca: Cornell University Press, 2000).

68 Levinson, *The Box*, 18, 24. On the ILWU and port strikes in the 1930s, see Bruce Nelson, *Workers on the Waterfront: Seamen, Longshoremen, and Unionism in the 1930s* (Urbana: University of Illinois Press, 1988), 127–155; Gerald Horne, *Red Seas: Radical Black Sailors in the United States and Jamaica* (New York: New York University Press, 2005), 35–56; David Selvin, *A Terrible Anger: The 1934 Waterfront and General Strikes in San Francisco* (Detroit: Wayne State University Press, 1996), 88–112.

69 Levinson, *The Box*, 80.

70 Arthur A. Sloane, *Hoffa* (Cambridge: Cambridge University Press, 1991), 350–410; for Teamster membership, see Nelson Lichtenstein, *The State of the Union: A Century of American Labor* (Princeton: Princeton University Press, 2002), 145; Bonacich and Wilson, *Getting the Goods*, 210.

71 Dubofsky, *State and Labor*, 217–223; Lichtenstein, *The State of the Union*, 162–166.

72 Fones-Wolf, *Selling Free Enterprise*, 257–284; R. Alton Lee, *Eisenhower and Landrum-Griffin: A Study in Labor–Management Politics* (Lexington: University Press of Kentucky, 1990), 45–73.

5

LOST OPPORTUNITIES, 1961–1981

Labor, New Social Movements, and Economic Change

In Manhattan, in 1969, hard-hatted construction workers confronted anti-war protesters in what the media widely advertised as a clash between "working men" and college kids. Skilled white working men, the construction workers wore hats decorated with the American flag, yelled obscenities, and roughed up the protesters, who were privileged, white, male, and critical of their government. The Nixon administration prided itself on winning the allegiance of white workers, even while their Democratic opposition could not muster the votes of anti-war youth. As a symbol of the conservatism and patriotic fervor of the working class, the hard-hat protests signaled that the political spectrum had shifted to the right, even while the labor movement's power to hold workers' political loyalties waned.[1]

The "hard hat riots," protests that occupied but a few days and a few hundred people, loom large in historians' accounts of increasing conservatism among American workers. A media event more than an historical turning point, such clashes had, as their underpinning, the conflict between traditional labor politics and rising social movements that were focused outside the workplace and beyond class conflict. The 1960s and 1970s witnessed the coming of age of important social movements on the Left and the Right, including the new conservatism, civil rights and black power, women's liberation, Native American and Chicano rights; and protest movements against the Vietnam War, for nuclear disarmament, environmental protection and reproductive freedom, and gay and lesbian rights. These social movements engaged issues of class inequality and social injustice that had been the concerns of a labor movement which, however, did not see them as central to its purpose. According to many observers, American politics no longer gave priority to the redistribution of income but focused instead on social equality, as shown by the rise of the black power movement and second wave feminism. They also argue that redistributive politics came to an end, in class terms, as the

New Deal coalition slowly fell apart and lost power.[2] Political debates about racial inequality, environment, and peace engaged few labor union voices. While this summary does not do justice to the complex political landscape of the time, many commentators agree that labor and class struggles had diminished importance and "identity politics" had taken their place by the end of the 1970s.

History written from this perspective ignores crucial workplace struggles in the civil rights and black power movements, working-class activism in the anti-war movement, and the revival of labor feminism in the period.[3] It also equates a small subset of working-class white men who opposed the anti-war movement, feminism, and the environmental movement with "the working class" as a whole. Like the hard-hat protesters, or "Joe the Plumber" campaigning for John McCain in the 2008 election, these voices received disproportionate media—and scholarly—attention, in large part because they gave blue collar credibility to conservative candidates. The "silent majority," as surely someone quipped, was neither silent nor a majority.[4]

During the 1960s and 1970s, ordinary women and men experienced changes in the labor force, politics, government, and the economy that had profound effects on their lives. Even as labor unions had to grapple with divisions that existed among workers in the same plant and industry, labor leaders faced difficult strategic and political choices born of the central questions of the time: How did dependence on defense production, a fact of American economic life since World War II, affect the nation's ability to withdraw from conflicts such as the war in Vietnam, sign disarmament pacts, or downsize the army? How would a declining need for defense workers affect the level of unemployment and union power? Should established seniority rights that protect workers from job loss and employer retribution outweigh the demand for equal opportunity and equal pay for minority and women workers? How should primarily white and predominantly masculine trade unions adapt to the increasing number of women of all races in the labor force? Against the perceived competition of immigrant workers, could American workers re-imagine solidarity and union organizing, or would they feel compelled to draw the line against undocumented workers and foreign trade? In a time of growing awareness of ecological crises—from toxic waste dumps and occupational hazards to oil spills, strip mining, and climate change, could employers successfully leverage jobs against demands for environmental regulation? How then should local and state governments—and labor—respond to environmental blackmail?[5]

These vexing questions arose against a backdrop of enormous economic, political, and cultural changes that troubled individual workers. So, too, did the rise of the public sector and the expansion of government, which introduced new rights and regulations into the economy and also opened the door to new opportunities for women and African American workers in local and federal government jobs. Even as the Nixon administration loosened trade restrictions and created an environment in which American workers were disadvantaged, the same workers disconnected these policies from their political affiliation and fought, instead, against "big government." Many working-class men and women believed there were good reasons to support the conservative backlash against foreign-made goods and workers who were "out of place"—"others" who were undocumented, female, and/or of a different race. At the same time, immigrant workers were not new or different in the 1960s, and government's growth was largely in the area of providing new services to ordinary people. The "doubling effect" of fear of the foreign—whether in the form of workers or in the shape of a new car, clothing, or television—diminished over time among working- and middle-class voters and consumers. Indeed, by the 1990s, big box stores—including conservative corporate giant Wal-Mart—increasingly sold foreign-made goods from Central America and Asia.[6]

Fears of the foreign, the criminal, the dangerous and the different continued to echo in American culture and in the political campaigns aimed at working- and middle-class voters. Pet food, athletic shoes, children's bikes, and cell phones made in China came to dominate in the mass market; immigrants from the Philippines, the Middle East, and Honduras challenged the boundaries of sense and solidarity. In this sense, political rhetoric in the United States—including union campaigns that targeted foreign workers and goods, government benefits, and services—deepened divisions among workers. The AFL-CIO's Cold War opposition to the labor Left in Latin America, Africa, and Asia laid the groundwork for a grassroots suspicion of foreign workers. Fear of what lay beyond our shores (or under the radar) undermined any hope for a unified labor politics.[7]

Public Employee Unionism in an Era of Social Upheaval

The intersection between social movements of the time with changes in the economy and society reshaped the labor movement in ways that were not foreseen. Trade policy, party realignment, globalization, and neoliberalism aside, the one social movement that sustained labor power in these decades was only marginally connected to civil rights and the women's movement. Instead, labor campaigns to organize and mobilize public employees occurred at the beginning of the 1960s. Two crucial Supreme Court decisions and Executive Order 10988 strengthened the political hand of labor and opened the door for the organization—and collective action—of public employees, the fastest growing sector of the labor force. Like *Brown v. Board of Education*, *Baker v. Carr* (1962), and *Reynolds v. Sims* (1964) were the result of a rights revolution that reframed questions of power and broadened our democratic vision. The landmark court decisions required states to reapportion state legislatures to more accurately reflect the population. In doing so, they recuperated much of the power lost between election campaigns and legislative agendas. The labor movement, through such figures as lawyer-activist August "Gus" Scholle, understood that labor's inability to move its political agenda—specifically in the area of public employees—was rooted in the disproportionate power of rural, less densely populated districts to set the legislative agenda and limit the extent of change. The Supreme Court required states to represent more fairly city districts, and a small avalanche of legislation beneficial to individual workers and to labor unions poured through state legislatures. There was renewed hope that public employees might gain the right to collective bargaining within the emerging liberal welfare state.[8]

The growth in the public sector made some of these changes inevitable. After World War II, as social security, veterans' benefits, college loans, and federal aid to dependent children expanded, so did the number of workers in local, state and government employment. These workers knew their rights better than most. They tended, given job requirements, to have better education and greater knowledge of government. Their lack of protection against unfair labor practices and exclusion from federally supervised union elections that had been granted under the Wagner Act did not go unchallenged. By the 1940s, the American Federation of State, County and Municipal Employees (AFSCME) had some success in organizing workers as did the Building Service Employees Union and the United Public Workers. Post-World War II teacher unions fared even better, but the threat of dismissal, permanent unemployment, fines, and jail time kept most public employees from violating laws that prohibited them from striking. State laws that suppressed public worker activism and strikes now became the focus of union demands for repeal.[9]

At the state level, New York and Wisconsin led the way. Then, in 1962, President John F. Kennedy issued Executive Order 10988 (Employee Management Cooperation in the Federal Service) that allowed federal public employees to form unions and to collectively bargain on wages and working conditions. The order signaled a new era in public sector labor relations. Individual states passed acts such as Michigan's Public Employee Relations Act (1965), which overrode laws that prohibited public employees' unions and barred public employees from striking. While the laws imposed stiff fines and penalties on public workers who went out on strike, the symbolic opening of the public realm encouraged unions to organize public employees. It expanded opportunities for workers to protest and strike. Across the nation, following rapid growth in public sector unions, especially in teaching and urban transport, led the way to intense strikes and protests, such as the Memphis Sanitation Workers strike in 1968, teachers' strikes, and the national postal strike of 1970.[10]

A major consequence of an expanded public sector and the unionization of government employees was that more minority men and women of all races became unionized public employees. That meant that the wages and benefits of the most disadvantaged segments of the labor force gradually increased. Working women on average saw an increase in their wages, job security, and benefits; so, too, did minority working men and women. The black middle class expanded and had increased political presence, as did women of all races, especially in the Democratic party. The Democratic party had supported the expansion of education and the welfare state, and of the public work force. Democratic party officeholders generally supported the labor movement and the unionization of public employees, and Democratic presidents and congresses supported affirmative action. These changes affected the labor movement on a broad scale, slowly increasing the representation of women and minority men in leadership and among union members. Public sector unionization became the engine of social and political equality through the involvement of public employees in the labor movement's fastest growing unions—the SEIU, AFSCME, and the American Federation of Teachers. By the late 1970s, the growth of these unions outpaced and overshadowed all other unions, except the Teamsters.

Changes Beyond the Public Sector

The history of labor in the 1970s underlines how the labor movement has been forced to adjust to and integrate new challenges in the economy, from the introduction of the first power spinning machines and looms to the new digital age. It is no accident that the word "Luddite," a term that referenced technological resistance and machine-breaking in the eighteenth century, has been applied to labor unions and their leaders. The introduction of new technology often has displaced workers, whether it was the steam drill slashing the need for labor in the mines or new conveyer belts reducing the need for workers to manually shift cattle and hog carcasses or lift automobile engines. There was, however, no single moment of technological transformation. Rather, cohorts of workers had to address the introduction of new machines over time, as business owners and managers sought to drive down the costs of labor.[11]

The last decades of the twentieth century saw fundamental shifts in where labor was located, how work was organized, and what adaptations were required; and these changed the environment of unionism. In automobile manufacture, these changes, combined with increased energy costs, led to fundamental restructuring of the industry. U.S. automakers General Motors, Chrysler, and Ford relocated the production of certain parts and models to right-to-work states and the borderland Maquilladoras region. Japanese automakers Toyota and Honda built new plants in Indiana and Ohio, and non-union states in the South. In the electronics industry, the manufacture of televisions and electrical parts were similarly dispersed, even as Japanese firms began to dominate the market for radios, televisions, and stereo components. In steel, while U.S. industry remained entrenched in older plants and resisted updating their technology, Japanese steel slowly took over the market. In each industry and community where deindustrialization took place, there were massive job losses. In Detroit, where the American automobile industry maintained its headquarters, over 100,000 regional production jobs were lost.[12]

In the 1960s and 1970s, these changes were attributed to one word: computers. Computer-guided machines performed new tasks (robotics that reduced production work), and calculators supplanted manual methods of computation, from double-entry book-keeping ledgers to adding machines. Information storage, once bound in ledgers or organized in files, was slowly transferred to magnetic tape, computer disks, and other electronic media. Over time, these changes reduced the need for clerical workers, including file clerks, typists, and bookkeeping accountants, even while temporarily increasing the need for software engineers and consultants. The field of telecommunications gradually saw the introduction of remote switches, phone machines, and phone banks; later firms created domestic and off-shore call centers, some with robo-calling capacity, which drastically reduced the need for telephone workers and on-site secretaries. Down the line, the expansion of computing through the Internet decreased the need for retail clerks, librarians, receptionists, and even delivery persons and drivers, since on-demand services had less need for on-call workers. Automation, and computerization, thus affected the labor force in ways that increasingly intensified the work load and working hours of employees while at the same time reducing employment needs and opportunities. It eventually meant the migration of clerical—and even technological jobs—to off-shore and foreign facilities.[13]

These new technologies had repercussions for workers and the working environment beyond the level of employment. In Silicon Valley and in the Maquilladoras region, the new electronics industry that took off in the 1970s caused a shift in the labor force with the recruiting of younger women as factory operatives. It also brought into the lives of workers, their families, and their communities new environmental hazards. The soldering of circuit boards, their etching with chemicals, and the resulting exposure caused escalating worker injuries and illnesses with long-term effects on workers' health. The use of silicon and plastics in automobile manufacture and the continual exposure to heat, airborne dust, and metal particles underwrote higher rates of occupational cancer for workers in foundries and on the assembly line. Chemicals used in manufacturing new cars presented their own hazards, as chemically treated wood, paint fumes, and silicon dust permeated the air of paint shops and metal forges, eroding the health of workers in the new robotic age. The introduction of computer-aided machine production did not fundamentally alter the workplace environment but also did not moderate the toxic impact of chemicals on workers' bodies.[14]

Despite these technological advances, much labor remained manual and personal. In the service, agriculture, and extractive industries, working men and women continued to lift, move, wash, serve, pick, and shovel. In secondary manufacturing, workers in garment and light manufacture and food processing completed much of their work in machine-aided production. To fill the gaping need for physical labor, employers primarily sought out the cheapest workers. The 1960s and 1970s witnessed the culmination of labor migration that had begun earlier in the century, as African American and white workers from the South became a permanent part of the Northern labor force by the 1960s; but others soon joined them. Puerto Rican migrants and Cuban and Dominican refugees, Asian migrants from the

Philippines and, later, Vietnam and Cambodia, came to the United States in these prosperous decades. A growing number of these workers were women employed in service work. This diverse labor force created challenges for labor unions that went beyond the physical presence of new workers to the central question of what the labor movement ought to be—an organization dependent upon and catering to its current members to whom it provides service and advocacy, or a social movement with goals of recruiting new members and addressing their needs in a changing political and economic environment.[15]

The Lost Civil Rights Legacy and the Labor Movement

As historians Robert Korstad and Nelson Lichtenstein have argued, the labor movement had led the country in fighting for the political and economic rights of African American and other minority workers at critical times in its past. Powerful municipal unions such as 1199 and District 65 displayed an interracial solidarity that both embraced racial equality and represented how labor and racial struggles were intertwined. But with the conservative backlash, the labor movement began to lose that edge by the mid-1950s. Anti-communist campaigns, especially in the South, targeted unions as well as political radicals and the NAACP. The emerging civil rights movement, while it allied with national labor leaders in its broader politics, gradually decentered its labor agenda. Historian William Jones argues that it was only after King's assassination that the role of the Negro American Labor Council and other groups were slowly displaced from their role in the civil rights movement and its memory.[16]

Still, for every national affirmation of racial equality and labor solidarity—Martin Luther King in the Memphis Sanitation Workers strike or UAW president Walter Reuther walking with Cesar Chavez in the fields, there were local setbacks, contexts in which broad-based class solidarity foundered on union competition or worker prejudice. In Alabama, the UAW supported a segregated local, when it competed with the Machinists over membership. In union bargaining, gender and racial equity fell victim to seniority rules and geographic separation. The growth of dissident groups among labor's disenfranchised minority workers cost the labor movement time, political influence, and organizational momentum in these crucial decades. By the end of the 1970s, such groups as Teamsters for a Democratic Union (TDU), Miners for Democracy (MFD), and the Dodge Revolutionary Union Movement (DRUM) challenged labor leaders to bargain more aggressively and to make the labor movement more inclusive.[17]

The answer to labor's shortcomings was to reach out to minority workers and recruit new members. After decades of failed organizing, the United Farm Workers, under the leadership of Cesar Chavez and Dolores Huerta, signaled new forms of labor activism that combined civil rights work with community organizing and environmental activism. While more conventional labor leaders confined their attention to mass production industry, Chavez, Huerta, and others like them recruited migrant workers in the field and in the community. Nationally, they created broad social support through the Delano grape and lettuce boycotts and joined efforts to redress not simply work-related grievances but also the needs of the community. Later organizations like Justice for Janitors drew upon the merging of advocacy for undocumented and unprotected workers with labor organizing. In their buoyant organizing campaigns, there was less attention to the formalities of membership, maintenance of dues, and benefits; rather, diverging from bread-and-butter issues to address the needs of the community led to victories in a new field for labor.[18]

At the same time, while the Brotherhood of Sleeping Car Porters had assumed a major role in the civil rights movement of the 1950s and 1960s, more radical groups, such as the Dodge Revolutionary Union Movement (DRUM) and the League of Revolutionary Black Workers (LRBW), confronted national labor leaders on racial inequality and conflict. Drawing on models of black power, DRUM and LRBW forged important alliances within the black community but also with other networks of auto workers, hospital workers, newspaper workers and others; these networks spread far beyond Detroit.[19] Dissidents in the UAW laid the groundwork for widespread wildcat strikes in the 1970s, in Detroit and Lordstown and other automobile plants in the Midwest. Dissident autoworkers blamed labor's weakness on concessionary bargaining that disadvantaged new workers and made current workers vulnerable to successive wage and work force cuts. Challenging UAW leadership in New Directions,[20] they took on the troubled issues of occupational injuries and deaths related to the intensified pace of work in manufacturing. The computers that replaced workers had few safeguards against human endangerment. Producing cars at higher speeds increased productivity but also rates of worker injury and death. Workplace violence reached new heights, as angry workers confronted an unforgiving pace of work, intrusive supervision, and the powderkeg of fatigue and stress on the shop floor.[21]

Characterized as "American Petrograd," Detroit became the epicenter of worker discontent in the region. Black workers joined left-wing white workers in protests that demanded fundamental changes in auto factories and in union governance. African Americans who could find auto work, and their counterparts among Latino and Arab American communities, found significant barriers to promotion into higher skilled and better paid jobs. They continued to be employed in the most dangerous and unhealthy areas of auto plants, more often in foundries and parts factories than in the higher paid assembly plants. While some union locals, such as Ford Rouge Plant Local 600, embraced an agenda of political and economic equality, other UAW locals continued to see black militant unionists as part of the problem and opposed changing seniority rules, following affirmative action guidelines, or accepting black leadership. The CIO of the 1930s had been a leader in demands for racial equality. By the 1960s, its legacy locals had a more conflicted history.[22]

The failure here, while rooted in widely accepted beliefs about race and a history of conflict, was that labor leaders did not return to their CIO roots. By the 1970s, despite layoffs in the automobile industry, production continued to occupy significant territory in the vast landscape of American manufacturing. Unions such as the UAW, however, did little toward addressing racial and gender inequality as a way to forge a more powerful labor coalition. Instead, the labor movement, already faced with declines in domestic manufacturing and political opposition, resisted the imposition of any new standards for racial and gender equality, especially in the arena of seniority rights, hiring, and promotion. Their opposition strengthened as manufacturing employment continued to shrink, along with the absolute number of union jobs and union members.[23] As the economy and labor force changed, and minority and women workers comprised an increasing share of the labor force, unions not only were ill-equipped to organize them but assertively insisted that seniority rights overturned new rules about hiring, promotion, and pay. It would take two more decades before the labor movement began to understand the importance of "marginal" minority and women workers to the future of labor organizing.

It was the new generation of workers—the baby boom generation, shaped not so much by economic depression and world war as by the New Left and the counter culture—who began to break through these barriers. Suspicion of labor leaders, resistance to bureaucratic unionism, and reaction to the corruption of some unions and the lack of democratic process in others fueled internal struggles and demands for labor reform. The rank-and-file rebellions of the 1970s were not directed solely against employers but launched against what many workers saw as an unresponsive, undemocratic, and even corrupt union establishment that largely ignored younger workers. The baby boom generation, including those who "colonized" the factory floor and sought to stir working-class discontent, did not want their father's labor movement. Rather, they sought to forge their own way.[24]

The centers of labor activism in the 1970s were located far from Pengally Hall, where the workers of Flint gathered to form the UAW-CIO. Instead, labor activism was found in the fields and vineyards of California, in mill towns and coal towns in North Carolina and West Virginia, along interstate highways and at truck stops, at Love Canal and in the timberlands of Oregon, and in the cafeterias and bowling alleys of working-class communities. Workers' self-activity, central to the triumph of labor in the 1930s, now re-emerged as a generation of union dissenters, labor feminists, civil rights activists, and environmental advocates, faced an economy where wages were slowly stagnating, work environments were threatened with new hazards, and the ground was slowly shifting from mass production manufacturing to a service and information economy. The workers that labor unions tried to recruit were more racially diverse and politically divided, and younger, than at any time since the 1920s.[25] But the older genera-tion of labor leaders, who had set labor's priorities since the 1950s, now lacked both the vision and the desire to organize the young workers who wanted to join the movement.

Dissident Unionism

The UAW was not the only union experiencing new resistance on the shop floor and in the meeting hall. From the long mining strike of 1977–1978, which lasted 110 days, and the emergence of Teamsters for a Democratic Union to the feminist activism of flight attendants and protests on Secretaries' Day, young union dissidents sought to reform or topple the "New Men of Power," as sociologist C. Wright Mills called them. There were, as had been observed in the 1950s, many sources of worker—and especially young worker—discontent. First, as anti-union forces in the 1960s had noted, there were signs of corruption and, perhaps more importantly, disconnection in national unions. Not only did this affect the IBT, whose leader, Jimmy Hoffa, had been indicted for misuse of funds, malfeasance, and influence peddling, but also local construction, garment unions, and small manufacturing concerns strong-armed by protection rackets. By the mid-1970s, independent truckers turned against the Teamsters, and embraced deregulation and anti-government policies as a remedy.[26] The "corruption" of which AFL-CIO unions such as the UAW and the UMW were most often charged was in the realm of close—and inappropriate—relationships with industry, contracts that undersold workers' demands and allowed for management to escape, unscathed, from safety violations, increased workloads, and production speed-ups. Sweetheart deals between Hoffa and the operators of transit lines, or Tony Boyle, head of the UMW, and mine operators, particularly when they followed mine disasters, fueled worker resentment, especially among the young.[27]

The concessionary bargaining of labor leaders in the 1970s had its origins in the challenges many international companies faced during the energy crisis and the subsequent stagnation in the American economy. Manufacturing companies viewed foreign competition for markets as an incentive to look abroad not only for markets but for a new production base. In Mexico, China, Taiwan, the Philippines, Thailand, Honduras, and Guatemala, there were fewer constraints on management, lower wages, and, for the most part, no unions that intervened. However much these considerations weighed into collective bargaining, union leaders and negotiators accepted cuts in wages, work force, and a faster work pace, often in the face of rank and file opposition, as the price of global competition. After Taft-Hartley, collective bargaining and striking had been curtailed and the employer's "right to manage" took precedence over waning calls for shop floor democracy. The labor movement's political allies, moreover, made no headway on a labor law reform bill to restore labor's freedom of action. Nonetheless, the failure of the labor movement to more broadly address income inequality, racial discrimination, and worker health was among the principal causes for one of the strongest and longest-lasting strike waves in United States history, exceeded only by the postwar strikes of 1946 and 1959.

At the height of the 1970 strike wave, more than 66 million work days were lost due to work actions. UPS drivers went out on strike. So, too, did long-shoremen, in the longest waterfront strike in U.S. history. A half million truckers engaged in a wildcat strike in 1970 that lasted 123 days; coal strikes in 1974–1975 numbered 9,000, the overwhelming majority wildcat strikes, conducted without union authorization. In 1970, a national postal strike called out more than 200,000 postal workers. General Motors endured one of its longest strikes, as its Lordstown plant went out, joined by others. There were strikes among teachers, nurses, and other public employees. Many of the workplace actions were wildcats, strikes taken against contract obligations and in the face of labor leaders' opposition.[28]

In bituminous coal, miners, who had only recently won a favorable contract in 1974, went on strike in the winter of 1977. The 110-day strike marked a turning point for the mine unions. Despite great progress under the New Deal, mine jobs were in decline and the UMW weakened. The past decade already had done some damage. In 1969, the UMW had been rocked by the assassination of Joseph "Jock" Yablonski, who was challenging union leader Tony Boyle for the presidency. Boyle was implicated in the murder, and the democratic forces in the union appeared to be on the upswing. In mining communities, women and disabled miners had begun organizing around black lung disease and pressing for compensation and relief.[29] Local struggles such as the Brookside strike in 1973, against Eastover Coal and the Duke Power Company in Harlan County, Kentucky, had periodically disrupted the industry.[30]

Miners for Democracy had brought them a new leader in Arnold Miller, but Miller's combination of both autocratic decision-making (long a UMW tradition) and his eroding support among local affiliates weakened both the union and Miller. In 1977, with the oil crisis momentarily settled, and national coal consumption declining, the prospects for strike success were slim. The largest customers of union mines—utility companies and steel mills—laid in a large supply of coal prior to the strike. The UMW membership among coal miners also was in decline, from 67 percent union in 1974 to only 50 percent, a 17 percent drop in only four years. After months of negotiating, UMW locals rejected initial contract offers, which prompted President Jimmy Carter to seek an injunction against the strike. While the injunction was only a temporary measure, it seemed to have worked. By the end of March, the miners agreed on a contract that gave them immediate wage gains but also stripped away the right to strike over local issues and cost them health care and pension benefits.

In Lordstown, Ohio, the Chevrolet Vega plant was the site of a major strike in 1972, when the factory's 7,000 workers went out on a twenty-two-day strike. Costing General Motors $150 million, the Lordstown wildcat had been directed at plant management that had driven up the pace of work and a UAW leadership that seemed to care more about concessions than worker health, safety, and sanity. It was a disproportionately young work force that went out on strike, one where seniority rights, pension plans, and health care benefits were of less importance than treatment on the shop floor. The generational gap, noted between college kids and their parents, arose in the conflict among different generations of workers engaged in the same production work. Some of this difference was attributable to local conditions—Plant management, shift managers, did differ in how they approached and treated workers. There were, however, significant conflicts among unionists on issues of union democracy, work pace and compensation, and cultural differences in music, alcohol consumption, and work discipline. The Lordstown wildcat brought these differences to the surface at the same time as the strike created opportunities for the labor movement to respond to the changing workplace conditions.[31]

Ken Pfaff of the Teamsters, Jock Yablonsky, Arnold Miller, and, later, Rich Trumka of the United Mine Workers, Andy Stern and Anna Burger of the Service Employees International Union, John Wilhelm of the Hotel and Restaurant Employees, Bruce Raynor of UNITE-HERE, and Larry Cohen of the Communications Workers of America came of age in a labor movement ripe for reform. This cohort of labor organizers drew upon community-organizing experience gained from the New Left and capitalized on new opportunities to lead, even as the original CIO leaders approached retirement age. The neglected demands for equality among minority and women workers and the unmet needs of public service and clerical workers made new organizations and leaders both necessary and possible. Already, in unions such as the UAW, black trade unionists had demanded the union begin to break down racial barriers to hiring and promotion and grant greater access to higher paid and better skilled work. Women trade unionists were among the founders of the National Organization for Women, working with former labor journalist Betty Friedan. Now, these same women, in coalition with women labor lawyers, fought for equal pay legislation and filed employment discrimination suits based on Title VII of the Civil Rights Act. Inspired by women's liberation, Karen Nussbaum and other Boston-area feminists founded 9 to 5 to address the needs of unorganized women clericals.[32]

This activism faced concrete opposition not only from employers but from labor leaders. Under the banner of seniority rights, labor leaders challenged the application of equal opportunity to the unionized workplace. The majority of unions remained stubbornly resistant to electing or appointing minority workers and women leaders and assigned low priority to race- and gender-specific demands. Resistance to these demands began in union headquarters, where the generation of labor leaders who had come of age in the Great Depression held on to traditional attitudes about race and gender. While male union leaders worked with individual women and minority workers, many of those same leaders saw civil rights and feminist demands as undermining labor unity and cohesion, among them such stalwarts as Walter Reuther and Emil Mazey. The bulwark of labor's rights in the workplace, after all, had been in seniority as a form of employment security. As union leaders understood it, the last hired should be the first fired. It was at least one way to prevent discrimination against or retribution toward union workers. Just as unions had fought against veterans' preference in employment after World War II in a bid for "super-seniority" for fighting men, so too did unions view the demands of the Equal Pay Act and the Civil Rights Act as threatening hard-won union rights.[33]

For the skilled trades, there was entrenched opposition to minority hiring, rooted in craft traditions that went back to the nineteenth century in the practice of training and hiring trade apprentices from within a closed working-class community. Carpenters, pipefitters, electricians, carpenters, bricklayers, and stonemasons often had families in the trade. Fathers, brothers, sons, nephews, male cousins— craft fraternities often shared more than the language of kinship but actual family ties. As we saw among railroad workers, the skilled trades had racial/ethnic and gender codes that associated manly work and masculine skill with trade and trade union identities. This pattern went beyond the trades to oil drillers and steel workers but also to those most celebrated of fraternities— police, firefighters, and even, though not unionized, military men. White working-class masculinity in the 1970s claimed for itself strength, power, virtue, and rights forged in the line of fire and on the firing line.[34]

For both minority men and for women workers of all races, the barriers to entry existed in nearly all sectors of the labor force where white men predominated. During World War II, there had been hate-strikes against the employment of black workers and women. Minority men met with hostility, violence, or isolation; women faced sexual harassment and name-calling ("dollies" was not a compliment). By the 1970s, after more than a decade of civil rights activism, one might have predicted a less hostile response. And yet, women electricians were sent to do dangerous work with little or no training, egged on and often harassed by male co-workers who saw them as threats to their own—and their sons'—livelihood. The hazing—call it "initiation ritual"—that often accompanied entry into the trade or acceptance in the ranks of journeymen and master craftsmen—was visited upon women and minority male workers with a particular vengeance. These rituals were made all the more difficult by the fact it was harder to be prepared for them—women in the trades were fortunate if they could find one male mentor once they became apprentices; often they did not. Minority men and women who took on a new trade similarly were in need of patronage—and mentoring. Unlike new groups seeking entry, young white men who became apprentices in carpentry, electrical work, or pipe-fitting often grew up hearing, or specifically had been taught, trade secrets. Not unlike the women printers at the turn of the century, women and minorities who aspired to being skilled workers often had to "steal the trade."[35] For mainstream industrial unions, the challenges were far less about direct apprenticeship and hiring than they were about national union policies that sidelined issues of equity and equality in favor of contract maintenance and bargaining power.

Challenging the unions not only on grounds of workplace equality but also in terms of organizing and bargaining were workers of the baby boom generation, young in age but also familiar with forms of resistance unimagined in the heyday of the 1930s. Some of these workers were from black inner-city neighborhoods, where the issues of race and class merged with demands for better garbage removal and improved welfare benefits; some also had been part of the civil rights and student movements, organized anti-war protests during the Vietnam era, and worked in anti-poverty projects. Others took up the charge within their own home regions, enlisting in the effort to organize textile factories in the right-to-work South or fighting for black lung or brown lung compensation for poor and beleaguered miners and textile workers. They came to translate their political experience into working-class terms, finding in labor organizing an alternative to the slowly disappearing student Left.[36]

While unions like the United Auto Workers advanced the careers of a few women and minority leaders, they neglected the structural obstacles to greater workplace equality, preferring to leave in place department seniority, rather than plant seniority, sex segregated job postings, and the racial exclusion of specific occupational categories. Indeed, there was little or no internal pressure for white-only unions of skilled workers such as electricians, plumbers, and carpenters to take on minority apprentices or to assist minority workers in challenging civil service rankings and procedures. For such unions, worker solidarity meant that the workplace remained stratified by race, gender, ethnicity, and skill in ways that replicated societal inequality and left the structure unchanged. With the rise of new social movements, union resistance increasingly formed the basis of worker grievances and worker alienation.

The Other Labor Movement: Women and Labor in the 1970s and 1980s

The women's movement of the 1960s and 1970s had an influence on the labor movement that was equal to that of civil rights and the New Left. While there had been a long history of women in unions, working women were ignored as a target for organization, excluded from all but token leadership, and underpaid and unrecognized in labor unions as a whole. Stereotypes about women workers— that they worked for "pin money" or only worked until married—were challenged by the reality of a female labor force that was older, married, and more often than not carried parental responsibilities. Women, even those with children younger than five years old, were a growing segment of the labor market in the 1970s.[37]

By 1970, the majority of adult women had joined the labor force, whether in part-time or full time employment. The vast majority of women workers, however, were employed in jobs that were about 90 percent female—from retail sales of clothing, toys, and perfume to lower level food service (in family restaurants, truck stops, and fast food places), to the traditionally female professions of nursing, social work, and teaching. Cast in the manufacturing mold, coupled with a masculine labor union culture, unions before 1930 had little use for women as members, except to stave off non-union competition. In the decades between the Great Depression and the 1970s, women made inroads, becoming leaders in the nooks and crannies of the labor movement. In the 1940s in particular, both as a consequence of World War II but also in response to new institutional needs, women were visible as local and state leaders and as experts, especially in the fields of labor education, community relations, and labor economics.[38] As women workers began to constitute a growing proportion of the labor force, they presented an opportunity to the labor movement in the 1970s. Saleswomen, female waiters, flight attendants, nurses and hospital workers, and government clerks were the fastest growing sector of the labor force and the one area where the new energy of public sector unionism and social movement politics opened the door for new organization.

A central union in this transition was the United Auto Workers. The UAW, like many CIO unions, had a masculine union culture. The iconography of UAW workers played off the image of labor as a strutting, muscular, energetic man, fully capable of busting the heads of company guards and of dangling the top-hatted capitalist over the economic abyss.[39] In day-to-day terms, this language and imagery had little overt effect and, what is more, tended to reflect the reality of an auto industry not only dominated by white men in corporate leadership but also on the production line. Still, like other CIO unions, the UAW recognized female equality, the right to equal pay for women, and the necessity of incorporating women—as workers and as wives—into labor's political and community work. Not surprisingly, women existed in the upper echelons of the UAW, heading the women's department, community outreach, education, and even participating in the Executive Board, albeit one at a time. Women constituted in various sectors of automobile manufacturing as much as 40 percent of the work force, and they comprised a majority of union poll workers on election day.[40]

For the UAW, this tradition of female leadership can be dated back to the central role of the Women's Emergency Brigade in the Flint sit-down strike and other early sit-down strikes, a role now widely celebrated. A less public reason had to do with the recruitment of dynamic women leaders in the late years of the Depression and during and after World War II. Mildred Jeffrey, a social worker, had worked as an Amalgamated Clothing Worker organizer and labor educator in the 1930s. Jeffrey became the first director of the UAW Women's Bureau in 1944 and fostered women's participation in the union. In the crucial years of World War II, Jeffrey recognized the need for women to have access to child care and to be paid equally. In a similar fashion other women in the UAW, Olga Madar, Caroline Davies, and Lillian Hatcher contributed to the union in multiple ways—as advocates for racial equality, community participation, labor education, and political work. In each realm, they established themselves as champions of gender equality, both as working women themselves and as leaders within the union.[41]

The UAW had, prior to the 1970s, the same stance as other unions on the issue of the Equal Rights Amendment. Labor leaders, male and female, had long preferred state-level protective labor laws as a means for bettering women's condition. Limiting women's working hours, setting a female minimum wage, and barring women from certain dangerous—or potentially more immoral— occupations, such as miner or bartender guaranteed working women protections that they could not otherwise obtain. These laws had, for many women in female-dominated jobs, some basic rationale. A minimum wage for women protected them in jobs where the federal minimum wage did not. Moreover, the lack of other protections—health insurance, for example—seemed to require other state laws to prohibit the employment of women. For women unionists, the demand for equal rights at work threatened to undermine those same protections. Indeed, after woman suffrage was granted, the Supreme Court had invalidated a state minimum wage rate for women (*Adkins v. Children's Hospital*) on the presumption that the right to vote had lessened or eliminated women's disadvantages in wage demands. While the labor movement was not unified in opposing such sex-specific laws, many women labor leaders saw the Equal Rights Amendment as a means for undermining women's remaining protections. Up until 1970, despite their rejection of women's labor laws at the 1957 convention, the UAW generally sided with the opponents of the ERA.[42]

The difference may have well been in the inroads women made in the labor force. Taking on what had previously been male or predominantly male jobs, working women who belonged to the National Organization for Women, the Women's Equity Action League, and other feminist organizations demanded workplace equality. While some unions, including the Hotel and Restaurant Workers, which had many female-segregated locals, continued to oppose the ERA, the UAW, led by Millie Jeffrey and backed by the Michigan Democratic party caucus, threw its weight behind the ERA struggle nation-wide. At the 1970 convention, women delegates led the way for the union of Walter Reuther to support the ERA. Further, they challenged sex-specific bars to women's employment, including the fetal protection policies that preceded the *Johnson Controls* decision (1999), and pursued sex discrimination suits under Title VII of the Civil Rights Act of 1964.[43]

Further, it was UAW women who helped to organize and establish the Coalition of Labor Union Women (CLUW). In June of 1973, Olga Madar, the first woman president of the UAW, and Addie Wyatt of the United Food and Commercial Workers, another member of the 1940s cohort of women unionists, sought to establish a new organization to focus on working women's need for a voice in the labor movement. The following spring, over 3,000 women unionists from 58 unions met in Chicago to create CLUW. Their primary goal was to advocate for women's equality in the labor movement, from increasing women's membership to their election to union offices, pay and promotion in union work and in the workplace, support for affirmative action, and other legislation to improve working women's lives and their visibility in the labor movement.[44]

The resistance—or disinterest—of the mainstream labor movement to the participation of women workers—especially in women's occupations—led many feminists to seek alternate ways to address working women's needs. One such organization was Boston Working Women, also known as 9 to 5, an organization for women clericals headed by Karen Nussbaum. As women workers, they had less access or allegiance to broad-based women's organizations like the National Organization for Women or its local counterparts. Many women workers did, however, pay attention to legal suits and political campaigns for equal pay for equal work, equal opportunity, and comparable worth. More than that, the aspects of working in a woman's occupation, including sexual harassment and discrimination in hiring, promotion, and pay, played out in every woman's paycheck and in the workplace, often on a daily basis. How to transform the growing discontent among women workers, and to reconcile feminist activism with workplace action, was the brainchild of Karen Nussbaum, the child of a teacher and middle-class professional. She was working as a clerical worker at the time. Bringing together women clerical workers, at first in a women's organization, but later in SEIU's Local 925, to challenge female subordination, status, and opportunity in the workplace was Nussbaum's special brief. Issues such as technological unemployment, office computers, workplace injuries such as carpal tunnel and vision problems related to VDTs, and sexual harassment expanded the traditional union agenda and became the backbone of organizing campaigns in offices and on university and college campuses across the nation.[45]

The successful efforts to organize clerical workers in higher education were one result.[46] At Yale, Harvard, Columbia, the University of Minnesota, and Illinois, successful organizing led to some of the most innovative and effective labor union campaigns in recent decades. At Harvard, 3,700 clerical, service, and technical workers were organized under the auspices of an independent union led by Kris Rondeau. Eighty percent of the clericals at Harvard were women. By comparison, at the University of Minnesota 93 percent of clericals were women; at the University of Illinois there were similar percentages. Rondeau, the head of the campaign, began to organize the campus with the aid of seven other former organizers for UAW after a failed campaign. Using a one-on-one organizing method (with very little reliance on union literature), they managed to bring together the staff from diverse occupations and locations into a strong community-based union, employing cultural and political techniques, to recruit. The key issue in the campaign was not the $19,000 a year average salary, but child care availability and cost, health benefits, insurance, and pensions.[47]

Harvard's president, Derek C. Bok, was an eminent labor scholar; but despite already existing agreements with blue collar unions at the university, Bok resisted recognizing or negotiating with the Harvard Union of Clerical and Technical Workers. His opposition fueled an intensive anti-union campaign on campus, which argued that the new clerical union was a "disruptive force." Despite the alumni's negative reaction to Bok's anti-union tactics, the university went to court to enlarge the bargaining unit and pursued other legal tools to oppose the unionization campaign.[48]

As AFSCME head Gerald McEntee said, "As goes Harvard, so goes the unorganized white-collar sector of the economy." The campaign encountered many of the obstacles that clerical and white collar unions have in the past century— alienation from and hostility to unions, the difficulties of organizing women workers, who often carried a double burden of family and wage work, the professional or paraprofessional nature of the jobs and occupational identification, and the insensitivity, hostility and competition of established labor unions. But, as in other successful white collar campaigns, the union won out by employing innovative techniques and focusing on non-traditional issues.[49] In a hotly contested election, the union won. After defeating a court challenge, they were able to begin negotiations.[50]

In the Harvard campaign, assumptions about labor's goals, strategies, and constituencies were stripped away. Its lessons went beyond speculating whether public representation of labor, as well as of gender, impeded the organization of working men or women. In an interview, Kris Rondeau and Gladys McKenzie of AFSCME argued forcefully for the need to tailor unionism to the workers on a community basis, through person-to-person connections and with an emphasis less on issues than on what the workers wanted the union to be. As McKenzie said, "In our model, the goal is to build a community, not win an election." At Harvard, Minnesota, and other universities, the clerical and technical labor force was and remains predominantly female, which has meant that the community model was no longer a choice but a necessity and pointed the way to a revitalized labor movement through connections with other social movements and new constituencies.[51]

Women flight attendants present another example of how women belonged to and still were marginalized within unions. Although the first union of flight attendants was organized independently, by 1946, it had affiliated with the male-dominated Air Line Pilots Association (ALPA). From the beginning of commercial air travel, women had worked on airplanes serving food, protecting passengers, and guaranteeing smooth flights. They faced occupational barriers such as age limits for service, expectations of body weight and appearance, and rituals of care that relied on female subordination. The women's movement of the 1970s began to change the job, as women challenged age and body type limitations and more men were employed on airline carriers. In their relationship with the pilots union, it had been clear that women flight attendants' concerns and demands had little influence. It was, in the end, not through union action but in filing lawsuits for other protections (against discrimination and sexual harassment and for better pay and treatment) that flight attendants began to see substantive change. The labor movement was increasingly less relevant than the women's movement to women in the airline industry, because mainstream labor unions did not give their demands or needs priority.[52]

In a similar way, the labor movement's passive stance toward women's equality showed in both local and national struggles over women's working conditions, promotions, and pay. In the town of Willmar, Minnesota, eight women bank tellers went on strike at the Citizens' National Bank in December 1977. After bank management refused to consider them for promotion and pay adjustments, the women decided to strike. For these women, there was no union solution. Despite national union support, they did not fit within the rules of the National Labor Relations Act, which found the bank guilty of unfair labor practices but ruled that they were not the cause of the strike. The obvious discrimination against women tellers in pay and promotion also did not fit the narrow rules of the Equal Employment Opportunity Commission (EEOC). After nearly two years, the women were defeated. One returned to work for the bank at a lower rank and pay. The youngest teller, Glennis Ter Wischa, joined the ranks of organized labor as an organizer for AFSCME. The rest of the women remained in Willmar, despite the lack of community support.[53]

Most women's work lives resemble more those of the Willmar 8 than of women who are able, through their union membership, to command a decent wage and benefits. Women face sex discrimination in hiring, promotion, and pay. Some are subjected to personal harassment, and many believe they have few, if any options, if they want to retain their jobs. Women's lack of power in the workplace, however, is not solely based on their gender. Clearly, minority men and women workers, immigrant and undocumented workers, and youth and senior citizens (male and female) encounter discrimination, poor pay, and working conditions that include environmental hazards and personal abuse and bullying. Women in the home health care sector, to use one example, until recently had faced barriers to union organization in that they often worked alone, in private homes, and competed for jobs with other vulnerable workers. They have few public advocates. As with many service jobs, home health care is viewed as employment for the unskilled, for workers who have neither educational nor personal resources. Their primary work is categorized as menial labor and does not, from that perspective, require a high level of skills. Yet, home health care workers use in their work the "habits of the heart"—the affective labor and emotional intelligence that undergirds the wider service economy and which describes most women's work experience. Like the professions of teaching, nursing, and even retail sales, service work demands that women be present in their work in ways that are not seen in any other sector.[54] Unions become, for the women workers who have access to their benefits, one way in which to address the inequities of the service workplace.

Structural Changes: Defense and the Energy Crisis

At the end of the 1970s, the defense sector in manufacturing was threatened by changes in U.S. foreign policy, in particular the shifting of Cold War priorities and the spread of smaller scale conflicts. Even during the Vietnam conflict, U.S. armed forces slowly moved away from employing land armies into military strategies more dependent on missiles, aircraft, and electronics than on personnel. This shift affected the number of production workers hired and the number of military personnel that needed to be supplied. Defense plants like the one in Warren, Michigan, no longer had contracts requiring a full production crew.[55] Reductions in defense expenditures contributed to the decline in unionized manufacturing jobs as a whole.

Since the end of the Second World War, defense manufacturing had provided a bastion against recurrent depression. Millions of well-paid and unionized production workers were employed in auto and electrical plants that were engaged in defense production. Throughout the 1950s and 1960s, minor recessions were resolved in part through expanded defense production in weapons, vehicles, fighter jets and bombers, ammunition, and in atomic energy and chemicals. For workers in manufacturing, Cold War politics underwrote high levels of employment and decent wages. After the United States withdrew from Vietnam, defense needs declined, reaching a low point in 1976. Despite sustained investment in domestic military bases, military presence abroad, and sporadic foreign intervention, defense expenditures for goods and services fell to $180 billion and dropped to little more than 5 percent of the gross national product.[56] This temporary divestment meant a decline in hundreds of thousands of defense jobs. Continued social and political pressure for disarmament meant that defense spending did not so much decline as shift into needs that were less labor intensive in production and focused instead on high tech weaponry. The shift also undercut the power of unions in the defense sector. Altered defense strategies thus contributed to the slow shrinkage of American manufacturing in the 1970s, even as the end of the military draft drew young, disadvantaged working-age Americans into the volunteer army.[57]

Above all, the energy crisis of the 1970s altered the conditions of and relationships among labor costs, wages and benefits, and political power. The rising costs of oil and petroleum products, including specifically gasoline, exacerbated inflation. They changed consumer preferences for and automobile companies' production of cars. The Big Three automakers originally had experimented with smaller cars and more efficient engine designs, but believing that small cars could not generate the same revenues, American carmakers left that segment of the market to foreign companies.[58] By the 1960s, Volkswagen, Toyota, Datsun (later Nissan), and Honda designed cars for the U.S. market. They emphasized fuel efficiency for the growing number of environmentally conscious consumers, youthful design elements that contrasted with muscle cars such as the Mustang, Corvette, and Charger, and streamlined engineering. The Volkswagen Beetle (the "Bug") and Volkswagen vans were prototypes, long-associated with the new counter culture and environmental activism. The impact on autoworkers in the United States was not immediately clear, even as American carmakers experimented with their own take on smaller, hipper cars like the Chevrolet Corvair, the car featured in Ralph Nader's *Unsafe at Any Speed*.[59]

As a greater proportion of the American buying public turned to more fuel-efficient cars during the energy crisis of the 1970s, a greater number of cars on the road were foreign-made. The consequences for car manufacture and employment at the Big Three were devastating. Production jobs dropped steadily as the productivity gains from the 1950s and 1960s, the energy crisis, and a dwindling market share put automakers—and the United Auto Workers—on notice that conditions were changing. Following close on the decline in domestic automobile manufacturing were declines in related industries such as steel, rubber, and electrical parts as well as coal extraction, the core manufacturing unions of the AFL-CIO and the heroes of the 1930s labor resurgence.[60]

The response of Big Labor (unions like the UAW, the United Rubber Workers, United Steelworkers, United Electrical Workers, Oil, Chemical and Atomic Workers) was anemic at best. Caught in a downward spiral where work force numbers were maintained through a combination of outdated technology (the steel industry, in particular, had no incentive to retool its factories with new equipment), protective tariffs, and work rules, domestic manufacturers pressed for concessions in contract bargaining. Faced with the threat of manufacturing plants leaving their communities, unions accepted concessions on work force safety, the creation of wage tiers, and even lower wage and benefits packages for active workers, if they included backloaded pension and health care benefits for retiring union members. Politically, while unions like the UAW and the United Mine Workers pushed for new legislation (Clean Air and Clean Water Acts, the creation of the Environmental Protection Agency and the Occupational Safety and Health Administration, and improvements in worker compensation, including black lung compensation), they stepped back from any demands for a broader social contract.[61] Certainly by the end of the 1970s, faced with conservative opposition, labor unions dropped demands for full employment and gradually withdrew their demands for single-payer national health insurance. As long as union contracts held out the promise of health care, there was no demand for national health insurance or guaranteed income. Indeed, the labor movement's most pressing political demand—to revisit Taft-Hartley and reinvigorate the National Labor Relations Board and the Wagner Act—was set aside for room at the political table.[62]

Public Sector Unionism and the Crisis in the Public Sector

As we now understand, the political climate for unionism at the end of the Democratic ascendancy was conflict-ridden at best. On the one hand, the

AFL–CIO captained political resources that kept Democratic representatives in control of many state houses and the Congress.[63] They were able, through court cases and political action, to open the door to public sector unionism and to recruit in the space of a decade hundreds of thousands of public employees to organized labor. In the 1960s and 1970s, social workers, teachers, bus drivers and subway conductors, police, firefighters, hospital workers, and clerks in the county courthouses and state DMVs joined unions. Two of the fastest growing unions—the American Federation of State, County, and Municipal Employees (AFSCME) and the American Federation of Teachers (AFT), followed closely by the Service Employee International Union (SEIU)—became major factors in local and state politics, even as workers faced a new economic and political climate.[64]

At the same time, the labor movement was increasingly constrained by the limitations of the National Labor Relations Board. New definitions of labor membership that excluded growing numbers of workers, and the impact of the Taft-Hartley Act (1947) and the Landrum-Griffin Labor Management Reporting and Disclosure Act (1959), which created new layers of scrutiny for labor leaders, hampered political campaigns and restricted forms and scope of labor protests.[65] Added to these laws were state right-to-work laws and state laws that specifically prohibited public sector strikes and doled out severe penalties, including termination, for public employees who went out on strike. Finally, changing economic factors, including a movement calling for privatization of government services and the growing fiscal crises in major American cities, undermined the ground not only for public employees but for workers employed by private firms.[66]

In the public sector, the difficulties of balancing city budgets at a time of out-migration due to white flight and declining tax receipts meant that city governments had little room to meet what many considered the fair demands of public employees. With the coming of the baby boom, schools had become over-crowded. School teachers, clerks, and maintenance workers were, by the measure of their work and education, underpaid. City crime rates and urban arson, especially in the deteriorating urban core, increased; demands on fire, police, and other safety personnel also grew. In this crisis atmosphere, public education—and teachers' unions—loomed large. Government employee unions began to take the brunt of demands to reduce budgets, lower deficits, and cut non-essential public services. The American Federation of Teachers (AFT), the United Federation of Teachers, and the National Education Association, along with other unions of government employees, such as the Service Employees International Union (SEIU) and AFSCME, became the focus of criticism regarding both how schools performed and how they were compensated. While the economy in the early 1970s remained buoyant, public employee salaries, compared to private workers, thus stayed low. Many cities and states lacked the tax revenue and public support to raise them. What public workers received instead were good health insurance and pay-ahead promises of solid pensions and retiree benefits. When New York experienced a massive fiscal crisis in the 1970s, it bargained hard with public sector unions, privatizing some services, but extending, into the future, its obligations to its employees. Chicago, Detroit, and Cleveland were among other cities that made similar bargains.[67]

Economic Decline and Political Stasis

The stagnating economy of the 1970s and 1980s, shifts in trade policy, and the second wave of deindustrialization that followed the oil embargo were echoed in political defeats as labor unions lost power in the Democratic party coalition. Further, labor's lack of political clout was echoed in a lack of congressional and executive action on its behalf. Long postponed changes in labor law and single-payer national health insurance that would ease the burden on workers and employers were seen as ways to shore up increasingly disadvantaged unions. It wasn't, in the end, that no laws benefitting workers were passed; rather, the political climate for labor unions had grown more hostile and restrictive, making necessary a change in agenda and tactics.

By 1980 the most promising developments of the 1960s, including the surge in public sector employee unionism, were threatened. Strapped city and state governments sought to limit the gains of public employees, and finance capitalists used these crises to increase their political power. As David Harvey has argued, the 1970s crisis allowed organized business and finance to hold city governments such as New York hostage and remake them in what historian Joshua Freeman calls "counterrevolution from above."[68] Local governments opted to privatize some public services and weakened union wage and pension guarantees. Economic change and political defeat were accompanied by revitalized anti-union campaigns in the political sphere and increasing hostility directed at private sector unions. What is more, arguments for privatization of government services such as street and bridge construction, sanitation, education, and even mail delivery, as well as deregulation of key industries like telecommunications and air transportation, threatened to undermine and dilute the growth in public employee unionism that had balanced the losses in the private sector.

The election of James Earl Carter as president in 1976 and Ronald Reagan in 1980 brought retrenchment to a new level and left unionized workers increasingly vulnerable to anti-union forces. Opposition to organized labor as a whole was mirrored in the adamant refusal of these administrations to bargain with labor unions and the willingness of conservative Democrats and their Republican peers to appoint anti-union lawyers to the National Labor Relations Board and the federal bench. Anti-union campaigns had a long history. With the creation of the New Deal state and especially the passage of the Wagner Act, business interests once again targeted federal and local government protections of organized labor. Under the conservative Democratic administration of Jimmy Carter, labor unions had further diminished influence. They failed in their primary objective to revise

Taft-Hartley and re-energize the labor movement through new organization. Further, the push to deregulate industries, which began under Carter, and retrenchment from environmental, health, and safety provisions of federal legislation stripped resources from the Department of Labor and its agencies. It signaled that labor's political moment was long since gone.

Under Reagan the trend continued and deepened. Just as private conservative donors had backed anti-union congressmen and senators such as Barry Goldwater, so too did they turn their sights on the federal apparatus that maintained public sector union power.[69] These efforts culminated in the PATCO (Professional Air Traffic Controllers Organization) strike of 1981. The right of federal workers to strike had long been contested, and it was tested again in the postal strike of 1970. Still, PATCO members believed, strongly, that the president they supported in the election would negotiate with the union. President Reagan ended the strike by firing PATCO employees and hiring replacement workers.[70]

Anti-union sentiment had been pervasive and growing not only among corporate elites but in the general population since the 1950s. Union workers did earn higher wages, have greater control over their work processes, drew better vacation, medical, and pension benefits. They also were more publicly engaged, politically active, and voted overwhelmingly Democratic, as numerous studies had shown.[71] As G. William Domhoff has argued, "reducing union power became the primary concern for both moderates and ultraconservatives in the corporate community by 1968, whether the immediate issue was inflation, wage rates, profit margins, or foreign trade." These forces became more organized in the 1970s, and Reagan delivered the "final blow."[72]

Labor as the voice of the working class lacked the power to halt firings in the PATCO strike or to alter the slow erosion of progressive taxation. Under conservative Democratic president Bill Clinton, the labor movement was unable to stop or modify the North American Free Trade Agreement. As NAFTA's opponents predicted, the trade treaty accelerated the movement of manufacturing jobs overseas and into borderland regions.[73] Surviving through the war-prone years of the 2000s, labor survived the toxic neglect of the Bush administration and supported, with its vast resources, the campaign of relative newcomer and community organizer, Senator Barack Obama. Under the new president, labor's advocacy groups, however, could not push through a new round of labor law reform or have Congress pass the Employee Free Choice Act, considered to be the best chance at labor law reform since the 1940s.[74] The Free Choice Act would have altered the rules for NLRB union certification elections and restored some meaning to union organizing campaigns, the unrealized potential in the shifting economy of the late twentieth century. The Affordable Care Act that emerged in 2009 was structured as a complicated maze of private and public options and varied by state in its coverage and eligibility, a further disappointment from labor's single payer hopes for national health insurance.

For labor advocates, presidential antipathy to organized labor represented a sea change in labor movement survival. Without a doubt, the new visibility and power of elected officials and corporate leaders hostile to organized labor signaled that change. Yet, one can argue, the era of labor's decline stretched back to the immediate postwar period, with the passage of Taft-Hartley, the postwar employer offensive, including right-to-work campaigns, and the failure of labor to respond to the fast-moving changes in manufacturing, the vast expansion of public sector employment, the rapid increase of women and minority workers, and the continuing and vital role of immigrant workers in leading sectors of the economy, including service and construction. Both external political opposition and internal division and entrenchment contributed to the shrinking labor movement.

It is, however, equally true that the Reagan era did not, in fact, doom the labor movement to extinction. In many ways, the Carter and the Clinton administrations, Democratic bookends to the Reagan–Bush era, were equally periods of labor decline. They signaled the disappearing commitment of liberals to labor and working-class justice. What went wrong? How did the election of Democratic presidents, who came from the party of Franklin Delano Roosevelt and the Wagner Act, result in fewer labor rights? The answer, which we have indicated before, is the landscape of politics had changed. The labor movement had neither the resources nor the capacity to capture the same share of public assets nor the same level of public support. Whether one calls it the "thunder on the right," the resurgence of conservative ideology, or the rise of neoliberalism, the labor movement was no longer part of the debate.[75]

Conclusion

Stirred by generational change and sparked by concessionary bargaining and worsening working conditions, the "rank and file" rebellions of the 1970s were not led by unions but despite and even against them. Dissident worker organizations and wildcat strikes such as the one at Lordstown suggested new labor militancy, but the institutional labor movement was as much a target for young and minority workers' anger as it was a vehicle for their activism. This strike wave, however, has not been well-remembered in history textbooks, in the popular media, or in our political memory. More than a decade of rank-and-file organization and protest reshaped our economic landscape and gave rise to a new generation of labor and community activists. It also ended—with a resounding noise—in the 1981 defeat of the PATCO air traffic controllers' strike. This strike often serves as a coda for the wave of rank-and-file labor militancy of the 1970s.

It is worth noting, however, that much of the organizing that specifically involved women workers, especially in the public sector, only began by mid-decade and continued throughout the 1980s. Public sector unions, while chastened by privatization of some forms of public service, remained strong, despite PATCO.

In contrast, rank-and-file activism in industrial unions (characterized as the core of the 1970s rebellion) had considerably cooled down by the time of the 1981 PATCO defeat. Moreover, the PATCO strike itself was conflicted. PATCO members were among the most conservative forces in the labor movement and had endorsed candidate Reagan for the presidency. Their rebellion was all the more remarkable in that they shared political beliefs with the president who would, in the end, destroy their union. The flight—or movement—of manufacturing plants from their communities, new NLRB practices (Reagan's NLRB appointees were, to a man, business advocates and deeply suspicious of labor law practices ante-Reagan), and division and conflict within new social movements and political campaigns undermined labor movement unity and effectiveness.[76]

The PATCO defeat, however, helps to explain our emaciated labor relations system, in which a few unionized workers retain rights to benefits and decent salaries while most workers cannot rely even on government protections against injury and illness in the workplace. Individual mobility and bargaining account for what little power workers have. But more than PATCO was at fault. In the decade that followed World War II, workers in core industries experienced increased real wages that matched productivity growth but did not exceed it. Unionized workers made crucial income and wealth gains, but the gains were not widespread. Minority men and women workers of all races were denied access to skilled jobs and earned incomes significantly below those of white men. And the labor movement, whose leadership ranks were overwhelmingly white and male, did not address discrimination in hiring, promotion, and wages. Nor did they, after the collapse of Operation Dixie, use significant resources in campaigns to organize the unorganized. Indeed, public workers did their own organizing, as did migrant agricultural workers. Women clerical and retail workers were pretty much ignored until experienced feminist organizers turned to the white collar workplace, and the same story can be told about nurses, hospital workers, and social workers.

There is a lesson in this history—one about the power of worker self-organization and the necessity of a militant minority who can imagine new paths for organization. It also highlights another principle—that is, that a strategic plurality, represented in the coming of new workers into older unions, could either be employed for new gains or be aimed at maintaining the status quo. It was the latter that labor chose. A moribund—or inflexible and aging—labor bureaucracy had difficulty being as agile as some of the most hidebound of corporate leadership and resisted most forms of entrepreneurship among its members. Labor leaders such as Lane Kirkland and George Meany did not have the same incentives, nor did they fully comprehend the need for new organization. At the same time, local and community-based organizers, young and dissident as they were, had fewer resources. Big Labor might have responded to their energetic challenges with support, even as if these campaigns represented fundamental change in the labor movement itself.

Notes

1 Joshua Freeman, "Hardhats: Construction Workers, Manliness, and the 1970 Pro-War Demonstrations," *Journal of Social History* 26:4 (1993), 725–44; Jefferson Cowie, *Stayin' Alive: The 1970s and the Last Days of the Working Class* (New York: New Press, 2010), 125–166. Useful correctives might be found in Penny Lewis, *Hardhats, Hippies and Hawks: The Vietnam Anti-War Movement as Myth and Memory* (Ithaca: ILR Press, 2013), 159–186; Frank Koscielski, *Divided Loyalties: American Unions and the Vietnam War* (New York: Garland, 1999); and Christian G. Appy, *Working Class War: American Combat Soldiers and Vietnam* (Chapel Hill: University of North Carolina Press, 1993), 206–208, 254–255; Jerry Lembke, *The Spitting Image: Myth, Memory, and the Legacy of Vietnam* (New York: New York University Press, 1998), 27–70.

2 Steve Fraser, "The Labor Question," in *The Rise and Fall of the New Deal Order*, eds. Steve Fraser and Gary Gerstle, (Princeton: Princeton University Press, 1989), 55–84. This label is implied as well in the critique of new social movements. Alan Brinkley, *The End of Reform: New Deal Liberalism in Recession and War*, reprint ed., (New York: Vintage, 1996), has a more nuanced position, but even his account relies on a false dichotomy between social and economic reform.

3 For a correction, see William P. Jones, *The March on Washington: Jobs, Freedom, and the Forgotten History of Civil Rights* (New York: W.W. Norton, 2013); Donald Tibbs, *Black Power to Prison Power: The Making of North Carolina Prisoners; Labor Union* (New York: Palgrave Macmillan, 2012); Lauren Araiza, *To March for Others: The Black Freedom Struggle and the United Farm Workers* (Philadelphia: University of Pennsylvania Press, 2014); Risa L. Goluboff, *The Lost Promise of Civil Rights* (Cambridge, MA: Harvard University Press, 2007).

4 Adolph Reed, "Reinventing the Working Class: An Exercise in Elite Image Manipulation," *New Labor Forum* 13:3 (Fall 2004), 18–26. Compare the relative acceptance of this image in Jefferson Cowie, "Nixon's Class Struggle: Romancing the New Right Worker, 1969–1973," *Labor History* 43:3 (2002), 257–283.

5 Richard Kazis and Richard L. Grossman, *Fear at Work: Job Blackmail, Labor and the Environment* (New York, 1982) 1–150; Robert W. Gordon, "Environmental Blues: Working-Class Environmentalism and the Labor-Environmental Alliance, 1968–1985" (Ph.D. Dissertation, Wayne State University, 2004).

6 Nelson Lichtenstein, "Supply Chains, Workers' Chains, and the New Work of Retail Supremacy," *Labor: Studies in Working Class History in the Americas* 4:1 (2007), 17–31; idem, "Wal-Mart's Tale of Two Cities from Bentonville to Shenzhen," *New Labor Forum* 1:2 (2006), 9–19; *Wal-Mart: The Face of Twenty-First Century Capitalism*, ed. Nelson Lichtenstein (New York: New Press, 2005); Dana Frank, *Buy American: The Untold Story of Economic Nationalism* (Boston MA: Beacon Press, 2000).

7 Kim Scipes, *AFL-CIO's Secret War against Developing Country Workers: Solidarity or Sabotage?* (Lanham, MD: Lexington Books, 2011), shows the conflicting stands taken by the AFL-CIO in supporting military dictatorships while engaging in solidarity work with other international unions. See Robert Anthony Waters, Jr., and Geert van Goethem, *American Labor's Global Ambassadors: The International History of the AFL-CIO during the Cold War* (New York: Palgrave Macmillan, 2013).

8 Louis E. Jones, "The Rise of Public Sector Unionism in Detroit, 1947–1967" (Ph.D. Dissertation, Wayne State University, 2010), 114–176, 198–220. For background, see Joseph Slater, *Public Workers: Government Employee Unions, the Law, and the State, 1900–1962* (Ithaca: ILR Press, 2004), 158–204; Joseph A. McCartin, "Bringing the State's Workers Back In: Time to Rectify an Unbalanced U.S. Labor Historiography," *Labor History* 47:1 (2006), 73–94; idem, "Convenient Scapegoat: Public Workers under Attack," *Dissent* (Spring 2011), www.dissentmagazine.org/article/convenient-scapegoat-public-workers-under-assault, accessed February 7, 2016.

9 Jones, "Rise of Public Sector Unionism"; Slater, *Public Workers*, 71–124; McCartin, "Bringing the State's Workers Back In."

10 Steve Estes, *I AM A MAN: Race, Manhood and the Civil Rights Movement* (Chapel Hill: University of North Carolina Press, 2005), 131–152; Marjorie Murphy, *Blackboard Unions: The AFT and the NEA, 1900–1980* (Ithaca: Cornell University Press, 1992); idem, "Militancy in Many Forms: Teachers' Strikes and Urban Rebellions, 1967–1974," in *Rebel Rank and File: Labor Militancy and the Revolt from Below in the Long 1970s*, eds. Aaron Brenner, Robert Brenner, and Cal Winslow (New York: Verso, 2010), 229–250; Aaron Brenner, "Striking against the State: The Postal Wildcat of 1970," *Labor's Heritage* (Spring 1996), 4–27; Joshua Freeman, *Working Class New York: Life and Labor since World War II* (New York: New Press, 2000), 201–227; Jon Shelton, "Against the Public: The Pittsburgh Teachers Strike of 1975–1976 and the Crisis of the Labor–Liberal Coalition," *Labor: Working Class History of the Americas* 10:2 (Summer 2013), 55–75; Erik S. Gellman, "In the Driver's Seat: Chicago Bus Drivers and Labor Insurgency in an Era of Black Power," *Labor: Working Class History of the Americas* 10:2 (Fall 2014), 49–76; For a recent intervention to bring in prison labor, see Heather Ann Thompson, "Rethinking Working-Class Struggle through the Lens of the Carceral State: Toward a Labor History of Inmates and Guards," *Labor: Studies in the Working Class History of the Americas* 8:3 (Fall 2011), 15–45.

11 See David F. Noble, *Forces of Production: A Social History of Industrial Automation* (New York: Oxford University Press, 1986); Harley Shaiken, *Work Transformed: Automation and Labor in the Computer Age* (New York: Holt, Reinhart and Winston, 1985); Shosana Zubnoff, *In the Age of the Smart Machine: The Future of Work and Power* (New York: Basic Books, 1988); Kirkpatrick Sale, *Rebels Against the Future: The Luddites and Their War on the Industrial Revolution: Lessons for the Computer Age* (New York: Basic Books, 1996).

12 Joseph Atkins, *Covering for the Bosses: Labor and the Southern Press* (Oxford: University Press of Mississippi, 2011); Jefferson Cowie, *Capital Moves: RCA's 70-Year Quest for Cheap Labor* (New York: Metropolitan Books, 2001); William B. Adler, *Mollie's Job: A Story of Life and Work on the Global Assembly Line* (New York: Scribner's, 2001); Heather Thompson, "New Autoworkers, Dissent, and the UAW: Detroit and Lordstown," in Robert Asher and Ronald Edsforth, eds., *Autowork* (Albany: SUNY Press, 1995), 181–208; Ronald Edsforth, "Why Automation Didn't Shorten the Work Week: The Politics of Work Time in the Automobile Industry," in Asher and Edsforth, *Autowork*, 155–180; Jack Metzgar, *Striking Steel: Solidarity Remembered* (Philadelphia: Temple University Press, 2000).

13 On office workers and automation, see Katherine Turk, "Labor's Pink-Collar Aristocracy: The National Secretaries' Association's Encounters with Feminism in the Age of Automation," *Labor: Studies in Working Class History of the Americas* 11:2 (Summer 2014), 85–109; Harry Braverman, *Labor and Monopoly Capital: The Degradation of Work in the Twentieth Century* (New York: Monthly Review Press, 1973), 203–247; Joan M. Greenbaum, *Windows on the Workplace: Computers, Jobs and the Organization of Office Work in the Late Twentieth Century* (New York: Monthly Review Press, 1995); Rachel Grossman, "Women's Place in the Integrated Circuit," *Radical America* 14:1 (1980), 29–50. For workers' response, see Jean Tepperman, *Not Servants, Not Machines: Office Workers Speak Out* (Boston MA: Beacon Press, 1976).

14 David Naguib Pellow and Lisa Sun-Hee Park, *Silicon Valley of Dreams: Environmental Injustice, Immigrant Workers, and the High-Tech Global Economy* (Berkeley: University of California Press, 2002), 85–168; June Nash and Maria Patricia Fernandez Kelly, eds., *Women, Men and the International Division of Labor* (Albany: SUNY Press, 1983); Maria Patricia Fernandez-Kelly, *For We Are Sold, I and My People: Women and Industry in Mexico's Frontier* (Albany: SUNY Press, 1983). The epidemic of work-related cancer deaths due to toxic chemicals is explored in Alan Derickson, "'Gateway to Hell': African American Coking Workers, Racial Discrimination, and the Struggle Against

Occupational Cancer," *The Journal of African American History* 101:1–2 (Winter–Spring 2016), 126–149; David Rosner and Gerald Markowitz, *Deceit and Denial: The Deadly Politics of Industrial Pollution* (Berkeley: University of California Press, 2002), 168–194; Josiah Rector, "Environmental Justice at Work: The UAW, the War on Cancer, and the Right to Equal Protection from Toxic Hazards in Postwar America," *Journal of American History* 101:2 (September 2014), 480–502.

15 See Margaret Gray, *Labor and the Locavore: The Making of a Comprehensive Food Ethic* (Berkeley: University of California Press, 2014), on the shift in the labor force on Hudson Valley farms, from Caribbean, Slavic, and Mediterranean workers to Southern blacks and whites and, finally, since the 1980s, to Mexicans and Central Americans. Gray further shows how wages and working conditions on organic and inorganic farms differ primarily in the restriction or use of pesticides.

16 Robert Korstad and Nelson Lichtenstein, "Opportunities Lost and Found: Labor, Radicals, and the Early Civil Rights Movement," *Journal of American History* 75:3 (December 1988), 786–811; Leon Fink and Brian Greenberg, *Upheaval in the Quiet Zone: 1199/SEIU and the Politics of Healthcare Unionism*, 2nd ed., (Urbana: University of Illinois Press, 2009); Lisa Phillips, *A Renegade Union: Interracial Organizing and Labor Radicalism* (Urbana: University of Illinois Press, 2013). For a correction, see William P. Jones, *The March on Washington*, esp. xii; idem, "The Forgotten Radical History of the March on Washington," *Dissent* (Spring 2013), www.dissentmagazine.org/article/the-forgotten-radical-history-of-the-march-on-washington, accessed January 15, 2016.

17 See Linda Gail Housch-Collins, "Selling Bread and Freedom: The Aircraft Organizing Drives of the UAW in Birmingham, Alabama, 1943–1952," doctoral dissertation, University of Michigan, 1998, for the UAW's divergent local and national policies on interracial organizing; see also Nelson Lichtenstein, *Walter Reuther: The Most Dangerous Man in Detroit* (New York: Basic Books, 1995), 370–395.

18 Randy Shaw, *Beyond the Fields: Cesar Chavez, the UFW, and the Struggle for Justice in the 21st Century* (Berkeley: University of California Press, 2008); Margaret Rose, "From the Fields to the Picket Line: Huelga Women and the Boycott, 1965–1975," *Labor History* 31:3 (Summer 1990), 271–293; Richard W. Hurd and William Rouse, "Progressive Union Organizing: The SEIU Justice for Janitors Campaign," http://digitalcommons.ilr.cornell.edu/articles/895; Christopher Erickson, Ruth Milkman, Daniel Mitchell and Kent Wong, "Justice for Janitors in Los Angeles: Lessons from Three Rounds of Negotiations," *British Journal of Industrial Relations* 40:3 (2002), 543–567; Preston Rudy, "'Justice for Janitors,' not 'Compensation for Custodians': The Political Context and Organizing in San Jose and Sacramento," in Ruth Milkman and Kim Voss, eds., *Rebuilding Labor: Organizing and Organizers in the New Union Movement* (Ithaca: ILR Press, 2004), 133–149; Mario Garcia, *Memories of Chicano History: The Life and Narrative of Bert Corona* (Berkeley: University of California Press, 1998), on organizing undocumented workers. There has been a lively debate on Chavez and the UFW, with a fierceness that echoes debates about Walter Reuther. For contrasting views, see Frank Bardacke, *Trampling out the Vintage: Cesar Chavez and the Two Souls of the United Farm Workers* (New York: Verso, 2011).

19 Dan Georgakas and Marvin Surkin, *Detroit, I Do Mind Dying* (New York: St. Martin's Press, 1975); Darrel Enck-Wanzer, ed., *The Young Lords: A Reader* (New York: NYU Press, 2010), 185–194.

20 A.C. Jones, "Rank and File Opposition in the UAW during the Long 1970s," in Brenner et al., eds., *Rebel Rank and File*, 281–310.

21 Jeremy Milloy, "'Chrysler Pulled The Trigger': Competing Understandings of Workplace Violence During the 1970s and Radical Legal Practice," *Labour/Le Travail* 74 (Fall 2014), 51–88.

22 Kieran Taylor, "American Petrograd: Detroit and the Revolutionary League of Black Workers," in Brenner et al., eds., *Rebel Rank and File*, 311–334; Georgakas and Surkin, *Detroit, I Do Mind Dying*.

23 Judith Stein, *Running Steel, Running America: Race, Economic Policy and the Decline of Liberalism* (Chapel Hill: University of North Carolina Press, 1998), emphasizes the lack of an industrial policy in the United States and conflicts among civil rights liberals, but she also documents the structural context of these battles.

24 Stanley Aronowitz, *False Promises: The Shaping of the American Working Class*, reprint ed. (Durham: Duke University Press, 1991), was an early assessment. On colonizers and "salts," see Steve Early, "Organizing for the Long Haul: Colonizing to the Rescue," *Working USA* 16 (September 2013), 351–369; Salar Mohandesi, "Between the Ivory Tower and the Assembly Line," https://viewpointmag.com/2014/03/27/between-the-ivory-tower-and-the-assembly-line/, accessed September 9, 2015, which applies the colonizer model to contemporary organizing.

25 This generational change, barely noted in standard accounts of labor in the 1970s, emerges sharply from most recent studies. It is not, however, to romanticize the baby boomer generation; rather we should recognize that the labor movement's history was and is contingent. These were times of social movement activism, and that activism bled into the labor movement. The success of labor organizing was determined by many factors, including economic decline, political stagnation and the conservative drift, and the energy crisis that exposed the weaknesses of the postwar economy. Labor faced what then was a Democratic party that increasingly depended on a professional-managerial constituency and slowly abandoned its commitment to the labor politics of the New Deal. See Lily Geismer, *Don't Blame Us: Suburban Liberals and the Transformation of the Democratic Party* (Princeton: Princeton University Press, 2015).

26 William M. Adler, *Mollie's Job: The Story of Life and Work on the Global Assembly Line* (New York: Touchstone Books, 2000), 118–120; Dan La Botz, "The Tumultuous Teamsters of the 1970s," in Brenner et al., eds., *Rebel Rank and File*, 199–228; Shane Hamilton, *Trucking Country: The Road to America's Wal-Mart Economy* (Princeton: Princeton University Press, 2014). See also David Witwer, "The Racketeering Menace and Anti-unionism in the Mid-twentieth Century United States," *International Labor and Working Class History* 74 (Fall 2008), 124–147; idem, "The Landrum-Griffin Act: A Case Study in the Problems and Possibilities of Anti-Union Corruption Law," *Criminal Justice Review* 27:2 (Fall 2002), 301–320.

27 See William Serrin, *The Company and the Union: The "Civilized Relationship" between the General Motors Corporation and the United Automobile Workers* (New York: Knopf, 1973); Paul J. Nyden, "Rank and File Movements in the United Mine Workers of America, Early 1960s–Early 1980s," in Brenner et al., eds., *Rebel Rank and File*, 173–198.

28 Cal Winslow, "Overview: The Rebellion from Below, 1965–1981," 1–35, and Kim Moody, "Understanding the Rank and File Rebellion in the Long 1970s," 105–146, in Brenner et al., *Rebel Rank and File*; Glen Perusek and Kent Worcester, eds., *Trade Union Politics: American Unions and Economic Change, 1960s–1990s* (Atlantic Highlands, NJ: Humanities Press, 1995). See also Sheila Cohen, "The 1968–1974 Labour Upsurge in Britain and America: A Critical History and a Look at What Might Have Been," *Labor History* 49:4 (2008), 395–416.

29 Richard Fry, "Dissent in the Coal Fields: Miners, Federal Politics, and Union Reform in the United States, 1968–1973," *Labor History* 55:2 (2014), 173–188.

30 Fred Harris, "Burning Up People to Make Electricity," *Atlantic Magazine* (July 1974); Dylan Lovan, "No Union Mines Left in Kentucky, where Labor Wars Once Raged," Associated Press, September 5, 2015; https://bigstory.ap.org; see *Harlan County USA*, dir. Barbara Kopple (1976).

31 Aronowitz, *False Promises*, roots the 1970s rebellion deeply in generational psychology and cultural divisions.

32 Brenner et al., eds., *Rebel Rank and File*; see also Steve Early, *The Civil Wars of U.S. Labor: Birth of a New Workers' Movement or Death Throes of the Old* (Chicago: Haymarket Books, 2011). On Karen Nussbaum, see Lane Windham, "'A Sense of Possibility and a

Belief in Collective Power': A Labor Strategy Talk with Karen Nussbaum," *Labor: Studies in Working Class History in the Americas* 12:3 (2015), 35–51; on women in auto, electrical, and packinghouse workers' unions, Dennis Deslippe, *"Rights Not Roses": Unions and the Rise of Working Class Feminism* (Urbana: University of Illinois Press, 2000); Nancy Gabin, *Feminism in the Labor Movement: Women and the United Auto Workers, 1935–1970* (Ithaca: Cornell University Press, 1990).

33 See also Alan Draper, *Conflict of Interests: Organized Labor and the Civil Rights Movement in the South, 1954–1968* (Ithaca: ILR Press, 1994); Nancy Maclean, "The Difference a Law Makes," *Labor: Studies in Working Class History of the Americas* 11:3 (2014), 19–24; comments by Thomas Sugrue and Toure Reed, 25–29, 31–36. For the UAW, John Barnard, *American Vanguard: The United Auto Workers during the Reuther Years, 1935–1970* (Detroit: Wayne State University Press, 2004), 392–399, and Nelson Lichtenstein, *State of the Union: A Century of American Labor* (Princeton: Princeton University Press, 2002), 204–207. On veterans and seniority, see the Davis R.B. Ross, *Preparing for Ulysses: Politics and Veterans during World War II* (New York: Columbia University Press, 1969), 148–157; Aaron Levenstein, "Superseniority: Postwar Pitfall," *Antioch Review* 4:4 (Winter 1944), 531–543; Walter J. Couper, "The Reemployment Rights of Veterans," *Annals of the American Academy of Social and Political Science* 238 (March 1945), 112–121.

34 See Mollie Martin, ed., *Hard Hatted Women: Life on the Job* (Berkeley, CA: Seal Press, 1988, 1997); Peggie Carlson, *The Girls Are Coming* (St. Paul: Minnesota Historical Society Press, 1999); Susan Eisenberg, *We'll Call You If We Need You: Experiences of Women Working Construction* (Ithaca: ILR Press, 1999); Jane LaTour, *Sisters in the Brotherhoods: Working Women Organizing for Equality in New York* (New York: Palgrave, 2012); David Goldberg and Trevor Griffey, eds., *Black Power at Work: Community Control, Affirmative Action and the Construction Industry* (Ithaca: ILR Press, 2010). For stunning insights into the process of defending trade monopoly and male power, see Cynthia Cockburn, *In the Way of Women: Men's Resistance to Sex Equality in Organizations* (Ithaca: Cornell University Press, 1991).

35 Edith Abbott, *Women in Industry: A Study in American Economic History* (New York: D. Appleton, 1909), 254.

36 Peter B. Levy, *The New Left and Labor in the 1960s* (Urbana: University of Illinois Press, 1994); Mimi Conway, *Rise, Gonna Rise: A Portrait of Southern Textile Workers* (New York: Anchor Press, 1973); Robert E. Botsch, *Organizing the Breathless: Cotton Dust, Southern Politics and the Brown Lung Association* (Lexington: University Press of Kentucky, 1993).

37 Claudia Goldin, *Understanding the Gender Gap: An Economic History of American Women* (New York: Oxford University Press, 1992), 211–215; Alice Kessler-Harris, *Out to Work: A History of Wage-Earning Women in the United States* (New York: Oxford University Press, 1982), 310–319.

38 Dorothy Sue Cobble, *The Other Women's Movement: Workplace Justice and Social Rights in Modern America* (Princeton: Princeton University Press, 2004), stresses the opportunities for women in labor and for labor feminism in the 1940s and 1950s. Certainly, individual women leaders rose in the ranks of labor, but the labor movement as a whole did not devote additional resources to working women's status or condition.

39 Elizabeth Faue, "The 'Dynamo of Change': Gender and Solidarity in the American Labour Movement of the 1930s." *Gender and History* 1:2 (Summer 1989), 138–158; idem, "Shifting Labor's Loyalties: Redefining Citizenship and Allegiance," in P. Abbott, ed., *The Many Faces of Patriotism* (Boston MA: Rowman and Littlefield, 2006), 111–127. For how the ideology of masculinity was expressed in the practices and experiences of working-class men, see Steve Meyer, *Manhood on the Line: Working-Class Masculinities in the American Heartland* (Urbana: University of Illinois Press, 2016).

40 Ruth Milkman, *Gender at Work: The Dynamics of Job Segregation by Sex during World War II* (Urbana: University of Illinois Press, 1987), 84–98; Gabin, *Feminism in the Labor Movement*, 143–187; Cobble, *The Other Women's Movement*, 94–120, 145–179.

41 Catherine Hoffman, "Fighting for Equality: Women in the UAW, 1940–1970," M.A. essay, Wayne State University, 2005; Nicolette Wright, "'Enter the Black Rosie the Riveter': Lillian Hatcher, International Representative to the UAW," M.A. essay, Wayne State University, 2005; Melissa R. Luberti, "'Labor Was Where I Wanted to Be': Mildred Jeffrey and the Struggles of Women Auto Workers," M.A. essay, Wayne State University, 2010; Amy Bromsen, "'They All Sort of Disappeared': The Early Cohort of UAW Women Leaders," *Michigan Historical Review* 37 (Spring 2011), 5–40.

42 Gabin, *Feminism in the Labor Movement*, 188–228; Cobble, *The Other Women's Movement*, 190–195.

43 Ibid.; see also Josiah Rector and Elizabeth Faue, "'Fix the Workplace, Not the Worker': Labor Feminism and the Shifting Grounds of Equality in the Road to Johnson Controls," paper, Social Science History meeting, Chicago, November 2013; Deslippe, *"Rights, Not Roses"*, documents the UE and UPCWA discrimination suits.

44 Gabin, *Feminism in the Labor Movement*, 225–228; Cobble, *The Other Women's Movement*, 201–205.

45 Amanda Walter, "Becoming a Priority: Unionizing University Clerical Workers through SEIU District 925," M.A. essay, Wayne State University, 2013.

46 Among the many analyses of these university clerical and technical campaigns, see Lisa Oppenheim, "Women's Ways of Organizing: A Conversation with AFSCME Organizers Kris Rondeau and Gladys McKenzie," *Labor Research Review* 18 (1991), 45–60; John Hoerr, "Solidaritas at Harvard: Organizing in a Different Voice," *American Prospect* (Summer 1993), 67–82; Aldo Cupo, Molly Ladd-Taylor, Beverly Lett, and David Montgomery, "Beep, Beep, Yale's Cheap: Looking at the Yale Strike." *Radical America* 19 (1985), 5–19; Toni Gilpin, Gary Isaac, Dan Letwin, and Jack McKivigan, On Strike for Respect: *The Clerical and Technical Workers Strike at Yale University, 1984–85* (Chicago: C.H. Kerr, 1988); Richard W. Hurd, "Bottom-Up Organizing: HERE in New Haven and Boston," *Labor Research Review* 8 (Spring 1986), 5–20; Richard W. Hurd and Adrienne McElwain, "Organizing Clerical Workers," *Industrial and Labor Relations Review* 41 (April 1988), 360–373. On clerical workers, see Deborah E. Bell, "Unionized Women in State and Local Government," in Ruth Milkman, ed., *Women, Work and Protest* (New York: Routledge, 1984), 280–299; Cynthia Costella, "WEA're Worth It! Work Culture and Conflict at the Wisconsin Education Association Insurance Trust," *Feminist Studies* 11 (Fall 1985), 496–518.

47 "Broader Day Care is Aim of Harvard Union Drive," *New York Times* February 28, 1988, 24L; Lisa Oppenheim, "Women's Ways of Organizing; A Conversation with AFSCME Organizers Kris Rondeau and Gladys McKenzie," *Labor Research Review* 18 (1991), 45–60.

48 "Harvard Chief Battles Union Drive," *New York Times* May 16, 1988.

49 Hurd, "Learning from Clerical Unions."

50 Susan Pollack, "Harvard Goes Union," *MS Magazine* 16 (June 1988), 68; "Harvard Union Wins Case," *Boston Globe* October 25, 1988; see also "Harvard Concedes Victory of Clerical Workers Demanding a Union," *New York Times* November 5, 1988; Debra E. Blum, "After a Combative Campaign, Harvard and Its New Union Try Cooperation," *Chronicle of Higher Education* 35 (March 8, 1989).

51 Oppenheim, "Women's Ways of Organizing"; Hoerr, "Solidaritas at Harvard."

52 Kathleen Barry, *Femininity in Flight: A History of Flight Attendants* (Durham: Duke University Press, 2007).

53 *The Willmar 8* (1981), dir. Lee Grant.

54 Eileen Boris and Jennifer Klein, *Caring for America: Home Health Care Workers in the Shadow of the Welfare State* (New York: Oxford University Press, 2012); see also Arlie

R. Hochschild, *The Managed Heart: Commercialization of Human Feeling*, updated edition (Berkeley: University of California Press, 2012).

55 See Jean Alonso, *The Patriots: An Inside Look at Life in a Defense Plant* (Create Space, Independent Publishing Platform, 2011); Lisa Furtchtgott, "Constructive Annihilation: American Weapons Suppliers and the Remaking of Work, 1939–1989" (Ph.D. Dissertation, Yale University, 2015); Robyn Meredith, "Vast Plant for Tanks Has Closed," *New York Times* December 21, 1996.

56 The figure is in 1987 dollars. See Norman C. Sanders, "Employment Effects of the Rise and Fall of Defense Spending," *Monthly Labor Review* (April 1993), 3–10.

57 Reader Editorial Collective, "Introduction: The Nature of the Public Sector," in *Crisis in the Public Sector: A Reader* (New York: Monthly Review Press, 1982), 2–3; Michele Naples, Tom Riddell, and Nancy Rose, "The Crisis in Perspective," *Crisis in the Public Sector*, 19–28.

58 Thomas McCarthy, *Auto Mania: Cars, Consumers, and the Environment* (New Haven: Yale University Press, 2007); Jack Doyle, *Taken for a Ride: The Big Three and the Politics of Air Pollution* (New York: Four Walls Eight Windows, 2000), 99–126.

59 Paul Garzelloni, "The Struggle for the American Economy Car, 1960–2008: The Automakers, the UAW, and the Federal Government," M.A. thesis, Wayne State University, 2010; Ralph Nader, *Unsafe at Any Speed: The Designed-in Dangers of the American Automobile* (New York: Grossman Publishers, 1965).

60 Daniel Horowitz, *Jimmy Carter and the Energy Crisis of the 1970s* (New York: Bedford/ St. Martins, 2004); Karen Merrill, *The Oil Crisis of 1973–1974: A Brief History with Documents* (New York: Bedford/St. Martins, 2007); McCarthy, *Auto Mania*, 213–218; Doyle, *Taken for a Ride*, 127–194.

61 Robyn Muncy, "Coal-Fired Reforms: Social Citizenship, Dissident Miners, and the Great Society," *Journal of American History* 96:1 (June 2009), 72–98; Richard Fry, "Making Amends: Coal Miners, the Black Lung Association, and Federal Compensation Reform, 1969–1972," *Federal History* 5 (January 2013), 35–56.

62 Judith Stein, "Conflict, Change and Economic Policy in the Long 1970s," in Brenner et al., eds., *Rebel Rank and File*, 77–102; Lichtenstein, *The State of the Union*, 141–211. Marie Gottschalk, *The Shadow Welfare State: Labor, Business, and the Politics of Health Care in the United States* (Ithaca: ILR Press, 2000), shows that vocal advocates for a national health care system remained in AFSCME, OCAW, ACTWU, and the UAW in the 1970s; but by the Reagan era, many of the big AFL-CIO unions stopped actively lobbying. They "did little to mobilize their members to put serious pressure on the federation or the Democratic Party to endorse the Canadian-inspired route to reform." Ibid., 100–101.

63 Tracy Roof, *American Labor, Congress, and the Welfare State, 1935–2010* (Baltimore: Johns Hopkins University Press, 2011), chapters 4–5; Andrew Battista, *The Revival of Labor Liberalism* (Urbana: University of Illinois Press, 2008), 27–42.

64 Joseph A. McCartin, "'A Wagner Act for Public Workers': Labor's Deferred Dream and the Rise of Conservatism, 1970–1976," *Journal of American History* 95:1 (2008), 123–148; idem, "Convenient Scapegoat." See also Dana Goldstein, *The Teacher Wars: A History of America's Most Embattled Profession* (New York: Doubleday, 2014).

65 Melvyn Dubofsky, *The State and Labor in Modern America* (Chapel Hill: University of North Carolina Press, 1994), 197–231; Lichtenstein, *State of the Union*, 141–177. See also Joseph A. McCartin, "Pattern for Partnership: Putting Labor Racketeering on the Nation's Agenda in the Late 1950s," in Nelson Lichtenstein and Elizabeth Tandy Shermer, eds., *The Right and Labor in America: Politics, Ideology, and Imagination* (Philadelphia: University of Pennsylvania Press, 2012), 207–225.

66 Union for Radical Political Economics, *Crisis in the Public Sector: A Reader* (New York: Monthly Review Press, 1982), esp. 73–11, 203–260, 275–280.

67 *Crisis in the Public Sector*; Miriam Greenberg, *Branding New York: How a City in Crisis Was Sold to the World* (New York: Routledge, 2008), 97–131; see also Robert Fitch,

The Assassination of New York (New York: Verso, 1993), and, on teachers, Murphy, *Blackboard Unions*.

68 David Harvey, *A Brief History of Neoliberalism* (New York: Oxford University Press, 2005), 45; Joshua B. Freeman, *Working-Class New York: Life and Labor since World War II* (New York: New Press, 2000), 256.

69 Elizabeth Tandy Shermer, "Origins of the Conservative Ascendancy: Barry Goldwater's Early Senate Career and the Delegitimization of Organized Labor," *Journal of American History* 95 (December 2008), 678–709; Kim Phillips-Fein, *Invisible Hands: The Making of the Conservative Movement from the New Deal to Reagan* (New York: W.W. Norton, 2009), 185–212; Lawrence Richards, *Union-Free America: Workers and Anti-Union Culture* (Urbana: University of Illinois Press, 2010), esp. 93–124; Lichtenstein and Shermer, eds., *The Right and Labor in America: Politics, Ideology, and Imagination*, esp. essays by Friedman and Shermer, 79–97, 114–136.

70 Joseph A. McCartin, *Collision Course: Ronald Reagan, the Air Traffic Controllers, and the Strike That Changed America* (New York: Oxford University Press, 2011), 328–358.

71 Richard B. Freeman and James L. Medoff, *What Do Unions Do?* (New York: Basic Books, 1984).

72 http://www2.ucsc.edu/whorulesamerica/power/history_of_labor_unions.html; see also G. William Domhoff, *The Myth of Liberal Ascendancy: Corporate Dominance from the Great Depression to the Great Recession* (New York: Routledge, 2014).

73 John MacArthur, *The Selling of Free Trade* (Berkeley: University of California Press, 2001).

74 Susan Orr, "Democracy in the Cards: A Democratic Defense of the Employee Free Choice Act," in Lichtenstein and Shermer, eds., *The Right and Labor in America: Politics, Ideology, and Imagination*, 296–320.

75 Thomas Ferguson, *The Golden Rule: The Investment Theory of Party Competition and the Logic of Money-Driven Political Systems* (Chicago: University of Chicago Press, 1995), 275–346. Ferguson also has a coherent argument for why the balance of forces was different in the New Deal era. See ibid., 203–240.

76 For a discussion of PATCO, see "Debating Joseph A. McCartin's *Collision Course*," *Labor: Studies in Working Class History of the Americas* 9:4 (Winter 2012), 29–54.

6

LABOR'S STRENGTHS AND WEAKNESSES, 1981–PRESENT

In the midst of a long but increasingly successful organizing campaign at a Volkswagen plant in Chattanooga, Tennessee, a political firestorm was unleashed. Breaking with precedent, the Tennessee state government interfered in the union certification election. Elected officials threatened to withdraw government support and subsidies from the plant if the workers voted to unionize. This act, one that put state jobs at risk and served as an unwarranted third party intervention in private labor relations, was credited with the narrow union defeat at Volkswagen. When the union challenged the election, Volkswagen management, to the surprise of observers, supported the union's legal challenge. Management's support for the UAW's organizing campaign defied popular expectations that union growth necessarily results in capital flight. Political opposition to unionization clarified for many observers that private employers sometimes offered a less significant obstacle to labor organization than the hostility of anti-union politicians.[1]

Like the earlier progressive alliance between the labor and business leaders, cooperation between management and labor at Volkswagen conflicts with widely held assumptions about labor relations. Public understanding of strikes, labor organizing, and "buy union" campaigns roots them in an inevitable conflict between employers and workers. For most of the twentieth century, that relationship was mediated by the state. State, local, and federal governments have acted against workers and their unions but also at times for them, especially in the decades between the passage of the labor-friendly Wagner Act (1935) and the PATCO strike in 1981. On occasion, governors, mayors and judges held the line against overreaching employers. Private businesses have been divided about how to approach workers and labor unions. Many turned to state and federal governments to intervene and suppress labor conflict. For these reasons, the tripartite relationship among labor, capital, and government has meant that the labor movement, despite an early commitment to "pure and simple unionism," has sought to have government act to neutralize—if not mediate—workplace conflict.

The contemporary labor movement has inherited this complex relationship to government and private employers. As seen in the Volkswagen campaign, opposition to unions has both an economic and a political edge. For two decades after the New Deal, anti-union forces were held in check by a large working-class voting block and the economic power of unions, whose members made up nearly a third of the wage workers. The current political climate, by contrast, has made opposition to unions a centerpiece of conservative political platforms. The emphasis of labor leaders on maintaining members and winning contracts has contributed to the image of labor unionists as only "out for themselves." The legacy of union hostility to immigrant, minority, and women workers, and its neglect of low-wage and less skilled sectors, has resulted in tangible losses for labor and its public image. In equally powerful ways, legislatures and courts that were and are hostile to the labor movement stifled union organizing and stripped unions of resources and political power.

This chapter has as its object to analyze the weaknesses and strengths of labor historically and in the contemporary United States. By necessity, we will talk about the role of the state in shaping the labor movement. We will examine both the expansive social vision of labor and the more detrimental long-term effects of union efforts to exclude minority and women workers. We further will explore labor's relationship to the environmental movement and global activism as the most recent examples of strong alliances, missed opportunities, and competing visions within the labor movement. Finally, we consider labor's decline in light of its historical weaknesses.

While the numbers of workers belonging to a union in the 1980s and 1990s grew, they represented a shrinking proportion of the non-agricultural labor force. Labor, in the view of its political allies and opponents, is in free fall. How then does one explain the continued influence and role of labor unions in American politics? To what do we attribute union successes or even calculate labor opportunities, given the considerable resources of anti-union employers, an ever-constricting field of labor organization and loss of strike effectiveness, and resurgent conservative ideology, that account for the political strength of Republicans in controlling Congress and the White House for much of the late twentieth and early twenty-first century? What are the strengths and weakness of the labor movement that carry forward into the post-industrial economy of the twenty-first century?

American Labor Politics

We will begin by asking how class politics have been defined in the United States and in labor history. The measure of labor strength has been, for many historians and activists, the vitality or absence of class politics on a national scale. The lack of class rhetoric in American politics and the bogeyman of "class war," raised when progressive taxation, the minimum wage, and business regulation are discussed, seem ready markers of the lack of class awareness among working men and women in the United States. And yet, class experience and sensibility, as AFL president Samuel Gompers once argued, does not always or necessarily translate into political consciousness or class politics. In his autobiography, Gompers eloquently described the "class feeling" that comes of hard poverty, individual need, and family deprivation that many working-class people experienced. Still, class feelings—of deprivation and, some have argued, envy—acknowledged inequality but offered few options to change it, especially when coupled with a sense of middle-class belonging.[2]

In the United States, class politics have played out differently than they have in other industrialized nations. The segmentation of labor—as defined by labor economists Richard Edwards, David Gordon, and Michael Reich, and sociologists Ira Katznelson and Erik Olin Wright—kept workers divided along relatively fine lines of the work force.[3] In particular, intra-class divisions among ethnic groups and within occupational categories eroded the sense of shared experience working-class organizations could provide. Certainly, there has been no labor party in the United States to negotiate these divisions. But what many perceive as a problem— the absence of a class-based political identity or the lack of a labor voice in government—might be seen as a question of language.[4] It is not, we might argue, that people don't see or understand "class." Given the dominant themes of popular entertainment—upward mobility, lucky lottery wins, and class-based crime, we need to understand that the language of class—its images, metaphors, and formulas—is different in the American context, especially two-party democracy. "Winner-take-all" elections set real limits on the power of oppositional politics, and recent debates about inequality have not changed that. Still, there have been times in United States history when groups of workers adopted workingmen's, populist, and socialist parties as means for effecting change. For the majority of our history, though, class politics have taken form in a dominant political party, albeit in the language of democracy and not socialism.

In the years after the New Deal, there was a specific appeal to blue collar workers, and their middle-class peers, to support the Democratic party on class terms. This version of class politics was not radical. It did not take up the banner of socialism or entertain abolishing private property, and did not openly speak to class struggle. Its lack of public visibility seems less important than that the New Deal labor coalition had an agenda about creating opportunity across the broad spectrum of society. Class politics was about redistribution of wealth and progressively greater social and political equality; it saw the working-class political agenda as one in which race and gender inequality should matter little.[5] Even when, as in the Communist party, race equality or "the woman question" were addressed, unionists saw them as ultimately solvable within the larger labor agenda. The gospel of unity and unionism of the CIO in the 1930s required that workers ignore the most salient differences among them in order to build interracial unionism. Labor emphasized the struggle for equality between income-based redistribution (progressive taxation, social insurance, and the union wage) over what came to be called identity politics, which were solely rights-based and individual in nature.[6]

Labor politics was based on the idea of a unified working class with no consciously politicized racial, ethnic, or gender identities. It saw the inequality and unfair treatment that arose from gender, race, and immigration status as less important than working-class and labor interests.[7] Even as labor leaders and policies discriminated against some workers, they declined to consider race and gender discrimination as having priority in the labor agenda. They also refused to see that legislation and practices that instituted policies for affirmative action and gender equality benefited the working class. In other words, the labor movement sometimes forgot that workers might be women, African Americans, or immigrants.

As we have noted earlier in the book, this inability to talk about or acknowledge race and gender difference, coupled with a strong identification of the labor movement as white and male, gave support to employers who discriminated against women and minority workers. It also underwrote the hostility of some minority workers to labor as a whole. Black strikebreakers played a feared role in strikes in meatpacking, steel, and transportation, precisely because African Americans had been barred from jobs, especially skilled jobs, in those industries. Women "stole the trade" from men in printing and cigar making, because men would not teach them the necessary skills and, more importantly, excluded women from union membership. When, after the Civil Rights Act passed, labor unions fought affirmative action because it ran counter to seniority rights, they asked women and minority workers to stand for the seniority principle against their own interests. In doing so, they asked disadvantaged workers to support a principle of unionism that had repeatedly been used to exclude and discriminate against them. Some women and minority workers did stand for collective union rights, rather than individual civil rights. They supported labor leaders who did not believe gender or race inequality required state intervention and who asserted that equality would be reached without such measures.

The only counter-weight to labor's conflicted legacy was in the national political arena. Some labor leaders stood for the principle of gender and race equality, even while they failed to support specific measures to achieve it. The AFL supported woman suffrage as a right and advocated equal pay for equal work among men and women working the same job. In its national platform, the AFL resisted— sometimes unsuccessfully—pressure to segregate locals or exclude African Americans. The CIO, and the UAW in particular, came out in support of civil rights and racial equality. Walter Reuther marched with Martin Luther King and Cesar Chavez. By 1972, the UAW supported the Equal Rights Amendment. Still, such national policies did not affect the organizing priorities of the AFL-CIO. The federation devoted few resources to industries and occupations where women and minority workers dominated. Nor did the AFL-CIO and its constituent international unions increase the representation of women and minority men in labor's leadership councils until the 1980s.

In her book, *In the Way of Women*, sociologist Cynthia Cockburn analyzes how the formal inclusion of women in workplaces, occupations, and trade unions still can produce the same exclusion from leadership that characterizes other organizations in society. While her subject is British companies and unions, the same mechanisms operate in the United States. Networks of mentoring and influence, the language and practices of workplaces, and agendas for action and priorities reflect the legacy of male domination in the public sphere. They also reveal the resistance that some men have to the inclusion of women. Similarly, there are ways in which the subtle and subconscious cultures of business, trade unions, and political parties significantly exclude African Americans, Latinos, Asian Americans, and Native Americans. Race and gender inequality is deeply rooted in the rituals, customs, and practices of all social groups. Not surprisingly, the labor movement, like other groups, subconsciously retained and maintains these values and has not sufficiently addressed the costs of exclusion.[8]

Change and Resistance: The Iron Law of Oligarchy

At different historical junctures, the labor movement has collaborated with social movements to campaign for equal rights for women and minorities, in ways that strengthened, rather than weakened, union economic bargaining power and political clout. Indeed, as historians Nelson Lichtenstein and Robert Korstad have argued, the labor movement fought for civil rights long before the modern civil rights movement.[9] Dennis Deslippe, Nancy Gabin, Lisa Phillips, and Dorothy Sue Cobble have shown that labor in the twentieth century supported racial and gender equality as part of its political agenda. Collaboration and coalition with civil rights advocates and labor feminists broadened labor politics and, more importantly, signaled labor's understanding of its responsibility to organize and advocate for a diverse and complex working class.[10] The question then might be why such coalitions have limited impact on labor movement membership and influence.

As we saw in the last chapter, competing interests and differing priorities in such basic policies as seniority and promotion within the labor movement sparked conflict with civil rights organizations, women's advocates, environmental groups, and the immigrant rights movement. Many working-class men and women, like their middle- and upper-class peers, harbored prejudices about race, ethnicity, gender, religion, and sexual orientation. These prejudices went far beyond who would be included in the labor movement to the heart of labor's place in American culture. Who is allowed to be a union brother or sister matters. As labor advocates encountered the new conservatism, what one historian called "Thunder on the Right," they found surprisingly less unity among working-class people—black, white, or brown, male or female—on issues such as the role of government, social welfare, taxes, immigration and trade policy, and state police powers. Increasingly, labor leaders came to understand that an undivided working class might be impossible to achieve when working-class politics encompasses the world far beyond individual workplaces and national boundaries.[11]

In addition to encountering the changing gender and race composition of the labor force, the labor movement has, like other organizations, struggled to adapt to a changing economic and political world. In three separate periods of labor history, labor unions have had to confront structural and political changes that fundamentally changed the environment of labor relations and the calculus for successful labor action. The first, during the progressive period, brought the syndicalists of the Industrial Workers of the World into conflict with older forms of trade union organization. The second, during the 1930s, returned the labor movement, which had been weakened by its repression in the 1920s, to an earlier emphasis on organizing the unorganized and bringing new occupational and social groups into the labor movement. While labor unions opened their doors to black, Latino, and Asian American workers, and saw increasing numbers of women join unions during World War II, they remained largely white and male organizations. During the 1960s and 1970s, political parties disengaged from "the labor question" and a new generation of workers became estranged from labor activism in politics. In response, leaders of the powerful, centralized, and bureaucratic postwar labor movement further distanced themselves from their members. Not only was there less concern about rank-and-file members and grassroots union democracy, but union leaders were alienated from the new labor force—urban African American and Latino workers, new and returning women workers, and immigrant and undocumented workers, who continued to dominate agricultural and service work. Such distance caused labor leaders to lose credibility in politics as a whole and among workers in particular. In public opinion, labor unions lost ground, as unions were increasingly seen to be "out of touch" with a different economic world.

Economic Competition, the Environment, and "the Business Climate"

At the same time, since the 1950s, corporate leaders and business organizations focused their sights on marginalizing labor within the political and economic arena. Employers relocated factories in right-to-work states and, later, moved to low-wage countries. They developed public relations campaigns and funded political candidates who were aggressively anti-union. Business groups sought changes in trade policies and tariffs that allowed the outsourcing of manufacturing jobs. The economic changes of the 1970s, including the fuel crisis, high unemployment, and rising prices, put workers and unions on the defensive. Not only did state and federal governments seek to cut their budgets and taxes, meaning fewer services and fewer public sector jobs; but elected officials sought to privatize what services remained.

By the 1970s, conservative politicians, who argued about the adverse effects of the welfare state on manufacturing and investment, took the offensive. They advocated a loosening of environmental and labor regulations, new business tax incentives, and trade policies that rewarded overseas investment. In effect, the tax burden was shifted from corporations to individuals and from upper bracket taxpayers to lower income earners. These policies also gave greater financial incentives to employers and investors who took their business—and, with it, their jobs and payroll—off shore.[12]

Among the most important arguments here was about "the business climate"—what was, in effect, the context and cost of doing business. In straightforward business calculus, "the cost of doing business"—buying land, investing in machinery, paying license fees, acquiring permits, and paying taxes—is, in effect, investment that allows firms to grow and expand. Schools, roads, and public services in local communities help businesses to recruit workers but also to get them to work on time, deliver mail, and ship goods. At the same time, the land on which a business is built, the taxes they paid for the services they and their employees used, and the local and state government rules that they had to follow—from pollution controls and employer contributions to workers' compensation and labor laws—varied from state to state and region to region. In this difference, the cost of doing business in a federal system, where states and communities could grant land and tax abatements and waive regulations, was given new meaning. "Business climate" became watchwords for conservative politics in the 1970s.[13]

The business climate lobby responded as well with an anti-environmental agenda. By 1970, the environmental movement had achieved major goals in the Clean Air Act and the Clean Water Act. Requiring new pollution controls over water and airborne emissions, the acts were designed to address increasingly toxic levels of chemicals and lead in air and water. The Environmental Protection Agency was tasked with enforcing national standards for pollution controls. As with other federal regulations, there was enormous variability at the municipal and state levels. Under pressure to cut the federal budget, the EPA and other enforcement agencies saw reductions in their resources and staff. There simply were not enough inspectors nor enough agency staff to meet the national need. Enforcement became, to a great extent, dependent on the activism of local and regional groups, who themselves provided information gathered in street-level epidemiological studies unimagined by Congress but crucial to enforcement.[14]

Environmental Blues

Even as business forces sought to reduce or eliminate government regulation, workers were increasingly aware of the hazards and risks at the workplace.

Among the new opportunities for labor was to join with environmental justice organizations. In cases where workers were encountering, with direct impact, health risks and physical threats in the workplace from exposure to radiation, pesticides, and toxic chemicals, new biological pathogens, ventilation and mechanical failures, and accidental injuries and fatalities, labor unions had new grounds on which to challenge managerial authority and argue for union intervention and control. In the auto industry, the use of paints, lead, chemical adhesives, and wood fillers had created new carcinogenic risks; in the atomic energy field, radiation exposures from inadequate and failing uranium solders to the catastrophic radiation leak at Three Mile Island; in working-class communities new exposures to incinerator and smokestack gasses; near mines, smelters, and factories, coal, asbestos, and silicon dust, and in harvesting exposure to chemical pesticides aroused worker anger and awareness of the threat that work could present.[15]

Environmental concerns were at the heart of many labor struggles in the 1970s. It was not simply low wages that brought miners out in numbers in the 1972 strike at Brookside Mine in Harlan County. It was the epidemic of black lung among miners and continued safety concerns in non-union mines. For automobile workers, the toxic air of the foundry and the paint shop had given rise to escalating rates of workplace cancer; faster machine speeds spurred higher rates of workplace injuries and fatalities. In other cases—the BASF boycott in the chemical industry, the incidence of silicosis in hard rock mining, exposure to asbestos dust in manufacturing, brown lung among textile workers, or radiation levels in nuclear plants—workers now understood the connection between hazardous working environments and workers' well-being. By the mid-1970s, the UAW, the United Steel Workers, the United Mine Workers, and the Oil, Chemical, and Atomic Workers had made connections with environmental groups and the environmentalists in their own ranks.[16]

Labor was, however, faced with the opposition of business lobbyists and conservative politicians who sought to take labor, and government, out of the workplace. Since the 1970 passage of the Occupational Safety and Health Act, the agency had been chronically underfunded. Its mandate to protect workers from toxic chemicals, carcinogens, dangerous equipment, fire hazards, and, later, blood-borne pathogens has been notoriously hard to meet, since the agency has a limited staff. Created under the Nixon Administration, OSHA soon faced budgetary constraints similar to those of the EPA. In particular, growing conservative forces in Congress and the erosion of regulatory authority under presidents Carter and Reagan meant that workers had less protection in the workplace and in the community. As Charles Noble noted in *Liberalism at Work*, no sooner had the OSHA been established than its power to implement its mandate was limited by budget cuts and legal challenges. It had little enforcement power and diminished capacity to inspect workplaces. Between 1972 and 1975, the number of inspections increased from 17,000 to nearly 90,000. In the 1980s, under the Reagan administration, these statistics slowly dropped, to only about 57,000. In the Bush and Clinton years, moreover, OSHA inspections decreased sharply. By 1999, there were only 22,000 workplace inspections. Under Reagan, the number of OSHA inspectors dropped by one-fourth between 1981 and 1982, and the over all staff by 22 percent. Even more devastating, there was a sharp reduction in funding available for inspections by state agencies.[17] The result was an increase in work injuries, occupational diseases, and workplace fatalities. In 2010, workplace deaths amounted to nearly 5,000 a year, while 50,000 died from occupational diseases. Entering the Reagan era, labor and environmental advocates competed with well-funded campaigns claiming the priority of economic growth and freedom over regulation and welfare.[18]

Conflicting Priorities: Community and Work Environments

Despite robust environmental campaigns, there was a growing political debate on the impact of environmental regulation on communities. Once again, the implementation of new government guidelines for more fuel-efficient and environmentally cleaner automobiles, regulations that required scrubbers on smokestacks, and a gradual shift to alternative energy sources changed the calculus for governments and businesses. Investigations into polluting effluents and toxic waste dumps did raise the cost of doing business over the short term. For whatever benefit might be derived, pollution controls on air emissions and waste water discharge meant new business investment—costs that had not been forecast and that were now seen as unnecessary and unfair.

In addition, conservative business groups began to challenge environmental regulations that went beyond industrial and urban pollution. Conserving and preserving wild habitats and unpolluted and underdeveloped public land for the future was an abiding concern from the origin of the environmental movement. Protecting endangered species also was integral to the broad mission of the environmental movement, which sought to protect natural ecosystems and biodiversity. And yet, as opponents of environmental protection argued, such measures could hamper economic growth and development. Drilling and mining on public lands, culling public herds of wildlife, cutting public stands of timber should be seen, they argued, as legitimate uses of the public trust and drivers of prosperity. For a fee, it was argued, public resources would provide the engine for private development.[19]

In a classic trope, business groups—and their conservative labor allies—placed the economic welfare of workers and their families against the survival of endangered species and the condition of the public commons. In the Pacific Northwest, the welfare of the spotted owl was deemed a poor substitute for a robust timber industry.[20] Arctic drilling, and the oil it would produce, was more important than caribou or polar bears. New regulations on emissions from coal and steel plants were set up in a competition with the jobs that mining and manufacturing provided. By 2010, strong arguments for restricting carbon emissions in order to abate climate change were met with opposition from those who wanted cheap energy and the economic growth that comes from mining. "Clean coal," argue proponents, will allow both. "Clean coal," however, takes neither the deadly statistics of the mine industry nor carbon dioxide emissions into consideration.

Despite conservative calls for deregulation, workers and working-class citizens who were self-organized, motivated to do their own studies of the frequency and course of occupational and residential disease, and advocated for new safeguards became, by the end of the decade, the most successful source of workplace and community protection. Whether it was in the studies of workplace cancer conducted by UAW members, the black-lung studies conducted by union miners and allied doctors, or the nurses' research and advocacy for protections against needlestick injury—it has been workers who have countered demands for a better business climate with evidence on how that climate affects workers at the street level. Among those who lived along Love Canal in the 1970s, or in Flint in 2015, or in thousands of other communities affected by higher levels of lead, chemical dumping, or smog, it was and is grassroots activists who demanded and won protection from toxic environments.

The Human Environment: Undocumented Workers

One of the most contested legacies of the labor movement has been that of anti-immigrant activism, which surfaced at key points in United States history. Labor unions supported the Chinese Exclusion Act in 1882, a series of immigration restriction laws in the early twentieth century—in a strange political coalition with the Anti-Immigration League—and a crackdown on undocumented workers and an increase in border protection in the years since the 1965 Immigration Reform Act. Ironically, legislation that restricts immigration, meant to curb the import of cheap labor, has had little or no impact on the practice of contract labor in the United States. Further, the federal government created opportunities for the importing of labor during times of shortage, such as the Bracero program that brought in cheap agricultural labor from Mexico and Jamaica during and after World War II, or the granting of EB-3 visas to skilled workers. Hostility to new immigrant groups has waxed and waned, reflecting rates of economic growth but seemingly unrelated to the willingness of American citizens to take on the jobs in unskilled and low-waged labor in the fields, mines, and construction sites.[21]

Despite this legacy, progressive unions like the United Auto Workers were more supportive of immigration law reform under the Johnson administration in the 1960s. The existence of a large group of undocumented workers and increased labor demand required a rethinking of immigration policy. In 1965, Congress passed the Immigration Reform Act, which revised immigration quotas, repealed the more punitive features of the immigration laws of the 1920s, and sought to create fairer and more equitable immigration policies. The law opened the doors to increased immigration and also highlighted the need for labor— skilled and semi-skilled—in the economy.[22] Middle Eastern, Caribbean, and Asian immigration gradually increased, as did that from Mexico.

Political refugees from Vietnam and Cambodia, Central America, and eventually the Middle East swelled the ranks of immigrants in the United States, as did the brain drain from India, Pakistan, China, and the Philippines. By the late 1970s, however, the energy crisis, gradual deindustrialization, and an economic downturn changed the debate. Many working- and middle-class people saw the existence of immigrant labor (whether legal or undocumented) as a threat to the American way of life, and hostility to foreign-made goods and foreign labor again surfaced. The "made-in-the-U.S.A." language of labor unions turned the debate over imports and exports into a targeted campaign to exclude and expel foreign-born workers. By the 1990s, these sentiments were widely shared among the general population of workers who had, by that time, suffered more than a decade of stagnant wages and the loss of good-paying jobs. Hostility surfaced among candidates for political office, who sought to curry favor among lower middle-class voters by blaming those who were "different" and foreign.

There were, however, exceptions. The Service Employees International Union (SEIU), a union with a long history of organizing among maintenance and janitorial workers, understood that there were areas, chief among them Los Angeles, where private building maintenance employees were not only immigrants but, more often than not, undocumented workers. Undocumented workers have turned to worker centers and to self-organization, as in the 2006 marches to demand changes in immigration policy and, in particular, as a path to citizenship.[23] In cities throughout the country, undocumented workers constitute the vast majority of workers in the food service and hospitality industries, in construction and in agriculture. We have a long history of benefitting from this labor. The labor movement has a long history of contesting who belongs to and whom is represented by labor. It has divided over the issues of race and gender equality, argued about the status of immigrant and undocumented workers, and fought over the basis for labor's claims—from the labor theory of value, to "job consciousness," to the universal call that "an injury to one is an injury to all." At this moment in time, it is the struggles of undocumented workers that have raised these issues again.

Labor and Politics Today: Are We All in This Together?

Today, the labor movement is faced with several challenges, for which its legacies do not provide easy answers. The decline of labor union membership and influence since the 1970s reflects labor's weakness in the private economy and the public sector. Whether labor's weakness might have been limited with more energetic efforts to adapt to the changing economy is unknown. Among the unions that did grow during the late twentieth century were those connected to and working with community organizing, public sector activism, environmental coalitions, and rights campaigns for immigrant and undocumented workers. Public sector workers have been a major part of this growth, and, understandably, they have been the target of conservative politicians. In 1984, Newt Gingrich used a "$40-an-hour janitor" driving an SUV as a major symbol of government corruption in his Republican party convention speech; more recently, teachers who refused to work in rat-infested schools have been the subject of such ire. These are just some of the ways in which conservative state legislatures and business advocacy groups seek to privatize government services and disband or disenfranchise public employee unions.

Despite energetic organizing campaigns in the American Federation of Teachers (AFT), the Service Employees International Union (SEIU), the American Federation of State, County and Municipal Employees (AFSCME), the Hotel and Restaurant Workers (HERE), and garment unions (UNITE: later UNITE-HERE), labor union membership continued its decline from its high point in the 1954, when nearly 35 percent of the labor force was unionized. Since 1970, when it had declined to 29.6 percent, union members as a proportion of the labor force have declined to 11 percent. In the private sector, only 6.7 percent of workers were unionized in 2015. Public sector gains partly offset private sector losses during the past few decades, but even public sector unionism has declined to 35.2 percent in 2015 from a high of 40.2 percent in 1976. With pressure to cut the size of government and to privatize government services from maintenance and janitorial service to social work, prisons, and charter schools, public sector unions have lost both numbers and influence.[24]

This decline has several causes: The anti-tax rhetoric of the 1970s, moves toward privatization of public services and assets (as recently as 2015 and 2016 with the Flint water crisis and the privatization of municipal water supplies in New Jersey), the anti-union campaigns that began with the right-to-work movement in the 1940s (and continuing today) and the charges of union corruption and undue political influence that began in the 1950s and continue unabated today. Structural changes in the U.S. economy account for much of these changes, but another significant factor has been not the undue political influence of labor unions but rather the decline of union influence in shaping the agenda and action of the Democratic party, its primary political alliance since the New Deal.

In his book, *Prisoners of the American Dream*, Mike Davis put the full weight of the argument on labor's misguided faith in the Democratic party, given its failure to bring home the bacon—or at least to reinstate post-1935 federal protections for workplace organizing and mediation of labor relations. He argues that this "barren marriage" has cost the labor movement flexibility and weakened its resolve to challenge anti-union campaigns and to improve worker benefits and state provisions. While he also chides the labor movement for its failure to support racial and gender equality, and rails against its moribund bureaucracy, his political argument summarizes the thrust of labor left thinking.[25]

The redemptive power of labor parties, despite the recent poor performance of such parties in the United Kingdom, Germany, and France in defending workers' rights, continues to be a myth that feeds the labor Left. Certainly, more forthcoming support for labor unions—beyond verbal affirmations to real legislation—would enhance the potential of labor organizing and labor politics. As Thomas Piketty shows in *Capital in the Twenty-first Century*, European workers still have better wages and benefits than their American counterparts, despite retrenchments that have occurred since the 1980s. Intergenerational mobility also remains higher in Europe than in the United States, in contrast to the immediate postwar years. European labor parties have given workers better health care and social wage policies than in the U.S.[26] But if that is true, then why don't American workers create a labor party? Why is it that, in 2015, we can have labor supporters of the centrist Hillary Clinton, old-style Democrat Joe Biden, nominative socialist Bernie Sanders, and—ironically—working class supporters as well of Donald Trump and former H-P CEO Carly Fiorina?

Three explanations might suffice. First, we can look toward an old explanation that has, over the years, served to explain "American exceptionalism" in politics. Labor economist Selig Perlman thought early white manhood suffrage was a major reason why labor and class politics have been only minor themes in our two-party political system. White workers generally did not work to win the vote, and they exercised it in ways that reflected more than their class status— ethnicity and race, religion, and community generally have played a more important role in working-class politics. Early on, workers bonded with the Democratic party. With few exceptions, whatever labor leadership has existed generally has lined up with the Democratic party and its agenda.[27]

Wage workers, for most of American history, have not been a majority—first and foremost because the United States was an agrarian nation that relied heavily on slave and family labor. In the twentieth century, salaried and contract workers constituted significant segments of the working population and often possessed different or contradictory interests than workers in regular wage employment. Moreover, there was a kind of undertow to the politics of class position. If the United States was the "land of opportunity," then that opportunity—accessible to many wage-workers—to own a piece of property, run a small business, win the lottery and invest the winnings, get educated and move into the middle class, or work one's way up from the shop floor, meant that class identity was neither stable nor certain. The workman of today was the businessman of tomorrow.

Skilled workers in the decades that stretched between the Gilded Age and World War I certainly believed that social mobility was the great gift of American citizenship. Leaders of the Knights of Labor, to use one example, showed a remarkable capacity to move back and forth across the class line. In Minneapolis, for instance, Jack McGaughey, a powerful voice for the workingman, became an assistant state labor commissioner and, later, a grocer. Timothy Brosnan, a shoemaker, later haberdasher, became a state legislator in Montana. And John Lamb, a fiery editorial writer and district assembly statistician for the KOL, became a statistician for Washington State. All of them retained their progressive politics, but none of them remained entrenched in working-class politics that bore a passing resemblance to their European peers. Similarly, in times of labor's most rapid growth, working-class leaders experienced social mobility, from Gompers in his ascent to the National Civic Federation and presidential counsel through labor journalists like Harvey O'Connor of the Federated Press and John Brophy of the United Mine Workers and the CIO.[28]

Between World War II and 1970, social mobility increased both in the United States and in Europe. For American workers, the G.I. Bill, while not providing for universal education for returning veterans after the war, still provided for a measure of upward mobility through educational grants, home and business loans, and veterans' preference in public and even private employment. The National Defense Security Act expanded higher education, providing low-interest loans to a broad swath of the American public. Expanded public funding for higher education, and the jobs that it supported, bolstered the prospects of working-class children, especially from union families, in ways that supported some measure of intergenerational upward mobility.[29] After 1970, however, economist Piketty argues, intergenerational class mobility in the United States declined in direct relation to rising inequality. For most of the twentieth century, then, "the available data suggest that social mobility has been and remains lower in the United States than in Europe."[30] The relative losses of American workers suggest a political cause.

Finally, it must be emphasized, unionized workers, and workers who might be unionized, were and are an interest group, not a voting bloc. That interest group lined up with a party that needed the votes of other interest groups and independent voters as well. This political fact placed limits on the extent to which labor could drive its agenda through Congress, state legislatures, or even city councils. Ironically, groups that advocated for business interests—chambers of commerce, businessmen's associations, the National Association of Manufacturers, and National Civic Federation, the Business Roundtable, and the American Enterprise Institute—did not encounter the same charge of pursuing private interests, because their political rhetoric relied deeply on the sanctity of private property, which gave cover to a multitude of individual and individuated political claims.[31]

Second, there's the disturbing fact that many workers do not vote for their interests—at least not their interests as labor unions define them. It is difficult, in a global economy dominated by international corporations for individuals to figure out what their interests are or how legislation reflects their interests or stymies them. For a worker at Caterpillar in the 1991 strike, what was most evident was that the company outsourced much of its labor, cut wages, and locked out its striking employees to hire replacement workers, because it could in fact hire cheaper labor.[32] How did workers come to understand that as an issue that fit into electoral decisions between Democrats and Republicans? Some time in the 1970s, small changes in foreign trade policies made possible the slow, incremental growth of manufacturing across a global workshop. Local workers voting in those years saw national presidential candidates who presented themselves, one more American than the other, as committed to American prosperity but utterly vague about what those things meant in terms that ordinary people—even those with Ph.D.'s—could understand. The mystery of international finance that allowed economic blackmail to downsize work forces, slash wages, and shift tax burdens from corporate capital gains to income and sales taxes was not clear; nor did the labor movement necessarily make the connections between these changes and a union card.[33]

It is not, as Thomas Frank would have it, that there's something wrong with Kansas or with the working-class voters that he and Democratic pragmatists Thomas and Mary Edsall refer to. Kansas as a state might have voted in a governor who has, over the space of his term, stripped the state of revenue and state citizens of benefits, but it is not an outlier. Other states—Red and Blue, Republican and Democrat—have elected governors and legislators who have embraced a vision of government in which "the commons" is not an arena to be protected but rather to be leased out. Attacks on minimum wage and support for "right to work" laws were not exactly voiced by candidates in working-class districts. Rather, politicians have been remarkably successful in compartmentalizing the concerns and interests of all voters within their larger political claims. Sometimes this has been expressed within a politics of fear—the other side is going to take your guns (rather than defend your union job)—and sometimes within a nationalist politics that sees collective interest groups as inherently anti-American. Labor is only out for itself, while "we" protect your freedom.

Third, there have been significant changes in the political process that have both limited labor's power and altered the calculus of politics. Those running for office in the years since the Reagan administration have been charged with fundraising as their principal obstacle to running for public office, a fact that has served a few large national unions well but the labor movement as a whole or workers individually significantly less well. What some after World War I called "money madness" has taken over political campaigning and the political agenda. In 2010, the Supreme Court decision in *Citizens United* declared invalid the restrictions on individual giving to political campaigns. It also permitted, through the back door, the growth of so-called "dark money," or political funds that could be donated to political parties and candidates without naming donors or, presumably, their specific political interests. Political candidates, ever more dependent on campaign donors to pay the escalating costs of campaigning in a media age, could accept donations and escape scrutiny on how such funds influenced their campaigns or their actions once in office.[34]

Not surprisingly, efforts to change the calculus between workers and employers, such as the Employee Free Choice Act, designed to allow unions to more easily organize workers, have met fierce opposition in this era. More recently, a whole new spate of "right to work" laws have been passed from Indiana and Michigan to Wisconsin and West Virginia, states that were once at the heart of labor's political and economic strength. Fierce local fights over the living wage such as "the fight for $15" have met equally fierce opposition; other efforts to strip away public employee rights and undercut prevailing wage laws that guaranteed union wages to all employees in construction and other industries have been introduced across the country. Opposition to labor unions has centered in the Republican party and other conservative groups such as the Tea Party and ALEC; labor support has waned among legislators otherwise occupied with re-election.[35]

The political conflicts between conservative businessmen and labor in the post-Clinton era came to a head in Wisconsin. In 2011, recently elected Governor Scott Walker, who ran for election promising not to attack labor unions, introduced a bill into the state legislature that effectively stripped public employee unions of their rights. That year, Madison, Wisconsin, became the epicenter of what some hoped would be the "Arab Spring" of American labor. Seventy thousand public workers and their allies occupied the state capitol to protest the imposition of a new set of restrictions on public employee unions that effectively undermined public employee unions under the rubric of the right to work but also, more importantly, demonizing public workers as "takers" of public resources and feeders at the public trough. Social workers, teachers, building guards and maintenance workers, clerks at the DMV and the county courthouse–every public employee group except police, firefighters, and the state highway patrol lost pension benefits, paid a greater portion of their health care costs, and lost their ability to grieve workplace misconduct. Governor Walker took up what he presented as a moral crusade against public employees who were, effectively, painted in similar ways as welfare cheats had been two decades before.[36] The bill that restricted public employee unions, creating in effect a "right to work" limitation on union dues, and restricting bargaining passed, despite elegant political maneuvers to limit Walker's power. By 2015, private unions faced a similar attack as Governor Walker, who had survived a recall campaign and been reelected, now pushed a right-to-work law and a broader anti-union agenda through the state legislature. It signaled, for the *New York Times*, the end of the labor movement.[37]

There are also signs of life in the labor movement, shoots that are green, networks that are growing, arguments that are being refurbished and regenerated to persuade workers to join a social movement that has, for nearly 150 years, been an advocate for all working people, despite its occasionally limited and biased vision. The campaigns for a $15 minimum wage, for a path to citizenship for undocumented workers, to pay public school teachers better and to give them better support, to modify the burdens of workers who are on parole and who, as convicted felons, have few rights, to address the problems in labor law and to bring better benefits to all workers: these are but a few examples of how the legacy of labor continues to this day—in advocating for the poor, those who lack workplace democracy, the disenfranchised voter and the non-union worker. In the broader arena, there is opposition to government austerity programs, to trade agreements that threaten jobs in the United States (the TransPacific Trade Pact), and to disproportionate military expenditures that neither reflect security needs nor allow us to invest in the domestic economy.

Conclusion

The documentary film, *With Babies and Banners*, captured one of the pivotal moments of the Flint Sit-Down Strike of 1937. After weeks of the standoff between company forces and union strikers, the United Auto Workers took a bold gambit. They asked the women of the Emergency Brigade, as a diversionary tactic, to picket one assembly plant, while they arranged to effectively shut down another, Chevrolet #4, which was more vital to production. Even as General Motors with the support of the local police was ejecting strikers from one building, the more central facility was brought under union control. After a two-month long sit-down strike, GM ceded victory to the upstart union. The bold decision to capture factories and face down General Motors, then the largest corporation in the United States, assured success in one of the most massive organizing strikes in American labor history and inspired hundreds of sit-down strikes between 1936 and 1939. Like the strikers in Lawrence, Massachusetts, before them, the auto workers of Flint showed innovation in their tactics and solidarity in the integration of even marginalized workers, the unemployed, and non-working women into the community on strike.[38]

Those who analyze the Flint Sit-Down strike point to a number of reasons for its success. The UAW struck General Motors during a particular political moment. With the New Deal at its zenith, crucial changes in labor law, bold union strategy and the participation of radical trade unionists, the CIO's "gospel of unity and unionism" unified working-class men and women from different ethnic, racial, and religious backgrounds and capitalized on the militancy and esprit de corps of the United Auto Workers in its early years. These strengths, which faded when the UAW and the CIO became "Big Labor," are cited as the primary causes for the resurgence of labor during the Great Depression. They also explain the continued national political influence of labor, even during the anti-communism of the Cold War years. Historian Mike Davis, and left labor critics such as sociologist C. Wright Mills and activist lawyer Staughton Lynd have argued that the ascendant labor bureaucracy—and its toxic alliance with the Democratic party—contained the seeds of labor's decline.[39] Other historians such as David Brody, Bob Zieger, and Sue Cobble have countered that workplace contractualism, and acceptance of government intervention in labor relations, assured the survival of labor unions in the last half of the twentieth century and made possible the emergence of women and minority leaders within labor.[40] Still others have suggested that the labor movement was inadequate as a vehicle for recruiting and politicizing those on the margins of the working class— unemployed or irregularly employed workers, migrant and undocumented laborers, minority and women wage-earners, and professional and managerial employees.[41]

Together these critics have asserted that the New Deal order in labor relations powerfully answered the needs of a specific segment of labor—white ethnics in industrial work—but did not address the needs of those outside primary industry. Those same workers lost out when industries began to decline, the labor force shifted and unions lost their power in collective bargaining and in the Democratic party agenda. Labor's loss of economic and political power occurred against the backdrop of an economy serviced by an increasingly diverse labor force, in which manufacturing played a diminished role. Most workers were employed in service industries, and the broader world was challenged by environmental degradation.

As previous chapters have shown, the American labor movement was slow to adapt to the shifting form and organization of the economy. Businesses and corporations had positive incentives to innovate. Moreover, most employers understood that, of the factors of production, labor was the most flexible in cost and the most vulnerable to competition. Over the course of the nineteenth and twentieth centuries, changes in work organization and machine and information technology presaged seismic changes in the landscape of labor relations. Labor's response was, generally, resistance—whether through resignation, migration, or, more rarely, soldiering and machine-breaking. Relatively consistently, skilled workers and their trade unions only reluctantly and belatedly developed the legal, organizational, and political tools suited for the times. More significantly, they kept marginal and non-union workers from gaining recognition in the work-place. Stubborn resistance to change, which Thomas Geoghegan argued is a chief characteristic of "Mastodon Labor," has remained a dominant union response to employer strategies.[42]

Long after excluded immigrant, minority, and women workers attained critical mass in the labor force and anti-union campaigns made industrial unionism increasingly obsolete, national labor unions kept their sights on maintaining membership, rather than capitalizing on new organizing opportunities. As AFL-CIO president George Meany explained, "Why should we worry about organizing groups of people who do not want to be organized? … Frankly, I used to worry about the size of membership. But quite a few years ago, I just stopped worrying about it, because to me, it doesn't make any difference."[43] Hide-bound labor leaders like Meany were, in a sense, only operating according to a script long familiar with scholars of social movements. What sociologists Max Weber and Roberto Michels termed "the iron law of oligarchy" fixed the structure and held the leadership of the labor movement in place.

One of the principal sources of division and discord in the labor movement, as we have noted, is rooted in its dual character, first, as a social movement, which, in periods of vibrant growth, recruited, educated, and mobilized millions of workers and, second, as an institution, which accrued power, created and reinforced relationships with employers and government, defended its base, and served its members to the exclusion and sometimes detriment of other workers. The dual—and even contradictory—character of the labor movement—broadly inclusive and democratic and at the same time exclusive and bureaucratic—has engendered the most fervent supporters and vehement critics for labor unions and for workers. While claiming to be the voice of the working class, that labor movement has on occasion silenced its members and critics and also failed to incorporate the diversity of workers within its leadership and even its agenda.

The tension between these two impulses—to organize the unorganized and to fight in a narrow sense for labor's interests—has shaped labor and working-class history and the broader outlines of American democracy. As a social movement mobilized to fight for fair wages and for social justice, the labor movement has inspired millions. Taking shape in a multitude of organizational forms, labor, and its advocates, pushed for a social welfare state that addressed the sources of poverty and disease, powerlessness and alienation with entitlements such as social security pensions, workers' compensation, unemployment insurance, and public education. It fought for economic opportunity that would ensure political equality. That meant laws to protect workers in plants, factories, stores, and fields; to protect the environment and to restore communities; to guard against abuses in the workplace and fight, however tentatively, for race and gender equality.

At the same time, under different leaders and in different contexts, labor organized aggressively for immigration restriction, racial segregation and discrimination in the workplace, reinforced already existing gender inequality, and fought for the granting of government and private employment benefits to the privileged few—white men of native birth or old immigrant roots, with property rights in their skill and political identities that made them the natural allies of business owners and employers, not marginal, temporary, or unskilled workers. In this role, the labor movement did exhibit strength. Exclusive unions meant tighter control over entry into the labor market, less competition for jobs, and greater bargaining power. But it also left labor open to accusations of racism, sexism, and xenophobia. Moreover, it simply made labor, whether in the craft unions of the AFL or in the Big Labor era in postwar America, seem greedy. It left them open to accusations of corruption, market manipulation, and unfair labor practices. Big Labor, for all its power, lost the public relations war because it could only claim to speak for a privileged segment of workers.

Notes

1 Mike Elk, "Volkswagen Isn't Fighting Unionization—but Leaked Docs Show Right-Wing Groups Are," *In These Times* November 13, 2013; Steven Greenhouse,

"Outsiders, Not Plant, Battle UAW in Tennessee," *New York Times* January 29, 2014; Gabe Nelson, "Must-Win for UAW; The Big Volkswagen Vote in Chattanooga Has Huge Implications for the Industry, Organized Labor," *Automotive News* February 10, 2014; Harold Meyerson, "Chattanooga Showdown," *The American Prospect* February 10, 2014; Mike Elk, "Tennessee Lawmakers Threaten to Block Subsidies if VW Plant Unionizes," *Working In These Times* February 11, 2014; "Historic Election Brings Outside Interference in the Vote of Chattanooga Volkswagen Workers," *UAW News* February 14, 2014; Steven Greenhouse, "VW Vote is Defeat for Labor in South," *New York Times* late edition, February 15, 2014; Alexandra Bradbury, "Minority Union at Volkswagen, For Now," *Labor Notes* July 23, 2014.

2   Samuel Gompers, *Seventy Years of Life and Labor: An Autobiography*, vol. 1 (New York, 1925, reprint 1957), 383; see also Elizabeth Faue, *Writing the Wrongs: Eva Valesh and the Rise of Labor Journalism* (Ithaca: Cornell University Press, 2002). For a more contemporary account, see Jonathan Cobb and Richard Sennett, *Hidden Injuries of Class* (New York: W.W. Norton, 1972); Correspondents, *Class Matters* (New York: Times Books, 2005).

3   Richard Edwards, David Gordon, and Michael Reich, *Segmented Work, Divided Workers: The Historical Transformation of Work in the United States* (Cambridge: Cambridge University Press, 1982); Ira Katznelson, *City Trenches: Urban Politics and the Patterning of Class in the United States* (Chicago: University of Chicago Press, 1981); Erik Olin Wright, *Classes* (London: Verso, 1985). See also Ruth Milkman, *Gender at Work: The Dynamics of Job Segregation by Sex during World War II* (Urbana: University of Illinois Press, 1987).

4   Werner Sombart, *Why Is There No Socialism in the United States* (New York: Macmillan, 1976. [1906]); Selig Perlman, *A Theory of the Labor Movement* (New York: Macmillan, 1924); Mike Davis,*Prisoners of the American Dream: Politics and the Economy in the History of the US Working Class* (London: Verso, 1986). See the wide range of historiographical essays, including Eric Foner, "Why is There No Socialism?" *History Workshop* 17 (April 1984), 57–80; essays in J. Carroll Moody and Alice Kessler-Harris, eds., *Perspectives on American Labor History: The Problems of Synthesis* (DeKalb: Northern Illinois University Press, 1990), among others.

5   Richard Oestreicher, "Urban Working-Class Political Behavior and Theories of American Electoral Politics, 1870–1940," *Journal of American History* 74 (1988) 1257–1286; idem, "The Rules of the Game: Class Politics in Twentieth Century America," in Kevin Boyle, ed., *Organized Labor and American Politics, 1894–1994: The Labor-Liberal Alliance* (Albany: SUNY Press, 1998), 19–50.

6   Marion Crain and Ken Matheny, "Labor's Identity Crisis," *California Law Review* 89 (2001) 1767–1846. Many studies of the New Deal capture these political compromises. There were moments in which left unionists called for racial equality and even equal pay for women, as Robin D.G. Kelley records in *Hammer and Hoe: Alabama Communists during the Great Depression* (Chapel Hill: University of North Carolina Press, 1990), 138–151. For claims to a longer legacy, see William P. Jones, "Something to Offer," *Jacobin* (August 2015): www.jacobinmag.com/2015/08/debs-socialism-race-du-bois-socialist-party-black-liberation/. As I have pointed out, these cases remained sidebars to the larger discussion. The marginalization of such claims, and the naming of women workers and minorities as "other than" working class, has created barriers to gender and race equality on the Left.

7   This critique is shared by many scholars, including David Roediger, *Towards the Abolition of Whiteness: Essays on Race, Politics and Working-Class History* (London: Verso, 1994); Paul Buhle, *Taking Care of Business: Samuel Gompers, George Meany, Lane Kirkland, and the Tragedy of American Labor* (New York: Monthly Review Press, 1999). For a critique of the scholarship, see Barbara J. Fields, "Whiteness, Racism, and Identity," *International Labor and Working-Class History* 60 (Fall 2001), 48–56; see also

Barbara Fields and Karen Fields, *Racecraft: The Soul of Inequality in American Life* (New York: Verso, 2012).

8 Cynthia Cockburn, *In the Way of Women: Men's Resistance to Sex Equality in Organizations* (Ithaca: ILR Press, 1991); see also Elizabeth Faue, "Paths of Unionization: Community, Bureaucracy, and Gender in the Minneapolis Labor Movement of the 1930s," in Ava Baron, ed., *Work Engendered: Toward a New History of American Labor* (Ithaca: Cornell University Press, 1991), 296–319; and Jeffrey Hearn and Wendy Parkin, "Gender and Organizations: A Selective Review and Critique of a Neglected Area," *Organization Studies* 4:3 (1983), 219–242.

9 Robert Korstad and Nelson Lichtenstein, "Opportunities Found and Lost: Labor, Radicals, and the Early Civil Rights Movement," *Journal of American History* 75:3 (December 1988), 786–811; see also Robert Korstad, *Civil Rights Unionism: Tobacco Workers and the Struggle for Democracy in the Mid-twentieth Century South* (Chapel Hill: University of North Carolina Press, 2003).

10 Nancy Gabin, *Feminism in the Labor Movement: Women and the United Auto Workers, 1935–1975* (Ithaca: Cornell University Press, 1990); Dennis Deslippe, *Rights, Not Roses: Unions and the Rise of Working-Class Feminism, 1945–1980* (Urbana: University of Illinois Press, 2000); Lisa Phillips, *A Renegade Union: Interracial Organizing and Labor Radicalism* (Urbana: University of Illinois Press, 2012); Kathleen M. Barry, *Femininity in Flight: A History of Flight Attendants* (Durham: Duke University Press, 2007); Dorothy Sue Cobble, *The Other Women's Movement: Workplace Justice and Social Rights in Modern America* (Princeton: Princeton University Press, 2004).

11 Underneath this narrow analysis is the pessimism about the intellectual and political capacities of working people that is woven into Western culture. All too commonly paired with smug self-righteousness, the bias surfaces even among labor historians. Two recent correctives are John Bowe, *Gig: Americans Talk about Their Jobs* (New York: Broadway Books, 2001), and Mike Rose, *The Mind at Work: Valuing the Intelligence of the American Worker* (New York: Viking, 2004). Jefferson Cowie's *Stayin' Alive: The 1970s and the Last Days of the Working Class* (New York: New Press, 2012), steers between what we can only call "workerism" and his blame-the-victim analysis of working-class decline. For Cowie, Bruce Springsteen plays the same role as William Blake does in E.P. Thompson's *The Making of the English Working Class*. He becomes an alternative, if equally monolithic, working-class icon. Extraordinary musician though Springsteen is, focusing on him rather misses the point that working-class politics are diverse—not uniformly liberal or conservative. We should note that unionized workers tend to vote more liberally than their non-unionized peers and than many white-collar middle-class voters. That doesn't fit the smug assessment of conservative voters as working-class Neanderthals or of working-class voters as right-wing populists.

12 Judith Stone, "Conflict, Change, and Economic Policy in the Long 1970s," in Brenner et al., eds., *Rebel Rank and File: Labor Militancy and the Revolt from Below during the Long 1970s* (New York: Verso, 2010), 77–104.

13 For background, see Elizabeth Tandy Shermer, "'Take Government Out of Business by Putting Business into Government': Local Boosters, National CEOs, Experts, and the Politics of Midcentury Capital Mobility," in Kim Philips-Fein and Julian E. Zelitzer, eds., *What's Good for Business: Business and American Politics since World War II* (New York: Oxford University Press, 2012), 91–106.

14 Jason Corburn, *Street Science: Community Knowledge and Environmental Health Science* (Cambridge, MA: MIT Press, 2005).

15 Robert Gordon, "Poison in the Fields: The United Farm Workers, Pesticides, and Environmental Politics," *Pacific Historical Review* 68:1 (Fall 1999), 51–77; Robert Gordon, "'Shell No!': OCAW and the Labor Environmental Alliance," *Environmental History* 3:4 (October 1998), 460–487; Josiah Rector, "Environmental Justice at Work:

The UAW, the War on Cancer, and the Right to Equal Protection from Toxic Hazards in Postwar America," *Journal of American History* 101:2 (September 2014), 1–23; Steve Schwarze, "The Silences and Possibilities of Asbestos Activism: Stories from Libby and Beyond," in *Environmental Justice and Environmentalism*, edited by Ronald Sandler and Phaedra Pezzullo (2007), 165–188; Kristin Shrader-Frechette, "Risky Occupational Environments, the Double Standard and Just Compensation," in *Environmental Justice: Creating Equality, Reclaiming Democracy* (2005), 135–162.

16 Dan Georgakas and Marvin Surkin, *Detroit, I Do Mind Dying: A Study in Urban Revolution*, updated ed., (Boston MA: South End Press, 1999), gives several examples of environmental risks and demands on part of the dissident union members, as does Heather Thompson's *Whose Detroit?* (Ithaca, NY: Cornell University Press, 2001). Richard Fry, "Fighting for Survival: Coal Miners and the Struggle Over Health and Safety in the United States, 1968–1988" (Ph.D. dissertation, Wayne State University, 2010), drawing on the rich literature on coal miners, shows a similar linkage; Russell B. Olwell, *At Work in the Atomic City: A Labor and Social History of Oak Ridge, Tennessee* (Knoxville: University of Tennessee Press, 2008); Timothy J. Minchin, *Forging a Common Bond: Labor and Environmental Activism during the BASF Lockout* (Gainesville: University Press of Florida, 2002).

17 Charles Noble, *Liberalism at Work: The Rise and Fall of OSHA* (Philadelphia: Temple University Press, 1986); Peter Lurie, Marti Long, and Sidney M. Wolfe, "Reinventing OSHA: Dangerous Reductions in Enforcement during the Clinton Administration," Public Citizen Health Research Group, September 6, 1999, www.citizen.org/docum ents/1494.pdf; Mark Allen Eisner, Jeffrey Worsham, and Evan J. Ringquist, *Contemporary Regulatory Policy* (Boulder, CO: Lynne Rienner, 1999), 188–189; Sage Reference Editions, *Federal Regulatory Directory* (Thousand Oaks, CA: CQ Press, 2016), 321–322.

18 Jamie Smith Hopkins, "Unequal Risk: The Campaign to Weaken Worker Protections," Center for Public Integrity, www.publicintegrity.org/2015/06/29/17522/campaign-weaken-worker-protections, accessed September 6, 2016; David Michaels, *Doubt Is Our Product: How Industry's War on Science Threatens Your Health* (New York: Oxford University Press, 2008). For recent statistics, see AFL-CIO Safety and Health Department, *Death on the Job*, www.aflcio.org/Issues/Job-Safety/2012-Death-on-the-Job-Report, accessed May 2, 2012.

19 Patrick Alitt, *A Climate of Crisis: America in the Age of Environmentalism* (New York: Penguin Press, 2014) provides an overview since the 1950s. See also Brian K. Obach, *Labor and the Environmental Movement: The Quest for Common Ground* (Cambridge, MA: MIT Press, 2004).

20 Erik Loomis, *Empire of Timber: Labor Unions and the Pacific Northwest Forests* (Cambridge: Cambridge University Press, 2015), argues, persuasively, that common assumptions about workers opposing environmental regulations are too simple and ignore historical experience of labor and environmental cooperation and alliance.

21 Mai Ngai, *Impossible Subjects: Illegal Aliens and the Making of Modern America* (Princeton: Princeton University Press, 2003); Aviva Chomsky, *Undocumented: How Immigration Became Illegal* (Boston MA: Beacon Press, 2014); Gunther Peck, *Reinventing Free Labor: Padrones and Immigrant Workers in the North American West, 1880–1930* (Cambridge: Cambridge University Press, 2000); Zaragosa Vargas, *Labor Rights Are Civil Rights: Mexican American Workers in Twentieth Century America* (Princeton: Princeton University Press, 2007), 276–282; Cindy Hahamovitch, *No Man's Land: Jamaican Guestworkers in America and the Global History of Deportable Labor* (Princeton: Princeton University Press, 2011); Deborah Cohen, *Braceros: Migrant Citizens and Transnational Subjects in the Postwar United States and Mexico* (Chicago: University of Chicago Press, 2011), among others.

22 Ngai, *Impossible Subjects*, 266–268.

23 Victor Narro, Saba Waheed, and Jassmin Poyaoan, *Building a Movement Together Workers Centers and Labor Union Affiliations* (Los Angeles: UCLA Labor Center, 2015), www.labor.ucla.edu/publication/building-a-movement-together-workers-centers-and-labor-union-affiliations-2/.

24 U.S. Bureau of Labor Statistics, union affiliation data from the Current Population Survey, http://data.bls.gov/timeseries/LUU0204922700?years_option=all_years, accessed August 25, 2016.

25 Mike Davis, *Prisoners of the American Dream: Politics and Economy in the History of the American Working Class* (New York: Verso, 1986).

26 Thomas Piketty, *Capital in the Twenty-first Century* (Cambridge, MA: Belknap Press, 2014).

27 Selig Perlman, *A Theory of the Labor Movement in the United* States (New York: Macmillan, 1928); Sean Wilentz, "Against Exceptionalism: Class Consciousness and the American Labor Movement, 1790–1820," *International Labor and Working Class History* vol. 1 (1984), 1–24; Ira Katznelson and Aristide Zolberg, eds., *Working Class Formation: Nineteenth Century Patterns in Western Europe and North America* (Princeton: Princeton University Press, 1986); Seymour Martin Lipset and Gary Marks, *It Didn't Happen Here: Why Socialism Failed in the United States* (New York: Norton, 2001).

28 Elizabeth Faue, *Writing the Wrongs*, 36–40; see also Chapter 1. For the CIO era, diverse autobiographies and memoirs and standard biographies reveal comparable—if not greater—social mobility among labor activists. For contrast, see Daisy Rooks, "The Cowboy Mentality: Organizers and Occupational Commitment in the New Labor Movement," *Labor Studies Journal* 28:3 (Fall 2003), 33–61.

29 This is largely anecdotal, since there has been little scholarly interest in longitudinal studies of working class upward mobility. Still, the sheer growth of the college and university student population argues for this growth. Autobiographical statements, memoirs, and essays by working-class academics suggest some mobility.

30 Piketty, *Capital in the Twenty-first Century*, 484.

31 Here, see Kim Voss, *The Making of American Exceptionalism: The Knights of Labor and Class Formation in the Nineteenth Century* (Ithaca: Cornell University Press, 1984), which argues that the chief distinction between the U.S. and Europe was (and is) in the higher degree of business class organization in the United States. See also more recent work by Elizabeth Tandy Shermer and Kim Philips-Fein.

32 On Caterpillar, see "Caterpillar Faces Strike in Two Cities," *Wall Street Journal* November 4, 1991; "Caterpillar and Union Workers Remain Apart," *New York Times* November 11, 1991; "Caterpillar Workers Try to Defy Lockout," *Los Angeles Times* November 12, 1991; "Caterpillar Announces Layoffs," *Wall Street Journal* November 14, 1991; "Caterpillar Workers Stage Walkout at Engine Plant," *Wall Street Journal* February 24, 1992; "Caterpillar at Impasse," *New York Times* March 7, 1992; "Caterpillar and Union in Battle over Principles," *Los Angeles Times* March 16, 1992; "Caterpillar Bars Returning Workers from Factories," *Los Angeles Times* April 16, 1992; "Caterpillar's Trump Card," *New York Times* April 16, 1992; "Caterpillar Workers' Shock," *New York Times* April 16, 1992; "Caterpillar's Success in Ending Strike May Curtail Unions Use of Walkouts," *Wall Street Journal* April 20, 1992; "Caterpillar Hit with NLRB Complaint," *Los Angeles Times* September 26, 1992; "Recent Labor Contract Results Portend a Rough Bargaining Year for Unions," *Wall Street Journal* June 25, 1993; see also Stephen Franklin, *Three Strikes: Labor's Heartland Losses and What It Means for Labor* (New York: Guilford Press, 2000).

33 Stein, "Conflict, Change and Economic Policy." Lawrence Shoup, *Wall Street's Think Tank: The Council on Foreign Relations and the Empire of Neoliberal Geopolitics, 1976–2014* (New York: Monthly Review Press, 2015), argues that elites seem to possess a vision of a "race to the bottom" that underlies their agenda and fuels their politics.

34 Thomas Ferguson, "Party Competition and Industrial Structure in the 2012 Elections: Who's Really Driving the Taxi to the Dark Side?" *International Journal of Political Economy* 42:2 (2013), 3–41.

35 Steven Greenhouse, *The Big Squeeze: Tough Times for the American Worker* (New York: Anchor, 2009); David Rolf, *The Fight for $15: The Right Wage for a Working America* (New York: New Press, 2016), among others.

36 Shoup, *Wall Street's Think Tank*, 194–199; John Nicolls, *Uprising: How Wisconsin Renewed the Politics of Protest, from Madison to Wall Street* (New York: Nation Books, 2012); Michael D. Yates, *Wisconsin Uprising: Labor Fights Back* (New York: Monthly Review Press, 2012); Jason Stein and Patrick Marley, *More Than They Bargained For: Scott Walker, Unions, and the Fight for Wisconsin* (Madison: University of Wisconsin Press, 2013).

37 Dan Kaufman, "Fate of the Union," *New York Times Magazine* June 14, 2015, 40–45, 54–55.

38 Mary Heaton Vorse, *Labor's New Millions* (New York: Modern Age Books, 1938), 72–81; Sol Dollinger and Genora Johnson Dollinger, *Not Automatic: Women and the Left in the Forging of the Auto Workers Union* (New York: Monthly Review Press, 2000), 12–160.

39 C. Wright Mills, *New Men of Labor*, while admiring, restarted an old debate on bureaucratization. See Staughton Lynd, ed., *We Are All Leaders: The Alternative Unionism of the Early 1930s* (Urbana: University of Illinois Press, 1996), 1–26; Mike Davis in *Prisoners of the American Dream*, among others.

40 David Brody, *Workers in Industrial America: Essays on the Twentieth Century Struggle*, 2nd ed. (New York: Oxford University Press, 1993), 82–119; implicitly in Nelson Lichtenstein, *State of the Union: A Century of American Labor* (Princeton: Princeton University Press, 2002), among others.

41 Most studies of women in the labor movement suggest how the narrowness of labor's vision and organizational strategy discouraged and even prevented the activism of working women. Among minority workers, both male and female, the resistance of the labor movement to legislative and workplace remedies such as affirmative action, problematic in the context of union seniority has made the labor movement less effective as a vehicle for racial equality as well.

42 Thomas Geoghegan, *Which Side Are You On? Trying to Be for Labor When It's Flat on Its Back* (New York: Farrar Straus Giroux, 1991), 3.

43 George Meany, quoted in Arthur Shostak, *Robust Unionism: Innovations in the Labor Movement*, (Ithaca: ILR Press, 1991), 59.

CONCLUSION

The Legacy of Labor in American Politics

The United Auto Workers, one of the most powerful labor unions in United States history, has made its home since 1934 in the state of Michigan. The UAW owes its stature in labor history to the economic importance of the automotive industry. Walter Reuther, UAW president from 1946 to 1970, embraced the liberal welfare state, championed a national civil rights agenda, and became the epitome of responsible unionism. He was only one of a large cadre of leaders that emerged from the UAW to shape labor politics in these crucial decades. Such leaders as Emil Mazey, R.J. Thomas, Shelton Tappes, Horace Sheffield, Robert "Buddy" Battle, Mildred Jeffrey, and Lillian Hatcher also became national figures. Like the automobile industry that they unionized, UAW stalwarts had contradictory reputations. Reuther was as reviled as he was respected and became, from the perspective of Big Business, "the most dangerous man in Detroit." Viewed from the political Left, he was a corporate shill and virulent anti-communist.[1] In Detroit today, Reuther's name graces a labor archive and a freeway; but in 2012, Michigan adopted a right-to-work law that would have rattled the teeth of the UAW's avatar. Like the once solid union states of Wisconsin and Indiana, Michigan is no longer home to the union shop.[2]

Michigan, once part of the industrial heartland of the United States, is an appropriate place to conclude this study. The state has seen the rise and fall of labor unionism in the twentieth century, from the new unionism to the rise of the CIO, the emergence of public employee unions, and the 1970s labor rebellion as embodied in the Dodge Revolutionary Union Movement. While the labor movement has maintained a powerful political presence, the ills of the manufacturing sector and the loss of jobs have transformed labor's position and its agenda. Labor leaders target those trade policies and taxes that undermine domestic industry. They search for immigration reform that both protects

American workers and the undocumented workers who have earned a place at the table. Just as important, however, the future of work, and thus of workers and unions, bends toward service and information sector jobs. So, too, in Michigan, health care, financial services, and personal care are the basis of economic growth. Part-time and temporary workers, the "precariat" and "gigariat" have become visible in new ways. Workers in these sectors are not well unionized. Where unions do exist, they face challenges from conservative employers, resentful consumers, and the political will to privatize public sector jobs. This requires a new kind of labor politics, for unionism is a hard sell in an era of wage stagnation and declining real incomes.[3]

Still, at a time of rising inequality, the labor movement remains a potent voice in electoral politics and movements for social justice in the United States and around the globe. As I write in September 2016, 150 million workers just staged the largest strike in history in India. Prisoners have launched a nation-wide prison strike in over twenty-four states and forty facilities. Several cities have passed living wage ordinances. There have been major gains in addressing the needs and supporting the rights of undocumented workers, gay and lesbian workers, and the disabled. The Culinary Workers Union is organizing Trump hotel workers, taking on the property interests of a major political party candidate, in a town where only recently hotel and restaurant workers won a strategic victory. Drivers for car services Uber and Lyft are talking about organizing against their companies, which had been shielded from labor action by the drivers' status as independent contractors; and graduate students have won a critical court case for the right to organize—both victories challenging employee classifications that had long stymied labor organization.[4]

At the same time, labor faces ongoing battles over the privatization of govern-ment and the rights of public employee unions. Labor has played a visible role in the presidential campaign, but labor rights do not make the docket for the debate. Labor law reform—the Employee Free Choice Act—remains an unfulfilled goal. Real wages remain flat, despite modest income gains. The longer term consequences of a weakened, if still active, labor movement are growing income inequality and effective disenfranchisement. To rethink the American labor movement is to acknowledge we have reached a tipping point. Labor will either cease to exist as a political and economic force, or it will, in one form or another, re-emerge to address the needs of workers. We still do not know what the workplace future will be, nor whether workers can continue to earn a union wage in an uncertain global economy. This short chapter outlines the changes in the work force and the labor movement in the recent past, setting in historical context the current state of the American labor movement today.

Outsourcing, the Environment, and Worker Protections

There has been a significant shift in the American economy away from domestic manufacturing and toward greater dependence on imported goods. Changes in tax and trade policies have meant that the capital flight—not simply to the South but to the Maquiladoras border region and to factories in Asia and Central America—continues with devastating impact on the manufacturing sector. More damaging has been the power of retail giant Wal-Mart to set the parameters of the industrial economy, from "just-in-time" production to the price of labor through the supply chain. Not only manufacturing work but jobs in the service and financial sectors have been relocated overseas. Call centers in India and Ireland handle financial transactions and resolve consumer problems with computers and digital media.[5]

Changes in the global economy have proven more threatening to the labor movement than even the most far-seeing leaders had envisioned. The brief of American unions against outsourcing was and is not, however, only about the loss of wages or job opportunities. It involves the deterioration of workplace conditions in the United States and in other countries. American-based multinational corporations manufacture or purchase goods in factories that have no government regulation or private oversight. By the 1980s, electronics and clothing factories in maquiladoras in the United States–Mexico borderlands of Ciudad Juarez were found guilty of labor abuses. The global assembly line became known for its toxic chemical environments and occupational safety hazards. Undocumented workers in the United States often worked in similarly unregulated conditions, with long hours and hazardous working conditions. Their employment is often coerced with the threat of blackmail and deportation. The result has been increasing incidents where workplace hazards led to worker deaths, as in the deaths of workers in a factory fire in a North Carolina chicken processing facility in 1991 and the escalating toll of occupational injuries that the AFL-CIO annually chronicles in *Death on the Job*. Construction runs at breakneck speed, and unprotected workers die; poor regulation of oil platforms led to the *Deepwater Horizon* disaster that took eleven oil rig workers' lives and caused a major environmental crisis. Abroad, these hazards have escalated. In Savar, Bangladesh, the collapse of a building in Rana Plaza, where thousands worked, lived, and shopped, killed more than 1,100 workers and injured 2,500; a year later, more than 100 were killed in a garment factory fire in Dhaka. Among Chinese workers, there have been other incidents including, most devastatingly, mine collapses and a recent harbor facility explosion that killed eleven and wounded hundreds of others.[6]

Apart from the physical hazards of the workplace, where neglect has gone unchecked, there is pervasive wage theft, employee blackmail, working off the clock, low base wages, unregulated working conditions, and the abuse of authority that leads to workplace harassment, bullying, and sexual violence. These conditions exist in American workplaces, but our global economy has meant that work has shifted away from countries where there is strict observation of the rules to those countries that pay little attention to global labor agreements.

Union Defeats and Victories

Over the past few decades, the labor movement has faced key battles in several sectors. Looking at the roll of strikes, it becomes clear that the strike as a weapon with long-term consequences—either positive or negative—has almost disappeared.[7] The threat of capital flight—of companies moving their facilities—and the hiring of replacement workers for those who strike undermined targeted strikes in manufacturing. In the meatpacking industry, United Food and Commercial Workers Local P-9 went on strike in Austin, Minnesota, in 1986—the same town that Frank Ellis had organized in the 1930s. The strike generated support from broad sectors of society, including a corporate campaign designed to push at the boundaries of the Taft-Hartley Act and use consumer pressure to force the company to the bargaining table. It failed.[8] Replacement workers proved the end of strikes at Staley, Caterpillar, and Bridgestone/Firestone in the 1990s. Management threatened to use replacement workers again in the recent Verizon strike, which ended, instead, with a union contract.[9]

In the information sector, the Detroit newspaper strike lasted nearly a year, before the company broke the union; but the company had the upper hand throughout the walkout. Not only did political winds favor union-busting, but mass circulation newspapers, and the businesses which support them, have faced far greater problems than reporters and delivery vans striking. Revenues for print media were sinking long before the internet became a constant companion on cellphones and tablets. As with the broadcast television networks, print news media were upended by the expansion of cable networks, social media, and online news. They were no longer able to turn a profit, and the reporters and printers who struck the *Detroit News* and *Detroit Free Press* lacked leverage.[10] Organizing campaigns in other industries suffered the same fate. They could not compete with overseas producers, and they remained removed from the daily interactions of customers. Media coverage of strikes and organizing campaigns in industry tend to voice the concerns of those who fear the loss of jobs more than underpayment.

In the service sector, unions had somewhat greater power in the workplace, in part because they had no physical plant to strike. Rather, during the Teamster's United Parcel Service (UPS) strike of 1997, the mobility of drivers, the increasing dependence of business and private customers on private delivery service, and the personal relationship built between uniformed UPS drivers and clients put consistent and increasing pressure on UPS to settle the strike. The media-savvy campaign also preempted the parent company's capacity to shape the strike narrative.[11] In a similar fashion, the Verizon strike of 2016 ended in victory, in no small part because mobile phone companies have a continuous presence in customers' lives. One also suspects that customer discontent at the inconvenience and burden of cable service and billing put many against management, who appeared focused on laying off workers and stripping company payrolls at a time when good paying jobs were at a premium and corporate profits and executive salaries on the rise.

The Landscape of Labor Organization: Labor's Legacy and Its Promise

Shifts in political parties and voter allegiance weakened labor's political influence, and the passage of an election reform law and the Supreme Court decision that eviscerated it altered the role of money in politics and of labor as a counterbalance to that influence. A key goal in the politics that followed was a full-scale assault on the remaining strongholds of labor. The starving of the labor "beast,"[12] wherein state legislatures pass right-to-work laws, corporations engage in open union-busting and unfair labor practices, has led to a labor movement that constitutes less than 11 percent of the adult labor force. Labor possesses far less power than it did even at the end of the Reagan–Bush era, and has splintered into warring segments that no longer support each other or all workers.[13]

Public sector unionism, coming at a time of industrial union decline, was marginalized as a force within organized labor, even as public sector workers slowly became the majority of union members. The AFT, AFSCME, and SEIU (Service Workers' International Union) were the only unions to experience continued growth through the last thirty years of the twentieth century. Yet, at a time of fiscal crisis, both in the 1970s and in the 2008 recession, public employees became the target of state legislatures, conservative office holders, and tax reformers determined to smoke out the last remnants of a public welfare state. In politics and the media, labor lost ground, as stereotypes of overpaid and reactionary white working-class men became the chief symbol of a labor movement losing touch with contemporary American society.

In the losses that followed, as school teachers, custodians, librarians, and hospital workers were laid off, given heavier workloads, lost their pension funds, and attacked in political campaigns, it was women and minority workers, disproportionately employed in the public sector as mail delivery persons, school teachers, and DMV clerks who lost most spectacularly. Nor were they the only targets. Despite the weakness of private sector unions, Wisconsin governor Scott Walker pivoted from attacking public employees to promoting a new right-to-work law in 2015, leaving those private sector unions that had supported his political vendetta against public employees reeling. In decline, a labor movement that did not understand its own power (or lack thereof) in the political sphere had failed to understand that its heart and power base lay among the public employees who felt the brunt of anti-unionism.

If neither the stereotype nor the failure of labor to capitalize on new growth altered the other structural barrier to the labor movement—the declining industrial economy—there remained a groundswell of resistance that occurred far beyond the Wisconsin statehouse or the halls of Congress. Deindustrialization, outsourcing, and globalization constricted the movements of labor by the end of the twentieth century. Labor organizing, strangely resilient in the face of such challenges, found new outlets and forums and started to remake itself by century's end. The election of John Sweeney of the SEIU and the emergence of a new generation of labor leaders, among them Rich Trumka, Bill Fletcher, and Karen Nussbaum, opened the door for the new work force to be integrated into national labor strategies and politics. So too did new social movements that rose up to confront the challenges of young, undocumented, minority, and women workers. The Occupy Movement, Black Lives Matter, the movement for LGBT rights, the Fightfor$15 campaign for a higher minimum wage, and other movements, with links to labor's own rebellious past, emerged to ask labor's questions—and make labor's demands—in a new form and a new language.

The Rebirth of American Labor

The end of the labor movement has been predicted for more than four decades. Much ink and many hours have been spent arguing about how to expand the shrinking footprint of labor and restore to it bargaining power. As already mentioned, the proportion of the unionized labor force has declined to 11 percent. In general, both organized and unorganized workers have lost benefits, wages, and control over working conditions since the 1970s. Such losses were offset for a time by the growth of public sector unionism. Since the 1990s, public employees have seen their wages decline; and in 2011, they were faced with new laws that severely limited their capacity to bargain in Michigan, New Jersey, and Illinois. Public employees now pay an increasing share of benefit costs; and in some states, they have had to accept drastic pension cuts. The economic downturn of 2008 cost a hundred thousand teachers their jobs. Most of these were unionized. The reemergence of right-to-work legislation has further weakened public and private sector workers. Despite economic growth in the 1990s and economic recovery after 2009, real wages have been in decline since the conservative 1980s.

In the wake of *Citizens United* (2010), which prohibited limits on "dark money" in politics, it has been difficult to imagine a political strategy that will empower labor relations or an economic strategy that can win gains for industrial or service labor without fundamentally changing our economy. Insurgencies such as Occupy Wall Street and the 2016 presidential campaign of Vermont's Senator Bernie Sanders sought to tip the balance, but labor unions have been slow to join hands. The Roosevelt Institute's *Rewriting the Rules of the American Economy* has provided one template that has surfaced in the Democratic nominee's stump speeches. Economists Joseph Stiglitz and Thomas Piketty are now regularly quoted on the need to address inequality if we are to have economic growth. Addressing the inequality of political representation must follow.[14]

The labor movement—and allied social movements—have grown historically when the gap between the promises of employment and the reality of workers' lives becomes too great. Only when workers on the ground begin to organize does the labor movement come to embrace their cause and support them in the contest with powerful employers. Beginning in 2014, as fast food and retail workers at corporate giants like Wal-Mart and McDonald's began to organize, community activists got behind the new $15/hour living wage. Labor activists and educators joined campaigns to bolster low-wage home health care workers. College professors have supported adjunct instructors against their own administrations. And, in 2016, labor unions plunked down on the candidates their members believed best embraced their values and goals. Unions were not unified in their choice of which candidate to back, but they were unified around a platform for change.[15]

Struggles at the margin—whether of undocumented workers, paroled temporary workers in construction and city work, or the mobile work force in the fast food industry—are where the most dynamic—and, one might add, precarious—labor organizing is on-going. Workers' centers and the living wage movement are at the core of this "alt-labor" strategy.[16] It is not, however, a national strategy. Rather, as labor relations are increasingly de-institutionalized and the courts and state governments hostile to the rights of workers, workers' struggles have shifted to the only ground open to them. They have turned to temporary coalitions by necessity. These coalitions form and re-form to address specific injuries and not as the unfolding of a coordinated national campaign. This is not the mark of an empowered, organized labor movement but of the social movements that workers, their allies and families create when existing institutions are neither powerful enough nor committed enough to support them. "We Are All Leaders," declared the IWW and the CIO in their formative years. We all need to become leaders again.

Ironically, it is in the public realm where labor continues to have hope. Despite assaults on public employee unions, it is such unions—as the SEIU and AFSCME—that have remained the fastest growing and most sustained and sustainable unions in a time of union decline. Despite the targeting of public employees and the hostility directed at teachers, social workers, and clerks at the DMV, public workers' unions have been a mainstay of American labor for a reason. The conditions of their employment are determined by politics—of budgetary priorities, taxation, privatization—and by public opinion. Public employees have no choice but to remain organized. They have an understanding of the public realm that is required if the labor movement, its members, and its constituent unions are to find their footing again. Public workers, because they serve the public, must convey to that public what it is that they do and why it is important. Much as there has been an assault on public employees—public schools, hospitals, and social agencies—there also is the reality of public service. How can public employees tap these memories and reawaken a public and collective sense of what it is to work, to be a worker, and provide a service worth its reward?

What we are left with is the knowledge that, for all of the labor movement's failings, the cause of its declining influence is as much political as economic and technological. Improving the condition of workers in the United States and globally requires understanding how much of it is not the inevitable result of neutral economic forces but the political choices we have made. Historians are not, however, prophets and fortune-tellers. We can only speculate, not predict, what the future will bring. The movement toward new forms of worker organization has the capacity to sustain the labor movement at a time when the future of work and of our democracy is not known. From worker centers to teachers "Bargaining for the Common Good," ordinary working people have once again become the source of grassroots political innovation that we have not seen since the 1970s—or even since the New Deal. As this account reveals, the effort to restore workplace justice and labor's place in our democracy is not unique to our time. When we protest low wages, hazardous working conditions, mass incarceration, racial violence, the deportation of undocumented workers, or discrimination against women workers, we join the long history of labor struggles. To rethink and remake the labor movement, we must recognize that the struggle for justice is not just for ourselves but for the common good.

Notes

1 Nelson Lichtenstein, *Walter Reuther: The Most Dangerous Man in Detroit* (New York: Knopf, 1995), is the standard biography.

2 Ruth Milkman, "Back to the Future: U.S. Labour in the New Gilded Age," *British Journal of Industrial Relations* 51:4 (2013), 645–655, begins with a discussion of the Michigan and Indiana right-to-work laws. Michael D. Yates, ed., *Wisconsin Uprising: Labor Rights Back* (New York: Monthly Review Press, 2012), looks specifically at reaction to conservative attack on public employee unions; the right-to-work law in Wisconsin, passed in 2015, is still being contested in the courts.

3 Some recent analyses are Thomas Geoghegan, *Only One Thing Can Save Us: Why America Needs a New Kind of Labor Movement* (New York: New Press, 2014); Ruth Milkman and Ed Ott, eds., *New Labor in New York: Precarious Workers and the Future of the Labor Movement* (Ithaca: Cornell University Press/ILR Press, 2014); Kim Moody, "U.S. Labor: What's New, What's Not," *Against the Current* May 1, 2016; Alexandra Samuel, "A Labor Day Look at the Future of Work," September 6, 2016, http://daily. jstor.org/a-labor-day-look-at-the-future-of-work/; see also *Labor History* Symposium on Steven H. Lopez, *Reorganizing the Rust Belt: An Inside Story of the American Labor Movement*, in *Labor History* 46:3 (August 2005), 347–389.

4 Michael Safi, "Tens of Millions of Indian Workers Strike in Fight for Higher Wages," *The Guardian*, September 3, 2016, www.theguardian.com/world/2016/sep/02/india n-workers-strike-in-fight-for-higher-wages; "Inmates Are Kicking Off a Nationwide Prison Strike Today,"*Mother Jones* September 9, 2016, www.motherjones.com/poli tics/2016/09/national-prison-strike-inmates; Heather Ann Thompson, "Rethinking Working Class Struggle through the Lens of the Carceral State: Toward a Labor History of Inmates and Guards," *Labor: Studies in Working-Class History of the Americas* 8:3 (Fall 2011), 15–45. David Rolf, *The Fight for $15: The Right Wage for a Working America* (New York: New Press, 2016); Kitty Krupat and Patrick McCreery, eds., *Out at Work: Building a Gay-Labor Alliance* (Minneapolis: University of Minnesota Press, 2001); Jack

Healy, "Trump Campaign Workers Campaign for a Union, Over the Boss's Objections," *New York Times* July 29, 2016, www.nytimes.com/2016/07/30/us/trump-hotel-workers-campaign-for-a-union-over-the-bosss-objections.html?_r=0; Steven Greenhouse, "On Demand and Demanding," *American Prospect* 27:3 (Summer 2016), 41–48; David Moberg, "This is Huge: NLRB Rules Graduate Student Workers Can Unionize," *Working in These Times* August 26, 2016, http://inthesetimes.com/work ing/entry/19412/this_is_huge_nlrb_rules_graduate_student_workers_can_unionize.

5 Judith Stein, *Pivotal Decade: How the United States Traded Factories for Finance in the Seventies* (New Haven: Yale University Press, 2010); Jefferson Cowie, *Capital Moves*; Maria Patricia Fernandez-Kelly, *For We Are Sold, I and My People: Women and Industry in Mexico's Frontier* (Albany: SUNY Press, 1984); Nelson Lichtenstein, "Supply Chains, Worker Chains, and the New World of Retail Supremacy," *Labor: Studies in Working-Class History of the Americas* 4:1 (2007), 17–31; Erin Hatton, *The Temp Economy: From Kelly Girls to Perma Temps in Postwar America* (Philadelphia: Temple University Press, 2011); Reena Patel, *Working the Night Shift: Women in India's Call Center Industry* (Palo Alto, CA: Stanford University Press, 2010); Winifred R. Poster, "The Virtual Receptionist with a Human Touch: Opposing Pressures of Digital Automation and Outsourcing in Interactive Services," in Marion Crain, Winifred R. Poster, and Miriam A. Cherry, eds., *Invisible Labor: Hidden Work in the Contemporary World* (Berkeley: University of California Press, 2016), 87–112.

6 "Food Plant Fire Kills 25," *Los Angeles Times* September 4, 1991; Rick Jervis, "At Least 11 Workers Missing after La. Oil Rig Explosion," *USA Today* April 21, 2010; Ben Casselman, "Rig Owner and Riding Tally of Accidents," *Wall Street Journal* May 10, 2010; "BP Leak the World's Worst Accidental Oil Spill," *The Telegraph* August 3, 2010; David W. Chen, "Safety Lapses and Death Amid a Building Boom in New York," *New York Times* November 26, 2015; AFL-CIO Health and Safety Division, *Death on the Job* (2015); Dina M. Siddiqi, "Starving for Justice: Bangladeshi Garment Workers in a 'Post-Rana Plaza' World," *International Labor and Working Class History* 87 (Spring 2015), 165–174; Robert J.S. Ross, "Inside Bangladeshi Factories: The Real Story," *American Prospect* January 8, 2016, http://prospect.org/article/inside-bangla deshi-factories-real-story; "Tianjin Explosion; China Sets Final Death Toll at 173, Ending Search for Survivors," *The Guardian* September 12, 2015; Javier C. Hernandez, "Tianjin Explosions Were the Result of Mismanagement, China Finds," *New York Times* February 6, 2016.

7 Joe Burns, *Reviving the Strike: How Working People Can Regain Power and Transform America* (New York: Ig Publishing, 2011); Alex Gourevitch, "The Decline of the Strike," *Dissent*, 61:4 (Fall 2014), 142–147; Jake Rosenfeld, *What Unions No Longer Do* (Cambridge, MA: Harvard University Press, 2014), 84–99.

8 Peter Rachleff, *Hard Pressed in the Heartland: The Hormel Strike and the Future of the Labor Movement* (Boston MA: South End Press, 1999).

9 Stephen Franklin, *Three Strikes: Labor's Heartland Losses and What They Mean for Working Americans* (New York: Guilford Press, 2002); Cole Stangler, "400,000 Verizon Workers," *Nation* April 15, 2016; Jake Johnson, "The Bitter Consequences of Corporate America's War on Unions," *Common Dreams* May 16, 2016; https://portside.org; May 17, 2016; Elizabeth Mahony, "Long Live the Picket Line," *Jacobin* May 23, 2016; https://port side.org, May 25, 2016; Sarah Jaffe, "Why the Verizon Worker's Victory Is a Big Deal," *The Progressive* May 31, 2016.

10 Christ Rhomberg, *The Broken Table: The Detroit Newspaper Strike and the State of American Labor* (New York: Russell Sage, 2012).

11 Matt Witt and Rand Wilson, "The Teamsters' UPS Strike of 1997: Building a New Labor Movement," *Labor Studies Journal* 24:1 (Spring 1999), 58–72; Deepa Kumar, *Outside the Box: Corporate Media, Globalization, and the UPS Strike* (Urbana: University of Illinois Press, 2007).

12 Here I am drawing a parallel between the "starving of the beast" (of federal government) often referred to in anti-statist political propaganda and the "labor beast" targeted by such governors as Scott Walker (WI), Bruce Rauner (IL), Mike Pence (IN), and Rick Snyder (MI).

13 Steve Early, *The Civil Wars of U.S. Labor: Birth of a New Workers' Movement or Death Throes of the Old?* (Chicago: Haymarket Books, 2011).

14 Gideon Lewis-Kraus, "The Change Artists," *New York Times Magazine* July 24, 2016, 30–35, 47; Joseph E. Stiglitz, *Rewriting the Rules of the American Economy: An Agenda for Growth and Shared Prosperity* (New York: W.W. Norton, 2015); idem, "Inequality is a Choice," *New York Times* October 13, 2013; Thomas Piketty, *Capital in the Twenty-First Century* (Cambridge, MA: Belknap Press, 2014).

15 David Rolf, *The Fight for $15:* (New York: New Press, 2014); Jennifer Klein and Eileen Boris, *Caring for America: Home Health Workers in the Shadow of the Welfare State* (New York: Oxford University Press, 2015); Ruth Milkman and Ed Ott, *New Labor in New York: Precarious Workers and the Future of the Labor Movement* (Ithaca: ILR Press, 2014); Immanuel Ness, *Immigrants, Unions, and the New U.S. Labor Market* (Philadelphia: Temple University Press, 2010); Gretchen Braun, "Narrating the Job Crisis: Self-Development or Collective Action?" in Allison L. Hurst and Sandi Kawecka Nenga, eds., *Working in Class: Recognizing How Social Class Shapes Our Academic Work* (Lanham, MD: Rowman & Littlefield, 2016), 157–172; Justin Miller, "When Adjuncts Go Union," *American Prospect* June 30, 2015, http://prospect.org/article/when-adjuncts-go-union.

16 Josh Eidelson, "Alt-Labor," *American Prospect*, 24:1 (Jan/Feb 2013), 15–18; David Rolf, "Toward a 21st Century Labor Movement," *American Prospect* 27:2 (Spring 2016), 11–13; Janice Fine, *Worker Centers: Organizing Communities at the Edge of the Dream* (Ithaca: Cornell University Press, 2006). See also analyses by Ruth Milkman, *L.A. Story: Immigrant Workers and the Future of the Labor Movement* (New York: Russell Sage, 2006), and Kim Moody, *U.S Labor in Trouble and Transition: The Failure of Reform from Above and the Promise of Revival from Below* (New York: Verso, 2007).

BIBLIOGRAPHY

Primary Sources

Anderson, Mary. *Woman at Work: The Autobiography of Mary Anderson, As Told to Mary N. Winslow*. Minneapolis: University of Minnesota Press, 1951.

Argersinger, Jo Ann E. *The Triangle Fire: A Brief History with Documents*. Boston MA: Bedford/St. Martin's, 2009.

Barry, Raymond B. and Federal Writers Project, eds. *A Documentary History of Migratory Farm Labor in California*. Oakland, CA: Federal Writers Project, 1938, available at http://content.cdlib.org/ark:/13030/hb88700929/, accessed September 30, 2016.

Baxandall, Rosalyn, Linda Gordon, and Susan Reverby. *America's Working Women: A Documentary History, 1600 to Present*, Rev. ed. New York: W.W. Norton, 1995.

Bulson, Carlos. *America Is in the Heart: A Personal History*, Rev. ed. Seattle: University of Washington Press, 2014.

Commons, John R., Ulrich Bonnell Phillips, Eugene Allen Gilmore, Helen L. Sumner, John B. Andrews, American Bureau of Industrial Research, and the Carnegie Institution of Washington. *A Documentary History of Industrial Society, Vols. 1–11*. New York: Russell & Russell, 1958 [1910–1911].

Denby, Charles. *Indignant Heart: A Black Workers Journal*. Boston MA: South End Press, 1978.

Dubofsky, Melvyn and Joseph A. McCartin, eds. *American Labor: A Documentary History*. New York: St. Martins, 2005.

Flank, Lenny. *The IWW: A Documentary History*. St. Petersburg, FL: Red and Black, 2007.

Flynn, Elizabeth Gurley. *The Rebel Girl: An Autobiography, My First Life, 1906–1926*. New York: International Publishers, 1973.

Foner, Philip S., ed. *The Black Worker: A Documentary History from Colonial Times to the Present*, 2nd ed. Philadelphia, PA: Temple University Press, 1983.

Gompers, Samuel. *Seventy Years of Life and Labor: An Autobiography*, ed. Nick Salvatore. New York: ILR Press, 1984.

Haywood, William D. *The Autobiography of Big Bill Haywood*. New York: International Publishers, 1977, c.1929.

Honey, Michael K. *Black Workers Remember: An Oral History of Segregation, Unionism, and the Freedom Struggle*. Berkeley: University of California Press, 2000.

Jones, Mother. *The Autobiography of Mother Jones*. New York: Arno, 1969.

Kornbluh, Joyce, ed. *Rebel Voices: An IWW Anthology*. Reprint ed. Chicago: Charles H. Kerr, 1998.

Kraus, Henry. *The Many and the Few: A Chronicle of the Dynamic Auto Workers*. 2nd rev. ed. Urbana: University of Illinois Press, 1985.

Lynd, Staughton and Alice Lynd, eds. *Rank and File: Personal Histories by Working-Class Organizers*. Princeton, NJ: Princeton University Press, 1981.

Metzgar, Jack. *Striking Steel: Solidarity Remembered*. Philadelphia, PA: Temple University Press, 2000.

Nestor, Agnes. *Woman Labor Leader: The Autobiography of Agnes Nestor*. Rockford, IL: Bellevue Books, 1954.

Pesotta, Rose. *Bread Upon the Waters*. Reprint. Ithaca, NY: ILR Press, 1987.

Register, Cheri. *Packinghouse Daughter: A Memoir*. St. Paul: Minnesota Historical Society Press, 2000.

Terkel, Studs. *Working: People Talk About What They Do All Day and How They Feel About What They Do*. New York: New Press, 1972.

Trotter, Joe William, Jr., and Earl Lewis, eds. *African Americans in the Industrial Age: A Documentary History, 1915–1945*. Boston MA: Northeastern, 1996.

Vorse, Mary Heaton. *A Footnote to Folly: Reminiscences of Mary Heaton Vorse*. New York: Farrar & Rinehart, 1935.

Vorse, Mary Heaton. *Labor's New Millions*. New York: Modern Age Books, 1938.

Weisbord, Vera Buch. *A Radical Life*. Bloomington: Indiana University Press, 1977.

Secondary Sources: Books

Allen, Joan, Alan Campbell, Malcolm Chase, and John McIlroy, *Histories of Labour: National and Transnational Perspectives*. London: Merlin Press, 2010.

Anderson, Karen. *Wartime Women: Sex Roles, Family Relations and the Status of Women during World War II*. Westport, CT: Greenwood, 1981.

Andrews, Thomas. *Killing for Coal: America's Deadliest Labor War*. Cambridge, MA: Harvard University Press, 2008.

Arnesen, Eric. *Brotherhoods of Color: Black Railroad Workers and the Struggle for Equality*. Cambridge, MA: Harvard University Press, 2001.

Aronowitz, Stanley. *False Promises: The Shaping of American Working Class Consciousness*. Rev. ed. Durham, NC: Duke University Press Books, 1991.

Baron, Ava, ed. *Work Engendered: Toward a New History of American Labor*. Ithaca, NY: Cornell University Press, 1991.

Barrett, James. *William Z. Foster and the Tragedy of American Radicalism*. Urbana: University of Illinois Press, 1999.

Barry, Kathleen. *Femininity in Flight: A History of Flight Attendants*. Durham, NC: Duke University Press, 2007.

Bates, Beth Tomkins. *Pullman Porters and the Rise of Black Protest Politics in America, 1925–1945*. Chapel Hill: University of North Carolina Press, 2001.

Bates, Beth Tomkins. *The Making of Black Detroit in the Age of Henry Ford*. Chapel Hill: University of North Carolina Press, 2014.

Bernstein, Irving. *The Lean Years: A History of the American Worker, 1920–1933*. Boston MA: Houghton Mifflin, 1960.

Bernstein, Irving. *The Turbulent Years: A History of the American Worker, 1933–1941*. Boston MA: Houghton Mifflin, 1969.

Boris, Eileen and Jennifer Klein. *Caring for America: Home Health Workers in the Shadow of the Welfare State*. New York: Oxford University Press, 2012.

Boyle, Kevin. *The UAW and the Heyday of American Liberalism, 1945–1968*. Ithaca, NY: Cornell University Press, 1995.

Brenner, Aaron, Robert Brenner, and Cal Winslow, eds. *Rebel Rank and File: Labor Militancy and Revolt From Below during the Long 1970s*. New York: Verso, 2010.

Brody, David. *Steelworkers in America: The Nonunion Era*. Cambridge, MA: Harvard University Press, 1960.

Brody, David. *The Steel Strike of 1919*. Philadelphia, PA: Lippincott, 1965.

Brody, David. *Workers in Industrial America: Essays on the Twentieth Century Struggle*. New York: Oxford University Press, 1980.

Cameron, Ardis. *Radicals of the Worst Sort: Laboring Women in Lawrence, Massachusetts, 1860–1912*. Urbana: University of Illinois Press, 1993.

Cherney, Robert W., William Issel, and Kieran Walsh Taylor. *American Labor and the Cold War: Grassroots Politics*. New Brunswick, NJ: Rutgers University Press, 2004.

Cobble, Dorothy Sue. *The Other Women's Movement: Workplace Justice and Social Rights in Modern America*. Princeton, NJ: Princeton University Press, 2004.

Cohen, Lizabeth. *Making a New Deal: Industrial Workers in Chicago, 1919–1939*. New York: Cambridge University Press, 1990.

Cole, Peter. *Wobblies on the Waterfront: Interracial Unionism in Progressive-Era Philadelphia*. Urbana: University of Illinois Press, 2007.

Commons, John, David J. Saposs, Helen L. Sumner, E.B. Mittelman, Henry E. Hoagland, John B. Andrews, Selig Perlman, Don D. Lescohier, Elizabeth Brandeis Raushenbush, and Philip Taft. *History of Labor in the United States*, 4 vols. New York: The Macmillan Company, 1918.

Cooper, Patricia A. *Once a Cigar Maker: Men, Women, and Work Culture in American Cigar Factories, 1900–1919*. Urbana: University of Illinois Press, 1987.

Cowie, Jefferson. *Capital Moves: RCA's Seventy-Year Quest for Cheap Labor*. Ithaca, NY: Cornell University Press, 1999.

Cowie, Jefferson. *Stayin' Alive: The 1970s and the Last Days of the Working Class*. New York: New Press, 2010.

Currarino, Rosanne. *The Labor Question: Economic Democracy in the Gilded Age*. Urbana: University of Illinois Press, 2011.

Davis, Colin. *Power at Odds: The Railroad Shopmen's Strike of 1922*. Urbana: University of Illinois Press, 1997.

Davis, Colin. *Waterfront Revolts: New York and London Dockworkers, 1946–61*. Urbana: University of Illinois Press, 2003.

Davis, Mike. *Prisoners of the American Dream*. London: Verso, 1986.

Deslippe, Dennis. *Rights, Not Roses: Unions and the Rise of Working-Class Feminism, 1945–80*. Urbana: University of Illinois Press, 2000.

Dubofsky, Melvyn. *We Shall Be All: A History of the Industrial Workers of the World*. New York: Quadrangle Books, 1969.

Dubofsky, Melvyn. *The State and Labor in Modern America*. Chapel Hill: University of North Carolina Press, 1994.

Dubofsky, Melvyn and Warren Van Tine, eds. *Labor Leaders in America*. Urbana: University of Illinois Press, 1987.

Du Bois, W.E.B. *Black Reconstruction in America, 1860–1880.* New York: Harcourt Brace, 1935.

Early, Steve. *Civil Wars of U.S. Labor: Birth of a New Workers' Movement or Death Throes of the Old?*Chicago: Haymarket Books, 2011.

Faue, Elizabeth. *Community of Suffering and Struggle: Women, Men, and the Labor Movement in Minneapolis, 1915–1945.* Chapel Hill: University of North Carolina Press, 1991.

Faue, Elizabeth. *Writing the Wrongs: Eva Valesh and the Rise of Labor Journalism.* Ithaca, NY: Cornell University Press, 2002.

Filippelli, Ronald L. and Mark McColloch. *Cold War in the Working Class: The Rise and Decline of the United Electrical Workers.* Albany: State University of New York Press, 1995.

Fine, Sidney. *Sit-Down: The General Motors Strike of 1936–1937.* Ann Arbor: University of Michigan Press, 1969.

Fine, Sidney. *"Without Blare of Trumpets": Walter Drew, the National Erectors' Association, and the Open Shop Movement, 1903–1957.* Ann Arbor: University of Michigan Press, 1995.

Fink, Leon. *Workingmen's Democracy: The Knights of Labor and American Politics.* Urbana: University of Illinois Press, 1983.

Fink, Leon and Brian Greenberg. *Upheaval in the Quiet Zone: A History of Hospital Workers Union, Local 1199.* Urbana: University of Illinois Press, 1989.

Fones-Wolf, Elizabeth. *Selling Free Enterprise: The Business Assault on Labor and Liberalism, 1945–60.* Urbana: University of Illinois Press, 1994.

Forbath, William. *Law and the Shaping of the American Labor Movement.* Cambridge, MA: Harvard University Press, 1991.

Frank, Miriam. *Out in the Union: A Labor History of Queer America.* Philadelphia, PA: Temple University Press, 2014.

Fraser, Steve. *Labor Shall Rule: Sidney Hillman and the Rise of American Labor.* New York: Free Press, 1991.

Freeman, Joshua. *Working Class New York: Life and Labor Since World War II.* New York: New Press, 2000.

Friday, Chris. *Organizing Asian American Labor: The Pacific Coast Canned-Salmon Industry, 1870–1942.* Philadelphia, PA: Temple University Press, 1995.

Gabin, Nancy F. *Feminism in the Labor Movement: Women and the United Autoworkers, 1935–1975.* Ithaca, NY: Cornell University Press, 1990.

Gall, Gilbert. *The Politics of the Right to Work: The Labor Federations as Special Interests, 1943–1979.* Westport, CT: Greenwood, 1988.

Georgakas, Dan and Marvin Surkin. *Detroit, I Do Mind Dying: A Study in Urban Revolution.* New York: St. Martin's Press, 1975.

Gerstle, Gary. *Working-Class Americanism: The Politics of Labor in a Textile City, 1914–1960.* Cambridge: Cambridge University Press, 1990.

Glaberman, Martin. *Wartime Strikes: The Struggle against the No-Strike Pledge in the UAW during World War II.* Detroit, MI: Berwick Editions, 1980.

Glickman, Lawrence. *A Living Wage: American Workers and the Making of Consumer Society.* Ithaca, NY: Cornell University Press, 1997.

Goldberg, David J. *A Tale of Three Cities: Labor Organization and Protest in Paterson, Passaic, Lawrence, 1916–1921.* New Brunswick, NJ: Rutgers University Press, 1989.

Goldfield, Michael. *The Decline of Organized Labor in the United States.* Chicago: University of Chicago Press, 1987.

Green, James. *The World of the Worker: Labor in Twentieth Century America.* New York: Hill and Wang, 1980.

Green, James. *Death in the Haymarket: A Story of Chicago, the First Labor Movement, and the Bombing that Divided Gilded Age America*. New York: Pantheon Books, 2006.

Greene, Julie. *Pure and Simple Politics: The American Federation of Labor and Political Activism, 1881–1917*. Cambridge: Cambridge University Press, 1998.

Griffith, Barbara. *The Crisis of American Labor: Operation Dixie and the Defeat of the CIO*. Philadelphia, PA: Temple University Press, 1988.

Guglielmo, Jennifer. *Living the Revolution: Italian Women's Resistance and Radicalism in New York City, 1880–1945*. Chapel Hill: University of North Carolina Press, 2010.

Hahamovitch, Cindy. *No Man's Land: Jamaican Guestworkers in America and the Global History of Deportable Labor*. Princeton, NJ: Princeton University Press, 2011.

Hall, Jacquelyn, James Leloudis, Robert Korstad, Mary Murphy, Lu Ann Jones, and Christopher B. Daly. *Like a Family: The Making of a Southern Cotton Mill World*. Chapel Hill: University of North Carolina Press, 1987.

Halpern, Rick. *Down on the Killing Floor: Black and White Workers in Chicago's Packinghouses, 1904–1954*. Urbana: University of Illinois Press, 1997.

Higbie, Frank Tobias. *Indispensable Outcasts: Hobo Workers and Community in the American Midwest, 1880–1930*. Urbana: University of Illinois Press, 2003.

Honey, Michael K. *Southern Workers and Black Civil Rights: Organizing Memphis Workers*. Urbana: University of Illinois Press, 1993.

Jones, William P. *The Tribe of Black Ulysses: African American Lumber Workers in the Jim Crow South*, Urbana: University of Illinois Press, 2005.

Kazin, Michael. *Barons of Labor: The San Francisco Building Trades and Union Power in the Progressive Era*. Urbana: University of Illinois Press, 1987.

Kelley, Robin D.K. *Hammer and Hoe: Alabama Communists during the Great Depression*. Chapel Hill: University of North Carolina Press, 1990.

Kersten, Andrew E. *Labor's Home Front: The American Federation of Labor during World War II*. New York: New York University Press, 2006.

Kessler-Harris, Alice. *Out to Work: A History of Wage-Earning Women in the United States*. New York: Oxford University Press, 1982.

Korstad, Robert Rogers. *Civil Rights Unionism: Tobacco Workers and the Struggle for Democracy in the Mid-Twentieth Century South*. Chapel Hill: University of North Carolina Press, 2003.

Krupat, Kitty and Patric McCreery, eds. *Out at Work: Building a Gay-Labor Alliance*. Minneapolis: University of Minnesota Press, 2001.

Laurie, Bruce. *Artisans into Workers: Labor in Nineteenth-Century America*. New York: Hill and Wang, 1989.

Levinson, Marc. *The Box: How the Shipping Container Made the World Smaller and the World Economy Bigger*. Princeton, NJ: Princeton University Press, 2006.

Lichtenstein, Nelson. *Labor's War at Home: The CIO in World War II*. Cambridge: Cambridge University Press, 1982.

Lichtenstein, Nelson. *The Most Dangerous Man in Detroit: Walter Reuther and the Fate of American Labor*. New York: Basic Books, 1995.

Lichtenstein, Nelson. *The State of the Unions: A Century of American Labor*. Princeton, NJ: Princeton University Press, 2002.

Lichtenstein, Nelson and Elizabeth Tandy Shermer, eds. *The Right and Labor in America: Politics, Ideology, and Imagination*. Philadelphia: University of Pennsylvania Press, 2012.

Lipsitz, George. *Rainbow at Midnight: Labor and Culture in the 1940s*. Urbana: University of Illinois Press, 1994.

Loomis, Erik. *Empire of Timber: Labor Unions and the Pacific Northwest Forests*. New York: Cambridge University Press, 2016.

Lopez, Steven H. *Reorganizing the Rust Belt: An Inside Study of the American Labor Movement*. Berkeley: University of California Press, 2004.

Mathew, Biju. *Taxi! Cabs and Capitalism in New York City*. New York: New Press, 2005.

McCartin, Joseph. *Labor's Great War: The Struggle for Union Industrial Democracy and the Origins of Modern American Labor Relations, 1912–1921*. Chapel Hill: University of North Carolina Press, 1997.

McCartin, Joseph. *Collision Course: Ronald Reagan, the Air Traffic Controllers, and the Strike that Changed America*. New York: Oxford University Press, 2011.

Meier, August and Elliot Rudwick. *Black Detroit and the Rise of the UAW*. New York: Oxford University Press, 1979.

Milkman, Ruth. *Gender at Work: The Dynamics of Job Segregation during World War II*. Urbana: University of Illinois Press, 1987.

Milkman, Ruth, ed. *Women, Work and Protest: A Century of U.S. Women's Labor History*. New York and London: Routledge, 2013.

Milkman, Ruth and Ed Ott, eds. *New Labor in New York: Precarious Workers and the Future of the Labor Movement*. Ithaca, NY: ILR Press, 2014.

Miller, Sally M. and Daniel A. Cornford, eds. *American Labor in the Era of World War II*. Westport, CT: Praeger, 1995.

Milton, David. *The Politics of U.S. Labor from the Great Depression to the New Deal*. New York: Monthly Review Press, 1982.

Mink, Gwendolyn. *Old Labor and New Immigrants in American Political Development: Union, Party, and State, 1875–1920*. Ithaca, NY: Cornell University Press, 1986.

Montgomery, David. *Workers' Control in America: Studies in the History of Work, Technology, and Labor Struggles*. New York: Cambridge University Press, 1979.

Montgomery, David. *The Fall of the House of Labor: The Workplace, the State, and American Labor Activism, 1865–1925*. Cambridge: Cambridge University Press, 1987.

Moreton, Bethany. *To Serve God and Wal-Mart: The Making of Christian Free Enterprise*. Cambridge, MA: Harvard University Press, 2009.

Nadasen, Premilla. *Household Workers Unite: The Untold Story of African American Women Who Built a Movement*. Boston MA: Beacon, 2015.

Nelson, Bruce. *Workers on the Waterfront: Seamen, Longshoremen, and Unionism in the 1930s*. Urbana: University of Illinois Press, 1988.

Ngai, Mae. *Impossible Subjects: Illegal Aliens and the Making of Modern America*. Princeton, NJ: Princeton University Press, 2004.

Peck, Gunther. *Reinventing Free Labor: Padrones and Immigrant Workers in the North American West, 1880–1930*. Cambridge: Cambridge University Press, 2000.

Rachleff, Peter. *Black Labor in Richmond, 1865–1890*. Urbana: University of Illinois Press, 1984.

Rhomberg, Chris. *The Broken Table: The Detroit Newspaper Strike and the State of American Labor*. New York: Russell Sage Foundation, 2012.

Rosswurm, Steve, ed. *The CIO's Left-Led Unions*. New Brunswick, NJ: Rutgers University Press, 1992.

Ruiz, Vicki L. *Cannery Women, Cannery Lives: Mexican Women, Unionization, and the California Food Processing Industry, 1930–1950*. Albuquerque: University of New Mexico Press, 1987.

Russell, Thaddeus. *Out of the Jungle: Jimmy Hoffa and the Remaking of the American Working Class*. New York: A.A. Knopf, 2001.

Salerno, Salvatore. *Red November, Black November: Culture and Community in the Industrial Workers of the World*. Albany: State University of New York Press, 1989.

Santino, Jack. *Miles of Smiles, Years of Struggle: Stories of Black Pullman Porters*. Urbana: University of Illinois Press, 1991.

Schatz, Ronald. *The Electrical Workers: A History of Labor at General Electric and Westinghouse, 1923–1960*. Urbana: University of Illinois Press, 1983.

Seidman, Joel. *American Labor from Defense to Reconversion*. Chicago: University of Chicago Press, 1953.

Slater, Joseph. *Public Workers: Government Employee Unions, the Law, and the State, 1900–1962*. Ithaca, NY: ILR Press, 2004.

Stein, Judith. *Pivotal Decade: How the United States Traded Factories for Finance in the Seventies*. New Haven, CT: Yale University Press, 2010.

Stromquist, Shelton. *Reinventing "the People": The Progressive Movement, the Class Problem, and the Origins of Modern Liberalism*. Urbana: University of Illinois Press, 2006.

Stromquist, Shelton, ed. *Labor's Cold War: Local Politics in a Global Context*. Urbana: University of Illinois Press, 2008.

Taft, Philip. *The A F of L in the Time of Gompers*. New York: Harper, 1957.

Taillon, Paul. *Good, Reliable, White Men: Railroad Brotherhoods, 1877–1917*. Urbana: University of Illinois Press, 2009.

Thompson, Heather Ann. *Whose Detroit?: Politics, Labor, and Race in a Modern American City*. Ithaca, NY: Cornell University Press, 2001.

Tomlins, Christopher L. *The State and the Unions: Labor Relations, Law, and the Organized Labor Movement in America, 1880–1960*. Cambridge: Cambridge University Press, 1985.

Trotter, Joe W., Jr. *Black Milwaukee: The Making of an Industrial Proletariat, 1915–1945*. Urbana: University of Illinois Press, 1985.

Vargas, Zaragosa. *Proletarians of the North: Mexican Industrial Workers in Detroit and the Midwest, 1917–1933*. Berkeley: University of California Press, 1993.

Vargas, Zaragosa. *Labor Rights Are Civil Rights: Mexican American Workers in Twentieth Century America*. Princeton, NJ: Princeton University Press, 2004.

Weir, Robert E. *Beyond Labor's Veil: The Culture of the Knights of Labor*. University Park: Pennsylvania State University Press, 1996.

Witwer, David. *Corruption and Reform in the Teamsters' Union*. Urbana: University of Illinois Press, 2003.

Witwer, David. *The Shadow of the Racketeer: Scandal in Organized Labor*. Urbana: University of Illinois Press, 2009.

Zieger, Robert. *The CIO, 1935–1955*. Chapel Hill: University of North Carolina Press, 1995.

Zieger, Robert and Gilbert Gall. *American Workers, American Unions: The Twentieth Century*. Baltimore, MD: Johns Hopkins University Press, 2002.

Secondary Sources: Articles and Essays

Arnesen, Eric. "'Like Banquo's Ghost, It Will Not Down': The Race Question and the American Railroad Brotherhoods, 1880–1920." *American Historical Review* 99 (December 1994), 1601–1633.

Boyle, Kevin. "Auto Workers at War: Patriotism and Protest in the American Auto Industry, 1939–1945." In *Auto Work*, edited by Robert Asher and Ronald Edsforth, 99–126. Albany, NY: SUNY Press, 1995.

Collomp, Catherine. "Unions, Civics, and National Identity: Organized Labor's Reaction to Immigration, 1881–1897." *Labor History* 29 (Fall 1988), 450–474.

Cowie, Jefferson. "Nixon's Working Class: Romancing the New Right Worker, 1969–1973." *Labor History* 43 (2002), 257–283.

Crain, Marion and Ken Matheny. "Labor's Identity Crisis." *California Law Review* 89 (2001), 1767–1846.

Davis, Mike. "The Stop Watch and the Wooden Shoe: Scientific Management and the Industrial Workers of the World." *Radical America* 9 (January-February 1975), 69–95.

Dawson, Andrew. "The Paradox of Dynamic Technological Change and the Labor Aristocracy in the United States, 1880–1914." *Labor History* 20 (Summer 1979), 325–351.

Dawson, Andrew. "The Parameters of Craft Consciousness: The Social Outlook of the Skilled Worker, 1890–1920." In *American Labor and Immigration History, 1877–1920: Recent European Research*, edited by Dirk Hoerder, 135–155. Urbana: University of Illinois Press, 1983.

Di Girolamo, Vincent. "The Women of Wheatland: Female Consciousness and the 1913 Wheatland Hop Strike." *Labor History* 34 (Spring-Summer 1993), 236–255.

Dubofsky, Melvyn. "The 'Not So' Turbulent Years: A New Look at the 1930s." In *Life and Labor: Dimensions of Working-Class History*, edited by Charles Stephenson and Robert Asher, 205–223. Albany, NY: SUNY Press, 1986.

Faue, Elizabeth. "The 'Dynamo of Change': Gender and Solidarity in the American Labour Movement of the 1930s." *Gender and History* 1:2 (1989), 138–158.

Faue, Elizabeth. "Paths of Unionization: Community, Bureaucracy, and Gender in the Minneapolis Labor Movement of the 1930s." In *Work Engendered: Toward a New History of American Labor*, edited by Ava Baron, 296–319. Ithaca, NY: Cornell University Press, 1991.

Faue, Elizabeth. "United States of America." In *Histories of Labour: National and Transnational Perspectives*, edited by Joan Allen, Alan Campbell, Malcolm Chase, and John McIlroy, 164–195. London: Merlin Press, 2010.

Feldberg, Roslyn. "'Union Fever': Organizing among Clerical Workers, 1900–1930." In *Workers Struggles, Past and Present: A Radical America Reader*, edited by James Green, 151–167. Philadelphia, PA: Temple University Press, 1983.

Fields, Barbara J. "Whiteness, Racism, and Identity." *International Labor and Working-Class History* 60 (Fall 2001), 48–56.

Fink, Leon. "Labor, Liberty and the Law: Trade Unionism and the Problem of the American Constitutional Order." *Journal of American History* 74:3 (November 1987), 904–925.

Foner, Eric. "Why Is There No Socialism in the United States?" *History Workshop* 17 (Spring 1984), 57–80.

Friedman, Tami J. "Exploiting the North–South Differential: Corporate Power, Southern Politics, and the Decline of Organized Labor after World War II." *Journal of American History* 95 (September 2008), 323–348.

Fry, Richard. "Making Amends: Coal Miners, the Black Lung Association, and Federal Compensation Reform, 1969–1972." *Federal History* 5 (January 2013), 35–56.

Gordon, Robert. "'Shell No!': OCAW and the Labor Environmental Alliance." *Environmental History* 3 (October 1998), 460–487.

Gordon, Robert. "Poison in the Fields: The United Farm Workers, Pesticides, and Environmental Politics." *Pacific Historical Review* 68 (Fall 1999), 51–77.

Green, Venus. "Race and Technology: African American Women in the Bell System, 1945–1980." *Technology and Culture* 36 (April 1995), 101–144.

Grossman, James R. "The White Man's Union: The Great Migration and the Resonance of Race and Class in Chicago, 1916–1922." In *The Great Migration in Historical*

Perspective: New Dimensions of Race, Class, and Gender, edited by Joe WilliamTrotter, Jr., 83–105. Bloomington: Indiana University Press, 1991.

Hall, Jacquelyn Dowd. "Disorderly Women: Gender and Labor Militancy in the Appalachian South." *Journal of American History* 73:2 (1986), 354–382.

Hall, Jacquelyn Dowd, Robert Korstad and James Leloudis. "Cotton Mill People: Work, Community, and Protest in the Textile South, 1880–1940." *American Historical Review* 91 (April 1986), 245–286.

Harris, William H. "Federal Intervention in Union Discrimination: FEPC and West Coast Shipyards during World War II." *Labor History* 22 (Summer 1981), 325–347.

Hearn, Jeffrey and Wendy Parkin. "Gender and Organizations: A Selective Review and Critique of a Neglected Area." *Organization Studies* 4 (1983), 219–242.

Hepler, Allison. "'And We Want Steel Toes like the Men': Gender and Occupational Health during World War II." *Bulletin of the History of Medicine* 72 (Winter 1998), 689–713.

Huntley, Horace. "The Red Scare and Black Workers in Alabama: The International Union of Mine, Mill and Smelter Workers, 1945–1953." In *Labor Divided: Race and Ethnicity in United States Labor Struggles, 1835–1960*, edited by Robert Asher and Charles Stephenson, 129–145. Albany, NY: State University of New York Press, 1990.

Kessler-Harris, Alice. "Where are the Organized Women Workers?" *Feminist Studies* 3 (1975), 92–110.

Koistinen, Paul A.C. "Mobilizing the World War II Economy: Labor and the Industrial-Military Alliance." *Pacific Historical Review* 42 (November 1973), 443–478.

Korstad, Robert and Nelson Lichtenstein. "Opportunities Lost and Found: Labor, Radicals, and the Early Civil Rights Movement." *Journal of American History* 75 (December 1988), 786–811.

Levine, Susan. "Labor's True Woman: Domesticity and Equal Rights in the Knights of Labor." *Journal of American History* 70 (September 1983), 323–339.

Markowitz, Gerald and David Rosner. "More than Economism: The Politics of Worker Safety and Health, 1932–1947." *Millbank Quarterly* 64 (1986), 341–346.

McCartin, Joseph. "A Wagner Act for Public Workers: Labor's Deferred Dream and the Rise of Conservatism, 1970–1976." *Journal of American History* 95 (2008), 123–148.

Milkman, Ruth. "Organizing the Sexual Division of Labor: Historical Perspectives on Women's Work and the American Labor Movement." *Socialist Review* 49 (January-February 1980), 95–150.

Milkman, Ruth. "Back to the Future: U.S. Labour in the New Gilded Age." *British Journal of Industrial Relations* 51:4 (2013), 645–655.

Milkman, Ruth and Veronica Terriquez. "'We Are the Ones Who Are Out in Front': Women's Leadership in the Immigrant Rights Movement." *Feminist Studies* 38:3 (2012), 723–752.

Montgomery, David. "The 'New Unionism' and the Transformation of Workers' Consciousness, 1909–1920." *Journal of Social History* 7:4 (1974), 509–529.

Montgomery, David. "Workers' Control of Machine Production in the 19th Century." *Labor History* 17 (Fall 1976), 485–509.

Montgomery, David. "Labor and the Republic in Industrial America, 1860–1920." *Le Mouvement social* 111 (1980), 201–215.

Muncy, Robyn. "Coal-Fired Reforms: Social Citizenship, Dissident Miners, and the Great Society." *Journal of American History* 96 (June 2009), 72–98.

Nelson, Bruce. "Organized Labor and the Struggle for Black Equality in Mobile during World War II." *Journal of American History* 80 (December 1993), 952–988.

Nelson, Daniel. "Scientific Management, Systematic Management, and Labor, 1880–1915." *Business History Review* 48 (Winter 1974), 479–500.

Nelson, Daniel. "Origins of the Sit-Down Era: Worker Militancy and Innovation in the Rubber Industry, 1934–1938." *Labor History* 23:2 (1982), 198–225.

Oestreicher, Richard. "Urban Working-Class Political Behavior and Theories of American Electoral Politics, 1870–1940." *Journal of American History* 75 (1988), 1257–1286.

Rogin, Michael. "Voluntarism: The Political Functions of an Antipolitical Doctrine." *Industrial and Labor Relations Review* 15 (July 1962), 521–525.

Rooks, Daisy. "The Cowboy Mentality: Organizers and Occupational Commitment in the New Labor Movement." *Labor Studies Journal* 28 (Fall 2003), 33–61.

Schofield, Ann. "Rebel Girls and Union Maids: The Woman Question in the Journals of the AFL and IWW, 1905–1920." *Feminist Studies* 9 (Summer 1983), 335–358.

Shermer, Elizabeth Tandy. "Origins of the Conservative Ascendancy: Barry Goldwater's Early Senate Career and the De-Legitimization of Organized Labor." *Journal of American History* 95 (December 2008), 678–709.

Shor, Francis. "'Virile Syndicalism' in Comparative Perspective: A Gender Analysis of the IWW in the United States and Australia." *International Labor and Working Class History* 56 (1999), 65–77.

Strom, Sharon Hartman. "Challenging 'Woman's Place': Feminism, the Left and Industrial Unionism in the 1930s." *Feminist Studies* 9 (Summer 1983), 359–386.

Thompson, Heather Ann. "Rethinking Working Class Struggle through the Lens of the Carceral State: Toward a Labor History of Inmates and Guards." *Labor: Studies in Working-Class History of the Americas* 8:3 (Fall 2011), 15–45.

Tomlins, Christopher L. "AFL Unions in the 1930s: Their Performance in Historical Perspective." *Journal of American History* 65 (March 1979), 1021–1042.

Turrini, Joseph M. "The Newton Steel Strike: A Watershed in the CIO's Failure to Organize Little Steel." *Labor History* 38:2–3 (1997), 229–265.

Urofsky, Melvin I. "State Courts and Protective Legislation during the Progressive Era: A Reevaluation." *Journal of American History* 72:1 (June 1985), 63–91.

Vosko, Leah F. and David Scott Witwer. "'Not a Man's Union': Women Teamsters in the 1940s and 1950s." *Journal of Women's History* 13:3 (Autumn 2001), 169–192.

Wakstein, Allen M. "The Origins of the Open-Shop Movement, 1919–1920." *Journal of American History* 51 (December 1964), 460–475.

Wilentz, Sean. "Against Exceptionalism: Class Consciousness and the American Labor Movement, 1790–1820." *International Labor and Working Class History* 1 (1984), 1–24.

INDEX

Taylor & Francis eBooks

Helping you to choose the right eBooks for your Library

Add Routledge titles to your library's digital collection today. Taylor and Francis ebooks contains over 50,000 titles in the Humanities, Social Sciences, Behavioural Sciences, Built Environment and Law.

Choose from a range of subject packages or create your own!

Benefits for you

» Free MARC records
» COUNTER-compliant usage statistics
» Flexible purchase and pricing options
» All titles DRM-free.

Benefits for your user

» Off-site, anytime access via Athens or referring URL
» Print or copy pages or chapters
» Full content search
» Bookmark, highlight and annotate text
» Access to thousands of pages of quality research at the click of a button.

REQUEST YOUR FREE INSTITUTIONAL TRIAL TODAY

Free Trials Available
We offer free trials to qualifying academic, corporate and government customers.

eCollections – Choose from over 30 subject eCollections, including:

Archaeology	Language Learning
Architecture	Law
Asian Studies	Literature
Business & Management	Media & Communication
Classical Studies	Middle East Studies
Construction	Music
Creative & Media Arts	Philosophy
Criminology & Criminal Justice	Planning
Economics	Politics
Education	Psychology & Mental Health
Energy	Religion
Engineering	Security
English Language & Linguistics	Social Work
Environment & Sustainability	Sociology
Geography	Sport
Health Studies	Theatre & Performance
History	Tourism, Hospitality & Events

For more information, pricing enquiries or to order a free trial, please contact your local sales team:
www.tandfebooks.com/page/sales

Routledge
Taylor & Francis Group

The home of
Routledge books

www.tandfebooks.com